1984
10TH EDITION
THE COMPLETE HANDBOOK OF
PRO FOOTBALL

S0-AXR-409

Super Sports Books from SIGNET

1984
10TH EDITION
THE COMPLETE HANDBOOK OF
PRO FOOTBALL

EDITED BY ZANDER HOLLANDER

A SIGNET BOOK
NEW AMERICAN LIBRARY

ACKNOWLEDGMENTS

Joe Namath, Cookie Gilchrist, Franco Harris, Ken Anderson, O.J. Simpson, Greg Pruitt—plus the World Football League. It was 1975 and all were prominent that year in these pages. Now there's the USFL; Harris, Anderson and Pruitt are still at it and so is *The Complete Handbook of Pro Football*, celebrating its 10th annual edition.

For making this one happen, we thank the writers on the facing page along with Frank Kelly, Rich Rossiter, Pete Sansone, Jerry Schlamp, Dot Gordineer, Beri Greenwald, Lee Stowbridge, Steve Wisniewski, Peter Hollander, Phyllis Hollander, Westchester Book Composition, Elias Sports Bureau, Fran Connors, Roger Goodell, Jim Heffernan, Joe Browne and the NFL team publicists.

Zander Hollander

PHOTO CREDITS: Covers—Richard Pilling. Inside photos—George Gojkovich, Richard Pilling, Mitchell Reibel, UPI, ABC Sports, the New Jersey Generals, the various NFL team photographers (including Lou Witt and Robert Smith), Sports Photo Source and the colleges whose graduates are pictured in the draft section.

SIGNET, SIGNET CLASSICS, MENTOR, PLUME, MERIDIAN AND NAL BOOKS
are published by New American Library, 1633 Broadway
New York, New York 10019

First Printing, August 1984

1 2 3 4 5 6 7 8 9

PRINTED IN THE UNITED STATES OF AMERICA

NFL vs. USFL SuperDuper Bowl I

By JOE GERGEN

The game was one man's tribute to himself. Not that it was the first which Donald J. Trump had engineered in his lifetime. But this was a football show of unparalleled dimensions.

In addition to lifting the United States Football League to a level of popularity where it had forced a direct confrontation with the National Football League, the New York builder had personally provided a site of lavish proportions for the eagerly-awaited spectacle. The very first SuperDuper Bowl would be staged as the inaugural attraction at TrumpDome, the elaborate sports palace which had been completed in record time across the East River from Manhattan. The game would help to assure the fame of the stadium, which was the foundation of a massive urban complex Trump already had proclaimed as the eighth wonder of the new world. "Now your task," he informed newsmen and civic leaders at the dedication ceremony, "is to find seven others."

Not only would this would be the largest domed stadium in the world, seating 100,000 spectators, but it would be the first housed in a skyscraper. For, above the main arena and a smaller one capable of housing the Knicks and Rangers, which he had just purchased from the Madison Square Garden Corporation, the Trump organization was erecting 60 floors of shops, office space and cooperative apartments.

The starting price for the residences was $2 million, and Trump said 100 of them had been purchased before they went on public sale. Although all of them had extraordinary views of the Manhattan skyline and such amenities as 24-hour limousine service to midtown, the major inducement according to the builder was special elevators which would run from the apartments to the level

Like Satchel Paige, sports columnist Joe Gergen of Newsday *never looks back.*

Al Davis
Governor of California

Pete Rozelle
Los Angeles Raiders

of luxury boxes ringing the stadium. "Live football without leaving home," read the upscale ads in *The New York Times*.

Although the duplex and triplex apartments would not be finished for another year, the stadium had been available for practice the week before the game. And a splendid facility it was, all bronze and burnished right down to the gigantic "T" over each doorway and at the mouth of the players' entrance tunnel, in the flamboyant style of Trump Tower on Fifth Avenue. There even was a huge "T" painted in the middle of the artificial turf, although the NFL had won the right to paint its own insignia for the game.

It was one of Trump's few concessions. His team, the New York Trumps (formerly the New Jersey Generals), was representing the United States Football League in the game and was scheduled to move into TrumpDome for the start of the next season, the second the league would conduct in the traditional fall months. The USFL had altered its schedule the previous year so as to be prepared for this first meeting of league champions on Feb. 4, 1990, and had achieved surprising success at the box office.

Many thought this was due to general discontent with the NFL, which had been powerless to act as more and more franchises skipped out on cities where they had been founded for better deals in new regions. The Raiders had opened the door when they left Oakland for Los Angeles and in the next few years it spun round

J.R. Ewing Enterprises: Dallas Cowboys.

and round. In fact, the Colts had bolted on three occasions during the decade, first from Baltimore, then Indianapolis and, finally, Phoenix, each time in the middle of the night under the frantic orders of Bob Irsay. By the start of the 1989 season, during which it holed up in Albuquerque, the team was known throughout America as the Atchison, Topeka and the Santa Fe Colts.

The Saints, Browns and Bengals all had changed location in the 1980s. But, for shock value, perhaps nothing matched the uprooting of Green Bay. Since the team was publicly owned by the townsfolk, the Packers weren't free to go. But the city was another matter. For the promise of an 80,000-seat stadium and cheap land alongside a man-made lake in the Southwest, the citizens of the semifrozen Wisconsin community voted to resettle in the desert, at Sun Bay.

In short, the old alignments and rivalries had been sacrificed to better or even free stadium rentals. And while the NFL owners continued to seek larger and larger profits, the USFL had courted more and more pro stars. In addition to signing the last eight Heisman Trophy winners ("The League of the Heisman" was one

*George Steinbrenner
Cleveland Shipbuilders*

*Jim Brown
Los Angeles Raiders*

of the promotional gambits), the junior league had grabbed some of the NFL's top coaches and quarterbacks with percentage-of-ownership deals.

Joe Theismann had been one of the early converts, jumping to the Baltimore Federals, where he served as chairman of the board, quarterback and radio-television color analyst. The franchise, which had been an unmitigated disaster in the nation's capital, became an overnight success 40 miles to the north as Baltimoreans, stung by the loss of the Colts, flocked to "Join Joe in the Huddle," as the ads had proclaimed. Through use of a small remote microphone attached to his shoulder pads, Theismann brought a sense of immediacy to every play.

Elsewhere, Bill Walsh had revived the Oakland Invaders and Don Shula had joined his former fullback, Larry Csonka, in guiding the fortunes of the Jacksonville Bulls. The New Orleans Breakers, with an innovative coach in Dick Coury and a headliner in Marcus Dupree, had become a tremendous attraction upon the departure of the Saints. And Dan Marino and Joe Montana were throwing touchdown passes for enormous profit in Tampa Bay and Denver, respectively, their salaries partially bankrolled by a new pay-television network founded by Trump and USFL Commissioner Ted Turner.

George Steinbrenner also had been persuaded to throw in with the young league, getting a chance to exercise his football knowledge and renowned second-guessing as chief executive officer and part-time offensive coordinator of the Cleveland Shipbuilders. Steinbrenner also had purchased an apartment in the new Trump complex while Trump had been placed on the board of directors of American Shipbuilding.

Donald Trump with Generals' VP-Poetry, Herschel Walker.

The Trumps, led by quarterback Bernie Kosar, a Heisman winner at the University of Miami, had dominated the USFL in the 1989 season, their first and last at recently refurbished Shea Stadium. Although Herschel Walker, the team's first star, had become the club's vice-president and resident poet, he also took the occasion to play in home games and the playoffs. It was Walker's 85-yard run with a screen pass from Kosar which broke open the championship game against Denver.

The Dynasty, newly renamed after its purchase by John Forsyth's Carrington corporation, had been a surprise finalist in Montana's first year in the USFL. But the Trumps proved too deep and powerful in the course of a 35-20 victory at the Superdome in New Orleans.

The NFL's representative, the Raiders, had a far more difficult time in qualifying for the SuperDuper Bowl, the first ultimate football game to be held in New York since the 1962 NFL matchup between the Giants and Packers. After their previous Super Bowl victory over the Redskins in 1984, the Raiders had mellowed out. Many contended that the team's fortunes started to decline from the moment Al Davis announced his intention to run for governor of California on the Greaser ticket.

Davis' stunning victory over Richard Nixon and Jane Fonda in the general election, despite the unanimous loss of every precinct in Oakland, certainly signaled a profound change in the team he had virtually created. He sold the Raiders to a group of movie moguls, who immediately altered the team's image by dressing the players in avocado and magenta uniforms. The Raiders were so embarrassed in their first technicolor season that those who didn't quit in disgust were severely trounced in every game.

Bill Walsh
Oakland Invaders

Don Shula
Jacksonville Bulls

In time, the franchise pulled out of Los Angeles and began drifting about the state, much in the manner of itinerant beach bums. Their wanderings, in fact, led them to be called the Anaheim, Azusa and Cucamonga Raiders as well as Raiders of the Lost Park. The people in Oakland no longer wished to be identified with Davis, not even on a historical basis.

It was Pete Rozelle, the same man who as NFL commissioner had challenged Davis' right to transfer the franchise to Los Angeles, who finally restored the team to its rightful position in the standings. After serving nearly 30 years in the commissioner's job, Rozelle resigned at the conclusion of the 1988 season and, as Davis once had predicted, acquired the rights to Los Angeles. But the team he wanted for the Coliseum was, of all things, the Raiders.

Not only did he order them back into the black-and-silver uniforms of bygone days but he set about luring some of their most famous and feared players out of retirement, including 40-year-old Lyle Alzado, 41-year-old Ted Hendricks and 41-year-old Jim Plunkett. He even toyed with the idea of activating 61-year-old George Blanda to kick placements but Blanda pulled a leg muscle getting out of bed on the first day of training camp and missed the critical first four weeks of competition.

The Raiders started slowly in the regular season as the team's old men seemed rusty. Most of the attention in the NFL was focused on the Dallas Cowboys, who had been sold a second time in five years, this time to Larry Hagman's J.R. Ewing Enterprises. Texas Stadium had been renamed South Fork in Hagman's honor but the team continued winning as if nothing had changed. And,

Bill Bradley
President of the U.S.

Joe Theismann
Baltimore Federals

for the players, nothing had, because Tom Landry was starting his 30th season as head coach.

Only the Redskins, behind a 350-pound-per-man offensive line nicknamed the Pachyderms, caused the Cowboys any trouble in the National Conference. The Raiders had to rally late in the season to clinch a playoff spot but then demolished the Patriots, Chiefs and Chargers to qualify for the last NFL championship game to carry the title Super Bowl.

Dallas held a tenous lead through the first half but the Raiders, said to be inspired by coach Ben Davidson's assault on Landry's hat (he tore it into small pieces which he then proceeded to eat) before the start of the second half, harkened back to their aggressive style of yesteryear. In the span of one minute, they were whistled for three personal fouls. By the end of the third quarter, they had stomped down the field for three touchdowns, en route to a 31-17 triumph.

Nor did their behavior improve in New York as they prepared for SuperDuper I. On their first night in town, Davidson led them to a biker hangout in Brooklyn where they got in their last heavy workout before the game. They followed the next night by terrorizing the Guardian Angels on the subways and, finally, in a light mood, trashed Studio 54 where several prominent athletes had come to a bad end in the 1980s. "We're ready," Davidson said while being booked. Yet the Raiders hadn't held one single football practice at TrumpDome.

Trump's team was much more conscious of its image. The owner, referred to as "Mr. T" by many of his employees and peers in the USFL, had considered outfitting the Trumps in tuxedo-style uniforms for the game but was dissuaded by the argument that the colors would have been almost identical to those of the Raiders. He insisted, however, that the ushers and concessionaires be fitted for formal attire and even authorized the employment of the New York Philharmonic in pregame festivities.

Yet, much of the hype in the week prior to the game centered around Kosar, the kid quarterback whose taste in clothes ran to jeans and T-shirts. It so happened that on Monday Kosar had been making an appearance at Bloomingdale's when he was called to the telephone. A close friend had been seeking a loan to finance an East Side co-op and needed a cosigner. "Don't worry," Kosar said to the banker at the other end, "I'll guarantee it."

The conversation was overheard by the manager of the women's shoe department and passed along to an acquaintance who was an assistant city editor at a New York tabloid. One day later, the story appeared on the front page under the screaming headline, "Bloomie Bernie Guarantees Trumps' Triumph." For Wednesday's edition, Kosar was photographed in his apartment on a circular bed set atop a white llama rug, both of which had been purchased for the quarterback by the paper. By Thursday, he had become Broadway Bernie and by the weekend, he was a cult figure.

The Raiders, of course, were impressed by none of this. Davidson showed his disrespect for the whole affair by wading into the string section of the Philharmonic early Sunday and scaring the cellists half to death. Then, on the Trumps' first play from scrimmage, Alzado nearly unscrewed Walker's head along with his helmet. In the same series, Kosar was sandwiched in the backfield by Howie Long and Hendricks, who wrestled him to the ground and then yelled, "Make a wish," as each grabbed a leg and began to twist. A hail of bullets by the heavily armed team of officials stopped the Raiders from terminating the contest on the spot.

Although Walker saw only limited duty thereafter, Kosar's passes kept the Trumps in the game, offsetting breakaway runs by Marcus Allen and his backup, Jim Brown, who had returned to pro football in 1989 to reclaim the career rushing record from Franco Harris. The teams exchanged leads into the fourth quarter when a 52-yard field goal by the Trumps' Ali Haji-Sheikh tied the score for the first time at 27-27.

The rally by the Trumps might have ended there if it hadn't been for Mark Gastineau's sack of Kosar on what appeared to be New York's last possession in regulation time. Gastineau, plucked by the Raiders from the scrap heap when the sad-sack Jets finally grew tired of his antics, nailed the quarterback at the Trumps' 22-yard-line on third down. However, the Raiders were penalized

Olympian Carl Lewis leaps for SuperDuper touchdown.

50 yards (five yards for each Gastineau hop and holler) under the twice-strengthened "hot dog" rule.

After Gastineau had been sedated, strapped onto a stretcher and wheeled to the clubhouse, the Trumps struck quickly for the go-ahead touchdown. On second down from the Raiders' 25, coach Walt Michaels sent in the man he called his "Trump card." Kosar faked a handoff, looked left and then threw to his right for the goal line. Carl Lewis, a triple-gold medalist in the previous two Olympics, took off at the 10-yard line and, in the course of extending his world long-jump record to 31 feet, caught the winning pass and tumbled forward into the end zone. Haji-Sheikh, who had bolted the lowly Giants for an efficiency apartment in the chi-chi Trump Plaza on the fashionable East Side, accounted for the final point in the 34-27 upset.

Donald J. Trump toasted himself with champagne in the royal box above the 50-yard line, where his guests included President Bill Bradley and House Minority Leader Jack Kemp, a former quarterback. The ticker-tape parade on lower Broadway might have been the grandest moment of his life but the exaltation didn't last long. Along with two other developers, he had placed a bid for the renovation of the Manhattan Bridge. His plan called for a magnificent structure which would provide luxury apartments for 1,000, dwarf the revered Brooklyn Bridge nearby and, of course, carry the name Trump Bridge.

Alas, for the first time in a decade, he was thwarted in his efforts to recast New York in his image. A headline in one Wednesday paper said it best: "Bridge Bid Won: No Trump."

"THE MARCUS ALLEN I KNOW"

By JACK DISNEY

Marcus Allen first caught my attention on a balmy Los Angeles evening in September 1978. USC had a big lead over Michigan State, and, early in the fourth quarter, Trojan football coach John Robinson began to clear his bench.

Those of us seated in the Memorial Coliseum press box already were at work on our story leads when a reserve USC quarterback pitched the football to this freshman running back from San Diego.

Marcus Allen latched on to the ball, burst through an opening, saw daylight off his left shoulder and cut accordingly. But he got tangled up in his own feet and the next thing you knew, the eager 18-year-old was sprawled face down on the Coliseum grass. Right out there in the open field. What a way to begin.

Out of curiosity, I reached for my USC media guide and looked up "No. 9—MARCUS ALLEN, Defensive Back, 6–3, 195."

The guide noted that he had been a quarterback and safety in high school and, judging by the description, Allen was meant to be a defensive back at USC. He'd been named as California Prep Athlete of the Year and made some high-school All-America teams.

But this wasn't so unusual on the USC team. Not with a freshman team. Not among a freshman class that included Chip Banks and Roy Foster, who would become first-round NFL draft choices. Besides, a quarterback/ball-carrier named Timmy White, who hailed from New Jersey, was the reputed blue-chipper in this class.

Allen? Well, the guide said he had maintained a 3.3 average in high school and had been voted the Christian Athlete of the Year in San Diego County for his activities with the Young Men's Club, School Gospel Choir and Young People's Bible Club.

As a sportswriter and columnist for the Los Angeles Herald Examiner *for a quarter of a century, Jack Disney has seen it all— USC football, the Dodgers, Angels, Lakers and now the newest home team, the Raiders.*

Marcus Allen ran off with the Super Bowl MVP trophy.

These were interesting off-the-field credentials, to be sure, but Marcus Allen's inauspicious college debut was not what I would be writing about. The big man in my story was Charles White, the tailback who mostly remained upright that night.

Three years later, Marcus Allen would win the Heisman Trophy while destroying the NCAA record for yards gained rushing in a single season. Four years later, as a Los Angeles Raider, he would be NFL Rookie of the Year and an All-Pro. And five years later, on Jan. 22, 1984, he would break the Super Bowl rushing record and be named MVP for leading the Raiders to the championship over the Washington Redskins.

Two things seem to combine to make Allen so special. First, he is an exceptional athlete. Second, his adaptability, temperament and self-control allow him to draw the most from his natural ability.

Before the Super Bowl in Tampa Bay, I asked a Raider assistant coach to assess the things Allen does best in order. The answer might surprise you. He said (1) catch the football; (2) block; (3) run with the ball.

He overlooked the erstwhile high-school quarterback's skill at throwing the option pass.

When Allen was a senior at USC, John Robinson called him "the finest athlete I've ever seen or been around."

And Raider teammate Vann McElroy says, "The thing about Marcus is that he's got his head on straight."

Those closest to 24-year-old Marcus LaMarr Allen are struck by his mature sense of priorities and his willingness to accept the Raiders' nonstar system.

At USC, Allen, in effect, had been groomed for the Heisman Trophy since his sophomore season. Interviews his senior year were accorded the panache due a superstar, which Marcus indeed had become.

The Raiders, however, do little to promote Allen. Or any other player. Marcus is just another face on promotional posters, another silver and black uniform on the face of the club's media guide.

He is distinctive, nevertheless, and you could probably pick him out in a numberless jersey on the Raider practice field even if you'd never seen him before.

They used to call it charisma when Arnold Palmer was in his prime. Palmer had that purposeful walk from tee to green that just told you he was someone special.

You could have picked Pelé out on a soccer field if you didn't know his number. Something about the man's persona.

There is something, too, about Allen's graceful, gliding carriage that similarly distinguishes him—whether he's running with the football or simply walking back to the huddle.

Greg Pruitt, the former Cleveland running star, has become Allen's backup since joining the Raiders. He remembers Charles White, Allen's Heisman predecessor, coming to the Browns from USC.

"I had been starting and in he came," says Pruitt. "All I wanted was the opportunity to lose my job with the Browns, not just give it to someone else.

"But White thought he knew it all. And even after he didn't perform well, he still had the same attitude. Needless to say, he and I didn't get along."

Allen's approach, says Pruitt, has been just the opposite.

"Marcus is open-minded and he asks me for advice," explains Pruitt. "It makes my role easier to take because of Marcus himself. He came off a great college career, a great rookie season, and now Super Bowl MVP, and I still see him keeping the same perspective."

Marcus is extremely watchful of his public image and is often characterized as being guarded and aloof.

He remembers an article written about him as a sophomore at USC that portrayed him—at least, in Allen's estimation—as being cocky and brash. Maybe he overreacted, Marcus admits. But, since that time, he tends to become guarded in his interview responses.

With those he trusts in the press, remarks are often followed by, "That was off the record, of course." The next 10 minutes might be spent in convincing Marcus there was nothing harmful in what he had said.

The fact is, the private Marcus isn't so much different than the public Marcus. He is a fun person, mindful of others, and, if he ever falls into a depression, it is neatly camouflaged by what seems an ever-present smile.

When first interviewing Allen when he was 19, I noted how often he laughed. I wondered, if the laughter had been a product of nervousness. Unlikely. Marcus hasn't stopped laughing.

In an interview with Gwen Jones of the Los Angeles *Herald Examiner* before Super Bowl XVIII, the laughter was evident when Allen was asked about women in his life.

Q: What about a girlfriend?

A: Nobody wants me.

Q: What did you say?

A: Nobody wants me.

Q: Who're you kidding? You're intelligent, handsome, affluent and have potential, and you tell me nobody wants you. You must have women crawling all over you! What about the groupies? You certainly must get lots of fan mail.

A: (Laughs.) My mail comes from little kids.

Q: Have you perhaps built up a wall that no one can penetrate?

A: (Pause.) I think I fell in love a long time ago and it didn't work out. I got hurt. Maybe I'm scared to fall in love again. Maybe it is a defense. That's the honest truth.

Q: Well, tell me, what qualities do you admire in women?

A: (Chuckles) Intelligence, beauty, great personality. The All-American type. Someone you can bring home to mother. It would help if she cooked. (Laughs) Seriously, I admire career-minded women who are independent thinkers but who have respect for and like what I do. And I would have the same attitude about her work.

Allen, who is entering the third year of his three-year Raider contract (an estimated $1 million and bonus clauses, plus an option year), lives alone in the fashionable Brentwood section of Los Angeles.

Soon after signing as a rookie, he supervised the construction of a condominium tailored for his needs. He owns a Ferrari and a Ford Bronco as well as a wardrobe of stylish, if not flamboyant, clothes.

"I like to dress," he says, "but I'm not the best-dressed. I like to be classy and conservative."

He dates often and has been exposed to the Hollywood scene. O.J. Simpson is a close friend. Marcus occasionally hits the night-clubs, but he'd just as soon be among a gathering of friends at home.

He seldom drinks and disdains drugs. "I don't do any of that," he says. "I got drunk once when I was in college. It was terrible. I was sick for two days. I'm fortunate to neither need nor want drugs even though they were readily available in the community where I grew up. I've seen people go crazy over drugs, literally lose their minds. I don't want any of that. It's not for me."

Marcus was the second oldest of six children born to Gwen and Harold (Red) Allen in the area surrounding San Diego's Abraham Lincoln High School.

"The community is loaded with talent," says Vic Player, coach of the Lincoln High Hornets, usually one of San Diego's football powers. That's where Marcus made his early mark. Player calls him "one in a million." He cites as a contributing factor the Allen family. "They are very religious and close-knit," he says.

Red Allen, an independent contractor who built the family's cozy home in 1963, remembers Marcus being consumed by sports as a youngster. "He'd come home from football practice and start playing basketball behind the house," says Red. "When it was his week to wash the dishes, I'd have to beat him out of the backyard to get him into the kitchen. He later told one reporter he was going to turn me in for child abuse."

Gwen Allen, a registered nurse, says sports always came easy for Marcus. "He was a natural," she says. "But it was only when he learned to discipline himself that he began to do better and better. Marcus has that confidence. He knew exactly what he could do and had the determination to do it."

Player adds: "I'm used to kids who can run the 100 in 9.5 or 9.6. Marcus, well, he was 10-flat, or maybe 9.9. I thought Robinson would end up putting him back at fullback. But Marcus is just too good an athlete. He sets goals for himself, and he decided 'I am John Robinson's tailback,' and that determination was enough."

Speed—or its want—always seems to have been Allen's hurdle. Too slow, his detractors kept saying. The Raiders didn't think so. They were breathless, in fact, to find him still available when

Marcus' 191 yards rushing set a Super Bowl record.

choosing 10th in the NFL's 1982 college draft. As a footnote, I've seen every college and pro game in which Allen has played, and I can't ever recall him being caught from behind.

Marcus was earmarked for tailback at USC almost from the day he arrived, and to play anywhere else at Southern Cal is strictly a supporting role. The defensive-back scheme was scrapped in a hurry.

"We knew from the beginning Marcus was going to be special," remembers John Robinson, who has gone on to coach the Rams. "You didn't have to be a mystic, though, to realize that.

"There was just something about the man that was evident right away. I suppose it was his ability to compete. Everything told us he was the kind of person we wanted at tailback."

After his freshman season as White's backup at tailback, Marcus spent a sophomore season of apprenticeship at fullback while White ran for the Heisman Trophy. Allen wasn't ready to displace White. Just the same, Robinson wanted him in the lineup.

After Marcus took up residency at tailback in his junior year, there were those who felt Allen still would have made a good fullback. Addressing a supporter's group several games into the 1980 season, Robinson opened proceedings with a question.

"OK," said the USC coach, "how many of you think I should move Marcus Allen back to fullback and play Michael Harper at tailback?"

When the murmur subsided among some 400 people present,

Robinson counted perhaps 60 hands extended. He seemed to savor the moment, and, after dramatic pause, he said:

"When the next assistant coach's job opens, I don't want to hear from any of you people with raised hands."

One year later, Marcus Allen was well on his way to rushing into the NCAA history book with his 2,342 rushing yards plus 12 other NCAA records.

There was hardly an award Marcus didn't win in 1981. On the plane flying to New York for the Heisman Trophy dinner, he mentioned one that had been overlooked.

"Know what happened to me the other day?" he said, and he proceeded to tell about backing out of his driveway and hearing a frightening sound.

"I'd forgotten to close the car door," said Allen. "It got caught in some shrubbery. Tore a big hole in the door on the driver's side." He laughed and laughed some more.

"No doubt about it," said Marcus, "I qualify for the Numbskull-of-the-Month Award. Hands down."

Even then, on his way to receiving college football's greatest salute, Allen was able to keep his perspective.

He had been in training camp with the Raiders for less than two weeks in Santa Rosa, Cal., when veteran players began to respect him.

It would be Gene Upshaw's 16th and last season with the Raiders, and already he was talking as if he was witnessing a once-in-a-lifetime experience.

"Allen was the first draft choice I've ever been excited about," said Upshaw, the four-time All-Pro offensive tackle, "and now that I've seen what he can do, I'm even more excited.

"You look at film of Marcus carrying the ball in our practices and you can see an excitement among our offensive linemen that hasn't been there before."

"Maybe I shouldn't be saying this," Lyle Alzado said, "but it's true. He reminds me so much of O. J. Simpson. I mean, the way he moves, and he's strong, too. I think he's going to be just great."

Ted Hendricks: "I think this guy is going to be our offense. They should give him the ball all the time. I only hope he's as durable as he was in college."

Tom Flores, the Raider coach, would see to it that Allen had the ball most of the time in 1982 and, by the strike-shortened season's end, the Heisman winner had won over his professional contemporaries. His 14 touchdowns in nine games made Allen the first non-kicker to lead the league in scoring since Simpson in 1975.

If Allen figured to pick up in 1983 where he had left off the season before, the pickings weren't so good. As the season unfolded, Marcus found his rushing average and his number of carries lessening.

Defenses seemed keyed only on him. He missed the Redskin game with a hip pointer. His fumbling increased. His longest scrimmage run the entire season would be for 19 yards. Meanwhile, just a county away, a rookie running back was stealing the thunder: Eric Dickerson for John Robinson's Rams in Anaheim.

In his frustration, Marcus sought out Raider owner Al Davis about carrying the football more. Davis said something like, "You want to run more? Run after practice."

"Mr. Davis explained that he didn't want to beat me up," Allen would say later. "He wants me around."

It was the kind of reasoning that looked good when the 1983 playoffs began. Allen exploded for 121 yards on 13 carries against the Steelers. He set a Raider record while averaging 9.3 yards a carry.

Against Seattle in the AFC championship game, Marcus rushed for 154 yards on 25 carries, caught seven passes for an additional 62 yards, and, all of a sudden, his team was in the Super Bowl.

"He's beginning to see the repetition of the same things," Greg Pruitt was explaining of the revitalized Allen. "Eventually, there won't be a defense he hasn't experienced."

Allen hadn't played against the Redskin defense, No. 1 in the league against the rush, but it made little difference. His 191 yards on 20 carries against Washington in Tampa Bay were a Super Bowl record.

As he awaited the 1984 season, Marcus maintained a relatively low profile. For a Super Bowl hero, anyway. He kept in shape over the winter. "I had worked so hard the winter and spring before that I was tired," he noted. "Then, when things weren't going so well, I became overzealous and overanxious." There was to be a more controlled approach this time.

Meanwhile, his perspective seemed in check.

"I'm very fortunate," said Marcus Allen, "but I realize that what I have today can be gone tomorrow. I always remember that. The way I see it, we're here on earth on borrowed time. I'm not what I'm supposed to be as a Christian, but I do believe in God with all of my heart.

"Like everybody else, I go out and sin. However, I realize where my strength comes from every day. And the success I have had and hope to have comes from God. He's taken care of me during my football career and throughout my life."

For a guy who once couldn't keep his feet straight, the head seems to be doing just fine.

O.J.'s World of Monday Night Football

By FRANK KELLY

He was accustomed to flying through airports and winning awards. But in his rookie season on Monday Night Football, O.J. Simpson discovered that landing in a convertible is a lot easier than settling comfortably into a seat in the broadcast booth.

Like most rookies, the former Heisman Trophy winner and All-Pro running back struggled at the beginning. But like Darryl Strawberry of the New York Mets, he overcame the unfamiliarity, adjusted to the pressure and came on strong at the end.

Simpson candidly admits he had problems at first, attributing his slow start to an odd combination of laziness and overeagerness.

"When I stopped playing [in 1979], I got away from speaking spontaneously; with movies and commercials, it's all rehearsed. I became a lazy speaker. When I was thrown into a situation where I had to speak spontaneously, it was a tough transition. It sometimes got so bad that by halftime I was babbling."

The situation was aggravated by physical problems. "I developed polyps on my throat," Simpson said, "and that caused me to begin speaking from down here [indicating his broad chest]. I got together with a speech guy and he told me I wasn't using my voice properly. I'm a natural baritone and speak from the throat. The doctor said I was aggravating the condition by going to discos; he said to avoid them, and try to speak more nasally. I followed his advice, and after I had the polyps removed, I recovered my normal speaking voice."

Simpson said some of the voice problems were caused by pressure—his eagerness to succeed in his new role.

O.J., of course, had been behind the mike before. With ABC Sports, he'd covered track and field at the 1976 Olympic Games in Montreal; worked on a variety of "Wide World of Sports" events, including the Hula Bowl, and he'd been a commentator

Frank Kelly is tube-fed as TV/Radio sports columnist of the New York Daily News.

Tips from Howard Cosell to O.J. as Frank Gifford observes.

on "The Superstars," an event he won in 1975. The 37-year-old Simpson also worked for five years at NBC Sports, where his football coverage included two Rose Bowl telecasts. But Monday Night Football represented his biggest challenge.

"He was a little awkward at first," Frank Gifford says of his new colleague. "I was impressed with how hard he worked to prepare himself for a game and how much he knows about football. A lot of former athletes really don't know that much about the game. But sometimes he had too much information in his head—in the Monday Night format, his role calls for him to be more analytical."

Simpson concurs. "It took a while for me to determine my responsibilities. I tended at first to try to relate everything I knew about a player or a team. I learned eventually to give facts at the right time—to illustrate a point.

"At the Pro Bowl, Carlos Carson [Kansas City wide receiver] dropped two passes when he was wide open. I mentioned that his first five receptions had gone for touchdowns, then said he's the kind of receiver who can make you or break you."

When you're breaking in as a broadcaster, your colleagues can help to make you or break you. Simpson said that both Gifford and Howard Cosell helped him overcome his early-season slump.

"I was under a lot of pressure early in the season," he said, and I wasn't enjoying it. Why do it if you're not having a good time?"

Simpson, whom Gifford describes as "an up guy," was becoming a down guy. He says both Cosell and Gifford were sympathetic and understanding. Gifford advised him to relax and be himself—to avoid trying to impart too much information. "It was a matter of me determining in my head what is my responsibility in the booth," Simpson says.

Cosell, Simpson says, was always supportive. "We'd sit down after a game and have a drink and critique the broadcast. He was always positive."

The media critiques were not, however. "The most difficult part was reading the newspapers on Tuesday and Wednesday after my first outings. It was like I was back in the line—but not carrying the ball. I couldn't break a run in the fourth quarter and change my review."

Another thing that confused Simpson was the viewer reaction. "He was taken aback by the results of the tremendous exposure he got on Monday Night Football," said Gifford. "He would say something on the air and get a positive letter and five negative ones, a total reverse of reaction. That kind of thing stunned him."

Simpson admits that a lot of the criticism was justified, but he was able to turn it around in the second half of the season. "A lot of the same critics who had given me bad reviews started writing about how much I had improved. That made me happy."

What turned it around? Simpson mentions a point in the eighth game of the season—the infamous 20-20 overtime tie between the New York Giants and St. Louis Cardinals. Both teams kept botching scoring opportunities and it got so ludicrous that "I looked at Don [Meredith] and he looked at me and when it went into overtime, we just began having fun.

"It became just a joke; it was absolutely impossible to say something positive. So we decided to be entertaining. It was a revelation."

Simpson's confidence had begun to build the previous week, when he, Gifford and Meredith worked a wild game between the Packers and Washington Redskins at Green Bay. "I was just glad to be in the booth," said Simpson. "When there are enough big plays, it's easy to be interesting."

Simpson found it interesting—and challenging—to work with Cosell. "With Gifford and Meredith," he said, "they'd kid me and I'd kid back. But the weeks I knew I was going to be on with Howard, I'd prepare harder. If he was on and I wasn't, I'd have the benefit of listening to his story line. If I didn't agree with him, it would make me analyze why I thought the way I did. It helped

O.J. in his glory days with the Buffalo Bills.

me; it made me a more informed analyst."

For his part, Cosell thinks Simpson's strengths as an analyst are his "contemporary credibility—he's not that far removed from the playing field"—and his native intelligence.

Cosell recalled that early in the season he had said on the air that there were two power teams—Washington and the Los Angeles Raiders—and two finesse teams—Dallas and Miami— among the NFL's elite, and that the power teams would usually win. "O.J. picked up on that and used it in later broadcasts when I wasn't there," Cosell said. One reason for Simpson's early difficulties, Cosell suggested, was that "it took him awhile to learn when to get in and when to get out of on-air discussions."

As he polished these skills and gained confidence, Simpson says, he began to enjoy the job more. "It would have been a long offseason if I hadn't improved," he said. "If I can work all season like I did at the end, I'll be happy."

Asked what areas he felt needed improvement, Simpson mentioned "proper word delivery" and being "concise and quick" with his commentary.

What about the future? "My contract is up next year," he said. "It's up to Roone Arledge [ABC Sports president] whether I stay or not.

O.J. tuned up for airport commercials as a USC sprinter.

O.J. looks for a long run as analyst on Monday Night Football.

"I could easily see myself the next 10 or 15 years spending the fall doing Monday Night Football. I'll be able to have a connection with the game and the audience. For a football player—and I still consider myself one—it's a dream come true, the ultimate dream. Who wouldn't prefer to do Monday Night Football?"

Gifford and Cosell both feel Simpson will continue to improve. "He's never done anything he hasn't been successful at," noted Gifford. "There's no reason to think he can't be successful at this."

One of the things Simpson has been successful at is making commercials. The "flying through airports" spots were highly profitable for Hertz. But later campaigns were not as successful, so the car-rental firm brought Simpson back. "People weren't getting the message," says Simpson.

Noting the success of the "team approach" in beer commercials, the sponsor wanted to pair Simpson with another former athlete. "I was reluctant," admits Simpson, "I prefer to work alone." Then someone suggested pairing him with Arnold Palmer.

"I was flattered," said Simpson. "I didn't know him, but there's no one bigger in commercials. He's not just a former golfer—he's Arnold Palmer."

The ads, geared to a specific service or feature, have been getting a good response. "People are retaining the message."

O.J. Simpson no longer flies through airports in the ads, but he's more visible than ever, and he's on the way to winning his varsity letter as a pro football commentator.

Lawrence Taylor proved as formidable off the field as on.

Lawrence Taylor's Giant Trump

By BILL VERIGAN

Lawrence Taylor grabbed the blue inflated tackling dummy like it was one of the quarterbacks he sacks on Sunday afternoons. He threw it to the artificial turf in Giants Stadium, leaped on top and began pummelling it with his fists and feet. At last satisfied that he was the winner, he jumped up and started laughing while the other Giants at practice just shook their heads.

Frustration bubbled to the surface, then boiled over for Taylor last season. He was the angry young man of professional football.

One of the most gifted men ever to play the game, he was playing for one of the saddest teams in the league, a team with a 3-12-1 record. Moreover, the 6-foot-3, 237-pound linebacker was playing for a lot less money than many of his underachieving teammates.

It was Taylor's season of discontent, a season that will change him forever. Indeed, at the beginning, it appeared he would have no season at all.

He had come to the NFL as a relative innocent in 1981 out of the University of North Carolina, where he was a consensus All-American as an outside linebacker/defensive end. When the word was leaked out that his agent wanted $750,000 a year, some of the Giants' veterans suggested they should stage a holdout. They now claim that suggestion was made in jest, but it so upset Taylor that he sent a wire to the Giants' management asking not to be drafted. The veterans who had complained suddenly began calling Taylor to explain they had been misunderstood, and in the end, of course, the Giants made Taylor the second pick of the draft, right behind George Rogers, and wound up paying him much, much less than $750,000 a year.

For Bill Verigan the football season never ends. He covers the NFL in the fall, the USFL in the spring and whatever happens in between for the New York Daily News.

From his first scrimmage, he was by far the best player on the team, better than All-Pro linebackers such as Harry Carson and Brad Van Pelt. Points are awarded to the defense at scrimmages, two for causing a fumble, one for recovering it, three for a sack, and so on. Taylor had four sacks. He won the scrimmage 12-0. And he kept getting better.

He was the first rookie ever to be named NFL Defensive Player of the Year, then he repeated that honor the next year. Those honors didn't spoil him in the least. People who encountered him for the first time were always surprised at how unaffected he seemed to be.

Perhaps he still believed that good things happen to good people. He once said one of the biggest shocks of his life was finding out there was no Santa Claus. It happened back in the Taylor family's middle-class neighborhood in Williamsburg, Va., when he and one of his three brothers discovered their mother was stashing toys away in the attic before Christmas. He should have learned from that experience.

Instead, he waited for the Giants to come down the chimney and reward him for being such a good player during his first two seasons. He waited and waited and finally decided that he had to take matters into his own hands. All three of the Giants' other starting linebackers were making more than Taylor in 1982, according to the Players Association's base salary chart. Van Pelt was making $210,000, Carson $142,500 and Brian Kelley $120,000 while Taylor received $110,000. Incentive clauses pushed Taylor beyond $200,000, but that base salary stuck in his throat.

That's why he held out when training camp began a year ago. If the Giants had been smart, they would have appeased him. Instead, they let him fume. They never bothered to pick up the phone and give him a call. Some of his teammates who were closest to him were very worried that he would never return.

"I understood the consequences completely," Taylor said. "I used to say I was getting paid for having fun, but I got to see that professional football was a business. I also saw that I was just another asset."

He hated every minute of that holdout. He knew he belonged with the rest of the team. One day he showed up at practice and sat in the stands at the high school where the Giants were working out. He also came to the team's first preseason game and attracted as much attention as the players on the field. His replacement in that game, Andy Headen, had three sacks, and the Giants' management rubbed it in by saying the raw rookie might wind up as a permanent replacement.

Three days later, after forcing himself to stay away for three weeks, Taylor reported. It was no thanks to the Giants. Over lunch, a business associate had persuaded Taylor to let him act as an intermediary. The associate got them together, and Taylor was promised that his contract would be altered at the end of the season.

The promises were vague. They seemed to deal mainly with the incentive clauses, but nothing was in writing. Taylor remained skeptical, but his basic urges as a player overruled his judgment as a businessman.

The scars remained, though. The wounds were too deep to heal cleanly. One day he would make the Giants pay for those wounds, and that day was not far away.

Perhaps it would have been better if the Giants had not been so utterly pathetic during the season. Taylor was infuriated. He stopped talking to reporters because he feared that he might trample on his teammates' feelings the way he trampled blocking backs.

He skirmished with that tackling dummy, and occasionally he could be heard berating other players right through the closed door of the locker room after games.

After one particularly futile game, a tie against the St. Louis Cardinals on a Monday night, he hurled his helmet at a wall as he came off the field. The obscenities filled the hall as he told the team exactly what he thought. On the plane home, he was so depressed he told the coach, Bill Parcells, he just wanted to quit.

"It had gotten to the point where I was so hurt I didn't want to play football," he said. "I wanted to quit. When we got back to New Jersey, I sat with him in his car. We talked about a lot of things, personal things because we've been so close. I didn't want to hear about football, but he showed me why I should stay. He showed me what pride is."

Parcells would probably have paid anything it took to keep Taylor happy. Like Taylor says, they did have a special relationship. They had come to the Giants at the same time in 1981, and they had been the forces that drove the Giants into the playoffs that year. When Parcells became the head coach last season, he became aloof from many of his former defensive players. But he always had time to share with Taylor.

Taylor was one of the few men Parcells knew he could count on. When Carson got hurt, Parcells never hesitated to move Taylor inside. Other coaches might be fearful about toying with the best player and pass-rusher on the team, but Parcells showed no reluctance. Taylor openly wished he were back outside, but he played the new position like he had been there for his entire life.

It was a sacrifice that Taylor made for the good of the team. It was one more reason he chafed when some of his teammates refused to make sacrifices.

"A lot of times I got so mad I was ready to point fingers," he said, "but I couldn't do that. That's one reason I stopped talking to the press. I didn't want to say the wrong thing at the wrong time. A lot of our record you have to put on management, but you've got to look at the players, too, and a lot of them are not giving what it takes. It's no disgrace if you get beat by the guy across from you if you've done your best. But if you've given any less, it is a disgrace."

Considering the frustrations, Taylor was very vulnerable when the New Jersey Generals called. "My feelings were hurt," he said. Brig Owens, a friend in the Players Association, told him that the Generals seemed interested, and within hours his phone was ringing. The caller was Jim Gould, an advisor for the Generals and parttime agent.

Without ever telling his agent, Jim Paliafito, or former agent, Mike Trope, Taylor decided to pay a visit to the Generals. They were waiting for him with a check for $1 million, an interest-free loan that would become the down payment on an offer he couldn't refuse. Here was a team that made him feel wanted.

Although he still had a contract with the Giants that ran through 1987, he was being presented with a guaranteed deal for his future services. It seemed too good to be true. He signed the contract and took the check without blinking, and perhaps no one would have known if Donald Trump, the Generals' Fortune 500 owner, had resisted the impulse to have lunch with Taylor one day in Manhattan. Naturally enough, there were questions.

Taylor made it clear that he didn't really trust the Giants' management to live up to its promise to renegotiate. Even if it did, he didn't expect to get anywhere near as much as the Generals were offering.

However, Taylor wanted to renegotiate his contract with the Giants, so he asked Trope to see what they would offer. Perhaps the Giants already knew what the Generals had given him. No one will ever know for sure. At any rate, the Giants came up with a very similar deal. They also insisted that Taylor's contract be extended through 1989. Trope advised Taylor to accept the deal, and that's when Taylor had to admit he was already under contract to the Generals starting in 1988.

After weeks of indecision and haggling, the Giants bought back Taylor's contract with Trump. The episode must have been the most galling in the Giants' proud history. Here they were, paying off a team in an upstart, year-old league to get back one of their own players. How humiliating! Trump wound up getting $750,000, and the Giants wound up paying $2 million more than Taylor was asking for in training camp.

On the way to Giants, Taylor starred at North Carolina.

This time his teammates have no objections to Taylor's salary. They see it as a bargaining wedge when they want to negotiate with the Giants. The agent for Mark Haynes, a Pro Bowl cornerback who is entering his option year, said he expected his client's next salary to be based on what Taylor makes.

"If they want to win, they're going to have to pay some players," Taylor said, "but players are going to have to contribute more than they have. Some players on our team are a little bit overpaid."

For a team that is notoriously cheap, the Giants have had few contractual problems. They sign all of their draft choices, letting no one escape to the USFL, and they seldom have anyone of importance playing out an option.

However, last year there were frightening rumblings from some players who have been keys over the years, Carson and Van Pelt. Even before their salaries paled in comparison to Taylor's, they were asking to be traded. They could not stand losing any more.

Linebackers Taylor, Carson, Van Pelt and Brian Kelley became one of the most feared combinations of players in history. They were called the Crunch Bunch, and they even formed their own corporation to sell posters and other souvenirs. Recently, they held a party and sold the remaining 50,000 posters to a large corporation. Some of them obviously believed that the Crunch Bunch was breaking up.

Taylor is the heart of that unit, although he is by far the youngest. He doesn't want to see any of them leave.

But money alone will not make Taylor happy. He might have a $6.2-million deal that runs through 1989, but he wants something more. He wants to win.

Taylor is such a competitor that he loses sleep trying to figure out how to squeeze a few more points out of the video games he loves to play. He carries a golf club around the Giants' locker room and constantly works on his swing. Imagine what it must be like for him to play on a 3-12-1 team like the Giants.

"It's hard when you're faced with as much adversity as we were last year," he said. "When the primary word in your repertoire is losing, it's very hard. I never saw anything like last season. A lot of things came about. Our whole defensive line was struck down, and Harry Carson, too. And the offensive line didn't play up to its potential. And then there were the quarterback problems."

"I don't want to just say I play for the New York Giants. I want to be able to say I kick ass for the New York Giants. I'd love for our team to be able to say that. Now when you say you play for the Giants, you can tell what people are thinking. I want to be part of a winning team. I can hold my head up high knowing I've done my best, but that's nothing like hearing people say 'Ooooo, Wow!' when you say you play for the Giants. I've heard just that reaction when someone mentions the Raiders or the Cowboys. There are a lot of veterans on the Giants who will tell you they never experienced anything like the playoffs in 1981."

Those veterans had waited for years to be in the playoffs. Players like Carson and Van Pelt frequently talk about trades or retirement to vent their frustration. Taylor couldn't bear winding up like them.

"Harry Carson is one of the 10 or 12 guys who goes out every week and busts his butt," Taylor said. "It's frustrating when I look at Harry. I tell myself that I hope I never have to go through the things he did. He deserved better. He asked to be traded after last season, after putting in so many good years. He has to make his own decision, but I'd respect any decision he makes."

A linebacker's lot is never easy. Taylor is only 25—married, the father of two—and he appears indomitable. But he is preparing for his retirement. He kept that $1-million loan. The Giants had to pay it off. He has been investigating investments, from race horses to restaurants to real estate.

"A lot of guys in this game want to quit and can't afford to," he said. "I'll play out my contract, play hard every year. But when the game becomes a hassle, I don't want to be out there when I'm beat up and people say 'You should have seen him five years ago.'"

When he retires he will probably disappear the way he does during the offseason. He calls himself "a private person." He turns down 99 percent of the offers that come his way. He shuns interviews. He shuttles among Chapel Hill, N.C., where he went to school; Williamsburg, Va., where he grew up; and Upper Saddle River, N.J., where he now lives.

There are probably a lot of offensive players for other teams who wish he would slip away. They would have been relieved to see him in the USFL right now.

A lot of guys will probably remember getting hit by Taylor. He is fast enough to run down a receiver, strong enough to fight off an offensive lineman.

"There's nothing better than a real good, solid tackle," Taylor said. "I've put a couple of people out in my day, but I don't want anybody to get hurt. I always pray before a game that nobody gets hurt. It's okay to stun them, but I don't want any broken bones. I'm physical, but I'm not dirty."

Last year, he resorted to a tactic that didn't go down very well with opponents. After a sack, he occasionally ran over and taunted the opposing bench. Parcells told him to stop, but in a game Taylor is always slightly out of control. Unfortunately, the Giants were unable to back up his taunts last year. Taylor hopes this year will be different in many ways.

Coach Hugh Campbell and Warren Moon team up in Houston.

Houston's Moon Magic

By STEVE KELLEY

The waters of Lake Washington reflected the slate gray skies. Raw wind was kicking and the drizzle was beginning. It was a typical Washington winter afternoon and Warren Moon, one of the state's sporting resources, was spending it in typical fashion—sitting in his sweats on the University of Washington campus, hanging out, preparing for another round of workouts.

"This is me," the National Football League's new millionaire quarterback said as he watched a few hearty sailors wrestle with the Lake Washington winds. "I spend a lot of my time when I'm in Seattle around the university, talking with young people. I do

Steve Kelley, a sports columnist for the Seattle Times, *has been on the Moon voyage from the time Warren started turning jeers into cheers at Washington's Husky Stadium.*

The Moon family looks forward to a new voyage.

it because everyone around here is trying to shoot for where I am. If you keep yourself surrounded by people who are still striving to get to a certain point, you're always going to have your own goals fresh in your mind."

This is Moon's comfort zone. This is where he came to think when his whirlwind tour of National Football League cities got him confused. This is where he came for shelter when he got tired of hearing about tax shelters. He looks at home here whether he is pumping iron in the bowels of the athletic department building or sitting in the stands watching a University of Washington basketball game; whether he is throwing passes; or passing time.

This is where the dream began for him: the dream that was capped by his five-year, $6.5-million contract with the Houston Oilers.

When he first came here nine years ago, the name was Harold Moon. He was a junior-college transfer expected to turn new coach Don James into a winner. Harold Moon, the son of Harold Moon, Sr., who died when Warren was seven, preferred to be called Warren.

On a hot August afternoon, shortly after his arrival, he filled out a questionnaire. He was asked to describe his goals.

"To push the others going out for quarterback," he wrote. "To be No. 1 by Sept. 13, 1975. To be behind the ball in the Rose Bowl January 1."

Academic goals?

"Graduate on time in Society and Justice."

Financial goals?

"To establish a savings account; have enough money to go home with."

Long-range goals?

"When I graduate from UW, I would like to sign a six-figure contract in pro ball."

Would you believe seven figures? Everything in Moon's pro football life has unfolded as beautifully as a perfect rose. Rather than risk being drafted in the middle rounds of the 1978 National Football League draft, Moon signed three weeks before the draft with the Canadian Football League's Edmonton Eskimos. It was the beginning of a master plan that made him a truly free agent last winter. He led the Eskimos to five straight Grey Cups; then in his sixth season last year he threw 31 touchdown passes.

"I wouldn't call it a master plan, but I'm always looking a step ahead," Moon said. "If I ever wanted to come back to the NFL, I wanted it to be to the team of my choice. Things worked out extremely well. Not just me being a free agent, but the timing of me becoming a free agent this year. This is the best year possible for a player because of all the stuff going on in the USFL. I wanted to get out of my contract in Edmonton last year, but if I had, I would never have been in this good a position."

At Houston he will have his own radio and television shows. He also is expecting to move his chocolate-chip cookie business down from Edmonton. But part of his heart will remain in Seattle. It is here that he has continued a long, tumultuous love affair. There are those who think moving Moon to Houston is like placing the Space Needle in the Astrodome, as absurd as plopping Mount Rainier on a Texas prairie.

"I really did want to play in Seattle more than a lot of people thought," Moon said. "If the money and all of the guarantees had been equal, I probably would have come here. I wanted to play in Seattle more than I let on because of negotiating reasons. But I didn't want to put a lot of pressure on them. I didn't want to make it seem like they had to sign me. I knew how people reacted to me in this area. A lot of people wanted me here. If I went around making comments in the papers about how much I wanted to play here, I think it would have just put more pressure on the Seahawks and on myself."

Still, when negotiations between Seattle and Moon's agent Leigh Steinberg reached a dead end, Moon insinuated himself into the talks. He called Seattle owner Jim Nordstrom and general manager Mike McCormack. They listened politely, but refused to budge from their chiseled-in-stone policy not to award guaranteed contracts.

McCormack, an old-school negotiator whose tough stance fits Nordstrom's fiscal policies, simply argued, "If I gave one guaranteed contract, I'd have 48 other other guys wanting the same thing."

"I did some things on my own to try and make things work out," Moon said. "That's how much I wanted to play here. I was a little frustrated, but they had their policies. There are nine other quarterbacks who have some kind of guarantees. I think if the USFL stays around, you're going to see the majority of the NFL contracts guaranteed.

"The thing that really got me thinking about guaranteed contracts more than anything was the Washington Redskins. They won the Super Bowl two years ago and went back there this year. They've got their MVP quarterback [Joe Theismann] but they really wanted me to come there and play. I figured, if Theismann's not in a position where his job is secure, then I don't think there's a player in the league whose job is secure. I look at myself. I'm 27 and in a few years I'll be 30 and some other young, hotshot quarterback might be coming up on me. All of a sudden I'm expendable, just like all of a sudden Jim Zorn was expendable. I just wanted to protect myself as much as possible."

Moon's life in Seattle wasn't always this secure. Those were troubled waters he saw in 1975 when he looked from Husky Stadium to Lake Washington. Football is serious business at Washington. Don James was hailed as the savior come to resurrect the program. Moon was his quarterback. But their first season together, Washington finished 6–5. Moon didn't have the Huskies rising quickly enough. That noise he heard when he jogged onto the field may have sounded like *moooooon*, but it was *boooooo*.

"It got pretty bad," Moon said. "I didn't know everything that was going on because I tried to keep clear of the media. I didn't read the papers; didn't listen to many of the radio shows. Most of what I got was secondhand. But I had a lot of friends in the stands during the games who were confronted with a lot of different things. They got into more altercations about stuff than I did. They had arguments and fist fights because people were calling me names.

"My wife [Felicia] was in the middle of all of that. She even got into some shouting matches, but I never really asked her about it that much and she never really tried to share it with me because I had enough things on my mind."

Felicia, who had been Moon's Los Angeles High School sweetheart, was attending San Jose State when the fan pressure started building. Finally, she transferred to Washington to stand by her man. The booing of Moon was especially ugly because he was Washington's first black quarterback. Much of the criticism was racially motivated.

"When we weren't winning, the racism was blatant," Felicia said. "There were actually letters in the papers saying that Warren was coach James' token black. Fans would call him names in the stands. They would call him 'nigger.' Of course, when we won the Rose Bowl, things were fine again."

Moon saw the hypocrisy in all of this, but he still enjoyed the people around him. He understood that the ugliness was coming from a small band of thugs, the kind he would find anywhere.

"It all was tough, but the thing that made it good was that my teammates knew that I had the ability and that I was the best guy at the position. As long as I had those people in my corner, I wasn't going to give up. I think the experience made me a better person. It made me a lot stronger. I'm able to deal with a lot of adversity now because I had to deal with it at a young age.

"Tougher things actually happened to me in high school. I had my life threatened a couple of times by gangs because of the way I played on the football field. I grew up during the big gang movement in Los Angeles. Sometimes I had gangs of guys waiting around my car after games. I'd have to drive home with a friend and get my car in the morning. After those experiences and the things that happened to me at Washington, I think I can deal with most anything."

Moon was all class even when the Husky fans were acting all crass. It will be his charm as well as his arm that will make him a success in Houston.

"I got angry sometimes," he said. "There were some things I could have done, especially when it was all over and we started winning. I remember the USC game my senior year [1977]. I had just busted a 70-yard run that pretty much clinched the game and assured us the PAC-8 title. Everybody was chanting my name and then I remembered how, even early in the season, they had been booing me. I could have just flipped everybody off then. But I don't think that would have gained me anything in the long run. I have a little more class than that.

"Things have worked out well. I've had a lot of people come up to me and apologize. Even six years later they say they booed me when I was here and they apologize for the way they acted. If I had done some things I had in my mind to do then, I probably wouldn't be as happy as I am today."

Moon's smile, as much a part of him as his golden arm, tells everyone he's a happy man. He has been reunited in Houston with his Edmonton coach, Hugh Campbell. He has lifetime security. And he has a team that has nowhere to go but up.

"Having Hugh there made the decision easier for me," he said. "Having a guy I'm used to who is used to me. He knows how I'm going to react to certain situations. If I throw an interception, he would know better than anybody why I threw it. He would know how I was going to react in the next series. That helps. If he would say something derogatory, I would know why he said it. I wouldn't have to worry about why. That's important.

"Houston won only two games last year; so this has got to be a big challenge for me. I've never stepped down from a challenge in my life. That's one of the reasons I can go to Houston and feel good about it. I can be a part of something from the ground up, just like I was at Washington."

"One thing, it can't get much worse than it already is in Houston. It might have been a little tougher on me pressure-wise in Seattle. They went to the AFC championship game last season without me. The only thing left is the Super Bowl. If they don't go to the Super Bowl this time, it will be a big disappointment."

Moon announced his decision to go to Houston the same day another Challenger space craft whizzed into space. It marked the end of the NFL's Moon watch and the beginning of Moon's life as a millionaire.

"I'm pretty basic. My family is pretty basic," he said. "Everybody asks me what am I going to do with all that money. I really have nothing I want to go out and buy. I bought my mother a new home before Christmas. I've wanted to do that for a long time. I'm going to give her a lump sum of money so maybe she won't have to work so hard the rest of her life. I'm going to get my sister started in business. I'm going to do some things like that. But that's all.

"Money isn't the only reason I signed with Houston. I wouldn't have come down from Canada to the NFL if there wasn't a chance to win a Super Bowl. I would have gone to the USFL if it was strictly for the money. But the challenge of winning a Super Bowl really means something to me. I want to see how good I can be and the best way to do that is play with the best people there are to play with. That's what I'll be doing in the NFL. I wouldn't have found that out in the USFL."

INSIDE THE NFC

By PAUL ATTNER

PREDICTED ORDER OF FINISH

EAST	CENTRAL	WEST
Washington	Detroit	New Orleans
St. Louis	Chicago	San Francisco
Dallas	Green Bay	Los Angeles
N.Y. Giants	Minnesota	Atlanta
Philadelphia	Tampa Bay	

NFC Champion: Washington

Everyone already knows the good teams in the NFC: Washington, San Francisco, Los Angeles, possibly even Dallas yet. But maybe this is a time for a change in the conference. So let's look at the new intruders.

Keep your eyes on the likes of St. Louis, Chicago and New Orleans. Why? Because all three can be praised for intelligent drafting the last five years. Toss out this year's draft; it's too early to evaluate. But off the last half-decade, these three teams have carefully built a nucleus of fine players, much as New England is doing in the AFC. And these youngsters are about to mature.

Ironically, the Saints' Bum Phillips gained a reputation at Houston for hating the draft and, George Allen-like, depending too much on trades for older players. With the Saints, he stuck almost strictly with the draft until unloading his No. 1 last spring for quarterback Richard Todd, which well may be the last piece in the Saints' playoff puzzle. They've never qualified for postseason play, but that will change this year.

If Mike Ditka could stop long enough from kicking tables and hitting lockers and concentrate on coaching, he might find himself

---

Paul Attner plays the field as roving NFL correspondent for the Washington *Post.*

Dallas counts on another good year from receiver Tony Hill.

on the verge of playoff contention, too. The Bears are ready to make a run at Detroit, a little older club which also has been doing a good drafting job. The Lions may be a bit too strong this season for Chicago, but wait until the Bears can make full use of their 1984 draft crop.

St. Louis has had a horrible habit of starting off slowly and finding itself out of the playoff race before the season is half over. If the Cardinals can reverse that trait, they may be ready to jump ahead of the Cowboys. That's right, Dallas is teetering at that jumping off point; the Cowboys have enough holes to fall back to the rest of the pack and leave things to the also-aging Redskins. Tom Landry's decision at quarterback will do much to determine how well Dallas does. And if either John Riggins or Joe Theismann stumbles, the NFC race will become much more open than it appears now.

No matter, the upstarts are ready to take over. It's just a matter of time. Meanwhile, a shaky vote for the Redskins to make it three in a row in the NFC.

ATLANTA FALCONS

TEAM DIRECTORY: Chairman: Rankin Smith Sr.; Pres.: Rankin Smith Jr.; Exec. VP: Eddie LeBaron; GM: Tom Braatz; Dir. Pub. Rel.: Charlie Dayton; Head Coach: Dan Henning. Home field: Atlanta Stadium (60,748). Colors: Red, black, silver and white.

SCOUTING REPORT

OFFENSE: Dan Henning is committed to a one-back offense and the Falcons should execute it better this season. Quarterback Steve Bartkowski had his best season, overall, in his NFL career but he really isn't the mobile player Henning would like in the position. It will be interesting to see if Henning modifies things a bit to make Bartkowski more comfortable.

There is no need to do anything for William Andrews, who had a standout season and is almost perfect for the one-back approach. The only problem is, that leaves little time for backup Gerald Riggs, who has too much ability to stay on the bench. The offensive line, anchored by Mike Kenn and R.C. Thielemann, is solid although center Jeff Van Note is nearing the end of his career.

Stacey Bailey emerged as a quality receiver last year, but will Alfred Jackson come back from a shoulder injury and Alfred Jenkins from problems with chemical dependency? And will the Falcons find a tight end?

DEFENSE: Part by need, part by desperation, the Falcons turned to rookies last year to help out their defense. By season's end, five rookies (Andrew Provence, Dan Benish, Mike Pitts, John Rade, James Britt) all were starting. In this year's draft Atlanta again went for defenders, led by Oklahoma DT Rick Bryan.

The unit's progress will depend on how these players develop. Veteran tackle Mike Zele (knee), linebacker Al Richardson and tackle Don Smith (knee) all expect to return from injuries to challenge for their old starting spots. The Falcons want to upgrade their pass rush, which was limited to a mere 34 sacks last year.

In the secondary, Britt made a nice starting debut but fellow safety Tom Pridemore might have to scramble to keep his starting spot.

After finishing 25th overall and next-to-last in rushing defense, the entire unit has room for vast improvement.

KICKING GAME: Field goal specialist Mick Luckhurst is coming off his best season and punter Ralph Giacomarro was acceptable with a 40.3 average. White Shoes Johnson supplies the spirit and the talent with his dashing punt returns and the Falcons blocked six kicks in 1983. An improving unit.

THE ROOKIES: The Falcons went into the draft seeking defensive help; and that's what they got—all first-rounders from Oklahoma. How much help the rookies will be immediately is another question. DT Bryan may improve their pass rush and then there are DB Scott Case and LB Tom Benson. QB Ben Bennett, a sixth-rounder from Duke, could be their best pick.

OUTLOOK: Atlanta won three of its last five and knocked two teams out of the playoffs. That gives Henning an optimistic feeling about 1984, especially when considering the Falcons' first five

Billy Johnson soared with his punt returns and exciting catches.

FALCONS VETERAN ROSTER

HEAD COACH—Dan Henning. Assistant Coaches—Steve Crosby, George Dostal, Sam Elliott, Ted Fritsch, Bob Fry, Bob Harrison, Bobby Jackson, John Marshall, Gary Puetz, Dan Sekanovich, Jack Stanton.

No.	Name	Pos.	Ht.	Wt.	NFL Exp.	College
31	Andrews, William	RB	6-0	213	6	Auburn
82	Bailey, Stacey	WR	6-1	163	3	San Jose State
10	Bartkowski, Steve	QB	6-4	218	10	California
69	Benish, Dan	DT	6-5	265	2	Clemson
26	Britt, James	CB-S	6-0	185	2	Louisiana State
66	Bryant, Warren	T	6-7	270	8	Kentucky
23	Butler, Bobby	CB	5-11	175	4	Florida State
21	#Cain, Lynn	RB	6-1	205	6	Southern California
88	Cox, Arthur	TE	6-3	245	2	Texas Southern
89	Curran, William	WR	5-10	175	3	UCLA
50	Curry, Buddy	LB	6-4	228	5	North Carolina
51	Dixon, Rich	LB	6-2	235	2	California
71	Dufour, Dan	G	6-5	280	2	UCLA
58	Frye, David	LB	6-2	205	2	Purdue
34	Gaison, Blane	S	6-1	188	4	Hawaii
1	Giacomarro, Ralph	P	6-0	190	2	Penn State
36	Glazebrook, Bob	S	6-1	200	7	Fresno State
52	Harper, John	LB	6-3	230	2	Southern Illinois
30	Haworth, Steve	CB	5-11	190	2	Oklahoma
83	Hodge, Floyd	WR	6-0	190	3	Utah
85	Jackson, Alfred	WR	6-0	185	7	Texas
84	#Jenkins, Alfred	WR	5-9	155	10	Morris Brown
81	Johnson, Billy	WR	5-9	170	10	Widener
37	Johnson, Kenny	CB	5-11	172	5	Mississippi State
20	Jones, Earl	CB	6-1	175	5	Norfolk State
78	Kenn, Mike	T	6-7	255	7	Michigan
54	Kuykendall, Fulton	LB	6-4	228	10	UCLA
70	Lee, Ronnie	G-T	6-3	243	6	Baylor
55	Levenick, Dave	LB	6-3	220	2	Wisconsin
18	Luckhurst, Mick	K	6-0	180	4	California
49	Matthews, Allama	TE	6-3	230	2	Vanderbilt
87	Mikeska, Russ	TE	6-3	222	6	Texas A&M
62	Miller, Brett	T	6-7	275	2	Iowa
80	Miller, Junior	TE	6-4	240	5	Nebraska
15	#Moroski, Mike	QB	6-4	200	5	California-Davis
53	Musser, Neal	LB	6-3	223	4	North Carolina State
74	Pitts, Mike	DE	6-5	260	2	Alabama
27	Pridemore, Tom	S	5-11	186	7	West Virginia
72	Provence, Andrew	DT	6-3	265	2	South Carolina
59	Rade, John	LB	6-1	220	2	Boise State
56	Richardson, Al	LB	6-3	220	5	Georgia Tech
42	Riggs, Gerald	RB	6-1	230	2	Arizona State
33	Robinson, Bo	RB	6-2	235	6	West Texas State
67	Sanders, Eric	T	6-7	270	4	Nevada-Reno
61	Scully, John	G	6-6	255	4	Notre Dame
65	Smith, Don	DT	6-5	260	6	Miami
68	Thielemann, R.C.	G	6-4	252	8	Arkansas
43	Tutson, Tom	CB-S	6-1	180	2	South Carolina State
57	Van Note, Jeff	C	6-2	250	16	Kentucky
22	Williams, Richard	RB	6-0	205	2	Memphis State
79	Yeates, Jeff	DE	6-3	252	13	Boston College
86	Young, Benjamin	TE	6-4	225	2	Texas-Arlington
63	Zele, Mike	DT	6-4	250	6	Kent State

#Unsigned at press time

TOP FIVE DRAFT CHOICES

Rd.	Name	Sel. No.	Pos.	Ht.	Wt.	College
1	Bryan, Rick	9	DT	6-4	260	Oklahoma
2	Case, Scott	32	DB	6-1	185	Oklahoma
2	Benson, Thomas	36	LB	6-2	235	Oklahoma
3	McSwain, Rod	63	DB	6-2	190	Clemson
4	Malancon, Rydell	94	LB	6-2	219	Louisiana State

losses were by a total of only 19 points. This is a young, developing team with established superstars on offense. The key will be how well the sluggish defenses comes around.

FALCON PROFILES

STEVE BARTKOWSKI 31 6-4 218   Quarterback

His coach says "it would be difficult to play quarterback better than Steve Bartkowski did in 1983." . . . Had his finest season, leading the NFL with a pass efficiency rating of 97.6 . . . Tossed 22 touchdowns and only five interceptions for an interception ratio of 1.15, second best in NFL history . . . And this came despite troubles adapting to Dan Henning's new offensive philosophies . . . Even had to roll out some, not an easy task for a slow-footed quarterback . . . Born Nov. 12, 1952, in Des Moines, Iowa . . . Enjoys hunting, fishing . . . Good enough baseball player at U. of California to excite baseball scouts.

WILLIAM ANDREWS 28 6-0 213   Running Back

Falcons like to think he is the best all-around back in the league . . . Has statistics to back it up . . . Gained a club-record 1,567 yards last year to move into the NFL's top 25 career rushers with 5,772 yards . . . Had seven 100-yard games, including high of 162 against Miami . . . Also had 59 catches, second best on team . . . He was only a third-round choice out of Auburn, taken mainly for his blocking ability . . . But his talents are made just right for one-back offense . . . Henning loves his unselfish habits and his desire to keep on working . . . Born Dec. 25, 1955, in Thomasville, Ga. . . . Remains a small town citizen in the offseason.

BILLY JOHNSON 32 5-9 170   Receiver

This man has more lives than the neighbor's howling cat . . . Given up for good by the Houston Oilers, then rejected by Canada . . . They said his knees were too bad to allow him to play well again . . . Wrong . . . Became inspirational leader of Falcons last season . . . Caught two passes in 1982, and 64 in '83 to lead team in receiving . . . Who will forget his thrilling game-winning catch against the 49ers?... But did even more damage with his punt returns, rewriting Falcon record book with 489 yards... Born Jan. 27, 1952, in Bouthwyn, Pa.... Starred at Widener College... Teaches school in the offseason... Once played professional softball.

JEFF VAN NOTE 38 6-2 250   Center

Risen to the top in two professions... One of the league's best centers, and also top dog in the players' union... A peacemaker in the labor relations area, much needed following problems caused by players' strike in 1982 ... Has played in 201 NFL games... His only non-starting NFL appearance came in his rookie year, 1969... Has been in the Pro Bowl six times... Getting to point where he considers retirement every year... Born Feb. 7, 1946, in South Orange, N.J.... Does a lot of long-distance bike riding in the offseason... Started off as a running back at Kentucky, then became defensive end.

MIKE KENN 28 6-7 255   Offensive Tackle

Continues to rank as one of the elite tackles in the league... Solid in all phases and coaches love his consistency... Another Pro Bowl appearance, his fourth... Tough for his peers throughout the NFC to leave his name off the ballot... Never stops trying to get stronger, and this increased strength has made him a better player... Always had the quickness... Had a streak of 26 penalty-free games a few years ago... When he holds, it's a surprise... Born Feb. 9, 1956, in Evanston, Ill... A gourmet cook, real estate dabbler and former No. 1 choice from Michigan.

MICK LUCKHURST 26 6-0 180   Placekicker

Had his best season as a pro, making 17 of 22 field goals, including 11 of his last 13 tries... "I feel I am one of the best kickers in the league," he says... Beat out incumbent Tim Mazzetti three years ago... Kicked at the U. of California, where he missed only three field-goal tries his senior year... Born March 31, 1958, in Redbourne, England... Wife is a pro golfer on LPGA tour... Excellent rugby player who led California to national championship, winning tournament MVP award... Began college career at St. Cloud in Minnesota.

MIKE PITTS 23 6-5 260   Defensive End

Falcons' No. 1 1983 draft choice who finished strongly... Led team in sacks with 7½ even though he was not always a fulltime starter ... Was an early holdout but proved he was worth big bucks... Falcons thought he was the best defensive lineman available in the draft... Played mostly as standup defensive end at Alabama, including two years as backup to E.J. Junior... First-team All-American as senior... Born Sept. 25, 1960, in Pell City, Ala.... Communications major... Falcon coaches think he will develop into All-Pro very quickly.

BOBBY BUTLER 25 5-11 175   Cornerback

Now has 11 interceptions in three years after picking off four last year... By far his steadiest season... "I'm more comfortable," he says. "I'm doing the things I always felt I could do." ... Wore inconsistent tag for first two seasons in the league... But coaching-staff change helped when he fell under guidance of Jack Christiansen, Pro Football Hall of Famer... Former No. 1 pick from Florida State... Born May 28, 1959, in Boynton Beach, Fla.... Likes to play basketball in the offseason... Was track star in college and blocked seven kicks in college career.

BUDDY CURRY 26 6-4 228   Linebacker

A standout who was best player for the Falcon defense last year... Took on even more responsibility when Al Richardson was hurt in fourth week with a shoulder injury... Finished with 127 solo tackles to rank as the team's leading tackler for the fourth year in a row... Had 22 alone against San Francisco... Not supposed to be this good when he left North Carolina, where Lawrence Taylor was linebacking teammate... Born June 4, 1958, in Danville, Va.... His father was a football player at the University of Kentucky... Came back after serious knee injury at end of 1982 season.

JAMES BRITT 23 6-0 185   Safety

Another talented Falcon draft choice who had to step in and become immediate starter ... Wasn't sure in training camp whether he would be a safety or cornerback ... Could become a real defensive star in the league if he keeps developing ... Second-round pick after standout career at LSU, where he was first-team all-conference and three-time all-conference academic selection ... Graduated with 3.6 average in business administration ... Born Sept. 12, 1960, in Minden, La. ... Was high-school defensive player of the year his senior season ... Had injury problems in college, with two broken bones.

COACH DAN HENNING: Got mixed reviews from his first

season as NFL head coach ... His critics thought he was too stiff, too entrenched, especially with one-back offense ... His backers thought he set the stage for a Falcon comeback even though the team struggled at times during the year ... No-nonsense guy who has a dry sense of humor ... Very intense, intelligent, believes completely in what he is doing ... Improved his press relations ... Bases hope for improvement on year of progress, his own development ... Was an assistant coach under some good ones: Don Shula, Joe Gibbs, Bill Peterson ... Excellent handler of quarterbacks ... Born June 21, 1942, in New York City ... Attended William and Mary, where he was quarterback ... Son is a quarterback at University of Maryland.

BIGGEST PLAY

New Orleans coach Dick Nolan called it "one shot in a million." He was still shaking his head, not believing what he had just witnessed.

On Nov. 12, 1978, in New Orleans, the Falcons had been trailing most of the game to the underdog Saints. Atlanta knew a loss would probably mean playoff elimination.

Now, with 15 seconds remaining, the Falcons had the ball on their 43. And they had no timeouts. The scoreboard read: New Orleans 17, Atlanta 13.

Quarterback Steve Bartkowski called for "Big Ben Right"—a pass play designed to let one receiver tip the ball to another. Receivers raced down the field and Bartkowski simply threw the ball as high and as far as he could.

Wallace Francis got to the ball before three Saint defenders. He tipped it. Billy Ryckmann was supposed to be the trailer but he was delayed, so Alfred Jackson filled the role. He waited as the tipped ball eluded the Saints and fell into his hands on the 10, and he raced into the end zone for the winning touchdown.

INDIVIDUAL FALCON RECORDS

Rushing

Most Yards Game:	167	William Andrews, vs New Orleans, 1979
Season:	1,567	William Andrews, 1983
Career:	5,772	William Andrews, 1979-83

Passing

Most TD Passes Game:	4	Randy Johnson, vs Chicago, 1969
	4	Steve Bartkowski, vs New Orleans, 1980
	4	Steve Bartkowski, vs St. Louis, 1981
Season:	31	Steve Bartkowski, 1980
Career:	138	Steve Bartkowski, 1975-83

Receiving

Most TD Passes Game:	3	Alfred Jenkins, vs New Orleans, 1981
Season:	13	Alfred Jenkins, 1981
Career:	40	Alfred Jenkins, 1975-83

Scoring

Most Points Game:	18	Lynn Cain, vs Oakland, 1979
	18	Alfred Jenkins, vs New Orleans, 1981
	18	William Andrews, vs Denver, 1982
	18	William Andrews, vs Green Bay, 1983
Season:	114	Mick Luckhurst, 1981
Career:	270	Nick Mike-Mayer, 1973-77
Most TDs Game:	3	Lynn Cain, vs Oakland, 1979
	3	Alfred Jenkins, vs New Orleans, 1981
	3	William Andrews, vs Denver, 1982
	3	William Andrews, vs Green Bay, 1983
Season:	13	Alfred Jenkins, 1981
Career:	40	Alfred Jenkins, 1975-83

CHICAGO BEARS

TEAM DIRECTORY: Chairman: Edward B. McCaskey; Pres.: Michael B. McCaskey; VP/GM: Jerome Vainisi; Dir. Player Personnel: Bill Tobin; Dir. Marketing/Communications: Bill McGrane; Coordinator Media Relations: Ken Valdiserri; Head Coach: Mike Ditka. Home field: Soldier Field (65,793). Colors: Orange, navy blue and white.

SCOUTING REPORT

OFFENSE: The problem with the Bears last season on offense was Mike Ditka's temper and an inability to take advantage of scoring opportunities. Ditka swears he has his temper under control as much as it ever will be. Now maybe he can concentrate on that lack of points.

The Bears had one of the league's most effective offenses when total yardage is measured. But they scored 17 or less points nine times and 19 another. Part of the problem might have been youth but those youngsters—linemen Jimbo Covert, Jay Hilgenberg and Kurt Becker and receivers Willie Gault and Dennis McKinnon—are a year older and wiser now. So is quarterback Jim McMahon, who was benched by Ditka, then reinstated soon enough to lead the Bears to five wins in their last seven games.

McMahon needs to watch out for interceptions and he needs to make full use of Gault, the speedster who caught only two touchdown passes after the sixth game. The better McMahon gets, the more pressure it will take off Walter Payton, who rushed for 1,421 yards and threw for three touchdowns. Fullback Matt Suhey added two 100-yard games of his own.

DEFENSE: Ditka was upset after his rookie season two years ago that the Bears weren't consistent enough on defense. He demanded a change and got it last year. These weren't the old Monsters of the Midway, but they could be good enough to hold up if the offense increases its scoring production.

Middle linebacker Mike Singletary made the Pro Bowl as one of the few 4-3 middlemen left in the league. He heads a mobile linebacking group that includes Otis Wilson, one of those raw talents who may not function at his best in a disciplined system.

End Mike Hartenstine had his best year ever with 12 sacks, which helped make up for injuries to tackle Dan Hampton (knee and finger). A comeback performance by Hampton could give the Bears a more reliable pass rush and strengthen what, statistically, was among the eight best defenses in the league. Leslie Frazier,

Walter Payton raced for 1,421 yards and passed for three TDs.

a former free agent, was a pleasant surprise in the secondary with a team-high seven interceptions. Mike Richardson, a No. 2 1983 draft choice, wound up starting ahead of veteran Terry Schmidt at the other corner.

KICKING GAME: With Gault returning kickoffs, the special teams have to be in decent shape. He didn't record a TD return last year, but that will change. Ditka fired punter Bob Parsons in midseason and Ray Stachowicz was his lackluster (31.9) replacement. Bob Thomas was a so-so 14-of-25 on field goals. This is an area that needs help.

BEARS VETERAN ROSTER

HEAD COACH—Mike Ditka. Assistant Coaches—Jim Dooley, Dale Haupt, Ed Hughes, Jim LaRue, Ted Plumb, Johnny Roland, Buddy Ryan, Dick Stanfel.

No.	Name	Pos.	Ht.	Wt.	NFL Exp.	College
51	Atkins, Kelvin	LB	6-3	235	2	Illinois
7	Avellini, Bob	QB	6-2	210	10	Maryland
84	Baschnagel, Brian	WR	6-0	184	9	Ohio State
79	Becker, Kurt	G	6-5	270	3	Michigan
25	Bell, Todd	S	6-0	207	4	Ohio State
62	Bortz, Mark	G	6-5	267	2	Iowa
54	Cabral, Brian	LB	6-1	224	6	Colorado
74	Covert, Jimbo	T	6-4	271	2	Pittsburgh
95	Dent, Richard	DE	6-5	240	2	Tennessee State
22	Duerson, Dave	S	6-0	202	2	Notre Dame
88	Dunsmore, Pat	TE	6-2	230	2	Drake
64	Fada, Rob	G	6-2	258	2	Pittsburgh
45	Fencik, Gary	S	6-1	192	9	Yale
24	Fisher, Jeff	CB	5-10	195	4	Southern California
21	Frazier, Leslie	CB	6-0	189	4	Alcorn State
71	Frederick, Andy	T	6-6	265	8	New Mexico
4	Fuller, Steve	QB	6-4	198	6	Clemson
83	Gault, Willie	WR	6-0	178	2	Tennessee
29	Gentry, Dennis	RB	5-8	173	3	Baylor
99	Hampton, Dan	DT	6-5	270	6	Arkansas
90	Harris, Al	LB	6-5	250	6	Arizona State
73	Hartenstine, Mike	DE	6-3	243	10	Penn State
63	Hilgenberg, Jay	C	6-3	260	4	Iowa
32	Hutchison, Anthony	RB	5-10	180	2	Texas Tech
65	Jackson, Noah	G	6-2	265	10	Tampa
72	Janata, John	T	6-7	255	2	Illinois
98	Keys, Tyrone	DE	6-7	260	2	Mississippi State
82	Margerum, Ken	WR	6-0	180	4	Stanford
85	McKinnon, Dennis	WR	6-2	185	2	Florida State
9	McMahon, Jim	QB	6-0	187	3	Brigham Young
76	McMichael, Steve	DT	6-2	260	5	Texas
87	Moorhead, Emery	TE	6-2	220	8	Colorado
68	Osborne, Jim	DT	6-3	245	13	Southern U.
34	Payton, Walter	RB	5-11	204	10	Jackson State
20	Potter, Kevin	S	5-10	188	2	Missouri
53	Rains, Dan	LB	6-1	220	3	Cincinnati
27	Richardson, Mike	CB	6-0	188	2	Arizona State
81	Saldi, Jay	TE	6-3	230	8	South Carolina
44	Schmidt, Terry	CB-S	6-0	177	11	Ball State
57	Simmons, Dave	LB	6-4	225	4	North Carolina
50	Singletary, Mike	LB	5-11	230	4	Baylor
19	Stachowicz, Ray	P	6-0	185	4	Michigan State
26	Suhey, Matt	RB	5-11	217	5	Penn State
16	Thomas, Bob	K	5-10	175	9	Notre Dame
33	Thomas, Calvin	RB	5-11	220	3	Illinois
78	Van Horne, Keith	T	6-6	265	4	Southern California
80	Watts, Rickey	WR	6-1	203	6	Tulsa
43	Williams, Walt	CB	6-1	185	8	New Mexico
55	Wilson, Otis	LB	6-2	222	5	Louisville

TOP FIVE DRAFT CHOICES

Rd.	Name	Sel. No.	Pos.	Ht.	Wt.	College
1	Marshall, Wilber	11	LB	6-1	230	Florida
2	Rivera, Ron	44	LB	6-3	235	California
3	Humphries, Stefan	71	G	6-4	248	Michigan
4	Andrews, Tom	98	G	6-4	250	Louisville
7	Robertson, Nakita	179	RB	5-10	205	Central Arkansas

THE ROOKIES: No one had a better draft than the Bears. LB Wilbur Marshall of Florida was one the five best players available and could start immediately. Bear fans are going to love California LB Ron Rivera's intensity and Michigan guard Stefan Humphries comes from a polished college program, which could help his chances greatly.

OUTLOOK: Bears have been in a rut lately. They get off to such a bad start that no matter how well they finish, it doesn't matter. Key this season is stability: Ditka has to be less volatile and let his players perform with confidence. A playoff spot could be the reward if McMahon plays well.

BEAR PROFILES

WALTER PAYTON 30 5-11 204   Running Back

Wants to be remembered as football's Pete Rose . . . Always hustling, always giving his all . . . Amazes teammates with his consistency, his determination, his boyish enthusiasm . . . Still likes to lead fan cheers during key moments of games . . . Talked once about retiring early but now wants to go out as the NFL's all-time leading rusher . . . Picked up 1,421 yards last year to move ahead of O.J. Simpson into third place on all-time list . . . Both he and Franco Harris will go by Jim Brown if they stay healthy . . . Born July 25, 1954, in Columbia, Mo. . . . Active in charities and likes drums and privacy . . . Didn't start playing football until 11th grade.

JIM McMAHON 25 6-0 187   Quarterback

Considers himself the future of the franchise, but you couldn't know it at times last year . . . Mike Ditka benched him for Vince Evans, then finally put him back in the lineup, he says, for good . . . Cocky, handsome, outgoing: the perfect big-market quarterback . . . In two seasons ranks as the Bears' career passing leader with a 78.5 rating, putting him ahead of Sid Luckman, John Lujack and Bill Wade . . . He's completed 58 percent of his passes but has thrown too many interceptions (20) . . . Born

Aug. 21, 1959, in Jersey City, N.J.... Turned down basketball scholarship at Utah State to play at BYU... Has played every baseball spot save catcher.

WILLIE GAULT 23 6-0 178   Wide Receiver

A track man with a long football background ... Decided late to sign with the Bears, then became one of the NFL's most dangerous deep threats... Caught 40 passes for 836 yards and eight touchdowns... That's 20.9 yards a reception, which is one way to keep cornerbacks awake at night... "We didn't bring him here to lead the league in blocks," says coach Mike Ditka... A world-class sprinter and hurdler who thought he wanted to stick around for the 1984 Olympics... But family security proved more important... Born Sept. 5, 1960, in Griffin, Ga.... Had five career kickoff returns for touchdowns at Tennessee.

GARY FENCIK 30 6-1 192   Safety

Doesn't have to shoulder as much of the defensive burden as in the past... Has led Bears in tackling five times... Added two interceptions last season to give him 25 for career ... Made his first interception off Joe Namath... Not bad for a free agent from Yale... Born June 11, 1954, in Chicago... Works offseason for a pay-television company... Studying for master's in business... Once took course at Yale from Howard Cosell and studied in London in 1975... Active in many civic functions.

NOAH JACKSON 33 6-2 265   Guard

As Reggie McKenzie was to O.J. Simpson at Buffalo, this man is to Walter Payton at Chicago... No one seems to be able to beat him out of starting position no matter how old he gets... Once part of a truly outstanding offensive line but the unit's caliber has decreased recently... Known for his dependability and his endurance... Hardly ever injured... Traded by Colts, who picked him on the seventh round of the 1974 draft... Attended U. of Tampa, then went to Canada for three seasons... Born April 14, 1951, in Jacksonville Beach, Fla.... Hobbies include travel, soap opera, landscaping, golf.

MATT SUHEY 26 5-11 217   Running Back

Spending his career playing in Walter Payton's long shadow but he is making the most of it... Had a very quiet but competent 1983 season: 681 rushing yards, 49 catches for more than 1,000 combined yards... Lots of teams would like to have that kind of production from their second back... Had only 772 career rushing yards before last season, and 76 catches ... Favorite book: *Winds of War* by Herman Wouk... One of three brothers to play at Penn State, where father also played... Born July 7, 1958, in State College, Pa.... Avid squash player who is seeking MBA at Northwestern.

EMERY MOOREHEAD 30 6-2 220   Tight End

One of the smallest tight ends in the business, but bigger than two years ago, when he played the spot at 210... Even the Giants gave up on him after drafting him in the sixth round out of Colorado... But now he has caught 30 and 42 passes in back-to-back seasons to become competent pro... Also has added eight touchdowns over that span... Bears had him once, then cut him before bringing him back... A running back and flanker in college... Born March 22, 1954, in Evanston, Ill.... Has worked professionally in radio and television... Ran 36 times for Giants in 1979.

OTIS WILSON 26 6-2 222   Linebacker

Sometimes plays without the discipline his coaches want, but still a gifted talent... Gives the Bears a solid force on the left side... Was third in tackles last season with 100... Bears call him a "make it happen" player... Took a while for him to catch on as a rookie three years ago after a fine career at Louisville... Once had 25 tackles in college against Cincinnati ... Born Sept. 15, 1957, in New York City... Nickname is "Big O" and "The Stick"... Grew up in same neighborhood in New York City that produced John Brockington, Lloyd Free.

MIKE SINGLETARY 25 5-11 230   Linebacker

One of the few middle linebackers left in the league, but a throwback to the old days...Hard-hitting, solid, tough...Plays the middle like you should, and led the Bears in tackling with his reckless style...Second-round choice out of Baylor in 1981 who wound up starting by end of his rookie year...Was second in tackles last season...Bears worked a trade with San Francisco to get a chance to pick him...Player of the Year in the Southwest Conference in 1979 and 1980...Averaged 15 tackles a game for career...Born Oct. 9, 1958, in Houston... Likes classical music.

MIKE HARTENSTINE 31 6-3 243   Defensive End

Who can explain it?...Never really lived up to second-round potential for first eight years, then suddenly became a top-flight pass-rusher last year...Recorded a team-high 12 sacks from his end spot...Only had 35 career sacks going into the year, with a high of eight in 1979...Once graded 100 percent for his special-teams play against Detroit in 1982...Considered to be one of the league's strongest linemen...Born July 27, 1953, in Allentown, Pa....Has 48-inch chest, 34-inch waist, with body by weightlifting...Was consensus All-American at Penn State as 220-pound defensive tackle.

COACH MIKE DITKA: Struggled in 1983 to keep his massive

temper under control..."My biggest disappointment was me," he says...Frustrated by early fumbles and dropped passes, he yelled at everyone, including himself...Got so angry after a loss to Baltimore (who wouldn't?) that he broke his hand hitting it against a locker ...Finally took to wearing a tie, which for some reason kept him under better control...Didn't want to resort to the tie earlier because he thought people would say he was copying his former coach, Tom Landry...Maybe the new look in clothes helped since the Bears won five of their last six...Born Oct. 18, 1939, in Carnegie, Pa....Was All-American at Pittsburgh...Famed tight end who brought notoriety and new toughness to the position... Wants his players to perform in the same manner, but that's like Bart Starr asking his quarterbacks to play like an All-Pro... Tenth Bear coach in 64 years, and a particular favorite of late owner George Halas... His record 75 receptions for a tight end in 1964 held up for 16 years.

BIGGEST PLAY

This was in the NFL's first championship game—witnessed by 26,000 fans on Dec. 17, 1933, at Chicago's Wrigley Field.

Late in the fourth quarter, the New York Giants were leading the Chicago Bears, 21-16, and the Bears' battering-ram fullback, Bronko Nagurski, was trying to pull out one last score.

With the Bears on the Giant 36, quarterback Carl Brumbaugh handed off to Bronko, who threw a surprise pass to Bill Hewitt, one of the few players who didn't wear a helmet. Hewitt lateraled to Bill Karr. Behind a block from Gene Ronzani, Karr finished off a 25-yard run that gave the Bears a 23-21 victory.

The winner's share in that first title game was $210.23 each.

INDIVIDUAL BEAR RECORDS
Rushing

Most Yards Game:	275	Walter Payton, vs Minnesota, 1977
Season:	1,852	Walter Payton, 1977
Career:	11,625	Walter Payton, 1975-83

Passing

Most TD Passes Game:	7	Sid Luckman, vs N.Y. Giants, 1943
Season:	28	Sid Luckman, 1943
Career:	137	Sid Luckman, 1939-50

Receiving

Most TD Passes Game:	4	Harlon Hill, vs San Francisco, 1954
	4	Mike Ditka, vs Los Angeles, 1963
Season:	13	Dick Gordon, 1970
	13	Ken Kavanaugh, 1947
Career:	50	Ken Kavanaugh, 1940-41, 1945-50

Scoring

Most Points Game:	36	Gale Sayers, vs San Francisco, 1965
Season:	132	Gale Sayers, 1965
Career:	541	George Blanda, 1949-58
Most TDs Game:	6	Gale Sayers, vs San Francisco, 1965
Season:	22	Gale Sayers, 1965
Career:	87	Walter Payton, 1975-83

DALLAS COWBOYS

TEAM DIRECTORY: General Partner: H.R. Bright; Pres./GM: Tex Schramm; VP-Player Development: Gil Brandt; VP-Administration: Joe Bailey; Pub. Rel. Dir.: Doug Todd; Head Coach: Tom Landry. Home field: Texas Stadium (65,101). Colors: Royal blue, metallic blue and white.

SCOUTING REPORT

OFFENSE: The Cowboys weren't inefficient offensively last year, ranking fourth in the NFC by averaging 372 yards a game. But the longer the season lasted, the more predictable they became and the easier to stop. And there weren't that many games where

Tony Dorsett wound up fifth in the league in rushing.

everything worked so well that they just dominated an opponent in their old, effective manner.

Whether a change at quarterback is the answer remains to be seen. Certainly, Tom Landry will have pressure to switch from Danny White to untested but popular Gary Hogeboom. White threw too many interceptions last year and got into a habit of trying to force things to happen. Hogeboom has a stronger arm but no one knows if he can hold up over an entire season.

The offensive line is coming off a so-so performance even though Tony Dorsett had another decent year. But injuries hurt the unit's continuity. Depending on the health of Drew Pearson, the wide-receiving corps should be in good shape. Butch Johnson went to Houston in a trade for Mike Renfro. Doug Donley is a prospect and, one day, Landry may take full advantage of Tony Hill's skills.

DEFENSE: Almost everywhere you look, you can find question marks about the Dallas defense. Just think if the unit really didn't have any ability.

The Cowboys finished a dismal 10th in the NFC last season, almost unheard of for the former Doomsday boys. But age and inconsistency seems to be catching up with Dallas. And the Cowboys can't seem to handle physical, go-after-it opponents such as the Redskins or even Los Angeles in the playoffs.

Randy White and Ed Jones are no problem in the line but Harvey Martin has retired and John Dutton never has been that good. And there is no depth behind them. The linebacking corps is one of the weakest in Dallas memory. Bob Breunig isn't getting any outside help, so teams pound away on the wings until the Cowboys break. Rookie Billy Cannon Jr. will be a factor.

The secondary has its fine moments, especially Everson Walls. But if the Cowboys play too much man-to-man, they eventually get hurt. However, improved linebacking play would help this area greatly.

KICKING GAME: Rafael Septien continues to deliver, but Landry can't seem to get his punting situation straightened out. Because of injuries, Danny White wound up punting again in the playoffs. And Dallas never has been particularly strong covering or returning kicks.

THE ROOKIES: There will be a lot of pressure on Texas A&M's Cannon, the Cowboys' No. 1 choice, to break into the starting lineup right away. They have had some bad drafts lately and need immediate help at Cannon's linebacker post. He only played one

COWBOYS VETERAN ROSTER

HEAD COACH—Tom Landry. Assistant Coaches—Neil Armstrong, Al Lavan, Alan Lowry, Jim Myers, Dick Noland, Jim Shofner.

No.	Name	Pos.	Ht.	Wt.	NFL Exp.	College
31	Allen, Gary	RB	5-10	180	3	Hawaii
62	Baldinger, Brian	G	6-4	253	3	Duke
40	Bates, Bill	S	6-1	195	2	Tennessee
53	Breunig, Bob	LB	6-2	225	10	Arizona State
47	Clinkscale, Dextor	S	5-11	190	4	South Carolina State
61	Cooper, Jim	T	6-5	260	8	Temple
84	Cosbie, Doug	TE	6-6	236	6	Santa Clara
51	Dickerson, Anthony	LB	6-2	222	5	Southern Methodist
83	Donley, Doug	WR	6-0	173	4	Ohio State
67	Donovan, Pat	T	6-5	257	10	Stanford
33	Dorsett, Tony	RB	5-11	189	8	Pittsburgh
26	Downs, Michael	S	6-3	203	4	Rice
78	Dutton, John	DT	6-7	275	11	Nebraska
27	Fellows, Ron	CB	6-0	174	4	Missouri
58	Hegman, Mike	LB	6-1	228	9	Tennessee State
25	Hill, Rod	CB	6-0	182	3	Kentucky State
80	Hill, Tony	WR	6-2	198	8	Stanford
14	Hogeboom, Gary	QB	6-4	201	5	Central Michigan
77	Jeffcoat, Jim	DE	6-5	264	2	Arizona State
72	Jones, Ed	DE	6-9	275	10	Tennessee State
23	#Jones, James	RB	5-10	202	4	Mississippi State
57	King, Angelo	LB	6-1	230	4	South Carolina State
52	McLean, Scott	LB	6-4	233	2	Florida State
35	McSwain, Chuck	RB	6-0	191	2	Clemson
3	Miller, Jim	P	5-11	183	5	Mississippi
44	#Newhouse, Robert	RB	5-10	219	13	Houston
30	Newsome, Tim	RB	6-1	231	5	Winston-Salem
88	Pearson, Drew	WR	6-0	193	12	Tulsa
65	Petersen, Kurt	G	6-4	268	5	Missouri
75	Pozderac, Phil	T	6-9	270	3	Notre Dame
64	Rafferty, Tom	C	6-3	259	9	Penn State
82	Renfro, Mike	WR	6-0	184	7	Texas Christian
70	Richards, Howard	G	6-6	258	4	Missouri
50	Rohrer, Jeff	LB	6-3	232	3	Yale
66	Schultz, Chris	T	6-8	265	2	Arizona
68	Scott, Herbert	G	6-2	260	10	Virginia Union
1	Septien, Rafael	K	5-10	171	8	S.W. Louisiana
85	Simmons, Cleo	TE	6-2	225	2	Jackson State
60	Smerek, Don	DT	6-7	257	4	Nevada-Reno
20	Springs, Ron	RB	6-1	218	6	Ohio State
32	Thurman, Dennis	CB	5-11	183	7	Southern California
63	Titensor, Glen	C	6-4	260	4	Brigham Young
71	Tuinei, Mark	DT	6-5	270	2	Hawaii
24	Walls, Everson	CB	6-1	194	4	Grambling
59	Walter, Mike	LB	6-3	238	2	Oregon
5	Warren, John	P	6-0	207	2	Tennessee
11	White, Danny	QB-P	6-2	193	9	Arizona State
54	White, Randy	DT	6-4	263	10	Maryland

#Unsigned at press time

TOP FIVE DRAFT CHOICES

Rd.	Name	Sel. No.	Pos.	Ht.	Wt.	College
1	Cannon, Billy Jr.	25	LB	6-4	215	Texas A&M
2	Scott, Victor	40	DB	5-10	182	Colorado
3	Cornwell, Fred	81	TE	6-5	235	Southern California
4	DeOssie, Steve	110	LB	6-2	250	Boston College
5	Pelluer, Steve	113	QB	6-3	208	Washington

year at the position but some teams projected him as a future All-Pro.

OUTLOOK: Difficult to tell whether the Cowboys' down-slide has started, finally, or whether last year was a fluke. But certainly Dallas finished up poorly, which gives Landry and Co. real reason to be concerned. There was no fire by the playoffs, and that is a bad sign.

COWBOY PROFILES

DANNY WHITE 32 6-2 193   Quarterback

He can point to fine career statistics that rank him among the league's all-time best quarterbacks, but the fact remains: in his four years as a starter, the Cowboys haven't gotten to the Super Bowl...That's putting more and more pressure on him and sometimes he doesn't handle it all that well...His teammates respect him but they warm up better to Gary Hogeboom...Finished sixth in NFC passing ratings last year and did not make the Pro Bowl...Had 29 touchdowns but 23 interceptions, way too many for quarterback of his ability...Tends to take too many chances in pressure situations...Born Feb. 9, 1952, in Mesa, Ariz....A product of Arizona State...Sponsors annual golf tournament for Boy Scouts...Plays piano and sings.

GARY HOGEBOOM 26 6-4 201   Quarterback

Rarely has any player had so much written about him with so little to show on the field...His future based on an excellent second-half performance against the Redskins in the 1982 championship game...Had good preseason last year but coach Tom Landry still went with the more experienced Danny White...His teammates really like him and are pulling for him to have more playing time...Has told Landry he wants to be traded if he doesn't play more...Born Aug. 21, 1958, in Grand Rapids, Mich....A steal as a fifth-round draft choice from Central Michigan...Wants to become a home builder in the Dallas area.

RANDY WHITE 31 6-4 263   Defensive Tackle

No question he's on his way to the Hall of Fame...Automatic choice as All-Pro every year...He's that good and that consistent...Wasn't very pleased with 1982 so he came back last year lighter and meaner and played well...He's suffering a bit as the rest of the front four deteriorates...Seven straight Pro Bowl appearances...The only other Cowboy to make that many straight bowl appearances is Bob Lilly, who had 10 in a row...Quiet and under control off the field, he'd rather hunt or fish than create publicity...Born Jan. 15, 1953, in Wilmington, Del....Was Outland Trophy winner at Maryland, where he ranks as that school's greatest player.

TONY DORSETT 30 5-11 189   Halfback

Hard to believe he now is 30...Boyish good looks are deceiving...Holding up very well under punishment of his position...Gained 1,321 yards last year, just missing his second best pro season by five yards...When he gains 100 yards or more, the Cowboys are almost sure to win; when he doesn't, they struggle..."He's our catalyst," says Tom Landry ...When he wasn't doing much in the middle of the season, he indirectly knocked the blocking of his offensive line...The linemen didn't like it...Has more than 8,000 career yards and is certain to challenge for No. 1 spot if he stays healthy another four or five years...Born April 7, 1954, in Rochester, Pa....Heisman winner at Pittsburgh...Considered among best-dressed of celebrities.

RAFAEL SEPTIEN 30 5-10 171   Kicker

Broke his own club scoring record in 1983 with 123 points, beating 1980 mark of 121...Made 22 of 27 field goals and that was a record, too, of 81 percent, erasing Efren Herrera's 78 percent in 1976...Doesn't lack in confidence ...Just ask him how good he is and he'll tell you...Colts' Raul Allegre couldn't beat him out in training camp, but Cowboys may come to regret letting the younger kicker go...Must really bug NFL jocks who can't beat this fine player in racquetball...Born Dec. 12, 1953, in Mexico City...Has appeared in three movies and more than 40 commercials in Mexico...Wife is an opera singer.

EVERSON WALLS 24 6-1 194   Cornerback

Made the Pro Bowl for the third time in his three-year career even though he intercepted just four passes . . . Remember, he led the NFL in interceptions his first two seasons with 11 and seven . . . Has come a long way since being tabbed as a free agent out of Grambling by the Cowboys in 1981 . . . His teammates call him "Cubby" . . . Dennis Thurman says he is "superman" . . . Plays the most difficult position in pro football but has the right temperament and ability to be a standout . . . Earned a degree in accounting from Grambling, where he led the nation in interceptions his senior season with 11 . . . Born Dec. 28, 1959, in Dallas and was raised two miles from the Cowboys' practice field.

RON SPRINGS 27 6-1 218   Fullback

Better suited to play halfback, but the only way he's gotten into Cowboy lineup is to adapt to fullback . . . Not big enough for the spot but Dallas has learned to use him in unique ways . . . Would you believe he caught enough passes last year coming out of the backfield (73) to break the club record? . . . That's right, he's No. 1, not Bob Hayes or Drew Pearson or Tony Hill . . . Also ran for 541 yards to become one of the league's most versatile backs . . . Previous best year was 1981, when he ran for 625 yards and had 46 receptions . . . Born Nov. 1, 1956, in Williamsburg, Va. . . . They've named a street after him in his home town . . . Attended Ohio State, where he had injury problems his senior year.

TONY HILL 28 6-2 198   Wide Receiver

In the Cowboys' balanced offense, he's never had that sensational year enjoyed by some other of the league's elite receivers . . . Best has been 60 catches (twice), which isn't bad . . . Added 49 last season to rank behind Ron Springs . . . Got off to a troubled start when his name was linked to a drug problem in Dallas . . . Heatedly denies any link with drugs . . . Also had some injury problems during the season . . . "He's our big play man," says Tom Landry . . . Born June 23, 1956, in Long Beach, Cal. . . . Attended Stanford after playing quarterback in high school . . . Runs camp for underprivileged children in Long Beach.

ED (TOO TALL) JONES 33 6-9 275   Defensive End

Fighting desperately to maintain his quality play . . . Despite his size and strength, had just seven sacks last year to rank only third on the team . . . Not like his glory days when he was the most feared defensive end in the league . . . That's his lowest full season total since 1977 . . . His peers must have thought he played okay, though . . . They voted him to the Pro Bowl for the third straight year, all since he returned from year off to take up boxing . . . Was eighth on the team in tackles . . . Member of investment firm with three Cowboy teammates . . . Born Feb. 23, 1951, in Jackson, Tenn. . . . Attended Tennessee State . . . Has done some acting . . . Recorded a rhythm-and-blues record.

DOUG COSBIE 28 6-6 236   Tight End

In his second year as starter, made the Pro Bowl after catching 46 passes . . . Obviously, that was a career high for the six-year veteran who was playing behind Billy Joe DuPree . . . A third-round choice from Santa Clara, he felt badly when he moved ahead of DuPree . . . So all he does is break DuPree's team record for tight end catches . . . Had only 24 receptions in first three pro years . . . One of the Cowboys' most articulate players . . . Has degree in marketing and works for Dallas real estate company . . . Born Feb. 27, 1956 in Mt. View, Cal. . . . Also played at Holy Cross.

COACH TOM LANDRY: Last season had to be one of his most

painful since early expansion days . . . Primed his team for the Super Bowl from day one of training camp and then never got past the wild-card game . . . Even tried tougher discipline and a hardline approach and that didn't work . . . Says he hasn't given up and that the team is better than people think . . . But something seems to be missing from the old magic touch . . . Maybe everyone else in the league finally is catching up . . . Remains one of the two or three most respected coaches in the league, and one of the most highly regarded of all time . . . His fine sense of humor is finally coming out, thanks to some television commercials . . . Very religious and not hesitant to talk about his beliefs

...Born Sept. 11, 1924, in Mission, Tex....Graduate of the University of Texas...Also has industrial engineering degree from Houston...Even when he was a player for the New York Giants, he was helping design defenses which changed the game...Two more years and he should pass Curly Lambeau and become No. 2 on the NFL all-time coaching list, if Don Shula doesn't get there first.

BIGGEST PLAY

He never said anything he did was a matter of luck, but you knew Roger Staubach realized it wasn't all skill, either. At least not on December 28, 1975, when Roger and his Dallas teammates visited Minnesota for a divisional playoff game.

The Vikings were leading, 14-10, with 1:51 left. Minnesota

Everson Walls' interceptions dipped, but he made Pro Bowl.

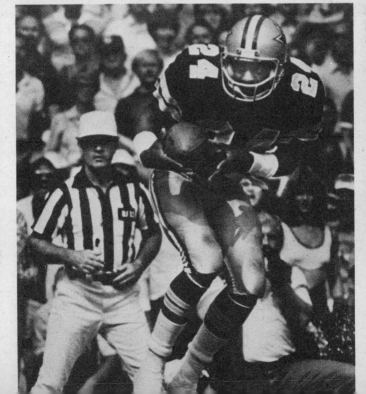

had been thoroughly in control, its Purple People Eaters controlling Staubach and Co. most of the afternoon. There wasn't a sense of panic within the Cowboy team but Dallas knew that time was certainly running out on its chances of advancing any further in their Super Bowl quest.

At midfield, Staubach dropped back and looked downfield for receiver Drew Pearson. Pearson fought off Nate Wright, pulled in the desperation pass on his hip at the five and backpedaled into the end zone with 24 seconds left.

The Cowboys won, 17-14. "A Hail Mary pass," said a laughing Staubach.

INDIVIDUAL COWBOY RECORDS

Rushing

Most Yards Game:	206	Tony Dorsett, vs Philadelphia, 1978
Season:	1,646	Tony Dorsett, 1981
Career:	8,336	Tony Dorsett, 1977-83

Passing

Most TD Passes Game:	5	Eddie LeBaron, vs Pittsburgh, 1962
	5	Don Meredith, vs N.Y. Giants, 1966
	5	Don Meredith, vs Philadelphia, 1966
	5	Don Meredith, vs Philadelphia, 1968
	5	Craig Morton, vs Philadelphia, 1969
	5	Craig Morton, vs Houston, 1970
	5	Danny White, vs N.Y. Giants, 1983
Season:	29	Danny White, 1983
Career:	153	Roger Staubach, 1969-79

Receiving

Most TD Passes Game:	4	Bob Hayes, vs Houston, 1970
Season:	14	Frank Clarke, 1962
Career:	71	Bob Hayes, 1965-74

Scoring

Most Points Game:	24	Dan Reeves, vs Atlanta, 1967
	24	Bob Hayes, vs Houston, 1970
	24	Calvin Hill, vs Buffalo, 1971
	24	Duane Thomas, vs St. Louis, 1971
Season:	123	Rafael Septien, 1983
Career:	585	Rafael Septien, 1978-83
Most TDs Game:	4	Dan Reeves, vs Atlanta, 1967
	4	Bob Hayes, vs Houston, 1970
	4	Calvin Hill, vs Buffalo, 1971
	4	Duane Thomas, vs St. Louis, 1971
Season:	16	Dan Reeves, 1966
Career:	76	Bob Hayes, 1965-74

DETROIT LIONS

TEAM DIRECTORY: Pres.: William Clay Ford; Exec. VP/GM: Russ Thomas; Dir. Football Operations/Head Coach: Monte Clark; Dir. Player Personnel: Tim Rooney; Dir. Pub. Rel.: Don Kremer. Home field: Pontiac Silverdome (80,638). Colors: Honolulu blue and silver.

SCOUTING REPORT

OFFENSE: The best thing that happened to the Lion offense since the end of the 1983 season was a February court decision. That verdict allowed Billy Sims to stay in Detroit and negated a contract with Houston of the U.S. Football League. With Sims, the Lions have the makings of a decent attack. Without him, it wouldn't be very pretty.

Still a Lion, Billy Sims aims for another 1,000-yard season.

Sims rushed for 1,040 yards and closed fast last year, with some standout pressure games. He has the size and strength to be a fine back in a one-back offense if the Lions are so inclined. Fullback James Jones had a good first year as Sims' running mate. But the Lions are not very good at quarterback. Eric Hipple threw six more interceptions than touchdowns and backup Gary Danielson has never proven to be more than an average player.

With young Jeff Chadwick and Leonard Thompson, the receiving corps is in good shape, but tight end Ulysses Norris is not another David Hill. With the improvement of center Steve Mott, the offensive line is one of the league's more solid units.

DEFENSE: The Lions wound up with one of the more solid defensive fronts in the conference, thanks to the unexpected play of third-round choice Mike Cofer from Tennessee. Cofer came on so fast that he moved into the starting lineup and allowed Monte Clark to move William Gay to defensive tackle, where he teamed with Doug English to provide decisive inside pass-rush pressure.

Another plus was the development of the secondary, an embarrassingly poor unit in 1982. In 1983, cornerbacks Bobby Watkins and Bruce McNorton played like veterans instead of second-year performers. And William Graham was an unexpected strength at safety. Suddenly, the Lion pass defense had some growl to it.

As long as Detroit stays with a 4-3, the Lions better improve their linebacking. Young Jimmy Williams has promise, so maybe there is hope for the unit, which was 11th best overall in the NFL but a stingy second in scoring defense.

KICKING GAME: The Lions are rarely sensational with their special teams, but they still are more than adequate. Eddie Murray made 25 of 32 field goals and rookie Mike Black had a 41-yard punting average. The Lions will be trying to improve their kickoff returning, which was among the worst in the conference.

THE ROOKIES: The Lions may have made three good early picks, especially with No. 1 Dave Lewis, the TE from California. Lewis will be expected to start soon, but he sometimes didn't play very hard at California. No. 2 Pete Mandley, a Northern Arizona receiver, and No. 3 Eric Williams, a Washington State DT, likewise were just as streaky in college.

OUTLOOK: Detroit won eight of its last 11 regular-season games and should have beaten San Francisco in the playoffs. Clark rid himself of some malcontents before 1983 and young players had

LIONS VETERAN ROSTER

HEAD COACH—Monte Clark. Assistant Coaches—Ed Beard, Don Doll, Fred Hoaglin, Bill Johnson, Ed Khayat, Joe Madden, Bill Nelson, Mel Phillips, Larry Seiple.

No.	Name	Pos.	Ht.	Wt.	NFL Exp.	College
54	Barnes, Roosevelt	LB	6-2	222	3	Purdue
11	Black, Mike	P	6-1	197	2	Arizona State
24	Bussey, Dexter	RB	5-11	210	11	Texas-Arlington
89	Chadwick, Jeff	WR	6-3	185	2	Grand Valley State
53	Cobb, Garry	LB	6-2	227	6	Southern California
66	Cofer, Mike	DE	6-5	245	2	Tennessee
50	Curley, August	LB	6-3	222	2	Southern California
16	Danielson, Gary	QB	6-2	196	8	Purdue
73	#Dawson, Mike	DT	6-3	258	9	Arizona
72	Dieterich, Chris	T	6-3	255	5	North Carolina State
58	Doig, Steve	LB	6-2	242	3	New Hampshire
70	Dorney, Keith	T	6-5	265	6	Penn State
61	Elias, Homer	G	6-2	255	7	Tennessee State
78	English, Doug	DT	6-5	258	9	Texas
57	Fantetti, Ken	LB	6-2	232	6	Wyoming
65	Fowler, Amos	C	6-3	253	7	Southern Mississippi
79	Gay, William	DE	6-5	255	7	Southern California
33	Graham, William	CB-S	5-11	191	3	Texas
67	Greco, Don	G	6-3	255	3	Western Illinois
62	Green, Curtis	DE	6-3	252	4	Alabama State
35	Hall, Alvin	CB-S	5-10	187	4	Miami (Ohio)
23	Harvey, Maurice	S	5-9	187	6	Ball State
17	Hipple, Eric	QB	6-2	196	5	Utah State
31	Jenkins, Ken	RB-S	5-8	184	2	Bucknell
21	Johnson, Demetrious	CB	5-11	190	2	Missouri
30	Jones, James	FB	6-2	228	2	Florida
32	Kane, Rick	RB	6-0	200	8	San Jose State
25	#King, Horace	RB	5-11	205	10	Georgia
43	Latimer, Al	CB	5-11	172	5	Clemson
82	Lee, Edward	WR	6-0	185	2	South Carolina State
64	Lee, Larry	G	6-2	260	4	UCLA
14	Machurek, Mike	QB	6-1	205	3	Idaho State
83	Martin, Robbie	WR-S	5-8	177	4	Cal Poly-Obispo
81	#McCall, Reese	TE	6-6	232	7	Auburn
29	McNorton, Bruce	CB-S	5-11	175	3	Georgetown (Ky.)
63	Moss, Martin	DT	6-4	252	3	UCLA
52	Mott, Steve	C	6-3	260	2	Alabama
3	Murray, Ed	K	5-10	175	5	Tulane
86	Nichols, Mark	WR	6-2	208	4	San Jose State
80	Norris, Ulysses	TE	6-4	232	6	Georgia
84	#Rubick, Rob	TE	6-2	228	3	Grand Valley State
20	Sims, Billy	RB	6-0	212	5	Oklahoma
71	Strenger, Rich	T	6-7	269	2	Michigan
39	Thompson, Leonard	WR	5-11	192	10	Oklahoma State
38	Thompson, Vince	FB	6-0	225	3	Villanova
55	#Turnure, Tom	C	6-4	253	5	Washington
34	Wagoner, Danny	CB-S	5-10	180	3	Kansas
27	Watkins, Bobby	CB-S	5-10	186	3	S.W. Texas State
59	Williams, Jimmy	LB	6-2	222	3	Nebraska

#Unsigned at press time

TOP FIVE DRAFT CHOICES

Rd.	Name	Sel. No.	Pos.	Ht.	Wt.	College
1	Lewis, David	20	TE	6-4	230	California
2	Mandley, Pete	47	WR	6-0	188	Northern Arizona
3	Williams, Eric	62	DT	6-5	255	Washington State
3	*Anderson, Ernest	74	RB	5-11	190	Oklahoma State
3	Baack, Steve	75	DE	6-3	240	Oregon

*Signed with USFL Oklahoma Outlaws

good seasons last year. Should that development continue, the Lions will again be a playoff factor.

LION PROFILES

BILLY SIMS 28 6-0 212   Running Back

There is a bumper sticker going around Houston that says, "I have a contract signed by Billy Sims."... We know he signed at least two, one with the Lions, one with the Houston team in the USFL... The court decided he could stay in Detroit, which was just fine with Billy, who picked up an extra $1 million in the Lions' agreement... No question he is the heart and feet of this NFL team... Put on a great display on national television last year with 106 yards rushing in the Thanksgiving Day blasting of Steelers... Born Sept. 18, 1955, in St. Louis... Gained 1,040 yards last year, third best in club history.

ERIC HIPPLE 26 6-2 196   Quarterback

One of the main reasons the Lions got to the playoffs last year, but then he was hurt and didn't play against San Francisco... Doesn't get much recognition round the league but his totals last season—204 of 387 for 2,577 yards—were among best in Lion history... The problem was, he had only 12 touchdown passes and 18 interceptions, which is a ratio coach Monte Clark certainly can't live with for very long... Can be confused by changing secondary coverages... Born Sept. 16, 1957, in Lubbock, Tex.... Has worked as a sportscaster on television during the offseason.

DOUG ENGLISH 31 6-5 258   Defensive Tackle

If Randy White isn't the best defensive tackle in the league, this man is... But has a decidedly low profile, probably because he plays for a less-than-sensational team... Doesn't do dances after sacks, just goes back to work... Had 13 sacks last year, a personal high, in eighth year... Took a year off in 1980 to work in the oil business and has been better since he returned . . . Born Aug. 25, 1953, in Dallas . . . Played on three SWC title teams at Texas . . . First name really is Lowell . . . Try calling him that.

KEN FANTETTI 27 6-2 232   Linebacker

The spirit of the Lion defense . . . Plays middle linebacker, one of the few 4-3 middle men in the business . . . Bright, cheerful, aggressive . . . Led the team in tackles for the fourth straight year with 182 . . . Now has started 65 straight games . . . Has been a starter since midway through his rookie year after outstanding career at Wyoming . . . A second-round pick in the 1979 draft . . . A communications major in college . . . Born April 7, 1957, in Toledo, Ohio . . . He has a career average of six tackles per game, a tough standard to keep matching.

WILLIAM GAY 29 6-5 255   Defensive Tackle

Coming into his own after six years in the league . . . As well as Doug English played last year, Lion teammates thought Gay played better . . . Voted him the team's defensive MVP award . . . Had 13½ sacks, fourth highest in the conference and a personal best . . . Gives the Lions a strong one-two pass rush from the inside, probably the best in the league . . . A former tight end at Southern California who didn't move over to defense until 1978, after he was traded from Denver to Detroit for Charley West . . . Born May 28, 1955, in San Francisco, Cal. . . . Was a linebacker in junior college.

GARY DANIELSON 32 6-2 196   Quarterback

Didn't start a game last season until the Lions entered the playoffs against San Francisco . . . Then had one of the worst first halves in playoff history with four interceptions . . . "Kept telling myself it was going to stop," he said . . . It did, in the second half, when he almost rallied the Lions to victory . . . Settled into a backup role now after starting for most of his first six pro years . . . Just can't seem to play consistently enough to hold off Eric Hipple . . . Born Sept. 10, 1951, in Detroit . . . Already establishing himself in second career as television sportscaster . . . Beats his former full-time job: sheet-metal worker.

ED MURRAY 28 5-10 175   Kicker

Will never forget late last December in San Francisco . . . Had a chance to give the Lions a belated Christmas gift . . . But missed a game-winning field goal against the 49ers in the play-offs . . . Broke the cardinal sin of kickers: he tried to adjust his style in the middle of the game . . . Just doesn't work . . . The miss over-shadowed what had been another fine season . . . Led the team in scoring with 113 points, fourth year in a row he has finished No. 1 . . . Finished sixth in the conference . . . Now has kicked 122 straight extra points, longest streak in the conference . . . Born Aug. 29, 1956, in Halifax, Nova Scotia . . . Was going to play soccer at Tulane before offered a football scholarship there.

BRUCE McNORTON 25 5-11 175   Cornerback

Didn't start until the ninth game last year . . . But still wound up leading the Lions in interceptions with seven . . . Twice he had two in one game and his total was a best for a Lion since 1976 . . . His performance gave a much-needed pick-me-up to a secondary which was expected to really struggle all last season . . . A second-year player drafted on the fourth round from Georgetown of Kentucky . . . Got the high draft nod after playing well in the Senior Bowl . . . Born Feb. 28, 1959, in Daytona Beach, Fla., where he was raised and still lives . . . Hand injury limited his playing time during first part of rookie year.

JAMES JONES 23 6-2 228   Running Back

The Lions had high hopes he would be able to move in immediately and provide blocking help for Billy Sims . . . But he wasn't expected to lead the team in receptions . . . He did just that, with 46 for 467 yards . . . He also added 35 carries for 475 yards and six touchdowns . . . Not bad production from a No. 2 back . . . And he is going to get better as the Lions keep using him more and more . . . Born March 21, 1961, in Pompano Beach,

Fla. . . . Named SEC's top blocking back in 1981 as standout at Florida . . . One of 10 children . . . Married his high-school sweetheart.

KEITH DORNEY 26 6-5 265   Offensive Tackle

One of the best in the business, but didn't get postseason nods last year because of injury problems . . . Started 12 of 16 games . . . Made the Pro Bowl in 1982 . . . First-round pick out of Penn State in 1979 . . . His teammates always impressed with his dedication to weightlifting . . . Named him Lifter of the Year in 1981 . . . Insurance and real estate major in college . . . Now does some real estate work during offseason in California . . . Born Dec. 3, 1957, in Macungie, Pa. . . . Began college career as starting center before moving out to tackle.

COACH MONTE CLARK: Has stood up under some wild and crazy situations in Motor City . . . Never seems to be on good relations with his general manager and someone always seems to be walking out of camp or leaving the team because of contract problems . . . Yet the Lions won the NFC Central title last year after getting off to a 1-4 start, and that was with Billy Sims in the middle of his contract squabble . . . It was the Lions' first Central Division crown and first title of any sort since 1957 . . . Also made the playoffs in 1982 . . . Signed a five-year extension that same year . . . Born Jan. 24, 1937, in Fillmore, Cal. . . . Now in his seventh season with the Lions, who also have shown great patience with him . . . Striking point about last season: he was willing to trade off many of his better-known players and go with younger, hungrier athletes . . . Played 11 years in the NFL as offensive lineman for San Francisco, Dallas and Cleveland . . . Attended USC . . . Oldest son, Bryan, is quarterback with San Francisco.

BIGGEST PLAY

The Lions had the ball at their own 20 with four minutes left in this NFL title game on Dec. 21, 1953, in Detroit. "Now if you'll just block a little bit, fellers, ol' Bobby'll pass you right to the championship," Bobby Layne told his teammates in the huddle.

They believed him but things certainly looked bleak for the defending champions. Cleveland had dominated the game for the most part and still had the momentum in the final quarter, a 16-10 lead, when Layne made his speech.

But Bobby was a man of his word. He opened the series with a pass to little-used Jim Doran, then completed another to the same man. Three more plays brought another first down and Layne called a timeout.

This was the same Doran who hadn't caught a touchdown pass all season, one year after being named the team's MVP. But he had primarily been a defensive player this year, and was on offense only because Leon Hart was hurt. Doran got wide open on the next play and grabbed Layne's pass for a 33-yard touchdown. Doak Walker kicked the extra point for the 17-16 margin that gave the Lions their second straight title.

INDIVIDUAL LION RECORDS

Rushing

Most Yards Game:	198	Bob Hoernschemeyer, vs N.Y. Yanks, 1950
Season:	1,437	Billy Sims, 1981
Career:	5,014	Dexter Bussey, 1974-83

Passing

Most TD Passes Game:	5	Gary Danielson, vs Minnesota, 1978
Season	26	Bobby Layne, 1951
Career:	118	Bobby Layne, 1950-58

Receiving

Most TD Passes Game:	4	Cloyce Box, vs Baltimore, 1950
Season:	15	Cloyce Box, 1952
Career:	35	Terry Barr, 1957-65

Scoring

Most Points Game:	24	Cloyce Box, vs Baltimore, 1950
Season:	128	Doak Walker, 1950
Career:	636	Errol Mann, 1969-76
Most TDs Game:	4	Cloyce Box, vs Baltimore, 1950
Season:	16	Billy Sims, 1980
Career:	42	Billy Sims, 1980-83

GREEN BAY PACKERS

TEAM DIRECTORY: Chairman: Dominic Olejiniczak; Pres.: Judge Robert Parins; Sec.: John Torinus; Assts. to Pres.: Bob Harlan, Tom Miller; Dir. Player Personnel: Dick Corrick; Dir. Pub. Rel.: Lee Remmel; Head Coach: Forrest Gregg. Home fields: Lambeau Field (56,155) and County Stadium, Milwaukee (55,958). Colors: Green and gold.

SCOUTING REPORT

OFFENSE: Offenses don't come more exciting than the one produced by the Packers. Like wide-open scoring? Like a lot of

Aging Lynn Dickey threw for most yardage in the NFL.

passing? Like quickness and talented players on display? The Pack has it all.

Last season, it scored a team-record 429 points and had the most efficient offense in the league, even if Bart Starr, replaced now by Forrest Gregg, insisted on staying with that old-fangled two-back set. Against Washington, the Packers rolled up 473 yards; against Tampa Bay, they tied a league record for points in a half with 49; they scored 40 points four times.

Quarterback Lynn Dickey is getting old—35—but he still can throw, especially as long as John Jefferson, James Lofton and Paul Coffman are around. All three caught at least 50 passes last year. Eddie Lee Ivery was the main running threat until a midseason drug problem. Now Gerry Ellis and both Jessie Clark and Mike Meade are the likely backfield of the future.

Rookie guard Dave Drechsler helped strengthen the line, which also saw tackle Greg Koch have a good year. Center Larry McCarren made the Pro Bowl.

DEFENSE: Gregg fooled around with offense for the most part when he coached at Cincinnati but he better change his speciality, now that he is with the Packers. This team needs defensive help badly.

Without an improvement from this unit, it will be hard for Gregg to get the club above the .500 level. For all the points they score, the Packers seem to give up just as many and sometimes quicker than they can counter.

The shopping list includes a couple of pass-rushers, a safety or two and a dominating linebacker. And that's just the start.

It will help if middle guard Terry Jones can come back from an Achilles tendon problem. He has good company in end Ezra Johnson, who had 15½ sacks in his best-ever season. End Byron Braggs must develop to replace the loss of Mike Butler to the USFL.

Mike Douglass, a very good linebacker, doesn't like it in Packerland and wants out. If he stays, it will be a plus. Cornerbacks Tim Lewis and Mark Lee are solid, but it seems the Packers likely will change at safety, now manned by Johnnie Gray and Mark Murphy.

KICKING GAME: If Jan Stenerud finally retires, the Packers will go with Eddie Garcia, whom they have been carrying just in case. Maybe Bucky Scribner is the punter they've been searching for. The return game is solid, if not spectacular.

THE ROOKIES: Expect both No. 1 Alphonso Carreker, a DE from Florida State, and No. 3 Donnie Humphrey, a DT from

PACKERS VETERAN ROSTER

HEAD COACH—Forrest Gregg. Assistant Coaches—Hank Bullough, Lew Carpenter, Virgil Knight, Dick Modzelewski, Herb Paterra, Ken Riley, Bob Schnelker, George Sefcik, Jerry Wampfler.

No.	Name	Pos.	Ht.	Wt.	NFL Exp.	College
59	Anderson, John	LB	6-3	229	7	Michigan
76	Bishop, Richard	NT	6-1	283	8	Louisville
72	Boyd, Greg	DE	6-6	280	7	San Diego State
73	Braggs, Byron	DE	6-4	270	4	Alabama
93	Brown, Robert	DE	6-2	250	3	Virginia Tech
19	Campbell, Rich	QB	6-4	219	4	California
88	Cassidy, Ron	WR	6-0	180	5	Utah State
33	Clark, Jessie	FB	6-0	233	2	Arkansas
82	Coffman, Paul	TE	6-3	225	7	Kansas State
52	Cumby, George	LB	6-0	224	5	Oklahoma
57	Curcio, Mike	LB	6-1	232	4	Temple
12	Dickey, Lynn	QB	6-4	203	14	Kansas State
53	Douglass, Mike	LB	6-0	214	7	San Diego State
61	Drechsler, Dave	G	6-3	264	2	North Carolina
31	Ellis, Gerry	RB	5-11	225	5	Missouri
85	Epps, Phillip	WR	5-10	155	3	Texas Christian
59	Favron, Calvin	LB	6-2	230	5	S.E. Louisiana
11	Garcia, Eddie	K	5-8	178	2	Southern Methodist
24	Gray, Johnnie	S	5-11	202	10	Cal State-Fullerton
65	Hallstrom, Ron	T	6-6	283	3	Iowa
69	Harris, Leotis	G	6-1	265	7	Arkansas
38	Hood, Estus	CB-S	5-11	189	7	Illinois State
25	Huckleby, Harlan	RB	6-1	201	5	Michigan
74	Huffman, Tim	G	6-5	282	4	Notre Dame
40	Ivery, Eddie Lee	RB	6-1	214	5	Georgia Tech
83	Jefferson, John	WR	6-1	204	7	Arizona State
99	Johnson, Charles	NT	6-2	265	4	Maryland
90	Johnson, Ezra	DE	6-4	259	7	Morris Brown
21	Jolly, Mike	CB-S	6-3	185	4	Michigan
63	Jones, Terry	DT	6-2	253	6	Alabama
64	Kitson, Syd	G	6-4	264	4	Wake Forest
86	Knafelc, Greg	TE	6-4	230	2	Notre Dame
68	Koch, Greg	T	6-4	276	6	Arkansas
67	Lapka, Myron	NT	6-4	260	3	Southern California
62	Laughlin, Jim	LB	6-1	222	5	Ohio State
22	Lee, Mark	CB	5-11	188	5	Washington
56	Lewis, Cliff	LB	6-1	224	4	S. Mississippi
26	Lewis, Tim	CB-S	5-11	191	2	Pittsburgh
80	Lofton, James	WR	6-3	197	7	Stanford
54	McCarren, Larry	C	6-3	251	12	Illinois
29	McCoy, Mike C.	CB-S	5-11	190	9	Colorado
39	Meade, Mike	RB	5-10	224	3	Penn State
37	Murphy, Mark	S	6-2	201	4	West Liberty State
44	O'Steen, Dwayne	CB	6-1	195	7	San Jose State
51	Prather, Guy	LB	6-2	229	4	Grambling
35	Rodgers, Del	RB	5-10	202	2	Utah
58	Rubens, Larry	C	6-1	250	3	Montana State
70	Sams, Ron	G	6-3	269	2	Pittsburgh
55	Scott, Randy	LB	6-1	222	4	Alabama
13	Scribner, Bucky	P	6-0	202	2	Kansas
78	Skaugstad, Daryle	NT	6-5	268	4	California
78	Spears, Ron	DE	6-6	255	3	San Diego State
10	#Stenerud, Jan	K	6-2	190	18	Montana State
67	Swanke, Karl	T-C	6-6	262	5	Boston College
34	Thomaselli, Rich	RB	6-1	205	3	W. Va. Wesleyan
75	Turner, Richard	DT	6-2	261	4	Oklahoma
17	Whitehurst, David	QB	6-2	205	8	Furman
50	Wingo, Rich	LB	6-1	227	5	Alabama
20	Winters, Chet	RB	5-11	204	2	Oklahoma

#Unsigned at press time

TOP FIVE DRAFT CHOICES

Rd.	Name	Sel. No.	Pos.	Ht.	Wt.	College
1	Carreker, Alphonso	12	DE	6-6	260	Florida State
3	Humphrey, Donnie	72	DT	6-3	275	Auburn
4	Dorsey, John	99	LB	6-3	233	Connecticut
5	Flynn, Tom	126	DB	6-0	195	Pittsburgh
6	Wright, Randy	153	QB	6-2	194	Wisconsin

Auburn, to break into the starting lineup, at least part time, this season. The Packers need defensive line help and both could be good enough immediately to fill that need.

OUTLOOK: The Packers have been rebuilding for so long now it has become a joke. This could be a pivotal year: if the defense improves, they could be in the playoffs. If not, look for more regression.

PACKER PROFILES

LYNN DICKEY 34 6-4 203   **Quarterback**

Did as much as he could to push the Packers into the playoffs last year . . . Had the best season of his 11-year career . . . Set five individual records, for most attempts (484), most completions (289), most yards gained (4,458), most touchdown passes (32) and most consecutive completions (18) . . . Also threw five touchdown passes against Houston to tie his own team record . . . He still had too many interceptions (29) to be as effective as he'd like . . . Born Oct. 19, 1949, in Paola, Kan., where the high school stadium is named afer him . . . Starred at Kansas State . . . Likes to play golf . . . Started pro career with Houston.

JAMES LOFTON 28 6-3 197   **Wide Receiver**

Acknowledged as perhaps the most gifted receiver in the league, even though his statistics sometimes don't rank him that high . . . One case where talent is not judged by figures alone . . . Made the Pro Bowl as a starter for the fourth straight year . . . Caught 58 passes for 1,300 yards, a stunning 22.4-yard average . . . His yardage total erased his own club record, set in 1981 . . . He twice has caught 71 passes . . . Known for his intelligence (Stanford), his athletic grace, his competitiveness . . . Does lots of charity work, especially for March of Dimes . . . Born July 5, 1956, in Los Angeles . . . Has advertising and public relations firm.

JOHN JEFFERSON 28 6-1 204   Wide Receiver

The Packers never have been able to put his talents to full use... He's one of the league's best, but his abilities have been overshadowed by James Lofton since he came to Green Bay... Caught 57 passes last year, one less than Lofton, but didn't even make it to the Pro Bowl... A much more fragile receiver whose particular flair is built around his wonderful leaping ability... Has worked out some of the kinks with quarterback Lynn Dickey, but now has to adapt to new coach... Born Feb. 3, 1956, in Dallas... All-American at Arizona State and former star with the Chargers.

MIKE DOUGLASS 29 6-0 214   Linebacker

His talents have been buried in Green Bay... Lack of national attention has prevented him from gaining true recognition for his talents... Led the team in tackles last year... Loves to blitz, where he can use his quickness to harass quarterbacks... Has had to overcome lack of height... Born March 15, 1955, in St. Louis... Vice president of public relations firm also owned by teammates James Lofton and John Jefferson... Has two Doberman pinchers and likes to bowl, cook and decorate... Drafted on the fifth round out of San Diego State.

EZRA JOHNSON 28 6-4 259   Defensive End

Talk about a comeback... Once had 20 sacks in a season (1978) and there were thoughts he would be a great one... Then injuries and a long slump ate into his reputation... But last year he arrived again, with 15½ sacks to easily be the Packers' best and rank among the tops in the league... He was coming off his best year since 1978, after getting five sacks and leading the defensive line in tackles in 1982... But no one associated with the Packers ever thought he would produce so well in 1983... Born Oct. 2, 1955, in Shreveport, La.... First-round draft choice out of Morris Brown.

TIM LEWIS 22 5-11 191   Cornerback

Here is one No. 1-round draft choice who paid off immediately... Broke into the Packers' starting lineup and produced quick results ... Had a team-high five interceptions despite being tested every week by opponent quarterbacks... Also showed off his running ability by returning those interceptions for 111 yards, a 22.2 average... Now the Packers want him to increase his tackling totals... Born Dec. 18, 1961, in Perkasie, Pa.... Was star at the University of Pittsburgh, where he was a two-year starter... Has 4.5 speed in the 40-yard dash plus good strength.

PAUL COFFMAN 28 6-3 225   Tight End

With all the great receivers surrounding him, he gets lost in the shuffle... But he is one of the league's most reliable, productive tight ends... Caught 54 passes last year, which is right on line with his normal career production... Now has 56, 55 and 54 receptions in his best years... Not particularly fast or flashy, but runs good routes and is so very reliable... And he benefits from all the attention defenses pay to Lofton and Jefferson... Born March 29, 1956, in Chase, Kan.... A free agent out of Kansas, he talked a Packer assistant into giving him a tryout.

SYD KITSON 25 6-4 264   Guard

Turned into perhaps the best player on the Packer offensive line after after spending the 1982 season on injured reserve with a neck problem... Injuries have hampered his development beginning in his 1980 rookie year... Was considered by the Packers to be the top guard in the 1980 group... Picked on the third round out of Wake Forest... Hurt a leg as a rookie and his neck as a second-year man... Born Sept. 27, 1958, in Orange, N. J.... Was a tight end early in his college career before moving first to tackle, then to guard... Enjoys golf, tennis, camping, sailing.

GERRY ELLIS 26 5-11 225   **Running Back**

Supplied what there was of the Packers' running game last year . . . Doesn't have breakaway speed, but gives the team the power short-yardage back it wants . . . Gets as much as anyone in the league out of limited ability . . . Gained 696 yards on 141 carries last season, a nifty 4.9-yard average . . . Second-best output in his career . . . Showed his versatility with 52 catches, again second-best ever for him . . . Born Nov. 12, 1957, in Columbia, Mo. . . . Free agent from Missouri . . . Pronounced Gary, not Gerry.

GEORGE CUMBY 28 6-0 224   **Linebacker**

Finally has managed to shake off injury problems long enough to put together two good back-to-back seasons . . . At one time, it seemed he never could stay healthy long enough to be consistent . . . Not the ideal height for a linebacker, but he has great athletic ability and he loves to hit . . . An All-American at Oklahoma, where his exploits late in his career are legend around Norman . . . Was third on the team in tackles last season . . . Born July 5, 1956, in LeRue, Tex. . . . A first-round draft choice in 1980 . . . His strength: quick reaction to the ball.

COACH FORREST GREGG: Says he finally has the job he always has wanted: coach of the Green Bay Packers . . . Probably one of the few men who could have replaced Bart Starr and not been caught in a lot of controversy in Wisconsin . . . But football people know he was getting restless at Cincinnati . . . He previously had made inquiries about an opening at Kansas City two years ago . . . The Bengals gave him a second chance after he was fired at Cleveland . . . A strict disciplinarian with a strong stare, he has modified his ways to get along better with his players . . . Produced a near Super Bowl champ at Cincinnati, where he was hampered by ownership interference . . . Has a sense of humor that doesn't always come out in interviews . . . Born Oct. 18, 1933, in Birthright, Tex. . . . Played college ball at SMU in the days of two-way tackles . . . Vince Lombardi called him the finest pro player he had ever seen . . . Played 14 years for the Packers and one season in Dallas . . . An All-Pro eight times.

BIGGEST PLAY

If a game has been played in colder conditions, nobody knows about it. It was bad enough on Dec. 31, 1967, in Green Bay: 16 degrees below zero with a wind chill factor of 46 below. Lambeau Field was frozen, and so were the players and fans. But championship games are not called off in the NFL because of weather. So they played on.

The Packers had won two straight NFL titles and the first Super Bowl. Another win would mean a record third title. But the Dallas Cowboys weren't cooperating. They had gone ahead, 17-14, and seemed on the verge of finally snapping the Packer jinx.

But Green Bay had one final shot. Quarterback Bart Starr drove the Packers to the Cowboy 11 with 71 seconds to go. Starr called a false trap, and Chuck Mercein bulled to the three. Now 54 seconds were left. Donnie Anderson got to the one for a first down with 30 seconds remaining. Twice, Anderson ran and twice he slipped inside the one. There were 16 seconds left.

Vince Lombardi wanted no part of kicking a field goal to force an overtime. The plan was for Starr to sneak over behind guard Jerry Kramer. Kramer made a memorable block, Starr scored and the Packers won, 21-17.

INDIVIDUAL PACKER RECORDS

Rushing

Most Yards Game:	186	Jim Taylor, vs N.Y. Giants, 1961
Season:	1,474	Jim Taylor, 1962
Career:	8,207	Jim Taylor, 1958-66

Passing

Most TD Passes Game:	5	Cecil Isbell, vs Cleveland, 1942
	5	Don Horn, vs St. Louis, 1969
	5	Lynn Dickey, vs New Orleans, 1981
	5	Lynn Dickey, vs Houston, 1983
Season:	32	Lynn Dickey, 1983
Career:	152	Bart Starr 1956-71

Receiving

Most TD Passes Game:	4	Don Hutson, vs Detroit, 1945
Season:	17	Don Hutson, 1943
Career:	99	Don Hutson, 1935-45

Scoring

Most Points Game:	33	Paul Hornung, vs Baltimore, 1961
Season:	176	Paul Hornung, 1960
Career:	823	Don Hutson, 1935-45
Most TDs Game:	5	Paul Hornung, vs Baltimore, 1961
Season:	19	Jim Taylor, 1962
Career:	105	Don Hutson, 1935-45

LOS ANGELES RAMS

TEAM DIRECTORY: Pres.: Georgia Frontiere; VP-Finance: John Shaw; Dir. Operations: Dick Beam; Adm. Football Operations: Jack Faulkner; Dir. Player Personnel: John Math; Dir. Pub. Rel.: Pete Donovan; Head Coach: John Robinson. Home field: Anaheim Stadium (69,007). Colors: Royal blue, gold and white.

SCOUTING REPORT

OFFENSE: Even though John Robinson put in a very up-to-date one-back offense last year after getting tight end David Hill from Detroit, that still doesn't mean the Rams were all that fancy.

As a rookie, Eric Dickerson rushed to NFL-leading 1,808 yards.

Robinson believes in basics, which means he used Eric Dickerson first, second and third and then went to the passing option.

This approach works as long as your guys are stronger up front than the other guys. Which is not always the case with the Rams, especially if defenses don't worry that much about the passing of Vince Ferragamo.

Robinson seems ready to alter his ways slightly for 1984. Dickerson, already perhaps the league's best runner and a mighty weapon, won't be forgotten. Robinson will always be, first and foremost, a runner's coach. But you might see more two-back sets and you might see Dickerson used more as a receiver. Something has to be done to help Ferragamo, who can go from great to bad as fast as any quarterback in the league.

One thing that would help is some improvement at wide receiver, where injuries and lack of ability took away Ferragamo's deep threat. For now, the team doesn't have a dominant receiver.

DEFENSE: This is not the Ram defense of old, when it could stay out on the field and crush opponents. That's one reason Robinson switched to a 3-4 last year, to try to shore up weaknesses. And that was a factor in his adopting a running attack that served to control the ball. The more time your offense is on the field, the less time your defense is left vulnerable. Makes sense, right?

The Rams are solid, if not spectacular. Jack Youngblood made a good transition from playing end in a 4-3 to playing one in a 3-4. Liked it so much he says he'll come back for another season. Linebackers Carl Ekern and Jim Collins moved to the front on the tackle chart, giving support to the use of a four-linebacker formation. And linebackers George Andrews and Mel Owens had contributing seasons.

The flip-flop of Johnnie Johnson and Nolan Cromwell at safety worked out better than expected, with Cromwell still going to the Pro Bowl. The acquisition of Gary Green from Kansas City should fill the void left by the death of Kirk Collins.

KICKING GAME: The Rams thought they had solved their field-goal problems by drafting Chuck Nelson but Mike Lansford wound up doing the kicking. John Misko had a decent 40.3 average. LeRoy Irvin remains one of the most explosive return men in the league.

THE ROOKIES: Last year, the Rams used trades to pick up Eric Dickerson. This year, the Rams used trades to take themselves out of the draft. They dealt away their No. 1 pick for veteran CB Gary Green and wound up not having a choice until the fifth

RAMS VETERAN ROSTER

HEAD COACH—John Robinson. Assistant Coaches—Bob Baker, Marv Goux, Gil Haskell, Hudson Houck, Jimmy Raye, Steve Shafer, Fritz Shurmur, Bruce Snyder, Fred Whittingham.

No.	Name	Pos.	Ht.	Wt.	NFL Exp.	College
35	Alexander, Robert	RB	6-0	185	3	West Virginia
52	Andrews, George	LB	6-3	225	6	Nebraska
62	Bain, Bill	T	6-4	285	10	Southern California
86	#Barber, Mike	TE	6-3	237	9	Lousiana Tech
96	Barnett, Doug	DE	6-3	250	3	Azusa Pacific
73	Bolinger, Russ	G	6-5	255	8	Cal State-Long Beach
50	Collins, Jim	LB	6-2	230	4	Syracuse
21	Cromwell, Nolan	S	6-1	200	8	Kansas
—	Crutchfield, Dwayne	RB	6-0	235	3	Iowa State
70	#De Jurnett, Charles	DT	6-4	260	8	San Jose State
88	#Dennard, Preston	WR	6-1	183	7	New Mexico
29	Dickerson, Eric	RB	6-3	218	2	Southern Methodist
71	Doss, Reggie	DE	6-4	263	7	Hampton Institute
55	Ekern, Carl	LB	6-3	222	8	San Jose State
80	Ellard, Henry	WR	5-11	170	2	Fresno State
84	#Farmer, George	WR	5-10	175	3	Southern U.
15	Ferragamo, Vince	QB	6-3	212	7	Nebraska
24	Green, Gary	CB	5-11	191	8	Baylor
82	Grant, Otis	WR	6-3	197	2	Michigan State
44	Guman, Mike	RB	6-2	218	5	Penn State
60	Harrah, Dennis	G	6-5	255	10	Miami
26	Harris, Eric	CB	6-3	202	5	Memphis State
81	#Hill, David	TE	6-2	230	9	Texas A&I
87	Hill, Drew	WR	5-9	170	6	Georgia Tech
72	Hill, Kent	G	6-5	260	6	Georgia Tech
47	Irvin, Le Roy	CB	5-11	184	5	Kansas
59	Jerue, Mark	LB	6-3	229	2	Washington
77	Jeter, Gary	DE	6-4	260	8	Southern California
20	Johnson, Johnnie	S	6-1	183	5	Texas
24	Jones, A.J.	RB	6-1	202	3	Texas
25	#Jones, Gordon	WR	6-0	190	6	Pittsburgh
9	Kemp, Jeff	QB	6-0	201	4	Dartmouth
76	Kowalski, Gary	T	6-5	275	2	Boston College
1	Lansford, Mike	K	6-0	183	3	Washington
51	Lewis, David	LB	6-4	245	8	Southern California
83	McDonald, James	TE	6-5	230	2	Southern California
69	Meisner, Greg	DT	6-3	253	4	Pittsburgh
6	Misko, John	P	6-5	207	3	Oregon State
13	Nelson, Chuck	K	5-11	175	2	Washington
22	Newsome, Vince	S	6-1	179	2	Washington
58	Owens, Mel	LB	6-2	224	4	Michigan
75	Pankey, Irv	T	6-4	267	5	Penn State
30	Redden, Barry	RB	5-10	205	3	Richmond
64	Shearin, Joe	G	6-4	250	2	Texas
78	Slater, Jackie	T	6-4	271	9	Jackson State
56	Smith, Doug	C	6-3	253	7	Bowling Green
37	Sully, Ivory	S	6-0	200	6	Delaware
54	Wilcher, Mike	LB	6-3	235	2	North Carolina
66	Williams, Eric	LB	6-2	235	8	Southern California
28	#Williams, Mike	CB	5-10	186	10	Louisiana State
85	Youngblood, Jack	DE	6-4	242	14	Florida

#Unsigned at press time

TOP FIVE DRAFT CHOICES

Rd.	Name	Sel. No.	Pos.	Ht.	Wt.	College
5	Stephens, Hal	133	DE	6-4	252	East Carolina
7	Radachowsky, George	188	DB	5-10	188	Boston College
8	Brady, Ed	215	LB	6-2	210	Illinois
9	Reynolds, George	242	P	6-0	188	Penn State
10	Vann, Norwood	253	TE	6-0	240	East Carolina

round, when they chose East Carolina DE Hal Stephens. Shades of George Allen.

OUTLOOK: Robinson thinks the Rams are on schedule to becoming a perennial contender. He needs improvement from his young players and some more speed on the outside. And he better add a dominant pass-rusher sometime soon to help out on defense.

RAM PROFILES

ERIC DICKERSON 23 6-3 218   Running Back

Coach John Robinson predicted he could become the league's next great running back, but probably no one expected him to emerge so quickly... The one person most responsible for the Rams' turnaround last season... Led the NFL in rushing with 1,808 yards while setting four club records... His 390 attempts were a league record... Gained over 100 yards nine times, including 199 against Detroit... And he caught 51 passes... Will be used more as a receiver this year... Only Simpson, Campbell, Brown and Payton have had better years... Has blazing speed and size of a fullback... Born Sept. 2, 1960, in Sealy, Tex.... Second pick in 1983 draft, out of SMU... Gained 311 yards in Texas high-school title game.

VINCE FERRAGAMO 30 6-3 212   Quarterback

For first time, didn't have to face a battle for starting position... John Robinson handed over offense to him and he responded splendidly ... Set Ram records for passes completed (274) and yards (3,276)... Completed 59 percent of his attempts and threw for 22 touchdowns... But there has to be concern over his 23 interceptions... Still remains slow on some reads and will force the ball into coverages... Born April 24, 1954, in Torrance, Cal.... Attended Nebraska after brief stay at California... Returned to NFL two years ago after rich, but unhappy stay, in Canadian League.

NOLAN CROMWELL 29 6-1 200   Safety

Switched spots last season with Johnny Johnson, moving from free to strong safety . . . Didn't bother him a bit, as he made the Pro Bowl after being picked three straight times at his old position . . . New coach John Robinson thought he had better talents for the new position, although the move was controversial . . . Had three interceptions and 91 tackles, to rank fourth on the team . . . Has 25 interceptions for career . . . Considered one of the league's better all-around athletes . . . Born Jan. 30, 1955, in Smith Center, Kan. . . . Avid outdoorsman and golfer . . . Former quarterback at Kansas.

JACK YOUNGBLOOD 34 6-4 242   Defensive End

The legend lives on . . . Even after 13 years, still a rock-solid player . . . In some ways, last season might have been his toughest . . . Had to make difficult transition from end in 4-3 to 3-4 . . . Cut down on his pass rush and made him more of a tackler, but still led the team in sacks with 10½ and had 53 tackles . . . One of the most cooperative, best-humored players in the league . . . Good-looking and charming . . . Even in the glaring lights of Southern California, has kept his country-boy ways . . . Likes to hunt and fish and owns a country store . . . Born Jan. 26, 1950, in Jacksonville, Fla. . . . Played Super Bowl XIV with broken leg.

DAVID HILL 30 6-2 230   Tight End

Came over from Detroit in late preseason trade that helped finish off the Rams' offense . . . To make one-back attack work, they needed a second tight end and he was the man . . . Caught 28 passes and added his blocking skills to help Eric Dickerson's runs . . . Lions finally gave up on him after hoping he would be Pro Bowl performer for years to come . . . Thought he was too inconsistent . . . A second-round pick out of Texas A&I in 1976 . . . Born Jan. 1, 1954, in San Antonio . . . A pleasant, outgoing man who relates well with the media . . . Became a popular Ram interview . . . Probably will be utilized more in Rams' attack this year.

MIKE BARBER 31 6-3 237   Tight End

Got to like a man who plays hard, says what's on his mind and earns a good living...Came over from Houston in 1982 and now has settled into a starring role with the Rams...Led the team in receiving last year with 55 catches, second highest in his career...Had only 31 receptions the two previous seasons...Tough, durable and sure-handed...Loves John Robinson's approach...Star at Louisiana Tech...Born June 4, 1953, in White Oak, Tex....State high-school hurdles champion... Works with prison inmates one weekend a month in offseason.

JACKIE SLATER 30 6-4 271   Tackle

Became the on-field guardian of Eric Dickerson...If you watched carefully, he was the guy who hovered over the young runner after tackles and helped him up...Knows a meal ticket when he sees one...A typical Rams' offensive lineman: big, mobile, strong...They all seem cut from a perfect mold...Rest of the conference recognized his play by selecting him to Pro Bowl for the first time...Born May 27, 1954, in Meridian, Miss....Teammate of Walter Payton's at Jackson State, where he also lettered in track...Third-round draft choice in 1976 who has been a starter since 1979.

DENNIS HARRAH 31 6-5 255   Guard

Not the biggest guard in the league, weight-wise, but you should see his physique...Has lived in the weight room for years and it shows...Strong, tough, loves to play, a coach's dream...Part of a line that allowed only 21 sacks, second lowest in the NFL, and blocked admirably for Dickerson...Maybe has lost a step from the days he was a Pro Bowl selection but still a solid player...Once didn't start until the ninth game (in 1980) because of injuries and still made the Pro Bowl...Born March 9, 1953, in Charleston, W. Va....Owns a popular night club in Long Beach, Cal.

BILL BAIN 32 6-4 285   Tackle

One of the league's more unusual stories... A journeyman player who usually has been overweight and a bit out of shape... But John Robinson knew him from USC and had him on the preseason roster... Then Irv Pankey got hurt and he suddenly became a starter at key left tackle position... And he held up well... Has played nine seasons, which shows what persistence can achieve... Born Aug. 9, 1952, in Pico Rivera, Cal. ... Second-round pick of Green Bay in 1975... Has played for five NFL teams... Began college career at Colorado.

CARL EKERN 30 6-3 222   Linebacker

Has had two major knee operations during seven-year career, which has cut into his consistency... But when he is healthy, he has been fine player... Led the team in tackles in 1981 and then came back to do it again last year with 130... Adapted well to the Rams' new 3-4 set.... Hurt his knee in the first poststrike game in 1982 and missed the rest of the season... A fifth-round choice in 1976... Born May 27, 1954, in Richland, Wash.... Attended San Jose State, where he was conference Player of the Year his senior season... Studying for MBA.

COACH JOHN ROBINSON: Given the title Miracle Worker

around Orange County... Took a sagging program and turned it into a playoff contender in one season with his philosophy of physical football... Immediately established a running game, even in this era of pass, pass, pass... His approach worked, too, although the Rams still have a way to go to be an elite team... One of the best in the league in relating to the press and doing public relations appearances... Likes to talk, to probe, to argue... A good-humored, easy-to-like man who lets his assistants have plenty of freedom in devising game plans and tactics... Was going to retire from coaching after successful tenure at USC... Had grown tired of recruiting and the constraints of college coaching... Has been coaching for 24 years, with stops at Oregon and the Oakland Raiders...His specialty always has been offense...Born July 25, 1935, in San Mateo, Cal....Says the major change in the new job "was taking a new freeway to work."

BIGGEST PLAY

A year before, Rams' pass-catcher Tom Fears had been compared to Green Bay's immortal Don Hutson. But now, slowed by knee problems, he was playing in the shadow of teammate Elroy (Crazy Legs) Hirsch, who had enjoyed a sensational season. And here they were on Dec. 23, 1951, in the final quarter of the NFL championship game against the Cleveland Browns at the Los Angeles Coliseum.

The Browns were the defending champs, the budding dynasty led by quarterback Otto Graham, flanker Dub Jones and placekicker Lou Groza. The Rams were the team of quarterbacks Bob Waterfield and Norm Van Brocklin, defensive end Andy Robustelli, power runners Deacon Dan Towler and Dick Hoerner, and long-bomb receivers Hirsch and Fears.

And now they were locked in a 17-17 tie. Van Brocklin had

Interceptions aside, Vince Ferragamo set some club marks.

entered the game as a replacement for Waterfield. The Browns had worried about the deep pass all afternoon, but the secondary really had been tested only once. Now it happened again. Fears went deep, Van Brocklin let go.

"It was the best-thrown pass I ever caught in my life," Fears said. The pass settled into Fears' hands 73 yards away. The Rams had a touchdown, the winning touchdown. And the only NFL title in their history.

INDIVIDUAL RAM RECORDS

Rushing

Most Yards Game:	247	Willie Ellison, vs New Orleans, 1971
Season:	1,808	Eric Dickerson, 1983
Career:	6,186	Lawrence McCutcheon, 1973-79

Passing

Most TD Passes Game:	5	Bob Waterfield, vs N.Y. Bulldogs, 1949
	5	Norm Van Brocklin, vs Detroit, 1950
	5	Norm Van Brocklin, vs N.Y. Yanks, 1951
	5	Roman Gabriel, vs Cleveland, 1965
	5	Vince Ferragamo, vs New Orleans, 1980
	5	Vince Ferragamo, vs San Francisco, 1983
Season:	30	Vince Ferragamo, 1980
Career:	154	Roman Gabriel, 1962-72

Receiving

Most TD Passes Game:	4	Bob Shaw, vs Washington, 1949
	4	Elroy Hirsch, vs N.Y. Yanks, 1951
	4	Harold Jackson, vs Dallas, 1973
Season:	17	Elroy Hirsch, 1951
Career:	53	Elroy Hirsch, 1949-57

Scoring

Most Points Game:	24	Elroy Hirsch, vs N.Y. Yanks, 1951
	24	Bob Shaw, vs Washington, 1949
	24	Harold Jackson, vs Dallas, 1973
Season:	130	David Ray, 1973
Career:	573	Bob Waterfield, 1945-52
Most TDs Game:	4	Elroy Hirsch, vs N.Y. Yanks, 1951
	4	Bob Shaw, vs Washington, 1949
	4	Harold Jackson, vs Dallas, 1973
Season:	20	Eric Dickerson, 1983
Career:	55	Elroy Hirsch, 1949-57

MINNESOTA VIKINGS

TEAM DIRECTORY: Pres.: Max Winter; VP/GM: Mike Lynn; Dir. Administration: Harley Peterson; Dir. FB Oper.: Jerry Reichow; Dir. Pub. Rel.: Merrill Swanson; Head Coach: Les Steckel. Home field: Hubert H. Humphrey Metrodome (62,212). Colors: Purple, white and gold.

SCOUTING REPORT

OFFENSE: The best news this season for the Vikings will be that all their key players remain healthy for Les Steckel, Bud Grant's successor as coach. You can criticize Minnesota for its

The arm is fine, but all hangs on Tommy Kramer's knee.

1983 performance but with most of the best players hurt, they had their excuses.

The most important player returning is quarterback Tommy Kramer, who missed most of the season with a bad knee. He has to be able to step in for beleaguered Steve Dils, who at least gained valuable experience playing for Kramer. Young Darrin Nelson proved his value as both a receiver and rusher and provides a darting one-two punch with Ted Brown, who is coming off a problem-plagued year.

If Joe Senser can rebound from a knee injury, tight end is in good shape. The Vikings need help at wide receiver, where they don't have the explosive player of years past. The offensive line is nothing sensational, but it is more than adequate and young tackle Curtis Rouse, all 300 pounds of him, could improve its quality nicely.

DEFENSE: Sometimes the Vikings recall the Purple People Eaters of the past. But too often, they seem a step slow and a muscle or two too weak. Maybe it is those slow-footed black shoes that they wear. Go to white, Vikings.

Grant thought two players—linebacker Matt Blair, cornerback Willie Teal—played well enough last year to be in the Pro Bowl, although they both missed out. They remain solid players and the Vikings can boast of a very good front line that includes veteran Charlie Johnson, Doug Martin and newcomer Neil Elshire. Mark Mullaney, James White and Randy Holloway provide depth.

A young, quick linebacker would be a nice addition and although the Vikings have added youth to the secondary, they still need more and No. 1 choice (1983) Joey Browner has to come on at safety.

KICKING GAME: Punter Greg Coleman had a standout season, averaging 41.5 yards to give the Vikings consistent performances from this vital position. Kicker Benny Ricardo scored 108 points and made 25 of 33 attempts. As usual, Minnesota has solid coverage teams.

THE ROOKIES: Keith Millard, the No. 1 pick, was considered a good defensive end for a 4-3 Washington State team. But the Vikings use a 3-4, so he will have to make an adjustment. But consider him insurance in case Doug Martin doesn't play because of contract problems. Baylor's Alfred Anderson (No. 3) should provide depth at running back, but he'll not be an All-Pro.

OUTLOOK: This will be an unusual year for Minnesota, trying to make it without Grant as coach. Steckel is an unknown quantity

VIKINGS VETERAN ROSTER

HEAD COACH—Les Steckel. Assistant Coaches—Tom Batta, Bud Bjornaraa, Dean Brittenham, Jerry Burns, Tom Cecchini, Ross Fichtner, Bob Hollway, John Michels, Bus Mertes, Dan Radakovich, Floyd Reese, Mike Sweatman.

No.	Name	Pos.	Ht.	Wt.	NFL Exp.	College
58	Ashley, Walker Lee	LB	6-0	240	2	Penn State
33	Bell, Rick	RB	6-0	205	2	St. John's (Minn.)
21	Bess, Rufus	CB	5-9	185	6	South Carolina State
59	Blair, Matt	LB	6-5	235	11	Iowa State
62	Boyd, Brent	G	6-3	275	5	UCLA
23	Brown, Ted	RB	5-10	210	6	North Carolina State
47	Browner, Joey	CB-S	6-2	205	2	Southern California
82	#Bruer, Bob	TE	6-5	240	6	Mankato State
87	Casper, Dave	TE	6-4	241	11	Notre Dame
8	Coleman, Greg	P	6-0	185	8	Florida A&M
7	Danmeier, Rick	K	6-0	183	6	Sioux Falls (S. D.)
12	Dils, Steve	QB	6-1	195	5	Stanford
73	Elshire, Neil	DE	6-6	260	4	Oregon
50	Fowlkes, Dennis	LB	6-2	230	2	West Virginia
32	Galbreath, Tony	RB	6-0	228	9	Missouri
61	#Hamilton, Wes	G	6-3	270	9	Tulsa
45	Hannon, Tom	S	5-11	195	8	Michigan State
75	Holloway, Randy	DE	6-5	255	7	Pittsburgh
51	Hough, Jim	G	6-2	275	7	Utah State
76	Irwin, Tim	T	6-6	285	4	Tennessee
65	Johnson, Charlie	NT	6-3	275	8	Colorado
52	Johnson, Dennis	LB	6-3	235	5	Southern California
89	Jones, Mike	WR	5-11	176	2	Tennessee State
83	Jordan, Steve	TE	6-3	230	3	Brown
9	Kramer, Tommy	QB	6-2	205	8	Rice
80	Le Count, Terry	WR	5-10	185	7	Florida
39	Lee, Carl	CB-S	5-11	185	2	Marshall
87	Lewis, Leo	WR	5-8	170	4	Missouri
4	Manning, Archie	QB	6-3	211	14	Mississippi
79	#Martin, Doug	DE	6-3	255	5	Washington
84	#McCullum, Sam	WR	6-2	195	11	Montana State
88	McDole, Mardye	WR	5-11	205	3	Mississippi State
54	#McNeill, Fred	LB	6-2	230	11	UCLA
86	Mularkey, Mike	TE	6-4	245	2	Florida
77	Mullaney, Mark	DE	6-6	245	10	Colorado State
20	Nelson, Darrin	RB	5-9	180	3	Stanford
49	Nord, Keith	S	6-0	195	6	St. Cloud, (Minn.)
22	Redwine, Jarvis	RB	5-10	205	4	Nebraska
1	Ricardo, Benny	K	5-10	170	7	San Diego State
78	Riley, Steve	T	6-6	260	11	Southern California
68	Rouse, Curtis	G	6-3	305	3	Tenn.-Chattanooga
57	Sendlein, Robin	LB	6-3	225	4	Texas
81	Senser, Joe	TE	6-4	235	5	West Chester (Pa.)
55	Studwell, Scott	LB	6-2	230	8	Illinois
29	Swain, John	CB	6-1	195	4	Miami
66	Tausch, Terry	T	6-5	275	3	Texas
37	Teal, Willie	CB	5-10	195	5	Louisiana State
27	Turner, John	S	6-0	200	7	Miami
72	White, James	NT	6-3	270	9	Oklahoma State
85	White, Sammy	WR	5-11	195	9	Grambling
11	Wilson, Wade	QB	6-3	210	4	East Texas State
34	#Young, Rickey	RB	6-2	200	10	Jackson State

#Unsigned at press time

TOP FIVE DRAFT CHOICES

Rd.	Name	Sel. No.	Pos.	Ht.	Wt.	College
1	Millard, Keith	13	DE	6-5	260	Washington State
3	Anderson, Alfred	67	RB	6-2	220	Baylor
5	Rice, Allen	140	RB	5-10	195	Baylor
6	Collins, Dwight	154	WR	6-1	210	Pittsburgh
7	Haines, John	180	DT	6-5	260	Texas

who will be trying to get the Vikings back into their usual playoff mode despite lack of quickness throughout the team.

VIKING PROFILE

TOMMY KRAMER 29 6-2 205   Quarterback

Major reason the Vikings didn't make it to the playoffs last year . . . Badly hurt a knee in the third game of the season and was out for the rest of the schedule . . . Without him, the team suddenly lost its offensive leader and its stability . . . Vikings say knee is healing ahead of schedule and he should be 100 percent for this year . . . Was off to a fast start, completing 67 percent of his attempts . . . It was to have been his year, now that he had settled down into domestic life and given up the nighttime fun . . . Rice graduate is one of 11 children . . . Born March 7, 1955, in San Antonio . . . Father coached at Texas Lutheran for six years.

TED BROWN 27 5-10 210   Running Back

Had a run-in with Bud Grant last season and suddenly found himself off the team briefly . . . Grant never gave reason why he disciplined him, or why he let him back . . . But if you check the Viking depth chart, he isn't listed as a starter . . . Had his good moments last year, especially when gaining 179 yards against San Francisco . . . Finished with 11 touchdowns and 476 yards rushing . . . Missed six games with a shoulder injury which cut into his production . . . Also had 41 receptions . . . Born Feb. 2, 1957, in High Point, N.C. . . . . Accidently shot himself in offseason, 1983 . . . Standout at N.C. State.

DARRIN NELSON 25 5-9 180   Running Back

People wondered how the Vikings could have drafted him No. 1 in 1982, but Stanford grad showed why last season . . . Finally got a chance to play and wound up being most consistent offensive threat on the team . . . Led in rushing with 642 yards and in receiving with 51 catches . . . . Ran 56 yards for a touchdown . . . Also led the NFC in kickoff-return average with 24.7 mark on 18 returns . . . First running back and seventh player chosen in the 1982 draft . . . Born Jan. 2, 1959, in Sacramento, Cal. . . . Cleveland's Ozzie Newsome and Cincinnati's Charles Alexander are his cousins.

JOE SENSER 28 6-4 235 — Tight End

Another of the Vikings' walking wounded from 1983 . . . Never did play a game last season after ruining a knee . . . There is hope that he will come back okay this year, because the Vikings desperately need him at tight end. . . . Considered to be one of the best pass-catchers at his position in the business . . . Four-year starter in both football and basketball at West Chester State . . . Majored in criminal justice . . . Born Aug. 18, 1956, in Philadelphia . . . Been troubled the last three years with a bad knee . . . Works with various charities in the offseason.

DOUG MARTIN 27 6-3 255 — Defensive End

Fifth in the NFC in quarterback sacks with 13 . . . Second outstanding year in a row after he had 10½ sacks in shortened 1982 season . . . Has learned how to use his quickness and experience even from the Vikings' 3-4 set . . . Has ability to play inside when the Vikings switch to a 4-3 in passing situations . . . Was a first-round draft choice in 1980 after being a star at the University of Washington . . . People around the league will tell you that the Vikings wanted to unload him in his early pro years . . . Born May 22, 1957, in Fairfield, Conn. . . . Brother George also made it to the pros, with the Giants.

MATT BLAIR 33 6-5 235 — Linebacker

In many ways, a symbol of the Viking Glory Past . . . Still one of the team's best players, but at his age, he should rank further down the list . . . Remains the consummate pro—always prepared, always trying . . . One of the few talented Vikings who didn't have an injury problem last season . . . Second on the team in tackles. . . . But this was the first time in seven years he didn't make the Pro Bowl . . . Born Sept. 20, 1950, in Honolulu . . . Freelance photographer and owns a trucking company—Matt Blair Express, Inc. . . . Runs a football camp, likes to play golf and chess and repair antique cars.

NEIL ELSHIRE 26 6-6 260　　　　Defensive End

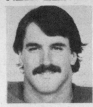

Here is a nice rags-to-riches story to help you swallow all those high salaries and holdouts a little better... Sat out senior year at Oregon with a bad knee, then signed as free agent with the Redskins... They thought he was a sleeper, but so did Vikings, who claimed him on waivers when the Redskins tried to clear him en route to spot on active roster... Then he hurt his knee in 1982 and missed more than half season... So all he did last year was beat out some bigger-name teammates and earn a starting position... Had 9½ quarterback sacks, second on the team... Born March 8, 1958, in Albany, Ore.... Has worked as lobbyist.

GREG COLEMAN 29 6-0 185　　　　　　Punter

Vikings' patience with this young punter has paid off... Not the longest kicker in the league, but his strength is consistency... Last year, he produced his best year yet, with a 41.5 average to rank fourth in the conference... And that was after he had a 41.1 average—his second highest—the previous season... Set three Viking records in 1983: most punts (91), most yards (3,780) and most inside the 20 (28)... Out of Florida A&M, he was a 14th-round draft choice by Cincinnati in 1976... Kicked a year for Cleveland before being released, then signed with the Vikings in 1979... Born Sept 9, 1954, in Jacksonville, Fla.... Had five future pros as teammates at Jacksonville High School.

STEVE DILS 28 6-1 195　　　　　Quarterback

Wound up as Viking starter for the last 13 games after Tommy Kramer hurt his knee early in the season... By far the most he has ever played in his five-year career... Mostly, he has been a holder on kicks... Completed 239 of 444 passes for 2,840 yards and 11 touchdowns last year... Threw 16 interceptions, which cut into his effectiveness... His first pro start, in 1980, he beat the Redskins, then in his second, in 1981, he set a club record with 62 passes... Attended Stanford, where he was teammate of Darrin Nelson... Born Dec. 8, 1955, in Seattle... Skis, plays tennis and golf.

CHARLIE JOHNSON 32 6-3 275   Middle Guard

One of the best trades in Viking history ...Came over in 1982 for a second-round draft choice after tiring of coach Dick Vermeil's boot-camp mentality...He must have known what was coming with the Eagles and Vermeil ...Not a particularly spectacular player, but lends both experience and leadership to a defense...Allowed the Vikings to play both 4-3 and 3-4 defensive sets...Born Feb. 17, 1952, in West Columbia, Tex....Had an Army tour in Vietnam after graduating from high school, then went to junior college and U. of Colorado...Three-time Pro Bowl performer.

COACH LES STECKEL: Hard to tell what was more surpris-

ing...That Bud Grant suddenly retired after 17 years as Vikings' head coach, or that he was replaced by this man...Not that he isn't qualified, but guessers weren't pointing to him as a likely Grant replacement...Seemed long-time offensive coordinator Jerry Burns was the likely assistant who would move up to the top job...But the Vikings sometimes like to pull off surprises...Should be interesting to see if the team can adapt to what should be a different approach from the ways of laid-back Grant...The new coach is a former Marine who served as an infantry officer in Vietnam in 1969 and 1970...He is known to be a lot more intense and demanding than Grant...Already has remade the coaching staff with Burns the only remaining member...Born July 1, 1946, in Whitehall, Pa....Another NFL coach who has no head-coaching experience...Was college assistant at Colorado and Navy before moving to 49ers in 1978 and then to Minnesota in 1979, where he handled receivers...A former Golden Gloves national boxing champion.

BIGGEST PLAY

Few teams are ever able to bail out from situations like the one that faced the Minnesota Vikings on Dec. 14, 1980, when they played host to the Cleveland Browns. Behind by a point, the

Vikings were on their own 20 with no timeouts remaining and just 14 seconds left on the clock.

If they lost the game, their chances of winning their 11th Central Division title in 13 years would be hampered severely. If they won, the Vikings' playoff trip would be clinched.

The Vikings had time for maybe two plays. On the first one, they lined up three wide receivers to the right and tight end Joe Senser to the left. Senser caught a pass from quarterback Tommy Kramer at the 30 and lateraled to running back Ted Brown, who was trailing the play. Brown finally was forced out at the Cleveland 46. Four seconds remained.

Again, three receivers lined up to the right. Kramer tossed the ball high and long. Minnesota's Sammy White tried to tip it but Cleveland's Thom Darden deflected it instead—into the arms of Ahmad Rashad, who caught it and backed in from the three for the Vikings' winning touchdown, 28-23.

INDIVIDUAL VIKING RECORDS

Rushing

Most Yards Game:	200	Chuck Foreman, vs Philadelphia, 1976	
Season:	1,155	Chuck Foreman, 1976	
Career:	5,879	Chuck Foreman, 1973-79	

Passing

Most TD Passes Game:	7	Joe Kapp, vs Baltimore, 1969
Season:	26	Tommy Kramer, 1981
Career	239	Francis Tarkenton, 1961-66, 1972-78

Receiving

Most TD Passes Game:	4	Ahmad Rashad, vs San Francisco, 1979
Season:	11	Jerry Reichow, 1961
Career:	45	Sammy White, 1976-82

Scoring

Most Points Game:	24	Chuck Foreman, vs Buffalo, 1975
	24	Ahmad Rashad, vs San Francisco, 1979
Season:	132	Chuck Foreman, 1975
Career:	1,365	Fred Cox, 1963-77
Most TDs Game:	4	Chuck Foreman, vs Buffalo, 1975
	4	Ahmad Rashad, vs San Francisco, 1979
Season:	22	Chuck Foreman, 1975
Career:	76	Bill Brown, 1962-74

NEW ORLEANS SAINTS

TEAM DIRECTORY: Owner: John Mecom Jr.; Pres.: Eddie Jones; VP-Administration: Fred Williams; Dir. FB Oper.: Pat Peppler; GM/Head Coach: Bum Phillips; Controller: Bob Landry; Dir. Pub. Rel.: Greg Suit. Home field: Superdome (71,330). Colors: Old gold, black and white.

SCOUTING REPORT

OFFENSE: The surprise addition of Richard Todd should both stabilize the Saints' offense and push them into the playoffs for the first time.

With Todd, Bum Phillips finally might loosen up the offense a bit and get away from the unpredictability and conservative tendencies that hurt it last season.

Now the Saints have a longball threat who can also restore their two-minute drill. And Todd's presence should make a better runner of George Rogers, who must be tired of all that gang-tackling and keying defenses on him.

New Orleans will work on its play-action passes to give Rogers a boost. They also want to cut down on their turnovers: they had 47 (25 interceptions and 22 fumbles) and they have to do better in tight games. Four more first downs in crucial situations last year and they would have had a 12-4 record.

DEFENSE: Three years ago, the Saints had the worst defense in the league. Last season, the unit finished second in the league. And it should get better, considering most of the key players are young and improving.

Everywhere Phillips looks, he sees better things. The Saints had a team-record 56 sacks and got an All-Pro year from linebacker Rickey Jackson. Only two of the team's eight losses were by eight or more points. And the unit gave up an average of 17 points a game, outstanding in this high-scoring era. The defense also forced 39 turnovers.

End Bruce Clark is sure to get better and that would help aging nose tackle Derland Moore. Jackson, Jim Kovach, Dennis Winston and Whitney Paul form a solid set of linebackers that should get even more dominant. When the Saints play well, they are extremely tough to run on, just manhandling offensive lines with ease.

When teams are forced to pass, they go against a now solid secondary that includes Johnnie Poe, Dave Waymer and Russell

George Rogers should benefit from presence of Richard Todd.

Gary. These guys are young and should prove more difficult for opposing quarterbacks in the years to come.

KICKING GAME: Russell Erxleben handles the punting duties with efficiency, if not with the spectacular kicks predicted for him when he left college. Morten Anderson seems to have the ability to be the Saints' placekicker for years to come. But the Saints' punt-coverage team made some major blunders in crucial games.

THE ROOKIES: With QB Todd representing their prime choice, the Saints took some gambles in the draft and came away with some question marks. Will No. 2 James Geathers, who didn't play much at Wichita State, become a legitimate TE? Will Georgia DB Terry Hoage show he is better than a standout college player?

OUTLOOK: The Saints came so close to their first playoff spot last year that it seems just the addition of Todd might put them across the threshold. Unless the Jets know something about Todd that we don't. Or unless Bum doesn't let go with the offensive reins like he should.

SAINTS VETERAN ROSTER

HEAD COACH—O. J. (Bum) Phillips. Assistant Coaches—Andy Everest, King Hill, John Levra, Carl Mauch, Lamar McHan, Russell Paternostro, Wade Phillips, Harold Richardson, Joe Spencer, Lance Van Zandt, John Paul Young, Willie Zapalac.

No.	Name	Pos.	Ht.	Wt.	NFL Exp.	College
7	Andersen, Morten	K	6-2	210	3	Michigan State
47	Austin, Cliff	RB	6-0	190	2	Clemson
50	#Bordelon, Ken	LB	6-4	226	7	Louisiana State
85	Brenner, Hoby	TE	6-4	240	4	Southern California
67	Brock, Stan	T	6-6	285	5	Colorado
75	Clark, Bruce	DE	6-3	275	3	Penn State
68	Clark, Kelvin	G	6-3	265	6	Nebraska
83	Duckett, Kenny	WR	6-0	187	3	Wake Forest
63	Edelman, Brad	G	6-6	265	3	Missouri
99	Elliott, Tony	NT	6-2	265	3	North Texas State
14	Erxleben, Russell	P	6-4	221	5	Texas
77	Fields, Angelo	T	6-4	314	4	Michigan State
46	Gajan, Hokie	RB	5-11	220	3	Louisiana State
20	Gary, Russell	S	5-11	195	4	Nebraska
88	Goodlow, Eugene	WR	6-2	190	2	Kansas State
72	Gray, Leon	T	6-3	270	12	Jackson State
86	Groth, Jeff	WR	5-10	175	6	Bowling Green
87	#Hardy, Larry	TE	6-3	230	7	Jackson State
62	Hill, John	C	6-2	260	13	Lehigh
57	Jackson, Rickey	LB	6-2	240	4	Pittsburgh
34	Johnson, Bobby	CB-S	6-0	191	2	Texas
60	Korte, Steve	G	6-2	270	2	Arkansas
52	Kovach, Jim	LB	6-2	225	6	Kentucky
21	Krimm, John	S	6-2	190	2	Notre Dame
64	Lafary, Dave	T	6-7	280	8	Purdue
93	Lewis, Gary	NT	6-3	260	2	Oklahoma State
98	Lewis, Reggie	DE	6-2	260	3	San Diego State
29	Lewis, Rodney	CB	5-11	190	2	Nebraska
59	Martin, Chris	LB	6-2	220	2	Auburn
84	#Mauti, Rich	WR	6-0	195	7	Penn State
19	Merkens, Guido	QB	6-1	195	7	Sam Houston State
74	Moore, Derland	NT	6-4	270	12	Oklahoma
55	Nairne, Rob	LB	6-4	227	8	Oregon State
66	Oubre, Louis	G	6-4	262	3	Oklahoma
51	Paul, Whitney	LB	6-3	220	9	Colorado
53	Pelluer, Scott	LB	6-2	220	4	Washington State
32	#Perry, Vernon	S	6-2	210	6	Jackson State
76	#Pietrzak, Jim	C	6-5	260	10	Eastern Michigan
25	Poe, Johnnie	CB	6-1	185	4	Missouri
58	Redd, Glen	LB	6-1	225	3	Brigham Young
38	Rogers, George	RB	6-2	229	4	South Carolina
41	Rogers, Jimmy	RB	5-10	190	5	Oklahoma
80	Scott, Lindsay	WR	6-1	190	3	Georgia
16	Stabler, Ken	QB	6-3	210	15	Alabama
27	Sternrick, Greg	CB	5-11	185	10	Colorado State
82	Tice, John	TE	6-5	242	2	Maryland
13	Todd, Richard	QB	6-2	206	9	Alabama
73	Warren, Frank	DE	6-4	275	4	Auburn
49	Wattelet, Frank	S	6-0	185	4	Kansas
44	Waymer, Dave	CB	6-1	195	5	Notre Dame
94	Wilks, Jim	DE	6-5	260	4	San Diego State
18	Wilson, Dave	QB	6-3	210	3	Illinois
45	#Wilson, Tim	FB	6-3	235	8	Maryland
30	Wilson, Wayne	RB	6-3	208	6	Shepherd (W. Va.)
56	Winston, Dennis	LB	6-0	230	8	Arkansas
89	Young, Tyrone	WR	6-6	190	2	Florida

#Unsigned at press time

TOP FIVE DRAFT CHOICES

Rd.	Name	Sel. No.	Pos.	Ht.	Wt.	College
2	Geathers, James	42	DE	6-7	263	Wichita State
3	Hoage, Terry	68	DB	6-3	196	Georgia
3	Anthony, Tyrone	69	RB	6-1	203	North Carolina
4	Hilgenberg, Joel	97	C	6-3	250	Iowa
5	Fields, Jitter	123	DB	5-8	185	Texas

SAINT PROFILES

RICHARD TODD 30 6-2 206　　　　　Quarterback

The Saints may have insured themselves their first winning season and playoff berth by acquiring this experienced quarterback from the Jets... With Ken Stabler and Dave Wilson both ailing, he will give this most important position some vitality... And maybe now the Saints will have a two-minute drill with some punch... Had best year ever in 1982 but last year was not very pleasant... When the Jets tumbled, he was blamed... Booed out of New York, as some critics put it... Passed for 3,478 yards but threw 26 interceptions and only 18 touchdowns... Born Nov. 19, 1953, in Birmingham, Ala.... Jets' No. 1 pick, out of Alabama, in 1976... Has pilot's license.

KEN STABLER 38 6-3 210　　　　　Quarterback

It was sometimes difficult to watch him play last season... His knees are so bad that you felt for the way he would stumble around... Still as tough as they come and a good leader but his fastball is now a slowball... With him in the lineup, the Saints have no real effective two-minute drill or long passing game... Said no to lucrative USFL offer in order to play again for Bum Phillips... Born Dec. 25, 1945, in Foley, Ala.... Led Alabama to NCAA title way back in 1965... His hair was dark then and Bear Bryant didn't welcome beards... A nice man who likes the laid-back life.

GEORGE ROGERS 25 6-2 229　　　　　Running Back

Another 1,000-yard plus season, but this was done very quietly... Had to deal with rumors about drug investigations and other off-the-field distractions, and his effectiveness was reduced... Not always healthy either, and that didn't help... Scored five touchdowns and caught just 12 passes... He needs to be more involved in the Saints' passing game... Why not a few more swing passes?... Born Dec. 8, 1958, in Duluth, Ga.... Heisman Trophy winner at South Carolina who set NFL rookie rushing record... It was broken by Eric Dickerson last year.

BRUCE CLARK 26 6-3 275   Defensive End

Came out of Canada to establish himself as quality NFL defensive player . . . Now he is expected to get better and better . . . Had 4½ sacks last year and should be able to double that, even working out of a 3-4 set . . . Gambled by going to Canada out of Penn State and came back with a very big contract . . . Was Packers' No. 1 choice in 1980 after consensus All-American career at Penn State . . . Born March 31, 1958, in Newcastle, Pa. . . . Saints had to trade No. 1 to Packers to get him . . . Works for local hotel during offseason.

DENNIS WINSTON 28 6-0 230   Linebacker

A really profitable trade for New Orleans . . . Since coming over form Pittsburgh, the man they call "Dirt" has been a stabilizing influence on Saints' defense . . . He plays tough and hard and often . . . Was the team's MVP in 1982 and came back last year to rank second in tackles with 217 . . . Is a standout special teams' player, too, where he can let his recklessness flow . . . Born Oct. 25, 1955, in Forrest City, Ark. . . . Standout at Arkansas, where he also played defensive end . . . One of eight children, he still lives in Fayetteville, Ark.

JIM KOVACH 28 6-2 225   Linebacker

His teammates voted him the defensive unit's MVP . . . Had 251 tackles last year, including 113 solo efforts . . . Also three sacks and eight pass deflections . . . And they said he was too slow and too preoccupied with off-the-field academic activities . . . A true scholar-athlete . . . Attends University of Kentucky medical school in the offseason and played his senior year at Kentucky while in med school . . . So calling defensive signals really isn't a very difficult challenge . . . Born May 1, 1956, in Parma Heights, Ohio . . . His hobby is golf.

DERLAND MOORE 32 6-4 270   Middle Guard

He's seen it all in New Orleans . . . Been with the worst teams and now he is trying to hang on to be part of the best Saints' team . . . He remembers when he wondered if the franchise would even make it through a season . . . Friendly, considerate, one of the team's most popular players . . . Also playing the best football of his career . . . Has to sit in the middle and take all that punishment, and this after having come in as a defensive tackle . . . Had 93 tackles last year and six sacks . . . Born Oct. 7, 1951, in Malden, Mo. . . . All-American at Oklahoma . . . Works with oil companies in offseason.

JOHNNIE POE 25 6-1 185   Cornerback

Came on very strongly last year to establish himself as a premier player at this position . . . Not the easiest era to stand out at cornerback, considering how much teams are throwing these days . . . Had seven interceptions to tie him for fourth best in the conference . . . Had only one previous interception despite starting for first two years in the league . . . Matter of building up his confidence . . . A tough way to get on-the-job training . . . Born Aug. 29, 1959, in East St. Louis, Mo. . . . Attended Missouri and was drafted on the sixth round in 1981.

RICKEY JACKSON 26 6-2 240   Linebacker

He was overshadowed in college by Pittsburgh teammate Hugh Green but he's carved out his own niche in pro football . . . The Saints love his hell-bent-for-leather style . . . Was a roving defensive end in college and still is learning how to play linebacker at this level, but he certainly has made great strides . . . Was fourth last season on the team in tackles and had 11 sacks . . . The Saints just let him go, like Lawrence Taylor, and see how many quarterbacks he can punish . . . Born March 20, 1958, in Pahokee, Fla. . . . Hobbies are checkers and fishing . . . Played on three state high-school football championship teams in Florida.

WAYNE WILSON 26 6-3 208   Fullback

His teammates recognized his value to the team in 1983 by voting him the offensive Player of the Year . . . That's right, he beat out George Rogers and Ken Stabler, among others . . . Always dependable, whether it's running, catching or blocking . . . Ran for 787 yards, scored nine touchdowns and caught 20 passes last year, and also returned 10 kickoffs and contributed some good special teams' play . . . Maybe even brushed off Bum's hats in his spare time . . . Born Sept. 4, 1957, in Montgomery, Md. . . . Attended tiny Shepherd College in West Virginia . . . A substitue teacher in offseason.

COACH BUM PHILLIPS: He hasn't produced a winning season or a playoff team in New Orleans, yet, but the fans do love him . . . Can't walk down Bourbon Street without offers of free beer with almost every step . . . Team had record number of sellouts last year, so he has to be doing something right . . . Has shown he can rebuild a team using the draft after turning Houston into a winner by trading for veteran players . . . Remains steadfast in his philosophy of keeping things simple and depending on defenses to win for him . . . A character who can get testy when pushed too hard on a subject . . . But with his witty sayings and common-sense approach, it is easy to see why he is a living legend in pro football . . . Born Sept. 29, 1923, in Orange, Tex. . . . Real name is Oail . . . You can see his face lots of places in New Orleans: he's doing a number of TV and billboard commercials . . . Loved it in Houston but New Orleans is probably one of the few places he didn't mind moving to this late in his career . . . A Marine Corps veteran who played guard at Lamar Junior College and Stephen F. Austin.

BIGGEST PLAY

They were an unlikely combination, these two New Orleans Saints.

One was the coach. His name was J. D. Roberts, and he had taken over earlier in the week for the fired Tom Fears. He had inherited a misfit team that, as usual, was going nowhere. And he knew there was little he could do to change things around.

The other was the field-goal kicker, Tom Dempsey, born with a malformed hand and foot. He was overweight but he had trained and trained and now he had become a pro kicker, using that bad foot to boom powerful kicks.

Roberts' first game as coach was following a familiar Saints pattern on Nov. 8, 1970. New Orleans was losing to Detroit, 17-16, with less than a minute left. The Saints had the ball, but couldn't even get to midfield. So Roberts sent in Dempsey.

The ball was placed down 63 yards away from the uprights. The kick never wavered. It was good, for an NFL record. Dempsey was smothered by his teammates and the Saints had a rare, sweet, victory.

INDIVIDUAL SAINT RECORDS

Rushing

Most Yards Game:	206	George Rogers, vs St. Louis, 1983
Season:	1,674	George Rogers, 1981
Career:	3,218	Chuck Muncie, 1976-79

Passing

Most TD Passes Game:	6	Billy Kilmer, vs St. Louis, 1969
Season:	23	Archie Manning, 1980
Career:	155	Archie Manning, 1971-81

Receiving

Most TD Passes Game:	3	Dan Abramowicz, vs San Francisco, 1971
Season:	9	Henry Childs, 1977
Career:	37	Dan Abramowicz, 1967-72

Scoring

Most Points Game:	18	Walt Roberts, vs Philadelphia, 1967
	18	Dan Abramowicz, vs San Francisco, 1971
	18	Archie Manning, vs Chicago, 1977
	18	Chuck Muncie, vs San Francisco, 1979
	18	George Rogers, vs Los Angeles, 1981
	18	Wayne Wilson, vs Atlanta, 1982
Season:	99	Tom Dempsey, 1969
Career:	243	Charlie Durkee, 1967-68, 1971-72
Most TDs Game:	3	Walt Roberts, vs Philadelphia, 1967
	3	Dan Abramowicz, vs San Francisco, 1971
	3	Archie Manning, vs Chicago, 1977
	3	Chuck Muncie, vs San Francisco, 1979
	3	George Rogers, vs Los Angeles, 1981
	3	Wayne Wilson, vs Atlanta, 1982
Season:	13	George Rogers, 1981
Career:	37	Dan Abramowicz, 1967-72

NEW YORK GIANTS

TEAM DIRECTORY: Pres.: Wellington Mara; VP/Treasurer: Timothy Mara; VP/GM: George Young; Dir. Pro Personnel: Tom Boisture; Dir. Pub. Rel.: Ed Croke; Head Coach: Bill Parcells. Home field: Giants Stadium (76,500). Colors: Blue, red and white.

SCOUTING REPORT

OFFENSE: Bill Parcells is quite aware that the only way his Giants will ever become contenders is to fix up a woeful offense that dragged even a talented defense down with it in 1983.

But where to start with this offensive fix? Quarterback is the logical place, and that's where Phil Simms is crying for a chance now that Scott Brunner has been traded to Denver. It would help if running back Butch Woolfolk could be consistent all year and if Rob Carpenter can come back from a knee injury. And Parcells has to find some receiver who can take the pressure off productive Earnest Gray, coming off his best season.

Tackle Brad Benson played well last season, but that can't be said about most of the rest of the line. Better years are expected from Gordon King and Bill Ard. And how about those turnovers? Too many, for one thing: 58 in all, including 27 fumbles. Once the Giants got inside the 20, it was almost certain they were going to give it up and quickly. Rookie OT Bill Roberts should help.

DEFENSE: After a strong finish the last part of the 1983 season, things seem in decent shape with the normally good Giant defense. But how long must this unit keep trying to carry the offense? Seems like it's been going on for years.

The Giants were second behind New Orleans in defense in the NFC, and were third in rushing defense behind Washington and Dallas, giving up just 3.5 yards a carry. And that was with a somewhat patched-up lineup, thanks to injuries.

One problem is the continued unhappiness of inside backer Harry Carson, who always wants out of New York. He missed five games with injuries last year but with him back, Lawrence Taylor can concentrate on the outside again. Brad Van Pelt isn't exactly excited about things in Giant land either, but like Carson, is tied up with a long-term contract. First-rounder Carl Banks comes in as an appealing all-around linebacker.

No. 1 safety choice Terry Kinard moved into a starting role and made good progress. This isn't a great secondary, but the Giants certainly have a lot more glaring problems facing them.

KICKING GAME: In rookie Ali Haji-Sheikh, the Giants had one of the game's best field-goal kickers last year. And he probably will get better. Leon Bright still doesn't call for fair catches and Dave Jennings still punts well, although not as well last season as he has in years past.

THE ROOKIES: Okay, so the Giants really didn't need another linebacker. But it was hard to pass up Michigan State's Banks,

Ali Haji-Sheikh set all-time NFL mark with 35 field goals.

GIANTS VETERAN ROSTER

HEAD COACH—Bill Parcells. Assistant Coaches—Bill Belichick, Tom Bresnahan, Romeo Crennell, Ron Erhardt, Len Fontes, Ray Handley, Pat Hodgson, Lamar Leachman, Johnny Parker, Mike Pope.

No.	Name	Pos.	Ht.	Wt.	NFL Exp.	College
67	Ard, Bill	G	6-3	250	4	Wake Forest
73	Belcher, Kevin	G	6-3	255	2	Texas-El Paso
60	Benson, Brad	T	6-3	258	7	Penn State
45	#Bright, Leon	RB	5-9	192	4	Florida State
64	Burt, Jim	NT	6-1	255	4	Miami
26	Carpenter, Rob	RB	6-1	230	8	Miami (Ohio)
53	Carson, Harry	LB	6-2	245	9	South Carolina State
74	Cook, Charles	NT	6-3	255	2	Miami
29	Currier, Bill	S	6-0	202	8	South Carolina
46	Dennis, Mike	CB	5-10	190	5	Wyoming
88	Eddings, Floyd	WR	5-11	177	3	California
37	Flowers, Larry	S	6-1	190	4	Texas Tech
83	Gray, Earnest	WR	6-3	195	6	Memphis State
6	Haji-Sheikh, Ali	K	6-0	172	2	Michigan
79	Hardison, Dee	DE	6-4	269	7	North Carolina
36	Haynes, Mark	CB	5-11	195	5	Colorado
54	Headen, Andy	LB	6-5	230	2	Clemson
27	#Heater, Larry	RB	5-11	205	5	Arizona
82	Hugger, Keith	WR	5-11	175	2	Connecticut
61	Hughes, Ernie	C	6-3	265	6	Notre Dame
57	Hunt, Byron	LB	6-5	230	4	Southern Methodist
13	Jennings, Dave	P	6-4	205	11	St. Lawrence
43	Kinard, Terry	S	6-1	195	2	Clemson
72	King, Gordon	T	6-6	275	7	Stanford
70	Marshall, Leonard	DE	6-3	285	2	Louisiana State
75	Martin, George	DE	6-4	245	10	Oregon
39	Mayock, Mike	S	6-2	195	3	Boston College
33	McDaniel, Le Charls	CB	5-9	170	4	Cal Poly-Obispo
76	McGriff, Curtis	DE	6-5	265	5	Alabama
52	McLaughlin, Joe	LB	6-1	235	6	Massachusetts
71	Merrill, Casey	DE	6-4	255	6	Cal-Davis
89	Miller, Mike	WR	6-0	182	2	Tennessee
85	Mistler, John	WR	6-2	186	4	Arizona State
20	Morris, Joe	RB	5-7	190	3	Syracuse
84	Mowatt, Zeke	TE	6-3	238	2	Florida State
81	Mullady, Tom	TE	6-3	232	5	Southwestern
77	Neill, Bill	NT	6-4	255	4	Pittsburgh
9	#Owen, Tom	QB	6-1	194	11	Wichita State
86	Perkins, Johnny	WR	6-2	205	8	Abilene Christian
17	Rutledge, Jeff	QB	6-1	190	6	Alabama
78	Sally, Jerome	DT	6-3	260	3	Missouri
80	Scott, Malcolm	TE	6-4	240	2	Louisiana State
44	#Shaw, Pete	S	5-10	183	8	Northwestern
11	Simms, Phil	QB	6-3	216	6	Morehead State
63	Steinfeld, Al	C	6-5	256	4	C.W. Post
65	Tautolo, John	G	6-3	260	3	UCLA
56	Taylor, Lawrence	LB	6-3	237	4	North Carolina
38	Tuggle, John	RB	6-1	210	2	California
68	Turner, J.T.	G	6-3	250	8	Duke
59	Umphrey, Rich	C	6-3	255	3	Colorado
10	Van Pelt, Brad	LB	6-5	235	12	Michigan State
87	Williams, Byron	WR	6-2	180	2	Texas-Arlington
25	Woolfolk, Butch	RB	6-1	210	3	Michigan

#Unsigned at press time

TOP FIVE DRAFT CHOICES

Rd.	Name	Sel. No.	Pos.	Ht.	Wt.	College
1	Banks, Carl	3	LB	6-4	230	Michigan State
1	Roberts, Bill	27	T	6-5	272	Ohio State
3	Hostetler, Jeff	59	QB	6-3	215	West Virginia
4	Goode, Conrad	87	T	6-6	275	Missouri
4	Reasons, Gary	105	LB	6-4	235	Northwest Louisiana

one of the best available players in the draft. He'll play inside, making the defense even better. Tackle Bill Roberts (No. 2, Ohio State) will have every chance to become a starter while West Virginia QB Jeff Hostetler is a good backup.

OUTLOOK: If you are looking for a team going nowhere fast, it's the poor Giants. One year they seem ready to become contenders, and then the bottom falls out. Some day, they will go out and hire a big-name, strong-armed coach and then maybe things will straighten out.

GIANT PROFILES

LAWRENCE TAYLOR 25 6-3 237 Linebacker

He is a great one on the field, and you have to admire his off-the-field talents, too...Used the USFL to maneuver the Giants into a massive contract extension that will make him an easy millionaire...And it cost the Giants money to buy out the USFL pact with New Jersey, too...Considered to be the league's premier linebacker and most threatening defensive player...Once again a Pro Bowl selection even though injuries forced him to play both inside and outside linebacker during the year...Born Feb. 4, 1959, in Williamsburg, Va....Led the team in tackles and was second in sacks...Was an All-American at North Carolina.

ROB CARPENTER 29 6-1 230 Running Back

Lost some of the running limelight last year to Butch Woolfolk...2Doesn't have the speed to be a premier NFL back but certainly has the strength and determination...Always seems to be unhappy about his contract or his playing time...Remember, it was much the same when he was with Houston...Came over to the Giants for a third-round draft choice in September 1981, and helped push team into a rare playoff appearance...Born April 20, 1955, in Lancaster, Ohio, and attended Miami of Ohio, where he gained 1,000 yards-plus his last two years...Picked up 624 yards and scored six touchdowns last year.

HARRY CARSON 30 6-2 245   Linebacker

There is a theory that if this man was happy with his place in pro football life, he wouldn't be nearly as good...How many times has he asked out of New York?...Maybe if he would stop making the Pro Bowl—he was named for the fifth time last year—he would be more likely trade bait...Gives the Giant defense respect in the middle...Third on the team in tackles last year despite injury problems...Born Nov. 26, 1953, in Florence, S.C....Defensive end at South Carolina State...Likes soap operas, music, fishing, trap shooting...Once appeared in TV soap opera, "One Life to Live."

MARK HAYNES 25 5-11 195   Cornerback

Made the Pro Bowl for the second straight year, putting him among the league's top cornerbacks...One of the few bright spots for the Giants in 1983, although he might not have played as well as he did in 1982...Intercepted three passes...Giant coaches say he has outstanding ability to "make up and catch up" when he is beaten by receiver on an initial move...He says he isn't an emotional player...A first-round draft choice who took some time to develop...Born Nov. 6, 1958, in Kansas City...Attended Colorado, where he switched from running back to cornerback.

BUTCH WOOLFOLK 24 6-1 210   Running Back

Took over last season as the Giants' No. 1 runner...Gained 857 yards on 246 carries and scored four touchdowns...Methodically took away major ball-carrying duties from Rob Carpenter...Set NFL record for most carries in a game when he had 43 against the Eagles while gaining 159 yards...When Carpenter hurt a knee and missed six games, he had to pick up the sagging Giant offense as well as he could...Gained 439 yards as a rookie after being Giants' No. 1 pick in 1982...Born March 1, 1960, in Milwaukee, Wis....Standout career at Michigan, where he also won four letters in track and qualified for the Olympic trials in 200-meter dash.

DAVE JENNINGS 32 6-4 205 **Punter**

Didn't have his usual Pro Bowl year . . . Averaged only 40.3 yards a punt, third lowest in his 10-year career . . . Maybe he was dragged down finally by the plight of the rest of the team . . . Still, he dropped 29 punts inside the 20 and had only one blocked . . . Just three years ago, led the league with a 44.8 average . . . Third cousin of White Sox catcher Carlton Fisk . . . A big Red Sox and Celtic fan and dabbles in sports broadcasting . . . Father is former president of Southern Connecticut State College . . . Born June 8, 1952, in New York City.

ALI HAJI-SHEIKH 23 6-0 172 **Placekicker**

Spectacular rookie season, surprising everyone in the league except perhaps himself . . . Drafted on the ninth round by the Giants, and that pick became a steal . . . Made the Pro Bowl and All-Pro . . . Set all-time NFL record with 35 field goals, beating Jim Turner's mark by one . . . Missed only seven all year, including tries from 66, 61 and 52 yards . . . At one point, was 21 of 22 . . . Set all types of club records and scored 127 points . . . Born Jan. 11, 1961, in Ann Arbor, Mich. . . . Attended Michigan, where he was a walk-on . . . Handled kickoffs as a freshman.

EARNEST GRAY 27 6-3 195 **Wide Receiver**

Moved from the ranks of the unproductive to the status of near all-star last year . . . Never had caught more than 52 passes in a season and his normal production was 25 . . . But suddenly burst out and pulled in 78 catches . . . That tied him for first place in the NFC with Roy Green and Charlie Brown, and easily broke the old club record of 68 held by Del Shofner since 1961 . . . Had five games of more than 100 yards—against the Redskins, Raiders and Dallas among others . . . Second-round pick in 1979 from Memphis State, where he had 97 career receptions . . . Born March 2, 1957, in Greenwood, Miss., where he still lives.

PHIL SIMMS 27 6-3 216   Quarterback

Although he played in just two games last season because of a fractured right thumb, he's now the Giants' No. 1 QB again . . . Rival Scott Brunner was traded to Denver, handing him job . . . Injuries limited Simms to just 13 passing attempts last year, none in '82 . . . This is sixth year and he's been hurt for most or all of four seasons . . . Former No. 1 draft choice from little Morehead State, he's shown brief glimpses of potential, including back-to-back 300-yard games in 1980 wins over Dallas and Green Bay . . . Born Nov. 3, 1956, in Springfield, Ky.

TERRY KINARD 24 6-1 195   Safety

Caused a little unrest with the Giants last season when veteran Beasley Reece quit the team after complaining coaches were favoring this rookie . . . Beasley was just recognizing the march of time . . . Giants were certain to turn over starting chores to this No. 1 draft choice from Clemson . . . He has the ability to be a star for years to come . . . Wound up with three interceptions and 70 tackles . . . Born Nov. 24, 1959, in Bitburg, Germany, where his father was in the Air Force . . . Grew up in Sumter, N.C. . . . Called "Special K" at Clemson, where he was a unanimous All-American.

COACH BILL PARCELLS: Not the best of rookie coaching seasons . . . Took over for tough-guy Ray Perkins with blessing of his players, but they took

a nose dive and he took lot of the heat . . . Maybe not a good idea for former defensive coordinators to become head coaches in this era of the NFL . . . Hasn't seemed to work for any recent team . . . He made some rookie mistakes, like picking the wrong guy to play quarterback and never seemingly getting things settled on offense . . . Safe for at least this season, but it's hard to think the franchise can tolerate another bad record . . . There have been too many of those for too long already, and it wasn't that long ago that it appeared the Giants were headed in the right direction . . . Twelfth Giant head coach . . . Born Aug. 22, 1941, in Englewood, N.J. . . . Linebacker at Wichita State, No. 7 pick of Lions, but became college coach instead . . . Six college jobs, including head coach at Air Force . . . Long-time Giant fan.

BIGGEST PLAY

Pat Summerall already was being fitted for goat's horns by the 63,192 fans in Yankee Stadium on a miserable afternoon on Dec. 14, 1958. This was a game the Giants had to win to force a playoff with the Cleveland Browns for the Eastern Conference title. But Summerall just missed a 31-yarder against those same Browns and now all Cleveland had to do was hold on for the last 4½ minutes and the championship would be decided.

But the Browns couldn't put it away. The Giants got the ball back one last time. But to make matters worse, a driving snowstorm made conditions all but unbearable. The sideline markers were covered and no one quite knew where the ball was at all times.

Still, Summerall paced the sideline, hoping for a chance to redeem himself. He got it. With time all but out, the ball at midfield—officially at the 49—he came on. This time his kick was good and the Giants won, 13-10.

INDIVIDUAL GIANT RECORDS

Rushing

Most Yards Game:	218	Gene Roberts, vs Chi. Cardinals, 1950
Season:	1,182	Ron Johnson, 1972
Career:	4,638	Alex Webster, 1955-64

Passing

Most TD Passes Game:	7	Y. A. Tittle, vs Washington, 1962
Season:	36	Y. A. Tittle, 1963
Career:	173	Charlie Conerly, 1948-61

Receiving

Most TD Passes Game:	4	Earnest Gray, vs St. Louis, 1980
Season:	13	Homer Jones, 1967
Career:	48	Kyle Rote, 1951-61

Scoring

Most Points Game:	24	Ron Johnson, vs Philadelphia, 1972
	24	Earnest Gray, vs St. Louis, 1980
Season:	127	Ali Haji-Sheikh, 1983
Career:	646	Pete Gogolak, 1966-74
Most TDs Game:	4	Ron Johnson, vs Philadelphia, 1972
	4	Earnest Gray, vs St. Louis, 1980
Season:	17	Gene Roberts, 1949
Career:	78	Frank Gifford, 1952-60, 1962-64

PHILADELPHIA EAGLES

TEAM DIRECTORY: Pres.: Leonard Tose; VP/Legal Counsel: Susan Fletcher; Dir. Player Personnel: Lynn Stiles; Dir. Pub. Rel.: Jim Gallagher; Dir. Communications: Ed Wisneski; Head Coach: Marion Campbell. Home field: Veterans Stadium (73,484). Colors: Kelly green, white and silver.

SCOUTING REPORT

OFFENSE: Maybe this says it all about the Eagle offense from 1983: coach Marion Campbell released his offensive coordinator, Dick Woods; his line coach, Jerry Wampfler, and his wide-receiver coach, John Becker. Campbell wants to shake things up and he already has started to do so.

Things can't get much worse for Philadelphia. The Eagles were woeful most of the season on offense, in part because of injuries to Wilbert Montgomery and John Spagnola, and in part because of talent problems. In the season finale against St. Louis, the Eagles scored a late-game touchdown for their only score, and managed only 14 rushing yards, six by punter Max Runager. Earlier, they picked up only 10 yards rushing against the Giants.

Quarterback Ron Jaworski was sacked an incredible 53 times, thanks to this sad running game. The only bright spot was receiver Mike Quick, whose 1,409 yards topped the NFL. Harold Carmichael is gone and rookie Kenny Jackson will get his chance. There is strength at guard (Ron Baker, Steve Kenny) but help is needed at tackle, where Dean Miraldi and Leonard Mitchell have the edge unless Jerry Sisemore gets healthy again. Placekicking is wide open.

DEFENSE: Philadelphia didn't waste any time here changing things. The defensive coaches are still around but linebacker Frank LeMaster and defensive end Carl Hairston have been traded off. LeMaster was coming off a knee injury anyway and Hairston, once a dominant player in the division, had lost his starting spot.

Campbell, who is a defensive specialist, will concentrate on trying to shore up his run defense, which hardly stopped anyone last season. He just needs more people to play up to the level of linebacker Jerry Robinson, one of the best around, and end Dennis Harrison, who had 11½ sacks last year. The Eagles could use another pass-rusher to help out Harrison.

Randy Logan lost his safety position during midseason and

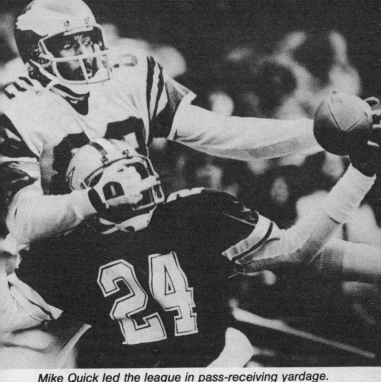

Mike Quick led the league in pass-receiving yardage.

probably will be a backup this year, if he stays. The Eagles are looking to people like strong safety Wes Hopkins to fill in some of the holes. There are plenty of holes: the Eagles gave up 340 yards a game and were last in the NFC in rush defense.

KICKING GAME: Franklin missed too many field goals last year and the Eagles finally gave up on him. The Eagles aren't that fond of punter Max Runager, either. And Campbell says he needs to bolster his return game. A lot of problems here, for sure.

THE ROOKIES: Penn State's Jackson is a superior talent who will provide the Eagles with a fine complement to Quick and good

EAGLES VETERAN ROSTER

HEAD COACH—Marion Campbell. Assistant Coaches—Fred Bruney, Chuck Clausen, Tom Coughlin, Harry Gamble, Frank Gansz, George Hill, Ken Iman, Ted Marchibroda, Billie Matthews.

No.	Name	Pos.	Ht.	Wt.	NFL Exp.	College
96	Armstrong, Harvey	NT	6-2	255	3	Southern Methodist
63	Baker, Ron	G	6-4	250	7	Oklahoma State
98	Brown, Greg	DE	6-5	240	4	Kansas State
71	Clarke, Ken	NT	6-2	255	7	Syracuse
57	Cowher, Bill	LB	6-3	225	4	North Carolina State
94	Darby, Byron	DE	6-4	250	2	Southern California
25	De Vaughn, Dennis	CB	5-10	175	3	Bishop
63	Dennard, Mark	C	6-1	252	6	Texas A&M
46	Edwards, Herman	CB	6-0	190	8	San Diego State
24	Ellis, Ray	SS	6-1	192	4	Ohio State
39	Everett, Major	RB	5-10	207	2	Mississippi College
67	Feehery, Gerry	C-G	6-2	268	2	Syracuse
29	Foules, Elbert	CB	5-11	185	2	Alcorn State
72	Fritzsche, Jim	T-G	6-8	265	2	Purdue
58	Griggs, Anthony	LB	6-3	220	3	Ohio State
26	Haddix, Michael	RB	6-2	225	2	Mississippi State
35	#Harrington, Perry	RB	5-11	210	5	Jackson State
68	Harrison, Dennis	DE	6-8	275	7	Vanderbilt
85	Hoover, Mel	WR	6-0	185	3	Arizona State
48	Hopkins, Wes	S	6-1	205	2	Southern Methodist
7	Jaworski, Ron	QB	6-2	196	11	Youngstown State
84	Kab, Vyto	TE	6-5	240	3	Penn State
73	#Kenney, Steve	G	6-4	262	5	Clemson
52	Kraynak, Rich	LB	6-1	221	2	Pittsburgh
41	Logan, Randy	SS	6-1	195	12	Michigan
64	Miraldi, Dean	T-G	6-5	254	2	Utah
74	Mitchell, Leonard	T	6-7	272	4	Houston
31	Montgomery, Wilbert	RB	5-10	195	8	Abilene Christian
34	Oliver, Hubie	FB	5-10	212	4	Arizona
62	Perot, Petey	G	6-2	261	5	NW Louisiana
9	Pisarcik, Joe	QB	6-4	220	8	New Mexico State
82	Quick, Mike	WR	6-2	190	3	North Carolina State
56	Robinson, Jerry	LB	6-2	225	6	UCLA
4	Runager, Max	P	6-1	189	6	South Carolina
87	Sampleton, Lawrence	TE	6-5	233	3	Texas
53	Schulz, Jody	LB	6-4	235	2	East Carolina
76	Sisemore, Jerry	T	6-4	265	12	Texas
88	Spagnola, John	TE	6-4	240	5	Yale
93	Strauthers, Thomas	DE	6-4	255	2	Jackson State
54	Valentine, Zack	LB	6-2	220	5	East Carolina
51	Wilkes, Reggie	LB	6-4	230	7	Georgia Tech
59	Williams, Joel	LB	6-1	220	6	Wisconsin-LaCrosse
32	Williams, Michael	RB	6-2	217	2	Mississippi College
22	#Wilson, Brenard	S	6-0	175	6	Vanderbilt
83	Woodruff, Tony	WR	6-0	175	3	Fresno State
89	Young, Glen	WR	6-2	205	2	Mississippi State
43	Young, Roynell	CB	6-1	181	5	Alcorn State

#Unsigned at press time

TOP FIVE DRAFT CHOICES

Rd.	Name	Sel. No.	Pos.	Ht.	Wt.	College
1	Jackson, Kenny	4	WR	6-0	173	Penn State
3	Russell, Rusty	60	T	6-6	295	South Carolina
4	Cooper, Evan	88	DB	6-0	175	Michigan
5	Hardy, Andre	116	RB	6-2	228	St. Mary's (Cal.)
6	Raridon, Scott	145	T	6-3	280	Nebraska

competition for Carmichael. But Philadelphia shouldn't expect as much help right away from talented but raw tackle Rusty Russell of South Carolina, their No. 3 choice.

OUTLOOK: The Eagles figured 11 wins last year wasn't out of the question, but it was. They will be fortunate now to be .500 this season, faced with a tough schedule and too much age at too many positions. And they are in a division where most teams are getting better.

EAGLE PROFILES

RON JAWORSKI 33 6-2 196   Quarterback

Maybe you don't realize it because he is booed in Philly, but this is a nice man with a fine sense of humor and the personality to absorb all the years of abuse...Maybe it would be best for him to go elsewhere, but a move now may be too late in his career...Not a spectacular 1983 season, but some of that is due to a bad offensive concept...Completed 235 of 446 passes for 3,315 yards, second-best yardage output of career ...Now has thrown for more than 20,000 yards in career ...Born March 23, 1951, in Lackawanna, N.Y....Partner in Ron Jaworski Sports Enterprises, which negotiates contracts and runs two golf courses.

WILBERT MONTGOMERY 29 5-10 195   Running Back

Missed 10 games because of a nagging knee injury...His absence really cut into the Eagles' effectiveness...They could make up for his loss over the short run but they don't have the depth to absorb a 10-game void...Managed only 139 rushing yards, just 10 more than quarterback Ron Jaworski...And that is after three 1,000-yard seasons in his seven-year career ...Eagles need him healthy to have chance of rebounding from dismal 1983...Born Sept. 16, 1954, in Greenville, Miss....Set NCAA record for career touchdowns (76) at Abilene Christian.

MIKE QUICK 25 6-2 190   Wide Receiver

Talk about having a surprise season... His first season in the NFL was a flop, with only 10 catches after being picked in first round of 1982 draft... Then he exploded for 69 receptions for 1,409 yards last year to put him among the league's elite receivers... Named to a starting spot on the Pro Bowl team by his NFC peers in recognition of his production... Broke four club records, including yardage, catches, most 100-yard receiving games (six) and most 100-yarders in a row (four)... His yardage total was the most in the NFL since Don Maynard's 1,434 in 1967... Born May 14, 1959, in Hamlet, N.C.... Standout at N.C. State with wonderful speed and hands... Likes to draw.

JERRY ROBINSON 27 6-2 225   Linebacker

Even when the Eagles struggled, he still played up to his usual high standard... Led the team in tackles (177) for the second straight year and was chosen the club's most valuable defensive player by his teammates... Recovered two fumbles and forced another two... Was a fine outside linebacker but probably plays better inside, where he has been stationed the last two seasons... Been helped by extra weight, adding 16 pounds over the last two years to help combat those big offensive guards trying to run him over... Born Dec. 18, 1956, in San Francisco ... Running back in high school and three-time All-American at UCLA.

JOHN SPAGNOLA 27 6-4 240   Tight End

Sometimes the best way to tell about the value of a player is to see what happens to his team when he is hurt... Eagles certainly found out how much they missed this productive tight end after he went down with a bad knee injury in preseason... Didn't play a game last year and the Eagles got just 20 catches from their tight ends... He must be able to come back this year if that position is to be upgraded... Was really coming into his own 1982, when he had 26 receptions in short season... Born Aug. 1, 1957, in Stroudsburg, Pa.... Was all-time pass-receiver at Yale... Served as a driver for Bill Bradley in the latter's suc-

ninth-round draft pick by the Patriots, he was released in that preseason and picked up by Eagles.

DENNIS HARRISON 28 6-8 275   Defensive End

Has put together good back-to-back seasons to play up to his ample ability . . . Tough to keep someone this size from doing at least occasional damage to the quarterback . . . Had team-high 11½ sacks last year, one more than the previous season . . . His 102 tackles were a career high, too . . . Easy going guy with a wonderfully pleasant personality and likeable disposition . . . Has to really push himself to be mean on the field . . . Born July 31, 1956, in Cleveland . . . State heavyweight wrestling champion in high school . . . Called "Bigfoot" by his teammates because of size 15 shoes . . . Vanderbilt grad.

ROYNELL YOUNG 26 6-1 181   Cornerback

Got his hands on a lot of passes last year (21) but only intercepted one, and he has to do better than that for the Eagle secondary to function at full blast . . . One of the more talented cornerbacks in the league, but maybe he was pulled down by team-wide slump . . . Had intercepted 12 passes in his first three years . . . First-round draft choice in 1980 from Alcorn State, the only college to give him firm scholarship offer . . . Active with the Fellowship of Christian Athletes . . . His 56 tackles last year ranked him ninth on the team . . . Born Dec. 1, 1957, in New Orleans.

MARK DENNARD 28 6-1 252   Center

Acquired by the Eagles in the offseason to fill hole at center created when veteran Guy Morriss was released. . . . Has a big hole to fill, since Morriss was one of the NFC's best for many seasons . . . Played behind Dwight Stephenson with the Dolphins after being a starter earlier in his five-year career . . . "He's a brawler, he'll do anything to get the job done," says Dolphin coach Don Shula . . . Born Nov. 2, 1955, in Bay City, Tex. . . . Been plagued with injuries during pro years . . . Academic All-America at Texas A&M.

JERRY SISEMORE 33 6-4 265 Tackle

With his long-time running mate Stan Walters probably going back into retirement, he's one of the last links on what once was a quality offensive line... Young horses like Joe Jacoby and Mike Kenn have begun dominating tackle spot in conference, but he once was among the elite... Played in two Pro Bowls... Missed one game last year because of a shoulder injury to cut into reputation as an ironman... Born July 16, 1951, in Olton, Tex.... One of best players in U. of Texas history... Enjoys sailing so much that he owns a marina on a lake near Austin.

COACH MARION CAMPBELL: Things looked so promising

for him when he took over for Dick Vermeil ... He instituted a different training camp, one with less work, more humor and shorter practices ... The players said they loved it and he appeared to be enjoying himself after a horrid coaching experience with Atlanta... Then everything fell apart in Philly, too... Injuries, a bad offensive concept and lack of talent combined to tumble the Eagles from their once lofty perch as a perennial contender... He's made some staff changes and vows things will be different this year... Campbell remains the most pleasant surprise about the Eagles' 1983 season... He showed humor he had kept hidden and he held up under the burden of losing better than many had anticipated... Born May 25, 1929, in Chester, S.C.... Attended Georgia, where he picked up "Swamp Fox" nickname after Francis Marion, hero of Revolutionary War.

BIGGEST PLAY

They were down to the final play of the NFL championship game between the Eagles and the Packers at Philadelphia's Franklin Field on Dec. 26, 1960. The Eagles had come from behind to take a 17-13 lead on Ted Dean's touchdown with 1:20 to play.

Now with seconds to go, Green Bay was on the Philadelphia

center and linebacker who had played nearly 60 minutes—knew that Packer quarterback Bart Starr would be making a last-ditch pass.

Starr tossed to Jim Taylor and the big Packer fullback took off, green jerseys bouncing off him as he pounded toward the Eagle goal line.

"I saw I had to get him," Bednarik would say afterward. "I hit him high with a bear-hug tackle."

And there on the nine-yard line, the Packers' title bid expired. The Eagles had won their third NFL championship. They haven't won one since.

INDIVIDUAL EAGLE RECORDS

Rushing

Most Yards Game:	205	Steve Van Buren, vs Pittsburgh, 1949
Season:	1,512	Wilbert Montgomery, 1979
Career:	5,680	Steve Van Buren, 1944-51

Passing

Most TD Passes Game:	7	Adrian Burk, vs Washington, 1954
Season:	32	Sonny Jurgensen, 1961
Career:	134	Ron Jaworski, 1977-83

Receiving

Most TD Passes Game:	4	Joe Carter, vs Cincinnati, 1934
	4	Ben Hawkins, vs Pittsburgh, 1969
Season:	13	Tommy McDonald, 1960 and 1961
	13	Mike Quick, 1983
Career:	79	Harold Carmichael, 1971-83

Scoring

Most Points Game:	25	Bobby Walston, vs Washington, 1954
Season:	114	Bobby Walston, 1954
Career:	881	Bobby Walston, 1951-62
Most TDs Game:	4	Joe Carter, vs Cincinnati, 1934
	4	Clarence Peaks, vs St. Louis, 1958
	4	Tommy McDonald, vs N.Y. Giants, 1959
	4	Ben Hawkins, vs Pittsburgh, 1969
	4	Wilbert Montgomery, vs Washington, 1978
	4	Wilbert Montgomery, vs Washington, 1979
Season:	18	Steve Van Buren, 1945
Career:	79	Harold Carmichael, 1971-83

SAN FRANCISCO 49ERS

TEAM DIRECTORY: Owner: Edward J. DeBartolo Jr.; Pres./Head Coach: Bill Walsh; Administrative VP: John McVay; Dir. Publicity: Jerry Walker. Home field: Candlestick Park (61,185). Colors: 49er gold and scarlet.

SCOUTING REPORT

OFFENSE: Statistics say that the 1983 49er offense was running on all gears, ranking high in most NFL categories. That was a distinct improvement over 1982. But a closer look says something else: inconsistency.

Once the 49ers got within scoring distance, all types of problems came up. They would make turnovers or they couldn't pick up short-yardage first downs. It's one area that coach Bill Walsh will have to work on for this coming year.

But he has a lot of strengths to ease the situation. Quarterback Joe Montana, who had another fine season, is quietly efficient and now ranks as the NFL's all-time ranked passer and career completion percentage leader. Dwight Clark is a superb possession receiver, but Fred Solomon's injury problems hurt the 49ers' long passing game. Wendell Tyler and rookie Roger Craig patched up what had been a poor running game. And tight end Russ Francis needs to be involved more in the passing game.

DEFENSE: Defensive coordinator George Seifert was recognized for doing a good job of maneuvering this unit from game to game, making it difficult for opponents to get a good line on 49er tendencies. His favorite ploy was to have his players jump in and out of positions, fake stunts and blitzes and try to take the edge off the thinking of quarterbacks.

It helped that he got fine seasons from first-year linebacker Riki Ellison, defensive ends Dwaine Board and Fred Dean and cornerback Ronnie Lott, who had to fill in at safety some games because of injuries.

But he didn't get helped by the team's contract negotiators, who couldn't sign middle guard Pete Kugler and linebackers Willie Harper and Bobby Leopold, all three of whom wound up in the USFL. The loss of Kugler, in particular, is damaging, since he finished the season strongly and was still improving.

Now it will be up to Seifert to make up for these holes—rookie Todd Shell is a start in this direction—while searching for a replacement for the aging Hacksaw Reynolds.

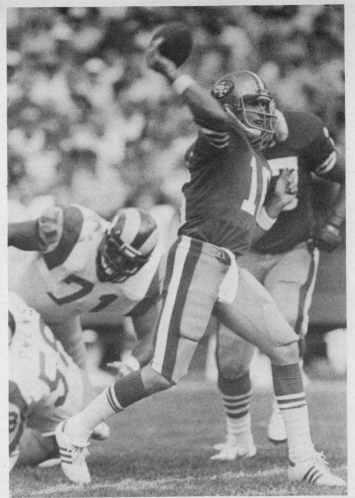

Joe Montana posted best completion percentage (64.5) in NFC.

KICKING GAME: Ray (The Bear) Wersching is a dependable placekicker who seemingly can go on forever and ever. He made 25 of 30 field goals last year and didn't miss any of his 51 conversion tries. There is a glaring weakness at punter, where Tom Orosz is the incumbent. The coverage teams are adequate, if not spectacular.

49ERS VETERAN ROSTER

HEAD COACH—Bill Walsh. Assistant Coaches—Jerry Attaway, Paul Hackett, Norb Hecker, Sherman Lewis, Bobb McKittrick, Bill McPherson, Ray Rhodes, George Siefert.

No.	Name	Pos.	Ht.	Wt.	NFL Exp.	College
68	Ayers, John	G	6-5	265	8	West Texas State
7	Benjamin, Guy	QB	6-3	210	7	Stanford
44	#Blackmore, Richard	CB	5-10	174	6	Mississippi State
76	Board, Dwaine	DE	6-5	248	5	North Carolina A&T
57	Bunz, Dan	LB	6-4	225	6	Cal State-Long Beach
6	Cavanaugh, Matt	QB	6-2	212	7	Pittsburgh
15	Clark, Bryan	QB	6-2	196	2	Michigan State
87	Clark, Dwight	WR	6-4	210	6	Clemson
47	Collier, Tim	CB	6-0	174	9	East Texas State
89	Cooper, Earl	TE-RB	6-2	226	5	Rice
33	Craig, Roger	RB	6-0	223	2	Nebraska
51	Cross, Randy	G	6-3	265	9	UCLA
74	Dean, Fred	DE	6-2	236	10	Louisiana Tech
62	Downing, Walt	C-G	6-3	270	7	Michigan
84	Durham, Darius	WR	6-2	193	2	San Diego State
50	Ellison, Riki	LB	6-2	220	2	Southern California
71	Fahnhorst, Keith	T	6-6	273	11	Minnesota
54	Ferrari, Ron	LB	6-0	212	3	Illinois
81	Francis, Russ	TE	6-6	242	9	Oregon
24	Gervais, Rick	S	5-11	190	4	Stanford
75	Harty, John	DT	6-4	263	4	Iowa
22	Hicks, Dwight	S	6-1	192	6	Michigan
28	Holmoe, Tom	CB-S	6-2	180	2	Brigham Young
—	Kelcher, Louie	NT	6-5	310	10	Southern Methodist
66	Kennedy, Allan	T	6-7	275	3	Washington State
55	Le Master, Frank	LB	6-2	238	10	Kentucky
42	Lott, Ronnie	S-CB	6-0	199	4	Southern California
53	McColl, Milt	LB	6-6	230	4	Stanford
43	McLemore, Dana	KR-CB	5-10	183	3	Hawaii
32	Monroe, Carl	RB-KR	5-8	166	2	Utah
16	Montana, Joe	QB	6-2	200	6	Notre Dame
60	Montgomery, Blanchard	LB	6-2	236	2	UCLA
25	Moore, Jeff	RB	6-0	196	5	Jackson State
63	Moten, Gary	LB	6-1	210	2	Southern Methodist
83	Nehemiah, Renaldo	WR	6-1	183	3	Maryland
3	Orosz, Tom	P	6-1	204	4	Ohio State
77	Paris, Bubba	T	6-6	295	2	Michigan
65	Pillers, Lawrence	DT-DE	6-4	250	9	Alcorn State
56	Quillan, Fred	C	6-5	266	7	Oregon
64	Reynolds, Jack	LB	6-1	232	15	Tennessee
30	Ring, Bill	RB	5-10	205	4	Brigham Young
61	Sapolu, Jesse	G	6-4	260	2	Hawaii
88	#Solomon, Freddie	WR	5-11	188	10	Tampa
72	Stover, Jeff	NT	6-5	275	3	Oregon
79	Stuckey, Jim	DE	6-4	253	5	Clemson
—	Tuiasosopo, Manu	DT	6-3	250	6	UCLA
58	Turner, Keena	LB	6-2	219	5	Purdue
26	Tyler, Wendell	RB	5-10	200	7	UCLA
14	#Wersching, Ray	K	5-11	210	12	California
27	Williamson, Carlton	S	6-0	204	4	Pittsburgh
85	Wilson, Mike	WR	6-3	210	4	Washington State
—	Wood, Mike	P-K	5-11	205	5	S.E. Missouri
21	Wright, Eric	CB	6-1	180	4	Missouri

#Unsigned at press time

TOP FIVE DRAFT CHOICES

Rd.	Name	Sel. No.	Pos.	Ht.	Wt.	College
1	Shell, Todd	24	LB	6-4	220	Brigham Young
2	Frank, John	56	TE	6-2	220	Ohio State
3	McIntyre, Guy	73	G	6-3	260	Georgia
4	Carter, Michael	121	DT	6-2	274	Southern Methodist
5	Fuller, Jeff	139	LB	6-2	209	Texas A&M

THE ROOKIES: Walsh provided the unexpected in making LB Shell of Brigham Young No. 1; he needs to get bigger to play in the NFL. Second-round TE John Frank of Ohio State and Georgia guard Guy McIntyre, No. 3, are strong candidates, and so is SMU DT Michael Carter, a great athlete.

OUTLOOK: The 49ers shook off a midseason slump last year and almost beat the Redskins to win the NFC title game. If they can make up for their defensive losses to the USFL, they should once again be a title contender.

49ER PROFILES

JOE MONTANA 28 6-2 200   Quarterback

Maybe he'll never match the magic of the 1981 season but he certainly didn't do badly last year... Made the Pro Bowl as a backup to Joe Theismann after passing for 3,910 yards by completing 332 of 515 passes... The yardage total was a team record; the others were personal bests... More important he had a fine touchdown-interception ratio (26-12), which better shows his accuracy and effectiveness... Not as outgoing as many quarterbacks... Prefers a private life where he can ride horses and relax... Born June 11, 1956, in Monongahela, Pa.... Only third-round draft choice out of Notre Dame.

DWIGHT CLARK 27 6-4 210   Wide Receiver

An injury against Dallas in the final game of the regular season may well have kept the 49ers out of the end zone... You just don't lose one of the game's best receivers and remain as strong... Suddenly, the 49ers' short and medium passing game wasn't the same... Still wound up with 70 catches for 840 yards and eight touchdowns.... Couldn't ask for a more cooperative, friendly man... One of the league's best interviews... Born Jan. 8, 1957, in Charlotte, N.C.... A 10th-round pick out of Clemson... Who will ever forget his game-winning catch against Dallas in the 1981 championship game?

WENDELL TYLER 29 5-10 200   Running Back

Bill Walsh went out on a limb when he traded for this fumble-prone back, saying he was the answer to the 49ers' running problems...In many ways, Walsh was right...Gained 856 yards between nagging injuries...That was the most yards by a San Francisco back since 1977...Also caught 34 passes to rank third on the team...And Tyler should be capable of playing better, since he twice gained more than 1,000 yards when he was with the Rams...49ers gave up two draft choices as part of the trade to the Rams...A UCLA product, he was born May 20, 1955, in Shreveport, La.

FRED DEAN 32 6-2 236   Defensive End

Got off a woeful start in 1983, but then, against New Orleans, he had an unbelievable eight sacks to help him finish among the league leaders with 17½...Just went crazy and the Saints couldn't handle him...That's the kind of athletic ability he has, but sometimes he doesn't seem to show up for games...Doesn't start, but comes in on passing situations and will be shifted around to try to confuse defenses...Once thought of as perhaps the league's premier pass-rusher but that reputation since has faded...Born Feb. 24, 1952, in Arcadia, La....Louisiana Tech grad who likes to read and write poetry.

DWAINE BOARD 27 6-5 248   Defensive End

Probably don't know this man that well, but he may be the MVP of the 49ers....How's that, you ask?...Well, when he plays, the 49ers usually win...When he is out with an injury, they usually lose...You can look it up ...Doesn't make a lot of tackles but he is very dependable and he mounts a fine pass rush... Had 13½ sacks last year...Also recovered five fumbles, so that gives you an idea of his ball instincts... Born Nov. 29, 1956, in Rocky Mount, Va....Standout at North Carolina A&T...Nickname is "Pee Wee"..."You should see my brother," he says.

RON LOTT 25 6-0 199   Cornerback

Made his third straight Pro Bowl, this one as a starter, yet many people feel he would be a better safety . . . Would allow him to use his size and strength to better advantage . . . No question he is one of the league's premier secondary players, no matter where positioned . . . Just a fine natural athlete who loves to play and seems to do his best in the big games . . . The 49ers depend on him for leadership. . . . Intercepted four passes last year and led the team in tackles by a wide margin . . . Born May 8, 1959, in Albuquerque, N.M. . . . All-American at USC.

RENALDO NEHEMIAH 25 6-1 183   Wide Receiver

He's impatient with his development since deciding to give up track career for pro football and the cash that goes with it . . . But he hasn't contributed all that much to the 49ers since signing with them two years ago . . . Caught 17 passes for 236 yards last year after eight receptions his first season . . . At least he proved he could come back after a hit . . . Was knocked cold against Atlanta and played the rest of the year. . . . Has the best speed in the game, even better than Willie Gault's, but having some trouble learning the 49ers' complex pass offense . . . Born March 24, 1959, in Newark, N.J. . . . World record-holder in 110 high-hurdles and still can run a 4.3, like he did at Maryland.

JACK REYNOLDS 36 6-1 232   Linebacker

Reminds you of that tough-minded, growling cop, Mick Belker, of "Hill Street Blues" . . . Always surly, but always professional and very, very tough . . . He should be tending to things on his island home in the Bahamas but he refuses to walk away from the game after 14 years . . . Despite coming out on passing downs last season, he still had 61 tackles and a sack . . . Gets frustrated when he can't make the tackles or the plays he once did . . . Always did function more on instinct and experience than raw skills . . . Born Nov. 22, 1947, in Cincinnati . . . Starred at Tennessee . . . Reportedly has garage full of notes on opponents . . . Lives to get to the 49er training complex and study films.

RUSS FRANCIS 31 6-6 242   Tight End

One of the game's true free spirits...Never has regained level he achieved as a Patriot ...Time off from football plus advancing age have cut into his skills...But he still can come up with the pressure catch and big play when he has to...Pulled in 33 passes last year, 10 more than in the strike-shortened season ...First-round choice of the Patriots in 1975 after stellar career at Oregon...Born April 3, 1953, in Seattle Wash....Former high-school quarterback who grew up in Hawaii...Licensed to fly helicopters and commercial multi-engine airplanes.

DWIGHT HICKS 28 6-1 192   Safety

Made the Pro Bowl for the third straight season...Says his goal is to be known as the best at his position...Not a bad aim for this former free agent who was drafted by the Lions in the sixth round, released, played in Canada, released, played in Philly, released and then signed with the 49ers...Had only two interceptions last year, first time in five years he had not led the team in that category...Returned one of those interceptions 62 yards for a touchdown...Born April 5, 1956, in Mount Holly, N.J....Four-letter man at Michigan...Has modeled and has interest in broadcast journalism.

COACH BILL WALSH: Having a hard time living up to his

own legend...When he came from nowhere and drove the 49ers to the Super Bowl title, he set a high standard to match...Now some critics sarcastically call him the "Genius" in reference to the label he carried through that glorious Super Bowl romp two years ago...But with a break or two this year, might have beaten the Redskins and returned to Super Sunday again ...Defenses have adjusted to his philosophies enough so he isn't quite dominating things as in the past, but the 49ers still can move the ball effectively and often...Facing another tough task this year trying to mend a defense hurt by losses to the USFL...Born Nov. 30, 1931, in Los Angeles...Soft-spoken, comes across sometimes as aloof...Didn't particularly like media criticism last year and lashed out about it near the end of the season . . . Came close to giving up coaching before last year, but now seems determined to stay with it for a while longer . . . Was an end at San Jose State, then started out as a high-school coach. . . . Was head coach at Stanford before becoming 49ers' 11th head coach.

BIGGEST PLAY

Earlier in the fourth quarter, Dallas had scored on a 21-yard pass from Danny White to Doug Cosbie to take a 27-21 lead. Now there were just five minutes left in this NFC title game on Jan. 10, 1982, and the Cowboys seemed well on the verge of once again advancing to the Super Bowl

But somebody forgot to tell Dwight Clark and Joe Montana that things were over. Crafty Montana, in the midst of a storybook season, began a drive at his own 11 against the Doomsday

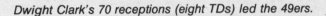

Dwight Clark's 70 receptions (eight TDs) led the 49ers.

Defense. Some effective running and a reverse by Fred Solomon had the ball at midfield. Two more completions and an end sweep gave the 49ers a third down at the Cowboy six with 58 seconds to go.

The Candlestick Park crowd was standing and screaming. And assistant coach wanted to run; coach Bill Walsh called a pass. Montana dropped back but was forced to his right and was under heavy pressure when he threw a high pass to the right corner of the end zone.

Somehow, the tall Clark leaped higher than he thought he could. He grabbed the pass, pulled it down and the 49ers had the winning touchdown, 28-27.

INDIVIDUAL 49ER RECORDS

Rushing

Most Yards Game:	194	Delvin Williams, vs St. Louis, 1976
Season:	1,203	Delvin Williams, 1976
Career:	8,689	Joe Perry, 1948-60, 1963

Passing

Most TD Passes Game:	5	Frank Albert, vs Cleveland (AAC), 1949
	5	John Brodie, vs Minnesota, 1965
	5	Steve Spurrier, vs Chicago, 1972
Season:	30	John Brodie, 1965
Career:	214	John Brodie, 1957-73

Receiving

Most TD Passes Game:	3	Alyn Beals, vs Brooklyn (AAC), 1948
	3	Alyn Beals, vs Chicago (AAC), 1949
	3	Gordy Soltau, vs Los Angeles, 1951
	3	Bernie Casey, vs Minnesota, 1962
	3	Dave Parks, vs Baltimore, 1965
	3	Gene Washington, vs San Diego, 1972
Season:	14	Alyn Beals (AAC), 1948
Career:	54	Gene Washington, 1969–76

Scoring

Most Points Game:	26	Gordy Soltau, vs Los Angeles, 1951
Season:	126	Ray Wersching, 1983
Career:	738	Tommy Davis, 1959-69
Most TDs Game:	4	Bill Kilmer, vs Minnesota, 1961
Season:	14	Alyn Beals (AAC), 1948
Career:	80	Joe Perry, 1948-60

ST. LOUIS CARDINALS

TEAM DIRECTORY: Chairman: William Bidwill; Pres.: Bing Devine; Dir. Pro. Personnel: Larry Wilson; Dir. Pub. Rel.: Curt Mosher; Head Coach: Jim Hanifan. Home field: Busch Stadium (51,392). Colors: Cardinal red, white and black.

SCOUTING REPORT

OFFENSE: As long as Neil Lomax keeps developing, and there is no reason he shouldn't, the Cardinals have high hopes of becoming a legitimate playoff team.

Lomax showed signs of greatness last season, throwing

Ottis Anderson had seven 100-yard games, caught 54 passes.

24 touchdowns and only 11 interceptions. He loves to run and throw on the run, and the Cardinals began letting him do both. You can't argue with the results.

If rookie receiver Clyde Duncan fills the bill, then the Cards will be able to build their offense on the pass—like the good old Jim Hart days—and complement it with the running of Ottis Anderson. That would take some of the pressure off this quality back and probably make him more productive.

Coach Jim Hanifan also has to shore up some offensive line problems. The Cardinal pass-blocking was horrid at times, and they must give Lomax better protection. Guards Joe Bostic and Terry Stieve and center Randy Clark all face challenges for their starting jobs.

DEFENSE: Coordinator Floyd Peters has a touch with pass-rushers. He made the Lions' front four famous and now he is doing the same thing with the Cardinal front wall.

Last year, Curtis Greer had 16 sacks, Bubba Baker 13½ and David Galloway 12. That's a lot these days from a front line, especially when other teams are relying on blitzing linebackers for their quarterback pressure. Even old man Elois Grooms turned in a good job at tackle despite being outsized almost every week.

The key to improvement of this unit will be linebacker E.J. Junior, who played both outside and inside last season. The Cardinals want him to stay in the middle permanently, and there is some feeling he could develop into an All-Pro. Cornerback Lionel Washington, in his rookie year, intercepted eight passes. Jeff Griffin, who had a broken arm last year, could strengthen the other side. Safeties Lee Nelson and Benny Perrin were one-two in tackles last season.

KICKING GAME: Punter Carl Birdsong made the Pro Bowl last year in a surprise development, but Neil O'Donoghue can't afford another inconsistent season like he had in 1983. Stump Mitchell is one of the league's best return men, and the Card special teams rank among the most solid around.

THE ROOKIES: The Cardinals wanted linebacking help from the draft, but instead got plenty of offensive players, beginning with WR Duncan of Tennessee, a speed burner with good size. Guard Doug Dawson and QB Rick McIvor, both from Texas, probably won't be much help for a while.

OUTLOOK: The Cardinals have to get off to a fast start to rid themselves of a longtime jinx. If they do, there is good reason to

CARDINALS VETERAN ROSTER

HEAD COACH—Jim Hanifan. Assistant Coaches—Chuck Banker, Tom Bettis, Don Brown, Rod Dowhower, Rudy Feldman, Dick Jamieson, Tom Lovat, Leon McLaughlin, Floyd Peters, Emmitt Thomas.

No.	Name	Pos.	Ht.	Wt.	NFL Exp.	College
58	Ahrens, Dave	LB	6-3	228	4	Wisconsin
51	Allerman, Kurt	LB	6-2	222	8	Penn State
32	Anderson, Ottis	RB	6-2	220	6	Miami
61	Audick, Dan	G	6-3	253	7	Hawaii
60	Baker, Al	DE	6-6	260	7	Colorado State
52	Baker, Charlie	LB	6-2	217	5	New Mexico
82	Bird, Steve	WR	5-11	171	2	Eastern Kentucky
18	Birdsong, Carl	P	6-0	192	4	S.W. Oklahoma
71	Bostic, Joe	G	6-3	265	6	Clemson
64	Clark, Randy	C	6-3	254	5	Northern Illinois
59	Davis, Paul	LB	6-3	210	4	North Carolina
73	Duda, Mark	DT	6-3	263	2	Maryland
31	Ferrell, Earl	RB	6-0	215	3	East Tennessee State
65	Galloway, David	DT	6-3	277	3	Florida
81	Green, Roy	WR	6-0	195	6	Henderson (Ark.)
75	Greer, Curtis	DE	6-4	258	5	Michigan
35	Griffin, Jeff	CB	6-0	185	4	Utah
78	#Grooms, Elois	DE	6-4	250	9	Tennessee Tech
39	Harrell, Willard	RB	5-8	182	10	Pacific
50	Harris, Bob	LB	6-2	205	2	Auburn
16	Heflin, Victor	CB	6-0	184	2	Delaware State
54	Junior, E. J.	LB	6-3	235	4	Alabama
89	La Fleur, Greg	TE	6-4	236	4	Louisiana State
16	Lisch, Rusty	QB	6-4	213	5	Notre Dame
15	Lomax, Neil	QB	6-3	214	4	Portland State
40	#Love, Randy	FB	6-1	205	6	Houston
47	Mack, Cedric	CB	6-0	190	2	Baylor
80	Marsh, Doug	TE	6-3	240	5	Michigan
76	Mays, Stafford	DE	6-2	250	5	Washington
87	McGill, Eddie	TE	6-6	225	3	Western Carolina
30	Mitchell, Stump	RB	5-9	188	4	Citadel
24	Morris, Wayne	RB	6-0	210	9	Southern Methodist
38	#Nelson, Lee	S	5-10	185	9	Florida State
11	O'Donoghue, Neil	K	6-6	210	8	Auburn
57	#Parlavecchio, Chet	LB	6-2	225	2	Penn State
23	Perrin, Benny	S	6-2	178	3	Alabama
82	Pittman, Danny	WR	6-2	205	5	Wyoming
70	Plunkett, Art	T	6-8	262	4	Nevada-Las Vegas
63	Robbins, Tootie	T	6-4	278	3	East Carolina
26	Schmitt, George	S	5-11	193	2	Delaware
56	Scott, Carlos	C	6-4	300	2	Texas-El Paso
53	Shaffer, Craig	LB	6-0	230	3	Indiana State
67	Sharpe, Luis	T	6-4	260	3	UCLA
84	Shumann, Mike	WR	6-1	185	7	Florida State
45	Smith, Leonard	S	5-11	190	2	McNeese State
44	Smith, Wayne	CB	6-0	175	5	Purdue
68	#Stieve, Terry	G	6-2	265	8	Wisconsin
83	Tilley, Pat	WR	5-10	178	9	Louisiana Tech
48	Washington, Lionel	CB	6-0	184	2	Tulane
55	Whitaker, Bill	LB	6-0	182	4	Missouri

#Unsigned at press time

TOP FIVE DRAFT CHOICES

Rd.	Name	Sel. No.	Pos.	Ht.	Wt.	College
1	Duncan, Clyde	17	WR	6-1	192	Tennessee
2	Dawson, Doug	45	G	6-3	267	Texas
3	McIvor, Rick	80	QB	6-3	210	Texas
4	Bayless, Martin	101	DB	6-2	195	Bowling Green
5	Leiding, Jeff	129	LB	6-4	240	Texas

believe this young, oncoming team could develop into a strong playoff club by mid-November.

CARDINAL PROFILES

OTTIS ANDERSON 27 6-2 220 Running Back

He's gained more than 1,000 yards in every full season he's played in the NFL since arriving in St. Louis as a No. 1 draft choice in 1979 . . . Has adjusted to a changing offensive line during his short career and still has kept up consistency . . . Had seven 100-yard games last year to give him 28 . . . Really hit his stride down the stretch, when he put together five 100-plus efforts in the final eight contests . . . Also caught 54 passes to set a club record . . . Born Jan. 19, 1957, in West Palm Beach, Fla. . . . First name was misspelled by doctor on birth certificate . . . Attended University of Miami before the Hurricanes were No. 1.

NEIL LOMAX 25 6-3 214 Quarterback

For a while, it didn't look as if the Cardinals had made a good draft choice picking him on the second round in 1981 . . . But near the end of last season, he came on so strongly that now he looks set for a long time . . . Had to change from a rollout passer at Portland State to a dropback stylist in the pros . . . Still can be confused by sophisticated defenses, but that is changing quickly . . . Completed 209 of 354 passes for a 59.0 percentage and a 92.0 quarterback rating . . . The latter two marks are club records . . . Passed for 24 touchdowns and only 11 interceptions . . . Born Feb. 17, 1959, in Lake Oswego, Ore.

ROY GREEN 27 6-0 195 Wide Receiver

No question, now one of the game's most consistent, dangerous receivers . . . And he has only been a full-time starter for two seasons . . . Followed up on a very good 1982 with a wonderful 1983, catching 78 passes for 1,227 yards and 14 touchdowns . . . He was fifth in yardage and sixth in catches in the league . . . Receptions and yardage were both club records... He caught five or more passes 10 times during the year... Born June 30, 1957, in Magnolia, Ark.... fourth-round pick out of Henderson State... First made name for himself by playing both ways, and sometimes also took turn on special teams.

CURTIS GREER 26 6-4 258   Defensive End

A first-round choice out of Michigan in 1980 who really blossomed last season... Was coming off an improved 1982 performance with seven sacks, but not even his coaches expected him to have 16 sacks last year... Among the league leaders, although he still doesn't get the recognition he deserves... That will come in time, especially if he keeps improving... Has had to adjust to playing both in a 3-4 and then a 4-3... Born Nov. 10, 1957, in Detroit... Has own radio show in St. Louis, playing jazz... During summers, works with disadvantaged children.

AL BAKER 27 6-6 260   Defensive End

Part of a surprising trade last season that saw him shipped from Detroit to the Cardinals ... Lots of talk about how he was finished and had lost his desire... But he put those rumors to rest with a good comeback year... Had 13½ sacks, which isn't quite the same as the 23 in his rookie year but at least it's an improvement on what he has done lately... Still has the ability to be a dominant player in the league when he puts his mind to it... Born Dec. 9, 1956, in Jacksonville, Fla... A second-round draft pick out of Colorado.

PAT TILLEY 31 5-10 178   Wide Receiver

The prototype complementary receiver ... Goes just perfectly with a speedy, fine athlete such as Roy Green... As soon as the defense begins worrying too much about Green, this guy can really kill you on the other side... Caught 44 passes for 690 yards last year, including a 71-yard touchdown romp for his only score... This was the first time in five years that he hadn't led the club in receiving... Born Feb. 15, 1953, in Marshall, Tex.... Played at Louisiana Tech and still lives in Shreveport, La., where he attended high school.

E. J. JUNIOR 24 6-3 235   Linebacker

After problems with drugs and run-in with NFL commissioner, he came back and had a fine third pro season... Tough go of it for a while, but he says he has straightened himself out... Played outside linebacker spot and finished third on the team in tackles with 86 and also added seven sacks, but will wind up in the middle in future... Look for the Cardinals to start using him more often on blitzes... He has the kind of quickness that can make quarterbacks miserable... A first-round draft choice in 1980 after an All-America career at Alabama, where he played defensive end... Born Dec. 8, 1959, in Sallsburg, N.C. ... Ester James is given name.

STUMP MITCHELL 25 5-9 188   Kick Returner

He's gradually easing into the Cardinal record book, erasing Terry Metcalf's old marks... Now has 107 career kickoff returns to tie Metcalf and 107 punt returns for a record, along with a record 947 punt-return yards... Had 38 returns for 337 yards in 1983... One of those exciting little men who is capable of breaking one for touchdown on every attempt... Got a chance to carry the ball 68 times from scrimmage and gained 373 yards, second on the team... Born March 15, 1959, in St. Mary's, Ga.... Standout running back at The Citadel... Given name is Lyvonia.

NEIL O'DONOGHUE 31 6-6 210   Kicker

Stands out as one of the tallest placekickers in the game's history... He's certainly had a roller-coaster career... Could have beaten the Giants on national television but missed a 19-yard field goal... Yet Jim Hanifan stuck with him and he finished strongly... Still too erratic for a long-term mortgage... Made 15 of 29 field goals and scored 90 points, second highest of seven-year career... Born June 18, 1953, in Dublin, Ireland, where his family still lives... Played soccer, rugby and hurling as a youngster... All-American soccer player at St. Bernard College before transferring to Auburn as a kicker.

CARL BIRDSONG 25 6-0 192   Punter

In only his third pro season, he made the Pro Bowl even though he didn't lead the conference in punting... His peers were impressed by his combination of good gross (41.5) and net averages (36.3) and the fact that the Cardinals had excellent special teams... A fine pickup for the Cards, who acquired him on waivers in 1981 from Buffalo... A free agent with the Bills after playing for Southwest Oklahoma State, where he averaged 43.5 his senior year.... Also a backup quarterback and placekicker in college... Born Jan. 1, 1959, in Kaufman, Tex.... Completing a degree in pharmacy.

COACH JIM HANIFAN: Every time it seems he may be headed out the door, his team puts things together and makes it easy for the Cardinals to retain him ... St. Louis won seven of its last 10 games to offset a horrid 1-5 start and finish a solid playoff contender for this season... He just has to do something about those bad starts, which have plagued the franchise for years... And he has to figure out a way to be more competitive with conference rival Washington, which now "owns" the Cardinals... A likeable, earthy guy who tells it like it is ... Not a whole lot of polish but he's friendly and cooperative and has a reputation for being a very good coach... Born Sept. 21, 1933, in Compton, Cal.... Former offensive line coach for the Cardinals who was hired away from the Charger staff... Was a receiver at the University of California and had a brief career in Canada before becoming an assistant coach at San Diego State.

BIGGEST PLAY

The Cardinals didn't know it then, of course, but it would be the last time they would appear in the playoffs for at least eight yers. But then, in 1975, things were a lot headier for St. Louis. Don Coryell was the coach and the Cardinals were climbing toward being a perennial league power.

They had made the playoffs the year before and wanted desperately to do it again. That's why this game against the Redskins on Nov. 16 in Busch Stadium was so important. Win it and they would all but lock up a postseason trip. Lose it to arch-rival Washington and the road would be much tougher.

Maybe that's why George Allen still steams when he thinks about this game and about St. Louis receiver Mel Gray.

The Redskins had the game locked up until Jim Hart tossed a tiny six-yard pass to Gray with six seconds left. It was to be the shortest TD pass of Gray's career—and the most controversial. The Redskins claim to this day that Gray never had possession, that Pat Fischer knocked the ball loose. But the officials said otherwise and the catch stood, tying the game at 17-17 at the end of regulation time.

Then Jim Bakken's 27-yard field goal after seven minutes of sudden-death overtime gave the Cardinals a 20-17 margin and they subsequently won the NFC East title.

INDIVIDUAL CARDINAL RECORDS

Rushing

Most Yards Game:	203	John David Crow, vs Pittsburgh, 1960
Season:	1,605	Ottis Anderson, 1979
Career:	4,920	Ottis Anderson, 1979-82

Passing

Most TD Passes Game:	6	Jim Hardy, vs Baltimore, 1950
	6	Charley Johnson, vs Cleveland, 1965
	6	Charley Johnson, vs New Orleans, 1969
Season:	28	Charley Johnson, 1963
Career:	205	Jim Hart, 1966-82

Receiving

Most TD Passes Game:	5	Bob Shaw, vs Baltimore, 1950
Season:	15	Sonny Randle, 1960
Career:	60	Sonny Randle, 1959-66

Scoring

Most Points Game:	40	Ernie Nevers, vs Chicago, 1929
Season:	117	Jim Bakken, 1967
Career:	1,380	Jim Bakken, 1962-78
Most TDs Game:	6	Ernie Nevers, vs Chicago, 1929
Season:	17	John David Crow, 1962
Career:	60	Sonny Randle, 1959-66

TAMPA BAY BUCCANEERS

TEAM DIRECTORY: Pres.: Hugh Culverhouse; VP/Head Coach: John McKay; VP: Joy Culverhouse; Dir. Administration: Herb Gold; Dir. Player Personnel: Ken Herock; Dir. Pro Personnel: Jack Bushofsky; Dir. Pub. Rel.: Rick Odioso. Home field: Tampa Stadium (72,812). Colors: Florida orange, white and red.

SCOUTING REPORT

OFFENSE: Critics may ask, what offense? Things couldn't get much worse than they were last year for the Bucs. Without quarterback Doug Williams, they lacked leadership and consistency from that most important spot. The irony was that the Bucs were willing to pay millions to Warren Moon when a much smaller offer would have allowed them to keep Williams.

Another double-figure year in sacks for Lee Roy Selmon.

Ex-Bronco Steve DeBerg joins Jack Thompson in the quarterback competition, but they need to be surrounded by a stronger supporting cast. The Bucs claim they have the talent, but that a season-long rash of injuries eliminated any chance for the unit to develop. Only time will tell if that is a correct assumption. Running back James Wilder certainly is a quality player and receiver Kevin House has been productive in the past. But Tampa has no quality tailbacks and its receiving corps is very shallow.

Coach John McKay only has to look at the statistics from 1983 to see the job ahead: last in total offense in the NFC (279.8) and last in rushing (84.6).

DEFENSE: Maybe the most amazing accomplishment—or the least recognized—was the fact Tampa Bay's defense managed to stay respectable last year even with no help at all from its offensive counterpart.

Consider how much the defense has to play, how quickly it was faced with bad field position, bad turnovers and no production from the offense. It probably should have fallen apart, but instead the proud Bucs finished in the middle of the statistical pack, ahead of even Dallas.

Maybe some of that was due to the fine play of end Lee Roy Selmon, who sets the tempo for the rest of the unit. He was helped by linebackers Scot Brantley and Hugh Green, who is one of the two best at the spot in the NFL. Beasley Reece played well at free safety after coming over from the Giants, helping a secondary that also suffered badly from injury problems.

KICKING GAME: Nothing symbolizes the plight of the '83 Bucs better than Bill Capece's downfall. He was a hero in 1982, but all but out in 1983 after making only 10 of 23 field goals 14d missing three extra points. Frank Garcia did a surprisingly good job as punter.

THE ROOKIES: The Bucs needed plenty of help from the draft but already had lost their No. 1 in the trade for Thompson. That puts a lot of pressure on Keith Browner, a confident LB from Southern California who may be overrated. The same could be said for DB Fred Acorn of Texas, drafted in the third round.

OUTLOOK: The Bucs lost five games by three points, nine by a touchdown or less and were beaten three times in overtime. So there is hope that 1983 was a fluke, although it will take a fine season by Thompson or DeBerg to help get Tampa on the winning track.

BUCCANEERS VETERAN ROSTER

HEAD COACH—John McKay. Assistant Coaches—John Brunner, Joe Diange, Boyd Dowler, Wayne Fontes, Abe Gibron, Jim Gruden, Kim Helton, Chip Myers, Howard Tippett.

No.	Name	Pos.	Ht.	Wt.	NFL Exp.	College
69	Arbubakrr, Hasson	DE	6-4	250	2	Texas Tech
46	Armstrong, Adger	RB	6-0	225	5	Texas A&M
30	Barrett, David	RB	6-0	235	2	Houston
82	Bell, Jerry	TE	6-5	225	3	Arizona State
83	#Bell, Theo	WR	6-0	190	8	Arizona
52	Brantley, Scot	LB	6-1	230	5	Florida
34	Brown, Cedric	S	6-2	200	8	Kent State
74	Bujnoch, Glenn	G	6-5	251	9	Texas A&M
78	Cannon, John	DE	6-5	260	3	William & Mary
3	Capece, Bill	K	5-7	170	4	Florida State
87	Carter, Gerald	WR	6-1	190	5	Texas A&M
28	Carver, Melvin	RB	5-11	215	3	Nevada-Las Vegas
23	Castille, Jeremiah	CB	5-10	175	2	Alabama
20	Colzie, Neal	S	6-2	205	10	Ohio State
33	Cotney, Mark	S	6-0	205	9	Cameron (Okla.)
58	Davis, Jeff	LB	6-0	230	3	Clemson
17	Deberg, Steve	QB	6-3	205	8	San Jose State
—	Dierking, Scott	RB	5-10	220	8	Purdue
62	Farrell, Sean	G	6-3	260	3	Penn State
5	Garcia, Frank	P	6-0	205	2	Arizona
88	Giles, Jimmie	TE	6-3	240	8	Alcorn State
53	Green, Hugh	LB	6-2	225	4	Pittsburgh
60	Grimes, Randy	G-C	6-4	265	2	Baylor
8	Hewko, Bob	QB	6-3	195	2	Florida
21	#Holt, John	CB	5-11	175	4	West Texas State
89	House, Kevin	WR	6-1	175	5	Southern Illinois
56	Johnson, Cecil	LB	6-2	235	8	Pittsburgh
51	Judie, Ed	LB	6-2	235	3	Northern Arizona
7	Komlo, Jeff	QB	6-2	195	6	Delaware
29	La Beaux, Sandy	S	6-3	210	2	Cal State-Hayward
76	#Logan, David	NT	6-2	250	6	Pittsburgh
64	Lowry, Quentin	LB	6-2	235	4	Youngstown State
24	Morris, Thomas	CB-S	5-11	175	3	Michigan State
1	Morton, Michael	KR-RB	5-8	180	3	Nevada-Las Vegas
86	Obradovich, Jim	TE	6-2	225	10	Southern California
26	Owens, James	RB	5-11	200	6	UCLA
75	Reavis, Dave	T	6-5	265	10	Arkansas
43	Reece, Beasley	S	6-1	195	9	North Texas State
66	Reese, Booker	DE	6-6	260	3	Bethune-Cookman
74	Sanders, Eugene	T	6-3	280	6	Texas A&M
63	Selmon, Lee Roy	DE	6-3	250	9	Oklahoma
22	Smith, Johnny Ray	CB-S	5-9	185	3	Lamar
72	Snell, Ray	G	6-4	265	5	Wisconsin
55	Spradlin, Danny	LB	6-1	235	4	Tennessee
70	Thomas, Kelly	T	6-6	270	2	Southern California
41	Thomas, Norris	CB-S	5-11	180	8	Southern Mississippi
14	Thompson, Jack	QB	6-3	220	5	Washington State
56	Thompson, Robert	LB	6-3	225	2	Michigan
81	Tyler, Andre	WR	6-0	180	3	Stanford
40	Washington, Mike	CB-S	6-2	200	9	Alabama
90	White, Brad	NT	6-2	255	4	Tennessee
32	Wilder, James	RB	6-3	220	4	Missouri
50	Wilson, Steve	C	6-4	270	9	Georgia
85	Witte, Mark	TE	6-3	235	2	North Texas State
54	Wood, Richard	LB	6-2	230	10	Southern California

#Unsigned at press time

TOP FIVE DRAFT CHOICES

Rd.	Name	Sel. No.	Pos.	Ht.	Wt.	College
2	Browner, Keith	30	LB	6-6	225	Southern California
3	Acorn, Fred	57	DB	5-10	178	Texas
4	Gunter, Michael	107	RB	5-11	206	Tulsa
4	Heller, Ron	112	T	6-6	256	Penn State
6	Washington, Chris	142	LB	6-2	220	Iowa State

BUC PROFILES

JACK THOMPSON 28 6-3 220   Quarterback

No one had a more difficult task in 1983 than this former Cincinnati Bengal... Had to come into the eye of a storm, trying to replace Doug Williams... The worse the Bucs played, the more the blame fell on him... Didn't have the greatest season, but certainly not the whole reason for the team's collapse... Completed 249 of 423 passes for 2,906 yards... Threw 18 touchdown passes and had 21 intercepted... Began as a backup to Jerry Golsteyn before claiming starting job... Was a No. 1 choice of the Bengals who had to learn behind the great Ken Anderson... Born May 18, 1956, in Pago Pago, American Samoa... Hence the nickname "Throwin' Samoan."... Played at Washington State.

STEVE DeBERG 30 6-3 205   Quarterback

Gets a new shot after on-again-off-again role with John Elway at Denver... Came off the bench to hand Denver two come-from-behind victories, but wondered when his reward would come. It finally did after the Broncos lost three straight... DeBerg moved in as the starter and only a late-season injury with three weeks to play got him out of the lineup. But he was back as the starter in Denver's playoff loss to Seattle... Born Jan. 19, 1954, in Oakland... Completed 55 percent of his passes, but the key point is he threw just seven interceptions... Accuracy with a game on the line has always been his problem, but he overcame it and a lack of arm strength to hold off Elway for a season.

HUGH GREEN 25 6-2 225   Linebacker

If you mention Lawrence Taylor in one breath, you better mention him in the next... The two are recognized as the best outside backers in the conference, if not the whole league ... Along with Jeff Davis, led the team in tackles and had five sacks... Ahmad Rashad says that he "scared me the most of all. All you see is two mean eyes staring out at you."... Bucs say they use him more in pass coverage than the Giants do with Taylor... Peers named him starter on the Pro Bowl team... Born

July 27, 1959, in Natchez, Miss. . . . Best lineman in football his senior year at Pittsburgh.

LEE ROY SELMON 29 6-3 250   Defensive End

Another perennial Pro Bowl selection . . . Just goes about his job quietly and professionally even when the rest of the team may be crumbling around him . . . Was in double figures with sacks once again . . . "I'm still trying to improve my techniques," he says . . . Has vigorous workout program year-round . . . Even likes to do offseason sprints. . . . Banker in the offseason who does his own contract negotiating . . . Was the team's first-ever first-round choice out of Oklahoma . . . Born Nov. 20, 1954, in Eufaula, Okla. . . . Personable, gracious and intelligent.

JEFF DAVIS 24 6-0 230   Linebacker

One of the few bright spots last season for the Bucs . . . Almost ignored in the draft because he wasn't tall enough, he is playing in the pros the same way he did with Clemson, when he helped the Tigers win a national title . . . Was a team leader in tackles as a first-time starter at inside linebacker . . . Runs a 4.7 40, bench-presses 450, has vertical leap of 36 inches, but scouts weren't that impressed . . . Bucs finally picked him on fifth round . . . Born Jan. 26, 1960, in Greensboro, N.C. . . . Intense on the field, easygoing off of it . . . Studying for degree at Clemson.

DAVE REAVIS 34 6-5 265   Offensive Tackle

In his seventh year as a pro, finally made a big name for himself, but not as a player . . . Seems he was on a plane taking off from Chicago and it developed engine trouble before leaving the ground . . . He played a major role in the evacuation, yanking open the escape hatch and catching some passengers jumping from the wing . . . "My adrenelin was pumping," he says, "but this has been blown out of proportion. A lot of people did what I did, too." . . . Retired briefly in 1982 but soon changed his mind and now plans on staying around for a few more years . . . Born June 19, 1950, in Nashville, Tenn. . . . Defensive lineman at Arkansas . . . Licensed commodities broker.

DAVID LOGAN 27 6-2 250   Middle Guard

One of the league's better little-known players... Shakes off injuries to anchor the middle of the Buc defensive front... Only Lee Roy Selmon had more sacks last year.... That's the same place he has occupied the last three years... Only a 12th-round draft choice out of Pittsburgh in 1979... Has degree in urban studies and hopes to learn sign language to communicate with deaf athletes... Also speaks to students about dangers of alcohol and drug abuse... Born Oct. 25, 1956, in Pittsburgh... Regarded as the team's biggest eater... Once ate a sandwich meant to be consumed by six people.

SCOT BRANTLEY 26 6-1 230   Linebacker

Pairs with Jeff Davis on the inside to give the Bucs an unlikely set of linebackers... Davis was considered too small to play in the pros and this guy had such a bad head injury at Florida that he was considered medically unfit... Bucs sought more medical opinions and got a favorable one, so they drafted him on third round in 1980... Gamble has paid off... Became a solid starter and was among top three tacklers on the team... Born Feb. 24, 1958, in Chester, S.C.... Parade Magazine picked him as best defensive high-school player in country in 1975... Runs youth football camp in summer.

KEVIN HOUSE 26 6-1 175   Wide Receiver

Without his buddy, Doug Williams, around to throw him those long bombs, he wasn't nearly as productive as the Bucs had hoped last season... Wound up catching 39 passes for a team-high 633 yards and four touchdowns... Had a long score of 74 yards... Just sometimes too fast for the present Tampa quarterbacks... And when the offensive line had injury troubles, protection wasn't good enough to let long patterns develop ... Good enough baseball player to be drafted by the St. Louis Cardinals... Born Dec. 20, 1957, in St. Louis, Mo. ... Attended Southern Illinois, working toward degree at South Florida.

SEAN FARRELL 24 6-3 260   Guard

Son of a successful surgeon...Earned nickname "Dirtman" from his relentless style...Plays with a belligerent, ungiving frenzy...Showed how important he was to the Bucs last year when his injury hurt offensive line...A first-round choice in 1982 out of Penn State, where he became dedicated to year-round workout program with Nautilus equipment...Born May 25, 1960, in Southampton, N.Y....Likes Wall Street and real estate and is learning how to fly...Wears jacket size 55.

JAMES WILDER 26 6-3 220   Running Back

Until he was injured, was on way to a wonderful season...Set NFL mark for carries in a game, which was later broken...At one point, he was the Buc offense, so John McKay just gave him the ball and let him go to work...Wound up gaining 640 yards on 161 carries and four touchdowns...Also caught team-high 57 passes, blocked well and carried the water buckets ...Has become the athlete the Bucs hoped for when they drafted him on the second round in 1981 out of Missouri...Has caught at least 48 passes the last three seasons...Member of high-school sprint relay team...Born May 12, 1958, in Sikeston, Mo.

COACH JOHN McKAY: One of the fascinating sidelights to

the Bucs' poor season last year was McKay's running battle with the critics and the fans ...Sometimes refused to talk to reporters and once seemed on the verge of challenging one to a fight...And he told the fans what they could do with their booing and harrassment ...Where is the man with the image of being a quick one-line artist?...He's a proud, sometimes belligerent man who isn't always as patient and forgiving as one might think...If he was thinking about moving permanently into the front office, he put those ideas behind him after last season...Doesn't want to go out with that black cloud hanging over his head...Doug Williams has blamed him indirectly for contract problems with the team...Born July 5, 1924, in Everettsville, W. Va....Avid golfer who takes full advantage of

Florida's weather . . . Big fan of John Wayne movies and loves to read.

BIGGEST PLAY

The Tampa Bay Bucs have not made it easy for themselves. They've lost more than they ever expected and even when they have won, they have had to struggle seemingly at every juncture.

This was never more evident than on Dec. 20, 1981, in the Silverdome in Pontiac, Mich. The Bucs should have clinched the Central Division title weeks before, but couldn't get the one necessary win they needed. Instead, they now had to beat the Lions in their noisy dome to win that championship and the Lions had won seven straight games in that stadium during the regular season.

Early in the fourth period, Tampa Bay held onto a 13-10 lead. Detroit was on its 32 when quarterback Eric Hipple dropped back to pass. Defensive end Lee Roy Selmon broke in from the blind side, sacked Hipple and forced a fumble. Nose tackle David Logan picked it up on one bounce and ran 21 yards for what became the winning touchdown.

INDIVIDUAL BUCCANEER RECORDS

Rushing

Most Yards Game:	219	James Wilder, vs Minnesota, 1983
Season:	1,263	Ricky Bell, 1979
Career:	3,057	Ricky Bell, 1977-81

Passing

Most TD Passes Game:	4	Doug Williams, vs Minnesota, 1980
	4	Doug Williams, vs Detroit, 1981
	4	Jack Thompson, vs Houston, 1983
Season:	20	Doug Williams, 1980
Career:	73	Doug Williams, 1978-82

Receiving

Most TD Passes Game:	3	Morris Owens, vs Miami, 1976
Season:	9	Kevin House, 1981
Career:	23	Jimmie Giles, 1978-83

Scoring

Most Points Game:	18	Morris Owens, vs Miami, 1976
Season:	79	Garo Yepremian, 1980
Career:	196	Bill Capece, 1981-83
Most TDs Game:	3	Morris Owens, vs Miami, 1976
Season:	9	Ricky Bell, 1979
	9	Kevin House, 1981
Career:	23	Jimmie Giles, 1978-83

WASHINGTON REDSKINS

TEAM DIRECTORY: Chairman: Jack Kent Cooke; Pres.: Edward Bennett Williams; Exec. VP: John Kent Cooke; GM: Bobby Beathard; Dir. Player Personnel: Mike Allman; Dir. Pub. Rel.: Charles Taylor; Head Coach: Joe Gibbs. Home field: Robert F. Kennedy Stadium (55,363). Colors: Burgundy and gold.

SCOUTING REPORT

OFFENSE: Football has never seen an offensive machine quite like what the Redskins threw at the rest of the NFL last year. They

It wasn't the best of Super Bowls for John Riggins and Co.

set a record for points scored and were nearly unstoppable most weeks. Just ask the Rams about the playoffs.

Everywhere defenses looked, there were problems. Joe Theismann developed into the league's best quarterback and, except for a bad finish against New York, he should have been below 10 interceptions for the year. When he wasn't passing to Charlie Brown or Art Monk, John Riggins was bulling over people, setting a league mark for touchdowns scored and enjoying the best season of his long career.

And the Hogs added to their reputation as the best line around. Remember this: other than tackle George Starke, this is a young, young unit which only can get better. Once Starke leaves, guard Mark May will move to tackle and no one will notice the difference.

The only cloud on the horizon is age: both Theismann and Riggins are getting old and there are no replacements in the wings.

DEFENSE: It was only a few years ago that the Redskins had the worst rush defense in the league, but how things have changed. Those stingy Washington players held opponents to just 80.6 yards a game on the ground last year, 13 less than any other team in the conference. The progress has been due both to a couple of injury-free seasons in a row and to addition of more talent.

The major problem is in the secondary, where the Redskins proved continually vulnerable to the deep pass. Rookie Darrell Green impressed everyone at one cornerback but Vernon Dean slumped and finally was benched, opening a glaring weakness. Safety Mark Murphy made the Pro Bowl but both Ken Coffey and Curtis Jordan struggled at the other safety. If Tony Peters is taken off suspension by the NFL, then the safety headaches will disappear quickly.

The return of Peters, coupled with the emergence of end Charles Mann and the maturing of some young linebackers would make the unit even stronger next season.

KICKING GAME: Even though Mark Moseley missed some important kicks last year, he still set an NFL record for kick scoring. Punter Jeff Hayes has never developed into the long-distance booter the Redskins had wanted, but the coverage teams remain among the strongest in the league.

THE ROOKIES: The Redskins traded off their No. 1 choice, then selected two defensive linemen in the second round, Bob Slater of Oklahoma and Steve Hamilton of East Carolina. But defensive line was considered a team strongpoint. Biggest gamble

REDSKINS VETERAN ROSTER

HEAD COACH—Joe Gibbs. Assistant Coaches—Don Breaux, Joe Bugel, Bill Hickman, Larry Peccatiello, Richie Petitbon, Jerry Rhome, Dan Riley, Wayne Sevier, Warren Simmons, Charley Taylor, LaVern Torgeson.

No.	Name	Pos.	Ht.	Wt.	NFL Exp.	College
58	Anderson, Stuart	LB	6-1	224	3	Virginia
53	Bostic, Jeff	C	6-2	250	5	Clemson
69	Brooks, Perry	DT	6-3	270	7	Southern U.
87	Brown, Charlie	WR	5-10	179	3	South Carolina State
65	Butz, Dave	DT	6-7	295	11	Purdue
41	Carpenter, Brian	CB-S	5-10	167	3	Michigan
48	Coffey, Ken	SS	6-0	190	2	S.W. Texas State
51	#Coleman, Monte	LB	6-2	230	6	Central Arkansas
54	#Cronan, Peter	LB	6-2	238	7	Boston College
32	Dean, Vernon	CB	5-11	178	3	San Diego State
86	Didier, Clint	TE	6-5	240	3	Portland State
26	#Evans, Reggie	RB	5-11	200	2	Richmond
89	Garrett, Alvin	WR	5-7	185	5	Angelo State
77	Grant, Darryl	DT	6-1	275	4	Rice
28	Green, Darrell	CB-KR	5-8	170	2	Texas A&I
68	Grimm, Russ	G	6-3	273	4	Pittsburgh
17	Hart, Jim	QB	6-1	210	19	Southern Illinois
5	Hayes, Jeff	P	5-11	175	3	North Carolina
8	Holly, Bob	QB	6-2	196	3	Princeton
61	#Huff, Ken	G	6-4	265	10	Noron
34	Hunter, Monty	S	6-0	202	3	Salem (W. Va.)
66	Jacoby, Joe	T	6-7	295	4	Louisville
22	Jordan, Curtis	SS	6-2	205	8	Texas Tech
55	Kaufman, Mel	LB	6-2	220	4	Cal Poly-Obispo
67	Kimball, Bruce	G	6-2	260	3	Massachusettes
50	Kubin, Larry	LB	6-2	238	3	Penn State
62	Laster, Donald	T	6-5	285	2	Tennessee State
12	Laufenberg, Babe	QB	6-2	195	2	Indiana
79	Liebenstein, Todd	DE	6-6	255	3	Nevada-Las Vegas
72	Manley, Dexter	DE	6-3	253	4	Oklahoma State
71	Mann, Charles	DE	6-6	250	2	Nevada-Reno
73	May, Mark	G	6-6	288	4	Pittsburgh
78	McGee, Tony	DE	6-3	249	14	Bishop (Tex.)
83	McGrath, Mark	WR	5-11	175	3	Montana State
76	Mendenhall, Mat	DE	6-6	255	3	Brigham Young
57	Milot, Rich	LB	6-4	237	6	Penn State
81	Monk, Art	WR	6-3	209	5	Syracuse
3	Moseley, Mark	K	6-0	205	13	Stephen F. Austin
29	Murphy, Mark	FS	6-4	210	8	Colgate
21	Nelms, Mike	WR-KR	6-1	185	5	Baylor
52	Olkewicz, Neal	LB	6-0	233	6	Maryland
23	Peters, Tony	SS	6-1	177	10	Oklahoma
—	Radford, Bruce	DT	6-5	280	4	Grambling
44	Riggins, John	RB	6-2	235	13	Kansas
80	Seay, Virgil	WR	5-9	175	4	Troy State
60	Simmons, Roy	G-T	6-3	264	5	Georgia Tech
74	Starke, George	T	6-5	260	12	Columbia
7	Theismann, Joe	QB	6-0	198	11	Notre Dame
88	Walker, Rick	TE	6-4	235	8	UCLA
85	Warren, Don	TE	6-4	242	6	San Diego State
24	Washington, Anthony	CB	6-1	204	4	Fresno State
25	Washington, Joe	RB	5-10	179	8	Oklahoma
47	Williams, Greg	FS	5-11	185	3	Mississippi State
84	Williams, Michael	TE	6-4	251	3	Alabama A&M
39	#Wonsley, Otis	RB	5-10	214	4	Alcorn State

#Unsigned at press time

TOP FIVE DRAFT CHOICES

Rd.	Name	Sel. No.	Pos.	Ht.	Wt.	College
2	Slater, Bob	31	DT	6-4	265	Oklahoma
2	Hamilton, Steve	55	DE	6-4	253	East Carolina
3	Schroeder, Jay	83	QB	6-4	215	UCLA
4	Smith, Jimmy	102	RB	6-0	205	Elon
5	Pegues, Jeff	125	LB	6-2	236	East Carolina

was QB Jay Schroeder of UCLA in the third round. He's been playing baseball for the last three years.

OUTLOOK: With the Super Bowl loss to the Raiders haunting his team, coach Joe Gibbs says the Redskins will be motivated more than ever this year. Remember, until that defeat, the league knew no more dominant team the last two years.

REDSKIN PROFILES

JOE THEISMANN 34 6-0 198   Quarterback

Remember all the talking he did in years past about how good he thought he was?...There was some laughter then, but not anymore ...Had a wonderful season in 1982 but was even better in 1983...Voted MVP of the league by most folks and was the top quarterback in the NFL...Again selected to the Pro Bowl ..."This is all a dream come true," he says ...Dreams of a Hollywood movie career and already has made film appearances...His 1983 stats were of star quality: 276 for 459 for 3,714 yards, 29 touchdowns, 11 interceptions...Born Sept. 9, 1949, in New Brunswick, N.J....Threw for 417 yards against the Raiders in the regular season...Ex-Notre Damer owns two restaurants and assorted other business ventures.

JOHN RIGGINS 35 6-2 235   Fullback

"The Diesel"...Chugs through defenses as if they were so many matchsticks...Remarkable career in which his best years have come at a time when most backs are retired...Probably ready to play his last season after signing massive two-year contract after 1982 campaign ...No. 5 rusher all-time with 9,436 yards and No. 3 carrier...Gained 1,347 yards last year to break club record...Scored 24 touchdowns, a league record, and had streak of 20 straight scoring games...How could he be left off Pro Bowl team?...Born Aug 4, 1949, in Lawrence, Kan. and played at Kansas...Still lives on a farm in hometown, loves to hunt, fish and stay to himself...One of sport's leading eccentrics.

MARK MOSELEY 36 6-0 205   Placekicker

Found it was impossible to match his dream-world 1982 season...Returned to the land of the mortals last season...But still didn't do badly...Led the NFL in scoring with 161 points, a league record for kickers...His 33 field goals was a team record and third highest in NFL history...His 62 PATS second highest ever....Now is sixth all-time in field goals made (242) and eighth in scoring...Beat the 49ers in the final minutes with a field goal to send the Redskins to the Super Bowl...Born March 12, 1948, in Laneville, Tex....Product of Stephen F. Austin...Owns a travel agency, western store, does some broadcasting, makes lot of civic appearances.

CHARLIE BROWN 25 5-10 179   Wide Receiver

Call his phone number and the answering voice says "Downtown Charlie Brown hasn't dropped one yet."...And he may be right...Amazing rise from unknown to all-star...Came out of South Carolina State as unheralded eighth-round pick and now has made Pro Bowl in his first two pro seasons....Caught 78 passes to break club record of 72 shared by Charley Taylor and Bobby Mitchell...His 1,225 receiving yards was third highest in team history behind two Mitchell outputs...Had 11 catches in regular-season win over Raiders, second best in team history...Born Oct. 29, 1958, in Charleston, S.C....Quietly confident...Standout basketball player.

DAVE BUTZ 34 6-7 295   Defensive Tackle

This inconsistent giant finally put together the season of his career last year...Got the Pro Bowl recognition that had eluded him the previous season...Had some very big games, especially against Dallas, but was buried by the Raiders in the Super Bowl...Come up for air now, Dave...When he is motivated, he's difficult to be blocked by one player...Born June 23, 1950, in Lafayette, Ala., and attended Purdue...Carves duck decoys as a hobby...Does a lot of charity work and is a banker in the offseason...Shoe size 12½EEEEEEE ...Nickname is "Bruno."

RUSS GRIMM 25 6-3 273   Guard

Became the middle man in a tug of war between the Redskins and the USFL's Pittsburgh Maulers . . . Hometown Pittsburgh boy who decided to turn down a guaranteed contract to stay in Washington . . . That's the kind of guy he is . . . Straight-forward, honest . . . Says there are more important things than money . . . Doesn't have agent . . . As long as his knees hold up, one of the league's best guards . . . Pro Bowl last year in his third season . . . The most talented of the Hogs . . . Born May 2, 1959, in Pittsburgh and attended U. of Pittsburgh . . . Likes outdoor life, including hunting and fishing.

MARK MURPHY 29 6-4 210   Safety

There always has been talk that the Redskins would like to find another free safety . . . But it will be hard to replace him after his quality 1983 season . . . Led the league in interceptions with nine, for 127 yards . . . Was a consensus All-Pro and was elected as a starter in the Pro Bowl . . . Had 18 interceptions in previous four seasons as a starter . . . Was second in tackles behind Neal Olkewicz after leading in tackles for four straight years . . . Born July 14, 1955, in Fulton, N.Y. . . . Keen mind, union leader, well-spoken, good-humored . . . Also plays a mean game of basketball . . . Colgate grad with future in politics.

DEXTER MANLEY 25 6-3 253   Defensive End

"Dr. D" . . . Came to training camp last year with a Mohawk haircut to make him different from anyone else . . . But his gift for gab probably has already done that . . . Finally went back to conventional haircut later in the season . . . When he is motivated, is one of the toughest pass-rushers in the league . . . But sometimes doesn't push himself hard enough . . . Had a late-season slump which had some Redskins worried . . . Born July 7, 1959, in Houston . . . Was a stand-up linebacker at Oklahoma State and a fifth-round draft choice by the Redskins . . . Will be pushed this year by the coaches and young Charles Mann, a talented backup defensive end.

JOE JACOBY 25 6-7 295   Offensive Tackle

Becoming a legend in his time . . . Takes a half-hour to get around him . . . The Gentle Giant . . . Soft-spoken, shy . . . But put him in a uniform and he is efficiently difficult to beat . . . Doesn't play mean, just well . . . Takes coaching extremely well and is constantly improving his technique . . . Ask Lyle Alzado how tough it is to block him for a full game . . . Came from nowhere after so-so career at Louisville . . . The Redskins signed him as a free agent and Joe Gibbs thought he was a defensive tackle . . . Born July 6, 1959, in Louisville, Ky. . . . Coaches Babe Ruth baseball team in offseason.

DARRELL GREEN 24 5-8 170   Cornerback

The jet from Texas . . . People wondered if he was too small to play in the pros but he soon showed that height makes little difference with this kind of athletic talent . . . Caught Tony Dorsett from behind in first pro game, and that made believers fast, including Dorsett . . . Has one of the best reaction times in the league . . . Got to a point where teams didn't challenge him that much, even as a rookie . . . Born Feb. 15, 1960, in Houston . . . Has run 100 meters in 10.08 . . . Played at Texas A&I, where he was a small college All-American.

COACH JOE GIBBS: Says it will take him a long time to forget one play . . . That screen pass at the end of the first half in the Super Bowl XVIII that was intercepted and returned for a Raider touchdown . . . He'll be criticized for it, but it also represents his style: aggressive, challenging, daring . . . Maybe this time being conservative would have been better, but the Redskins have won under him because he doesn't pull back . . . And that is a refreshing change . . . One of the new breed of coaches who think as much about player reactions as x's and o's . . . Has allowed the Redskins to function as team of personalities while also keeping rein on team discipline . . . Not an easy feat . . . Has emerged as one of the league's top coaches after only three seasons in the job . . . That's what is easy to forget . . . He's been to two Super Bowls, more than most coaches can dream

about... Born Nov. 25, 1943, in Mocksville, N.C.... Attended Cerritos (Cal.) Junior College and San Diego State... Taught Bible study to teenager juvenile delinquents during players' strike in 1982... Deeply religious... A real tough competitor.

BIGGEST PLAY

You have to remember how long it had been for Washington fans. Not since Sammy Baugh's heyday in the early '40s had they known what it was like to win a championship.

And now the wait might be extended some more. Their Redskins were trailing Miami, 17-13, early in the fourth quarter of Super Bowl XVII, played in late afternoon on Jan. 30, 1983 in

OT Joe Jacoby's blocking belies his gentle nature.

Pasadena, Cal. Washington had the ball at the Dolphin 43, facing a fourth-down-and-one situation. And time was running out.

Coach Joe Gibbs called for an end sweep, to go around the Redskins' powerful left side. John Riggins took the handoff from Joe Theismann, cut around end, shook off a Dolphin tackle and took off. No one was going to catch him. By the time he stopped, Riggins had recorded a 43-yard touchdown run, and when it was all over, the Redskins had won the Super Bowl, 27-17. All those years of frustration for the team and its fans had been wiped out.

INDIVIDUAL REDSKIN RECORDS

Rushing

Most Yards Game:	195	Mike Thomas, vs St. Louis, 1976
Season:	1,347	John Riggins, 1983
Career:	5,875	Larry Brown, 1969-76

Passing

Most TD Passes Game:	6	Sam Baugh, vs Brooklyn, 1943
	6	Sam Baugh, vs St. Louis, 1947
Season:	31	Sonny Jurgensen, 1967
Career:	187	Sammy Baugh, 1937-52

Receiving

Most TD Passes Game:	3	Hugh Taylor (5 times)
	3	Jerry Smith, vs Los Angeles, 1967
	3	Jerry Smith, vs Dallas, 1969
	3	Hal Crisler (once)
	3	Joe Walton (once)
	3	Pat Richter, vs Chicago, 1968
	3	Larry Brown, vs Philadelphia, 1973
	3	Jean Fugett, vs San Francisco, 1976
	3	Alvin Garrett, vs Lions, 1982
Season:	12	Hugh Taylor, 1952
	12	Charley Taylor, 1966
	12	Jerry Smith, 1967
Career:	79	Charley Taylor, 1964-77

Scoring

Most Points Game:	24	Dick James, vs Dallas, 1961
	24	Larry Brown, vs Philadelphia, 1973
Season:	161	Mark Moseley, 1983
	114	Mark Moseley, 1979
Career:	959	Mark Moseley, 1974-83
Most TDs Game:	4	Dick James, vs Dallas, 1961
	4	Larry Brown, vs Philadelphia, 1973
Season:	24	John Riggins, 1983
Career:	90	Charley Taylor, 1964-77

INSIDE THE AFC

By RON BORGES

PREDICTED ORDER OF FINISH

EAST	CENTRAL	WEST
Miami	Cleveland	L.A. Raiders
New England	Pittsburgh	Denver
Indianapolis	Cincinnati	Seattle
N.Y. Jets	Houston	San Diego
Buffalo		Kansas City

AFC Champion: L.A. Raiders

A professional football season has been scheduled this year so that it might as well be played, but the point is really moot. There may be 14 teams in the AFC but there is really only one that counts—the defending world champion Los Angeles Raiders.

The Raiders are not only the finest team in football, as they proved by dismantling the Washington Redskins in Super Bowl XVIII, but somehow they have managed to become an improved version of the finest team in football. This does not make them unbeatable as long as fumbles, interceptions, injuries and the Bermuda Triangle still exist. But it would take just such a four-way parlay to stop them unless the Denver Broncos' John Elway catches fire or Seattle proves that last year was not as much a freak of nature as Mount St. Helen's.

In the AFC East, the Dolphins will win because they always win. They win when their team is superior and when it is not, and this maxim will be tested this time if the Patriots continue to improve.

Ron Borges has covered pro football for newspapers on both coasts and now covers most closely the New England Patriots for the Boston *Globe.*

Miami will welcome another 16-sack season from Doug Betters.

New England should be this year's Seattle because it is young, talented, has a lust for victory (at last) and has the kind of schedule that should allow it to slip into the playoffs. The Bills cannot survive the loss of Joe Cribbs and the Jets cannot survive the loss of half their defense plus quarterback Richard Todd. Count them out quickly. Please.

This leaves only the Colts. If they could move as surreptitiously on the field as they did out of Baltimore, they'd win the Super Bowl in a walk, but they can't. Maybe next year.

Last we have the AFC Central, where the winters are bad and the teams are worse. It seems the Browns are ready to take over on the strength of a defense that will dominate if it finds a pass rush. As long as Chuck Noll is calling the shots, the Steelers will be in it, but as long as David Woodley is at quarterback instead of injured Terry Bradshaw, they won't be in it for long.

The Bengals helped themselves in the draft, which is a good thing because they needed it. The nucleus of their Super Bowl team of three years ago is still there, so Cincinnati remains dangerous but not dangerous enough.

Last (as always) we have the Houston Oilers. They shot the moon on quarterback Warren Moon and his presence behind a rock-hard young line will put points on the board and a few more wins in the standings. But who can save them from their defense? No one, that's who.

But so what? Who can save the AFC from the Raiders' Silver-and-Black Attack? You got it, no one.

BUFFALO BILLS

TEAM DIRECTORY: Pres.: Ralph Wilson; Exec. VP: Patrick J. McGroder; VP Adm./GM: Terry Bledsoe; VP/Player Personnel: Norm Pollom; VP/Pub. Rel.: L. Budd Thalman; Head Coach: Kay Stephenson. Home field: Rich Stadium (80,020). Colors: Scarlet red, royal blue and white.

SCOUTING REPORT

OFFENSE: Coach Kay Stephenson says he'll be going to the one-back offense more this season. Unfortunately, he no longer has one back to put in it.

Last year this would have been a wonderful plan because he had at his disposal one of the most versatile backs in the AFC— Joe Cribbs. But Cribbs shuffled out of Buffalo in a contract dispute for the USFL, leaving the Bills with a good idea but no one to execute it.

"You do not replace Joe Cribbs," Stephenson admits. "We hope we can find two backs who can gain 500 yards each."

Even if he does, Buffalo will still be 131 yards short of Cribbs' production, not to mention his club-leading 57 receptions. So that's the problem.

Stephenson is hoping Booker Moore, a No. 1 pick two years ago, and rookie Greg Bell will soften the loss. Moore may finally be at full health and ready to live up to his vast potential as a John Riggins clone. Since he gained just 275 yards in 1983 that may be a bit too much use of the rose-colored glasses.

So, what's a coach to do? Change his helmets.

Stephenson switched them from white to red in the hope it would decrease the incidents of mistaken identity that led quarterback Joe Ferguson to throw a career-high 25 interceptions. If Ferguson gets the helmets right, he has prime targets in Tony Hunter, 36 receptions as a rookie, and, if healthy again, Jerry Butler, 36 catches before suffering a knee injury that killed the second half of the season.

DEFENSE: Stephenson had more holes to patch then the Little Dutch Boy and the same amount of thumbs. However, Buffalo's tumble from second in the AFC to 12th in the NFL was far too steep a slide for the talent here, especially with the return of linebacker Jim Haslett and defensive end Sherman White.

Haslett, long the heart of the Bills' defense, is back from a disc injury. White, meanwhile, appears recovered from knee problems and will battle Ken Johnson for his old job. If White rejoins nose tackle Fred Smerlas and defensive end Ben Williams, the Bills won't finish 24th against the run again.

Overall, the linebacking is sound with Eugene Marve simply marvelous at inside linebacker and Haslett back.

The only real question is in the secondary. Rod Kush and Jeff Nixon return from injuries so a competitive situation is brewing at strong safety. That had been Steve Freeman's spot but he played Kush's old free-safety position so well he will probably stay there. The corners are set with Mario Clark and Charles Romes.

KICKING GAME: Nothing great here. Joe Danelo has a toehold on the placekicking job. Punter Greg Cater is consistent—his

Ex-Notre Damer Tony Hunter caught 36 passes as a rookie.

BILLS VETERAN ROSTER

HEAD COACH—Kay Stephenson. Assistant Coaches—John Becker, Milt Jackson, Monte Kiffin, Don Lawrence, Andy MacDonald, Miller McCalmon, Perry Moss, Jim Niblack, Bob Zeman.

No.	Name	Pos.	Ht.	Wt.	NFL Exp.	College
75	Acker, Bill	NT	6-3	255	5	Texas
84	Barnett, Buster	TE	6-5	235	4	Jackson State
73	Borchardt, Jon	G	6-5	255	6	Montana State
86	Brammer, Mark	TE	6-3	235	5	Michigan State
80	Butler, Jerry	WR	6-0	178	6	Clemson
67	Caldwell, Darryl	T	6-5	245	2	Tennessee State
7	Cater, Greg	P	6-0	191	5	Tenn.- Chattanooga
29	#Mario Clark	CB	6-2	195	9	Oregon
63	Cross, Justin	T	6-6	265	4	Western State (Colo.)
18	Danelo, Joe	K	5-9	166	10	Washington State
89	Dawkins, Julius	WR	6-1	196	2	Pittsburgh
70	#Devlin, Joe	T	6-5	250	8	Iowa
19	Dufek, Joe	QB	6-4	215	2	Yale
12	Ferguson, Joe	QB	6-1	195	12	Arkansas
28	#Flint, Judson	S	6-0	201	4	Memphis State
85	Franklin, Byron	WR	6-1	179	4	Auburn
22	Freeman, Steve	S	5-11	185	10	Mississippi State
53	Grant, Will	C	6-4	248	7	Kentucky
55	Haslett, Jim	LB	6-3	232	6	Indiana (Pa.)
49	Holt, Robert	WR	6-1	182	2	Baylor
25	Hooks, Roland	RB	6-0	195	8	North Carolina State
87	Hunter, Tony	TE	6-3	237	2	Notre Dame
28	Hurley, Bill	S	5-11	185	3	Syracuse
90	Hutchinson, Scott	DE	6-4	255	6	Florida
91	#Johnson, Ken	DE	6-5	253	6	Knoxville College
72	Jones, Ken	T	6-5	256	9	Arkansas State
50	Junkin, Trey	LB	6-2	221	2	Louisiana Tech
52	Keating, Chris	LB	6-2	223	6	Maine
21	Kennedy, Mike	S	6-0	195	2	Toledo
43	Kilson, David	CB	6-1	200	2	Nevada-Reno
10	Kofler, Matt	QB	6-3	192	3	San Diego State
42	Kush, Rod	S	6-0	188	5	Nebraska-Omaha
48	Leaks, Roosevelt	RB	5-10	225	10	Texas
82	#Lewis, Frank	WR	6-1	196	14	Grambling
59	Lumpkin, Joey	LB	6-2	230	4	Arizona State
61	#Lynch, Tom	G	6-5	250	8	Boston College
54	Marve, Eugene	LB	6-2	230	3	Saginaw Valley
58	Merrill, Mark	LB	6-3	234	6	Minnesota
34	Moore, Booker	RB	5-11	224	3	Penn State
88	#Mosley, Mike	WR	6-2	192	3	Texas A&M
38	Nixon, Jeff	S	6-3	190	5	Richmond
62	Parker, Ervin	LB	6-5	240	5	South Carolina State
40	Riddick, Robb	RB	6-0	195	3	Millersville (Pa.)
51	Ritcher, Jim	G	6-3	251	2	North Carolina State
26	Romes, Charles	CB	6-1	190	8	North Carolina Central
57	Sanford, Lucius	LB	6-2	216	7	Georgia Tech
76	Smerlas, Fred	NT	6-3	270	6	Boston College
56	Talley, Darryl	LB	6-3	231	2	West Virginia
	Taylor, Roger	T	6-6	275	2	Oklahoma State
24	Thompson, Gary	CB	6-0	180	2	Redwoods JC
81	Tuttle, Perry	WR	6-0	178	3	Clemson
41	#Villapiano, Phil	LB	6-2	225	14	Bowling Green
93	Virkus, Scott	DE	6-5	248	2	San Francisco City Coll.
65	Vogler, Tim	C-G	6-3	245	6	Ohio State
45	Walterscheid, Lenny	S	5-11	190	8	Southern Utah State
83	White, Sherman	DE	6-5	250	13	California
77	Williams, Ben	DE	6-3	245	9	Mississippi
27	Williams, Chris	CB	6-0	197	3	Louisiana State
23	Williams, Van	RB	6-0	208	2	Carson-Newman

#Unsigned at press time

TOP FIVE DRAFT CHOICES

Rd.	Name	Sel. No.	Pos.	Ht.	Wt.	College
1	Bell, Greg	26	RB	6-0	210	Notre Dame
2	Richardson, Eric	41	WR	6-2	188	San Jose State
3	Bellinger, Rodney	77	DB	5-8	185	Miami
3	McNanie, Sean	79	DE	6-5	250	San Diego State
3	Neal, Speedy	82	RB	6-2	245	Miami

punts seldom go 40 yards. Van Williams, who averaged 22 yards per return, and Robb Riddick (20.3) give Buffalo an unusually productive one-two return punch.

THE ROOKIES: Desperate for a runner to replace Joe Cribbs, the Bills gambled on Notre Dame's Bell on the first round. He is fast (4.5) and big (208), but has been nothing but injured throughout his career. He could be a Cribbs or a Booker Moore (always injured). Miami cornerback Rodney Bellinger has a chance.

OUTLOOK: Stephenson almost got his team into the playoffs in an ambulance last year. Perhaps he can do it this time with a little luck. But without Cribbs, Stephenson could be the casualty this time.

BILL PROFILES

JOE FERGUSON 34 6–1 195　　　　　　Quarterback

He has been given "seeing-eye" helmets this season in an attempt to reduce his interceptions . . . Buffalo changed its helmets from white to red because "so many clubs we play have white helmets," coach Kay Stephenson says . . . That would be fine if Ferguson hadn't had his worst game last year against the blue-and-gold helmeted Los Angeles Rams . . . Still, after throwing 25 interceptions, Joe surely needs some kind of help . . . After throwing for 2,995 yards in '83, Ferguson became one of only 20 NFL quarterbacks in history to amass over 25,000 yards passing . . . Born April 23, 1950, in Alvin, Tex. . . . Starred at Arkansas before Buffalo drafted him in 1973.

FRED SMERLAS 27 6-3 270　　　　　　Nose Tackle

Despite spending his autumn being hit from all sides, Smerlas made the Pro Bowl for the fourth straight time . . . Buffalo defense was decimated by injuries, but Smerlas was unaffected. He recorded six sacks and was generally acclaimed as the best in the AFC at his thankless position . . . Born April 8, 1957, in Waltham, Mass. . . . He is one of the strongest men in a league of strong men and has reputation for humor on and off the field... "It's always fun to match up with Fred," says Patriots' center Pete Brock. "You know he'll play hard and clean. Aside from that you don't know what he'll do."

BEN WILLIAMS 30 6-3 245   Defensive End

Probably deserved a trip to the Pro Bowl again, but with his team in collapse he went back to being unnoticed... Williams, of course, is used to that. He had 23 sacks in the 1980 and '81 season and no one even knew his name—except for the quarterbacks he was lying on top of... Had 10 more sacks last season... In the offseason Williams handles installment loans for a bank. When he comes to collect, there's no problem finding the check... Born Sept. 1, 1954, in Yazoo City, Miss.... Played for three different coaches while at the University of Mississippi... Intensive weight program started two years ago is just starting to pay off, so look out this season.

WILL GRANT 30 6-4 248   Center

Considered trying to become the largest defenseman in the National Hockey League but had to give up the sport after high school... "I kept outgrowing the equipment and pretty soon I was too big to turn and skate with anybody but Dorothy Hamill."... That doesn't sound so bad, Will... A four-year starter, unknown Grant forced Buffalo to move former No. 1 pick Jim Ritcher to guard... Grant was the 255th player taken in 1978 after a nondescript career at Kentucky... Born March 7, 1954, in Milton, Mass.... He began his college career at Idaho State. "I liked the snow," he says. "But I didn't like the football. I wanted to play on a higher level."

TONY HUNTER 24 6-3 237   Tight End

He will be hunted this season after breaking in with 36 receptions for 402 yards as a rookie... Numbers would have been higher had he not missed three games with shoulder and hamstring problems... Buffalo's top draft choice of a year ago after an All-America career at Notre Dame, where he played wide receiver, wingback and tight end... Born May 22, 1960, in Cincinnati . . . Set a Notre Dame record by averaging 25.6 yards per catch as a freshman . . . Hunter was the Ohio High School Player of the Year when he was a senior at Moeller High, where he first met Irish coach Gerry Faust.

JIM HASLETT 28 6-3 232   Inside Linebacker

The pain in his back was a pain in the neck for the Bills' defense . . . Haslett, who has been the heart of the Buffalo defense since 1979, missed 11 games with back problems and his team never recovered . . . If he doesn't, they may not again this season . . . He is considered suspect physically after having been lost for parts of the past two years . . . Born Dec. 9, 1955, in Pittsburgh . . . Once the linchpin of the "Bermuda Triangle," the middle of the Bills' defense where Haslett, Fred Smerlas and Shane Nelson once made runners disappear . . . Attended Indiana College. That's the one in Pennsylvania . . . Is he done after just five seasons? That's what has to be answered this year.

JERRY BUTLER 26 6-0 178   Wide Receiver

Butler was on his way to the finest season of his career when he went down with a knee injury against New Orleans that forced him out of the final seven games of the season . . . Butler had 36 receptions for 385 yards, a pace that would have left him with a career-high 64 receptions . . . Speed has always been his game, which is why a knee injury is doubly worrisome. But if he hasn't lost a step, he'll put fear back into the eyes of the cornerbacks who have to stop him . . . Born Oct. 12, 1957, in Greenwood, S.C. . . . He was so fast no one noticed him his first year of high school. He played the saxophone then, not football. But then someone saw him running to the music room and a star was born.

JUSTIN CROSS 25 6-6 265   Tackle

Once he had the impression that skiing was his game. Did fine until he began lifting weights and his skis began to bend at odd places . . . "I started getting heavy and kept breaking all my equipment," Cross said. "Finally the guy sponsoring me in races said he couldn't afford to keep me in skis so I retired." . . . Cross began working on his football and ended up becoming only the second player ever drafted out of Western College in Colorado... Born April 29, 1959, in Montreal... When Joe Devlin broke his ankle last year, Cross moved in. With or without skis, it will be tough to slide him back out.

BOOKER MOORE 25 5-11 224   Running Back

Life will be different for Moore this season... After carrying just 60 times a year ago for 275 yards, Moore will be looked upon as the man who must make Buffalo forget the departed Joe Cribbs... Cribbs is gone to the USFL, but the memory of his 1,131 yards rushing last year isn't... Moore has had some hard luck since being drafted No. 1 out of Penn State in 1981... He missed his rookie year because of Guillian-Barre Syndrome, a rare nerve disease... He returned to play in five games in 1982 and then became a starter last year by stepping in ahead of Roosevelt Leaks... Born June 23, 1959, in Flint, Mich.... Has the power of a bulldozer, but also the speed.

EUGENE MARVE 24 6-2 230   Inside Linebacker

Simply Marve-lous... Eugene led the Bills' defense with 200 tackles, including 136 first hits... One of the big surprises of 1982 when he came to Buffalo from Saginaw Valley State College and began hitting everything that came his way and much of what tried to go the other way... Got his chance after Shane Nelson was injured in Marve's rookie year... Made NAIA All-American at two positions, defensive and as a junior and linebacker as a senior... Born Aug. 14, 1960, in Flint, Mich.... In his less violent moments, Marve boxes as an amateur... He was a high-school rival of Booker Moore, a teammate he now cheers for.

COACH KAY STEPHENSON: Almost drowned in a sea of injuries during his head-coaching debut last year... Of the 49 players at his disposal, 22 missed at least one game through injury, including 10 starters... By season end he had to put together an offense with just two healthy wide receivers and one tight end... Still managed to keep Bills in the playoff picture until the season's final weekend, posting an 8-8 rec-.

ord after taking over for departed Chuck Knox
coach in the NFL at 39, Stephenson was born b.
DeFuniak Springs, Fla. . . . He coached Buffalo's qu.
der Knox for five years . . . Stephenson remains a qu.
heart, which is what he was while backing up Steve Sp
Florida . . . It will be difficult to throw without Joe Cribbs
to catch, but Stephenson doesn't intend to change his offens.
plans . . . He was Buffalo's starting quarterback for three games in
1968 and thus is the only former Bills' player to serve as their
head coach.

BIGGEST PLAY

There was 5:56 left to play in a relatively meaningless game
when suddenly the lights came on and pierced the gloom at Shea

Sack artist Fred Smerlas made fourth straight Pro Bowl.

was almost as if to announce that something special
t to happen.

Jets-Bills game meant little but the moment was history.
as late afternoon on Dec. 16, 1973, and O. J. Simpson was
nding in the huddle with his Buffalo teammates making ready
to assault a mountain no man had ever climbed.

"Let's go for two grand," guard Reggie McKenzie said to no
one in particular. It was something he had first said a half hour
earlier after Simpson had broken Jim Brown's single-season rushing record on a special play called "27."

That play had become the favorite of both Simpson and the
Bills, but the one that would take him over the peak called 2,000
was not.

Simpson took the handoff on a straight-ahead plunge into the
left side of the line behind McKenzie. And then he turned it into
something. He squeezed between two tacklers, pulled away from
a third and then ran over a fourth before being dragged down for
a seven-yard gain.

The quest was over. O. J. Simpson had rushed for over 2,000
yards. No one had done it before . . . and no one has done it since.

INDIVIDUAL BILL RECORDS

Rushing

Most Yards Game:	273	O. J. Simpson, vs Detroit, 1976
Season:	2,003	O. J. Simpson, 1973
Career:	10,183	O. J. Simpson, 1969-77

Passing

Most TD Passes Game:	5	Joe Ferguson, vs N.Y. Jets, 1979
Season:	26	Joe Ferguson, 1983
Career:	169	Joe Ferguson, 1973-83

Receiving

Most TD Passes Game:	4	Jerry Butler, vs N.Y. Jets, 1979
Season:	10	Elbert Dubenion, 1964
Career:	35	Elbert Dubenion, 1960-67

Scoring

Most Points Game:	30	Cookie Gilchrist, vs New York, 1963
Season:	138	O. J. Simpson, 1975
Career:	420	O. J. Simpson, 1969-77
Most TDs Game:	5	Cookie Gilchrist, vs New York, 1963
Season:	23	O. J. Simpson, 1975
Career:	70	O. J. Simpson, 1969-1977

CINCINNATI BENGALS

TEAM DIRECTORY: Chairman: Austin E. Knowlton; Pres.: John Sayer; VP/GM: Paul Brown; Asst. GM: Michael Brown; Dir. Player Personnel: Pete Brown; Dir. Pub Rel.: Allan Heim; Bus. Mgr.: Bill Connelly; Head Coach: Sam Wyche. Home field: Riverfront Stadium (59,754). Colors: Orange, black and white.

SCOUTING REPORT

OFFENSE: As long as Ken Anderson's arm stays intact and Chris Collinsworth's mind doesn't wander to that other league, the Bengals will score points. But will there be enough of them now that big Pete Johnson has gone to San Diego in the trade for little James Brooks?

Anderson rolls along year after year, passing as accurately as anyone who ever threw a football. Turk Schonert signed a big contract to back Anderson up and that's exactly what new coach Sam Wyche hopes he'll have to do.

Only 13 of Ken Anderson's passes were intercepted last year.

Johnson returned from his four-game suspension and battered his way to 763 yards and 14 TDs. He was power personified, the team's leading rusher for seven years. When Cincinnati refused to renegotiate his contract and he threatened to jump to the USFL, the Bengals said farewell. Size no matter, the 5-9 Brooks mustered 1,475 yards last year (516 rushing, 215 receiving, and 744 returning punts and kickoffs), so they hope he'll prove a bountiful Bengal.

Collinsworth is one of the best receivers in football. His problem will be concentrating on his work in Cincinnati when he knows he's headed for the USFL in January. But he's likely to produce another 1,000-yard season. Isaac Curtis is a question now because of his age but Steve Kreider, whose stats matched Curtis' last year, has youth and talent on his side.

The line is strong at tackles with All-Pro Anthony Munoz and Mike Wilson and at center with future All-Pro Dave Rimington. Guards are still a question, but maybe they should have to play without them considering the rest of the cast.

DEFENSE: The best in the NFL, according to the statistics. Cincinnati was second against the run and third against the pass (up from 22nd a year earlier). Obviously, there is no reason to make changes here and few are expected.

The only major one is replacing retired cornerback Ken Riley, who played 15 brilliant seasons. Ray Horton, a No. 2 pick last year, will handle that chore. He had five interceptions as a rookie and seems ready, although he may not be as ready as Riley.

The line is sound with Eddie Edwards a pass-rushing demon with 13 sacks. Ross Browner was less than sensational after returning from his suspension but Wyche is hopeful he can find the key to unlock his vast talents.

All the linebackers love to hit. They are a proven commodity, although there is a question mark where once stood Jim LeClair. Rick Razzano and Jeff Schuh will fight over his spot with Razzano having the edge. Linebacker Reggie Williams would be a star in this league if people noticed him. He had 7½ sacks and 90 tackles from his outside spot. Like the Beach Boys, he gets around.

KICKING GAME: Jimmy Breech doesn't have the leg for the long shots, but he's reliable inside 40 yards. Punter Pat McInally came back from a knee injury and returned to the form that once made him the best in the NFL. He averaged 43.1 yards per kick.

THE ROOKIES: Bengals had what could prove one of the best drafts ever. Arizona linebacker Ricky Hunley could step right in

BENGALS VETERAN ROSTER

HEAD COACH—Sam Wyche. Assistant Coaches—Jim Anderson, Bruce Coslet, Joe Faragalli, Dick LeBeau, Jim McNally, Dick Selcer, Bill Urbanik, Trent Walters, Kim Wood.

No.	Name	Pos.	Ht.	Wt.	NFL Exp.	College
40	Alexander, Charles	RB	6-1	226	6	Louisiana State
14	Anderson, Ken	QB	6-3	212	14	Augustana
61	Boyarsky, Jerry	NT	6-3	290	4	Pittsburgh
10	Breech, Jim	K	5-6	161	6	California
34	Breeden, Louis	CB	5-11	185	7	North Carolina Central
21	Brooks, James	RB	5-9	177	4	Auburn
79	Browner, Ross	DE	6-3	261	7	Notre Dame
67	Burley, Gary	DE	6-3	282	9	Pittsburgh
50	Cameron, Glenn	LB	6-2	228	10	Florida
11	Christensen, Jeff	QB	6-3	202	2	Eastern Illinois
76	Collins, Glen	DE	6-6	265	3	Mississippi State
80	Collinsworth, Cris	WR	6-5	192	4	Florida
85	#Curtis, Isaac	WR	6-1	192	12	San Diego State
73	Edwards, Eddie	DE	6-5	256	8	Miami
49	Frazier, Guy	LB	6-2	221	4	Wyoming
48	Gibler, Andy	TE	6-4	234	2	Missouri
22	Griffin, James	S	6-2	197	2	Middle Tennessee
44	Griffin, Ray	CB	5-10	186	7	Ohio State
66	Hannula, Jim	T	6-6	264	2	Northern Illinois
83	Harris, M. L.	TE	6-5	238	5	Kansas State
27	#Hicks, Bryan	S	6-0	192	4	Mc Neese
82	Holman, Rodney	TE	6-3	232	3	Tulane
20	Horton, Ray	CB	5-11	190	2	Washington
37	Jackson, Robert	S	5-10	186	3	Central Michigan
26	Kemp, Bobby	S	6-0	191	4	Cal State-Fullerton
28	Kinnebrew, Larry	RB	6-1	252	2	Tennessee State
86	Kreider, Steve	WR	6-3	192	6	Lehigh
69	Krumrie, Tim	NT	6-2	262	2	Wisconsin
47	Maidlow, Steve	LB	6-2	234	2	Michigan State
88	Martin, Mike	WR-KR	5-10	186	2	Illinois
87	McInally, Pat	P	6-6	212	9	Harvard
65	Montoya, Max	G	6-5	275	6	UCLA
60	Moore, Blake	C	6-5	267	5	Wooster
78	Munoz, Anthony	T	6-6	278	5	Southern California
68	Obrovac, Mike	T	6-6	275	4	Bowling Green
51	Razzano, Rick	LB	5-11	227	5	Virginia Tech
64	Rimington, Dave	C	6-3	290	2	Nebraska
15	Schonert, Turk	QB	6-1	190	5	Stanford
59	Schuh, Jeff	LB	6-2	228	4	Minnesota
25	Simmons, John	CB-KR	5-11	192	4	Southern Methodist
56	Simpkins, Ron	LB	6-1	235	4	Michigan
23	Tate, Rodney	RB	5-11	190	3	Texas
35	Turner, Jim	CB	6-0	187	2	UCLA
81	Verser, David	WR	6-1	202	4	Kansas
70	Weaver, Emanuel	NT	6-4	260	2	South Carolina
57	Williams, Reggie	LB	6-0	228	9	Dartmouth
77	Wilson, Mike	T	6-5	271	7	Georgia
32	Wilson, Stanley	RB	5-10	210	2	Oklahoma

#Unsigned at press time

TOP FIVE DRAFT CHOICES

Rd.	Name	Sel. No.	Pos.	Ht.	Wt.	College
1	Hunley, Ricky	7	LB	6-2	230	Arizona
1	Koch, Pete	16	DE	6-5	255	Maryland
1	Blados, Brian	28	T	6-6	295	North Carolina
2	Esiason, Boomer	38	QB	6-4	200	Maryland
3	Jennings, Stanford	65	RB	6-1	205	Furman

and hit somebody, as could Maryland defensive end Pete Koch. But the best move may have been scooping two projected first-rounders—Maryland QB Boomer Esiason on the second and Furman running back Stanford Jennings on the third.

OUTLOOK: The Bengals may roar mightily. They lost six of their first seven while trying to regroup from the suspension of four of their best players because of drug problems. But they rebounded with a 6-3 finish and may be the sleeper not only in the division but in the conference.

BENGAL PROFILES

CRIS COLLINSWORTH 25 6-5 192   Wide Receiver

This may be his Last Hurrah...In his three years in the NFL, Collinsworth has been All-Pro every season, but that could come to an end after this year because of a future contract he signed with the USFL's Tampa Bay Bandits for 1985...His new address was not on his mind last year. He caught 66 passes for a Bengal record of 1,126 yards, which broke the mark of 1,009 he set in his rookie year...He talks faster than most politicians and the press loves it...His long legs combine with the gift of great speed to make him one of the most deceptive deep threats in the NFL...Born Jan. 27, 1959, in Dayton, Ohio...He began his college career as a frewhman quarterback at Florida and threw a 90-yard TD pass. But he could do even more with his feet than his arm...His dad, Abe, played on Kentucky's 1958 national championship basketball team.

ANTHONY MUNOZ 26 6-6 278   Offensive Tackle

He had a down year but it looked like up to everyone else...Coaches who knew say he did not play as well as he had in the past, but he still made his third straight start in the Pro Bowl...Quickest moving monster since Loch Ness...It is that quickness that combined with his size that has made him the game's most intimidating blocker...Munoz was born Aug. 19, 1958, in Ontario, Cal....He missed his senior season at USC because of repeated knee problems. Somehow, however, he came back in time to play in the Rose Bowl and that courage was not lost on the scouts...Despite a medical record that could make a week of story lines for "General Hospital," Munoz was so adept at his job that the Bengals made him the third player selected in the 1980 draft.

KEN ANDERSON 35 6-3 212   Quarterback

Throws footballs through thimbles if asked... Anderson, the most accurate passer in NFL history when he completed 70.6 percent of his passes two years ago, wasn't far off the mark last season... He completed 66.7 percent, delivering 198 of 297 for 2,333 yards... He had only 13 passes intercepted... Perhaps age is showing, however. Last year was only the second time in 12 seasons that he attempted fewer than 300 passes... Born Feb. 15, 1949, in Batavia, Ill., just down the road from his alma mater, Augustana College... It's hard to believe anyone will be more accurate than Anderson was one afternoon in 1974 when he completed 20 of 22 passes against the Pittsburgh Steelers.

JAMES BROOKS 25 5-9 177   Running Back

Came from Chargers in Pete Johnson exchange in May... San Diego coach Don Coryell says little James is "tough as a boot." If you've ever bitten a boot, you know what he means... Size has never held him back. In fact, he has more uses than a Swiss Army knife... Last season Brooks totaled 1,475 combined yards rushing (516), receiving (215) and returning punts and kickoffs (744)... His one problem is a tendency to fumble... Born Dec. 28, 1958, in Warner Robbins, Ga.... He once had to share the football with both William Andrews and Joe Cribbs when all were in the backfield at Auburn... Despite seldom being in the limelight in college, he was the third back chosen in the 1981 college draft.

DAVE RIMINGTON 24 6-3 290   Center

Started slow as a rookie last season... By season's end, however, he was every bit as dominating as he had been while an All-American at Nebraska... He doesn't lift weights. He lifts weight machines... Rimington bench-presses 345 pounds and squats 650. He has lifted with the game's strongest man—Pittsburgh's Mike Webster—and did well enough. "He will be the best for a long time," Webster says of the man many expect will replace him one day on the All-Pro team... Born May 22, 1960, in Omaha, Neb.... Has intelligence as well as power going for him. He adjusted Nebraska's blocking assignments on his own late in a 1981 game with Missouri and that allowed the Cornhuskers to score the game's only touchdown.

REGGIE WILLIAMS 29 6-0 228   Outside Linebacker

The linebacker who keeps on coming... Speed is his game and quarterbacks are his aim... He had 7½ sacks last season and also was second in tackles with 90... An Ivy League man out of Dartmouth who plays like a Penn State linebacker... He was All-Ivy three times before coming to the Bengals in 1976... He holds Cincinnati's single-game record for tackles with 13... Born Sept. 19, 1954, in Flint, Mich.... He was runnerup to Joe Theismann as NFL Man of the Year for his charitable works... He keeps occupied with charcoal drawing and raising Great Danes.

EDDIE EDWARDS 30 6-5 256   Defensive End

He produced more sacks than a grocery-store clerk last year... Edwards led the Bengals with 13, many of which he credited to a new stance that has him charging lower into blockers... He hardly seemed to need any adjustments, however. He has led Cincinnati in sacks the past four years, averaging 10 per season... No one seems to understand why he hasn't yet made All-Pro. Obviously, no one is asking opposing quarterbacks... Born April 25, 1954, in Sumter, S.C.... All-American at Miami... Over half his solo tackles were sacks so his target is obvious.

GLENN CAMERON 31 6-2 228   Inside Linebacker

After a subpar year during the strike season, Cameron came back last fall and made his presence felt... He led the team with 103 tackles after making just 34 the previous year... Has been a 10-year starter since completing his college days at Florida... Born Feb. 21, 1953, in Miami... When not hustling to make a tackle, he's out hustling T-shirts. He runs a T-shirt company in Cincinnati along with former teammate Dave Lapham... He was an All-American and the Bengals' No. 1 pick in 1975.

PAT McINALLY 31 6-6 212   Punter

Put the foot and the knee back into the kicking game with a 43.1-yard average after slipping to 38.7 in 1982 because of constant knee problems... His hit song "Endlessly" could have been written about some of his punts, which seem to hang endlessly... He has been writing songs for three years now, which makes him most musically inclined Bengal since Mike Reid left the game to compose and play the piano... Also writes syndicated column on sports and fitness... Born May 7, 1953, in Villa Park, Cal.... A productive wide receiver at Harvard... Last year was the first since he turned pro in 1975 that he didn't catch a pass.

STEVE KREIDER 26 6-3 192   Wide Receiver

He can't be ignored any longer... His 42 receptions tied Isaac Curtis for second on the club... With Collinsworth possibly jumping to the USFL in 1985, Curtis showing his age at 33 and David Verser more disappointing than ever in his third season, the fleet-footed Kreider seems heir apparent for a starting job... Combines above-average speed with precision pass routes and intelligent reading of defenses... Born May 12, 1958, in Reading, Pa.... He was a Little All-American at Lehigh... Catching footballs is not all he can do. Kreider holds a master's degree in electrical engineering and is vice-president of a building and loan company.

COACH SAM WYCHE:

If he's judged by the company he's kept, Wyche should get the Bengals back to the Super Bowl in a hurry. Has played or coached under George Allen, Bill Walsh, Paul Brown, Jack Pardee, Don Coryell, Paul Dietzel, Raymond Berry and Ted Marchibroda... All he learned should be important as he enters his first season as a pro head coach... Last year Wyche took over Indiana's program from Lee Corso and went 3-8. That rebuilding job obviously had only begun, but when Forrest Gregg left Cincinnati for Green Bay, Wyche headed back to pro ball... He spent four years as Walsh's assistant with the 49ers, where he was credited with developing the skills of Joe Montana... Wyche was a walk-on at Furman in 1962. After graduation he began playing semipro football for the Wheeling, (W.Va.) Ironmen for a season before assisting Dietzel at South Carolina... The playing bug hadn't left him, though, and he was back in pads the next season after finally getting a shot at the NFL. Wyche lasted nine years as a backup quarterback for five teams, including the Bengals... Born Jan. 5, 1945, in Atlanta.

BIGGEST PLAY

There wasn't much mystery left in it at this stage. With 42 seconds to play and the Cincinnati Bengals trailing the Houston

---

INDIVIDUAL BENGAL RECORDS

Rushing

Most Yards Game:	160	Pete Johnson, vs Cleveland, 1978
Season:	1,077	Pete Johnson, 1981
Career:	5,419	Pete Johnson, 1977-83

Passing

Most TD Passes Game:	4	Greg Cook, vs Houston, 1969
	4	Ken Anderson, vs Cleveland, 1976
Season:	29	Ken Anderson, 1981
Career:	184	Ken Anderson, 1971-83

Receiving

Most TD Passes Game:	3	Bob Trumpy, vs Houston, 1969
	3	Isaac Curtis, vs Cleveland, 1973
	3	Isaac Curtis, vs Baltimore, 1979
Season:	10	Isaac Curtis, 1974
Career:	53	Isaac Curtis, 1973-83

Scoring

Most Points Game:	19	Horst Muhlmann, vs Buffalo, 1970
	19	Horst Muhlmann, vs Houston, 1972
Season:	115	Jim Breech, 1981
Most TDs Game:	3	Paul Robinson, vs Miami, 1968
	3	Bob Trumpy, vs Houston, 1969
	3	Doug Dressler, vs Houston, 1972
	3	Isaac Curtis, vs Cleveland, 1973
Season:	16	Pete Johnson, 1981
Career:	53	Isaac Curtis, 1973-83

Oilers, 27-24, there was only one thing to do—throw the ball to Isaac Curtis.

The Bengals had won six of their previous seven games. Now, on Nov. 4, 1976, they were rolling, finally threatening the supremacy of the Pittsburgh Steelers in the AFC's Central Divison.

So even with the Oiler defense geared to stop him, Curtis became the target of a short Ken Anderson pass. But it was short only until Curtis caught it.

One move and an Oiler defender was down. A quick cut back and a second Oiler was left tackling air. Both had been dropped without being touched. Isaac Curtis was alone and soon he was in the end zone with victory in his hands.

"It was the most electrifying run I can remember," says Bengal owner Paul Brown, a man who has seen more runs than most of us. "He took that pass and had no right to do much with it. But he made two cuts and accelerated and the game was over."

CLEVELAND BROWNS

TEAM DIRECTORY: Pres.: Art Modell; VP/Gen. Counsel: James Bailey; Asst. to Pres.: Ernie Accorsi; Dir. Player Relations: Paul Warfield; Dir. Player Personnel: Bill Davis; Dir. Operations: Dennis Lynch; Dir. Pub. Rel.: Kevin Byrne; Head Coach: Sam Rutigliano. Home field: Cleveland Stadium (80,098). Colors: Seal brown, orange and white.

SCOUTING REPORT

OFFENSE: "The apprenticeship is over," coach Sam Rutigliano says. "It's time for Paul McDonald to open his own store."

If this McDonald's is as successful as the original, there could be a golden arch over Municipal Stadium. But if he goes bust, he may take Rutigliano with him.

When Brian Sipe finally jumped to the USFL after last season, McDonald was handed his chance. Although he lacks the powerful arm of Sipe, Rutigliano is hoping McDonald's accuracy will make up for it. Arm strength alone doesn't get you into the playoffs. Sipe had a gun but often turned it on himself.

"In our nine victories, we fumbled three times and had eight interceptions," Rutigliano explains. "Those numbers were almost tripled (7 and 20) in the seven defeats. We're not designed to be a high-risk offense."

Cleveland's other problem was when it got the ball to its receivers they didn't have the speed to make it count. That may change with the addition of Duriel Harris from Miami. "We need speed," Rutigliano says. "Harris might be that player." Harris joins Ricky Feacher, young Henry Holt and sure-handed tight end Ozzie Newsome to form a solid but slow group.

McDonald will spend much of his time handing off to fullback Mike Pruitt. An unusual combination of power and speed, Pruitt pushed his 225 pounds over 1,000 yards for the fourth time in five years. He is perfectly designed for the one-back offense. Pruitt will be aided by the return of Charles White, who missed last season with a broken ankle, and Boyce Green, the unknown rookie who came in and ran for 497 yards. They'll run behind a successful line, if and when it's healthy.

DEFENSE: They can dominate with their linebackers, who are arguably the best four-man unit in football. Chip Banks is an All-Pro's All-Pro on the outside and Clay Matthews isn't far behind. Inside linebacker Tom Cousineau is fast becoming an All-Pro's All-Pro with Dick Ambrose solidly standing beside him.

Another 1,000-yard season for 225-pound Mike Pruitt.

If there is one thing this defense lacks, it's a fearsome pass-rusher. They traded with the Eagles for former All-Pro Carl Hairston and are hoping to make him the designated rusher. But to be honest, he's past his prime and has a gimpy knee. Nose tackle Bob Golic showed great promise in his first year at that position and Reggie Camp may be aided by Hairston's presence. Rutigliano is trying to light a fire under Keith Baldwin, who has all the tools, but can't find a match that works.

The secondary could use more speed, although cornerback Hanford Dixon is for real. Cleveland would like to see Rod Perry return to his All-Pro form but his knees won't let him. Expect Lawrence Johnson or Larry Braziel to end up on that corner.

KICKING GAME: Matt Bahr's 87.5 percent field-goal accuracy (21 of 24) was fourth best in history and he finished hot, hitting 17 of his last 18 and nine straight. Punter Steve Cox missed nine games because of brain surgery, but expects to be back.

BROWNS VETERAN ROSTER

HEAD COACH—Sam Rutigliano. Assistant Coaches—Dave Adolph, Joe Daniels, Jim Garrett, Howard Mudd, John Petercuskie, Tom Pratt, Dave Redding, Joe Scannella, Marty Schottenheimer, Darvin Wallis, Larrye Weaver.

No.	Name	Pos.	Ht.	Wt.	NFL Exp.	College
80	Adams, Willis	WR	6-2	200	5	Houston
52	Ambrose, Dick	LB	6-0	228	10	Virginia
61	Baab, Mike	C	6-4	270	3	Texas
9	Bahr, Matt	K	5-10	175	6	Penn State
99	Baldwin, Keith	DE	6-4	250	3	Texas A&M
56	Banks, Chip	LB	6-4	233	3	Southern California
88	Belk, Rocky	WR	6-0	187	2	Miami
47	Braziel, Larry	CB	6-0	184	6	Southern California
97	Brown, Thomas	DE	6-3	255	4	Baylor
49	Burrell, Clinton	S	6-1	192	5	Louisiana State
96	Camp, Reggie	DE	6-4	264	2	California
59	Carver, Dale	LB	6-2	225	2	Georgia
75	Contz, Bill	T	6-5	260	2	Penn State
50	Cousineau, Tom	LB	6-3	225	3	Ohio State
15	Cox, Steve	P-K	6-4	195	4	Arkansas
38	Davis, Johnny	RB	6-1	235	7	Alabama
64	De Lamielleure, Joe	G	6-3	260	12	Michigan State
54	De Leone, Tom	C	6-2	254	13	Ohio State
73	Dieken, Doug	T	6-5	252	14	Illinois
29	Dixon, Hanford	CB	5-11	182	4	Southern Mississippi
74	Farren, Paul	T	6-5	251	2	Boston University
83	Feacher, Ricky	WR	5-10	180	9	Mississippi Valley
10	Flick, Tom	QB	6-3	190	3	Washington
94	Franks, Elvis	DE	6-4	265	5	Morgan State
79	Golic, Bob	NT	6-2	260	5	Notre Dame
30	Green, Boyce	RB	5-11	215	2	Carson-Newman
31	Gross, Al	S	6-3	186	2	Arizona
78	Hairston, Carl	DE	6-4	260	9	Maryland-Eastern Shore
26	Hall, Dino	RB-KR	5-7	165	6	Glassboro State
84	Harmon, Mike	WR	6-0	208	2	Mississippi
—	Harris, Duriel	WR	5-11	184	9	New Mexico State
81	Holt, Harry	TE	6-4	230	2	Arizona
70	Hopkins, Thomas	T	6-6	260	2	Alabama A&M
68	Jackson, Robert E.	G	6-5	260	10	Duke
51	Johnson, Eddie	LB	6-1	215	4	Louisville
48	Johnson, Lawrence	CB	5-11	204	5	Wisconsin
89	Jones, Bobby	WR	5-11	185	7	No College
86	Manning, Wade	WR	5-11	190	4	Ohio State
57	Matthews, Clay	LB	6-2	230	7	Southern California
16	McDonald, Paul	QB	6-2	185	5	Southern California
82	Newsome, Ozzie	TE	6-2	232	7	Alabama
58	Nicolas, Scott	LB	6-3	226	3	Miami
40	Perry, Rod	CB	5-9	185	10	Colorado
43	Pruitt, Mike	RB	6-0	225	8	Purdue
72	Puzzuoli, Dave	NT	6-3	260	2	Pittsburgh
63	Risien, Cody	T	6-7	270	6	Texas A&M
22	Scott, Clarence	S	6-0	190	14	Kansas State
87	Stracka, Tim	TE	6-3	225	2	Wisconsin
12	Trocano, Rick	QB	6-0	188	4	Pittsburgh
42	Walker, Dwight	RB-KR	5-10	185	3	Nicholas State
55	Weathers, Curtis	LB	6-5	230	6	Mississippi
25	White, Charles	RB	5-10	190	4	Southern California
81	Whitewell, Mike	WR	6-0	175	3	Texas A&M

TOP FIVE DRAFT CHOICES

Rd.	Name	Sel. No.	Pos.	Ht.	Wt.	College
1	Rogers, Don	18	DB	6-1	206	UCLA
2	Rockins, Chris	48	DB	6-0	185	Oklahoma State
2	Davis, Bruce	50	WR	5-8	160	Baylor
4	Bolden, Rickey	96	TE	6-6	250	Southern Methodist
4	Brennan, Brian	104	WR	5-9	176	Boston College

THE ROOKIES: The Browns needed speed at wide receiver and in the secondary and they got it. UCLA defensive back Don Rogers is a first-rounder who should start. Oklahoma State's Chris Rockins, another corner, went next and will be in the hunt. So, too, will Baylor receiver Bruce Davis.

OUTLOOK: McDonald will determine how far Cleveland goes. Its defense will keep it in most games if the offense doesn't repeat its mental errors of a year ago. The Browns were 9-7 and just missed the playoffs. They'll be hard-pressed to do better this year unless Pittsburgh collapses.

BROWN PROFILES

CHIP BANKS 24 6-4 233 — Outside Linebacker

A Chip off no one's block but his own... If he continues to improve, they will have to create a new league for him... For the second straight year Banks was the only Brown to make the Pro Bowl. As a rookie in 1982 he was an all-star backup, but in '83 he moved in as a starter... Has phenomenal speed for a man his size, a fact highlighted by the 10 passes he defended... One of his three interceptions resulted in a 65-yard touchdown... Born Sept. 18, 1959, in Lawton, Okla.... Was an All-American at USC... Climaxed college career with 14 tackles and a 20-yard TD interception against Penn State in Fiesta Bowl... Sister nicknamed him "Chip"—really William.

OZZIE NEWSOME 28 6-2 232 — Tight End

He's the Wizard of Ozzie... Last season Newsome had 89 receptions, which was second in the NFL and the sixth-best performance of all time... Despite his numbers, though, NFL players didn't pick him for the Pro Bowl. "Every team we play had a goal of stopping Ozzie Newsome first," coach Sam Rutigliano said. "He was double-teamed and he caught 89 passes without another great receiver with him. He deserved to go." ... Newsome caught seven or more passes seven times last year... He has caught 50 or more passes in four of the last five seasons... Born March 15, 1956, in Muscle Shoals, Ala.... He was a two-time All-American at Alabama.

TOM COUSINEAU 27 6-3 225   Inside Linebacker

Tom Terrific really was . . . He finally decided to take the advice of his coach. "I told him to just try to play like a Pro Bowler," Rutigliano said. "He can't ever play well enough to earn what he's being paid." . . . Cousineau was the highest-paid defensive player in the game last year when he earned an estimated $500,000 in his second season since coming back to the U.S. from Canada . . . He led Browns in five categories—tackles (138), interceptions (4) and fumble recoveries (2) . . . Born May 6, 1957, in Bloomington, Ind. . . . Refused to play for the Buffalo Bills after ending his career at Ohio State, so he went into football exile in Montreal.

PAUL McDONALD 26 6-2 185   Quarterback

"This whole thing has developed like a novel," McDonald says of his career. "I'm ready and it's time for the next chapter." With Brian Sipe gone to the USFL, McDonald will write that chapter, but will it be "Hard Times" or "Breaking Away"? . . . Rode the pines for four years behind Sipe, although he managed to pick up a few starts the past two seasons . . . Last year he was just 32 for 68 for 341 yards, one TD and four interceptions . . . Such numbers are hardly a ringing endorsement, but his new contract and Sipe's departure are . . . Born Feb. 23, 1958, in Montebello, Cal. . . . He was a quiet winner at USC, but no one took his arm seriously. That's why he wasn't drafted until the fourth round.

CLAY MATTHEWS 28 6-2 230   Outside Linebacker

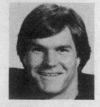

The Masked Man . . . On a team with Banks and Cousineau, this guy goes unnoticed. Especially by the people trying to block him . . . He was second on the team with 106 tackles and led the club with seven sacks . . . He is looked upon for big plays because teams are so often keying on Banks and Cousineau . . . He and younger brother Bruce were both All-Americans at USC . . . Born March 15, 1956, in Palo Alto, Cal. . . . He was rated the fifth-best prospect regardless of position in 1978 when he was the Browns' first draft pick . . . He's had more ankle problems than Ruffian, having been slowed by bone chips as a rookie and a broken ankle in 1982.

MIKE BAAB 24 6-4 270   Center

He's no barbarian but he roots for one. Baab collects Conan the Barbarian comic books...Collection now stands at 300..."I was at the barber shop in high school and the barber gave me one," Baab explains. "I saw this guy with muscles everywhere, chopping people up. I got interested. I never had a hobby before."...Some might say he still doesn't...One thing he does have is a job in Cleveland...He took over for 12-year veteran Tom DeLeone and the Browns felt he played as well as anyone in the AFC...Born Dec. 6, 1959, in Forth Worth, Tex....As a college center at Texas he had 19 "pins" his senior year, a pin being when he blocked his man to the ground.

BOB GOLIC 26 6-2 260   Nose Tackle

Converted from linebacker to the nose, but not by choice. "To play the nose you have to be unemployed or crazy," Golic once said. "I was unemployed. The other part is up in the air."...Browns picked him up in the fall of '82 after the Patriots released him...He was still a linebacker then. A slow one...Although he weighed just 240 at the time, Cleveland converted him to the nose and he survived because of his knowledge of leverage gained while a collegiate wrestler at Notre Dame...Born Oct. 26, 1957, in Cleveland...He was 14-4-1 as a wrestler with all four losses coming in the NCAA tournament...Wrestled teammate Tom Cousineau four times in high school, winning two and tying one.

MIKE PRUITT 30 6-0 225   Running Back

Browns officially went to one-back offense for the first time last season, but Pruitt's been the only man who counted since 1979...Cleveland's leading rusher the past five years...Has surprising speed (4.4 for the 40) for such a bulky man...Gained 1,184 yards, third best in the AFC. That was his fourth 1,000-yard season in the last five years...In just eight seasons as a pro he has become the 22nd player in history to rush for 6,000 yards...Born April 3, 1954, in Chicago...Oddly, he went unrecognized while at Purdue, where he was honorable mention All-Big Ten. Now he's All-World and climbing.

HANFORD DIXON 25 5-11 182   Cornerback

If he could catch something besides a cold, he'd be in the Pro Bowl... "My hands have not been my greatest assets," Dixon admits. "It seemed I was often in the right position but I ended up batting balls away, not catching them."... That explains why he finished the year with only three interceptions, which left him behind one linebacker and tied with another... Relies on speed to close on receivers... He can out run his mistakes, but not his hands... Born Dec. 25, 1958, in Mobile, Ala.... Starred at Southern Mississippi and was the first cornerback drafted in 1981.

Ozzie Newsome was second in NFL receptions in '83.

COACH SAM RUTIGLIANO: He has survived vocal attacks  from fans and the media who have not yet recovered from the Kardiac Kids of 1980 who nearly went to the Super Bowl...But Rutigliano's Browns may be ready to reach the playoffs again soon. "It's time for us to reload, but not rebuild," he says...What he must be careful with is not turning the gun on himself...Maybe the nicest head coach in football, although his patience wore thin with his critics at times last year...An NFL assistant with four teams before the Browns grabbed him in 1977. Two years later he was AFC Coach of the Year, an honor he won again in 1980...Born July 1, 1932, in Brooklyn, N.Y....Only the fifth head coach in Cleveland's history and he'd like to keep it that way a little longer. "Only six of the 27 other NFL teams had a better record than we did," he says...Played at Tennessee under General Bob Neyland and finished at Tulsa...Went from high-school coaching to college and pro assistant roles before being named head man with the Browns in 1978.

BIGGEST PLAY

It was hardly the longest run Jim Brown ever made. Still, when Cleveland Browns' owner Art Modell thinks about the greatest play in his team's history, only this one comes to mind.

"It was the most dramatic thing I've ever seen," Modell says now. "It was important because it helped give us a division championship, but it was memorable because Jim Brown just made up his mind he would not be tackled."

It was Nov. 21, 1965, and a record Cotton Bowl crowd of 76,251 had come to see if the defending world champions could hold a thin, one-game division lead against the Dallas Cowboys.

By late in the game it appeared they could not. The score was tied, 17-17, and the spark was gone until Jim Brown relit it.

With the ball on the Dallas three, Brown took a handoff and ran into three Cowboys. To escape, he circled to the six but was walled in and landed in the arms of linebacker Dave Edwards.

Edwards had Brown trapped, but somehow the powerful fullback spun free. But as he moved he was hit from both sides and began to fall. Brown placed his hand on the ground—back now on the three—and lunged forward, tumbling into the end zone with a game-winning score as four defenders dove on him.

"He was hit by all 11 defenders," Modell recalls. "It should have been a three-yard loss, but we needed a touchdown and Jim knew it so he got it."

INDIVIDUAL BROWN RECORDS

Rushing

Most Yards Game:	237	Jim Brown, vs Los Angeles, 1957
	237	Jim Brown, vs Philadelphia, 1961
Season:	1,863	Jim Brown, 1963
Career:	12,312	Jim Brown, 1957-65

Passing

Most TD Passes Game:	5	Frank Ryan, vs N.Y. Giants, 1964
	5	Bill Nelsen, vs Dallas, 1969
	5	Brian Sipe, vs Pittsburgh, 1979
Season:	30	Brian Sipe, 1980
Career:	154	Brian Sipe, 1974-83

Receiving

Most TD Passes Game:	3	Mac Speedie, vs Chicago, 1951
	3	Darrell Brewster, vs N.Y. Giants, 1953
	3	Ray Renfro, vs Pittsburgh, 1959
	3	Gary Collins, vs Philadelphia, 1963
	3	Reggie Rucker, vs N.Y. Jets, 1976
	3	Larry Poole, vs Pittsburgh, 1977
	3	Calvin Hill, vs Baltimore, 1978
Season:	13	Gary Collins, 1963
Career:	70	Gary Collins, 1962-71

Scoring

Most Points Game:	36	Dub Jones, vs Chicago Bears, 1951
Season:	126	Jim Brown, 1965
Career:	1,349	Lou Groza, 1950-59, 1961-67
Most TDs Game:	6	Dub Jones, vs Chicago Bears, 1951
Season:	21	Jim Brown, 1965
Career:	126	Jim Brown, 1957-65

DENVER BRONCOS

TEAM DIRECTORY: Owner: Patrick D. Bowlen; Dir. Player Personnel: John Beake; Dir. Pub. Rel.: Charles Lee; Dir. Publicity: Jim Saccomano; Head Coach: Dan Reeves. Home field: Mile High Stadium (75,100). Colors: Orange, blue, and white.

SCOUTING REPORT

OFFENSE: If you can get a copy of last season's final AFC passing statistics, save it. It will be the last year you see John Elway's name on the bottom of the list.

Elway seemed lost more often than Mr. Magoo in his rookie

Coach Dan Reeves tells John Elway he's got QB job for keeps.

year, completing just 47.5 percent of his passes, throwing twice as many interceptions as TDs (14 to 7) and being benched in favor of Steve DeBerg after five games. But do not be fooled. He's a player.

He hinted at what is to come this year in the season's final two games when he replaced the injured DeBerg and was 16 of 24 for 284 yards in a win over Cleveland and then led a comeback from a 19-0 fourth-quarter deficit against Baltimore with three TD passes and 345 yards.

He can't often do it alone, but that's what he's facing. His best running back is Sammy Winder, who is a workman but no game-breaker. If Gerald Willhite returns from injuries, there will be explosiveness in the backfield, but no matter how you slice it, this is not a class act.

Steve Watson has become a truly great receiver, having now had two 1,000-yard seasons in the past three years and now the Broncos have added Dave Logan from Cleveland, who will have to make up for the loss of the retired Rick Upchurch. Tight end is a problem. Denver used seven players there last year with Ron Egloff (who?) the starter, but young James Wright may be right there.

Coaches insist it all starts at the line and Denver has a chance to prove it. This is a quality group led by center Bill Bryan. Right now, it's these guys and Elway against the world.

DEFENSE: This was once a feared group and still is, although mostly by coach Dan Reeves, who fears what they may do to his playoff chances.

For 10 years Denver built its defense around seven-time All-Pro Randy Gradishar. Now he's retired and there is a hole the size of the Grand Canyon to fill. To compound the problem, underrated outside linebacker Bob Swenson may take his battered knee to the sidelines permanently. If so, Reeves has a rebuilding job similar to the one Japan faced in 1945.

Denver acquired Stan Blinka from the Jets to help and he'll fight Jim Ryan for Gradishar's job. Neither will erase his memory, however. At least Steve Busick and Tom Jackson are back, although Jackson is not what he once was.

The pass rush dropped off to 38 sacks. Barney Chavous, Rulon Jones and Rubin Carter return, but Carter's age is a question and Jones has broken more hearts than Joan Collins with his lackluster play the past two years. If he plays up to his capability, the rush will be back. If not, it's a bum's rush.

The secondary is the strong point. All-Pro Louie Wright returned to form, strong safety Dennis Smith has more knockouts

BRONCOS VETERAN ROSTER

HEAD COACH—Dan Reeves. Assistant Coaches—Marvin Bass, Joe Collier, Alex Gibbs, Stan Jones, Myrel Moore, Nick Nicolau, Frank Polsfoot, Mike Shanahan, Charlie West.

No.	Name	Pos.	Ht.	Wt.	NFL Exp.	College
74	Baker, Jerry	NT	6-2	297	2	Tulane
86	Barnett, Dean	TE	6-2	225	2	Nevada-Las Vegas
54	Bishop, Keith	C-G	6-3	260	4	Baylor
—	Blinka, Stan	LB	6-2	230	6	Sam Houston State
65	Bowyer, Walt	DE	6-4	245	2	Arizona State
12	Brunner, Scott	QB	6-5	200	5	Delaware
64	Bryan, Bill	C	6-2	258	7	Duke
58	Busick, Steve	LB	6-4	227	4	Southern California
68	Carter, Rubin	NT	6-0	256	10	Miami
79	#Chavous, Barney	DE	6-3	258	12	South Carolina State
59	Comeaux, Darren	LB	6-1	227	3	Arizona State
63	Cooper, Mark	T	6-5	267	2	Miami
55	Dennison, Rick	LB	6-2	215	3	Colorado State
21	Dupree, Myron	CB	5-11	180	2	North Carolina Central
85	Egloff, Ron	TE	6-5	227	8	Wisconsin
7	Elway, John	QB	6-3	202	2	Stanford
43	Foley, Steve	S	6-2	190	8	Tulane
31	Harden, Mike	S	6-1	192	5	Michigan
73	Hollingsworth, Shawn	T	6-2	260	2	Angelo State
60	#Howard, Paul	G	6-3	260	11	Brigham Young
28	#Jackson, Roger	S	6-0	186	3	Bethune-Cookman
57	Jackson, Tom	LB	5-11	220	12	Louisville
75	Jones, Rulon	DE	6-6	260	5	Utah State
3	Karlis, Rich	K	6-0	180	3	Cincinnati
8	Kubiak, Gary	QB	6-0	192	2	Texas A&M
76	Lanier, Ken	T	6-3	269	4	Florida State
—	Logan, Dave	WR	6-4	216	9	Colorado
41	Lytle, Rob	RB-TE	5-11	195	8	Michigan
66	Manor, Brison	DE	6-4	235	8	Arkansas
77	Mecklenburg, Karl	LB	6-3	250	2	Minnesota
29	Myers, Wilbur	S	5-11	195	2	Delta State
39	Myles, Jesse	RB	5-10	210	2	Louisiana State
24	Parros, Rick	RB	5-11	200	4	Utah State
34	Poole, Nathan	RB	5-9	212	5	Louisville
11	Prestridge, Luke	P	6-4	235	6	Baylor
—	Ramson, Eason	TE	6-2	234	6	Washington State
50	Ryan, Jim	LB	6-1	215	6	William & Mary
84	Sampson, Clinton	WR	5-11	183	2	San Diego State
82	Sawyer, John	TE	6-2	230	9	Southern Mississippi
49	Smith, Dennis	S	6-3	200	4	Southern California
78	Stachowski, Rich	DE-NT	6-4	245	2	California
70	Studdard, Dave	T	6-4	260	6	Texas
51	Swenson, Bob	LB	6-3	225	8	California
82	Thomas, Zack	WR	6-0	182	2	South Carolina State
67	Uecker, Keith	T	6-5	260	3	Auburn
81	Watson, Steve	WR	6-4	195	6	Temple
47	Willhite, Gerald	RB	5-10	200	3	San Jose State
45	Wilson, Steve	CB	5-10	195	6	Howard
23	Winder, Sammy	RB	5-11	203	3	Southern Mississippi
52	Woodard, Kenneth	LB	6-1	218	3	Tuskegee
87	Wright, James	TE	6-3	240	5	Texas Christian
20	Wright, Louis	CB	6-2	200	10	San Jose State

#Unsigned at press time

TOP FIVE DRAFT CHOICES

Rd.	Name	Sel. No.	Pos.	Ht.	Wt.	College
2	Townsend, Andre	46	DE	6-4	265	Mississippi
3	Lilly, Tony	78	DB	6-0	195	Florida
4	Robbins, Randy	89	DB	6-2	189	Arizona
6	Smith, Aaron	159	LB	6-2	223	Utah State
7	Kay, Clarence	186	TE	6-3	225	Georgia

than Larry Holmes, and Steve Foley is home free at safety. The only position up for grabs is right corner, where Mike Harden and Steve Wilson do battle again this summer.

KICKING GAME: Rich Karlis hit 21 of 25 field goals and is now 33 of 38 in two years. Punter Luke Prestridge slipped to a net average of 34 yards. Another slip like that and he'll slip out of the NFL. Zack Thomas now handles the returns. He's no Upchurch.

THE ROOKIES: When your first four picks are all defenders, it seems obvious you're worried. Unfortunately, even top pick Andre Townsend of Mississippi is a gamble at defensive tackle. Has shown constant improvement which, if it continues, could make him the draft's steal. Corners Tony Lilly of Florida and Randy Robbins of Arizona will get their chance to play.

OUTLOOK: It's all up to Elway. The Broncos will ride his arm as far as it will take them. A year ago they limped into the playoffs. Elway could throw them in this time . . . but only if the defense finds a way to replace Gradishar.

BRONCO PROFILES

JOHN ELWAY 24 6-3 202   **Quarterback**

He's The Franchise and then some, even though he suffered through a Rocky Mountain low as a rookie last season . . . Learned the hard way that life in the NFL isn't like life in the PAC-10, but his powerful arm and awesome physical tools make it clear his day will come . . . He was benched early in the season in favor of Steve DeBerg after several ineffective performances, but did throw for 1,663 yards . . . His problem was mistaken identity. He threw 14 interceptions . . . Born June 28, 1960, in Northridge, Cal. . . . Passed for nearly 10,000 yards while at Stanford . . . Also signed a one-year contract with the New York Yankees before his senior year of college. After not playing baseball for over a year he went to their Oneonta, N.Y., farm team and batted .318.

LOUIS WRIGHT 31 6-2 200   Cornerback

He's back, although some say he never left... After a subpar season in 1982, Wright led Denver with six interceptions and returned to the Pro Bowl for the fourth time... He also made over 100 tackles... Still one of the best coverage men in the game because he is one of the fastest. Still covers 40 yards in 4.4 seconds... Born Jan. 31, 1953, in Gilmer, Tex.... Denver's No. 1 selection in the 1975 draft after starring in football and track at San Jose State... Was a unanimous All-Pro in 1977, '78 and '79... He has only 17 career interceptions but that's not his fault. No one will throw at him.

STEVE WATSON 27 6-4 195   Wide Receiver

There's no meat on them bones but there's speed in them feet and footballs in them hands... Watson led the Broncos with 59 catches for 1,133 yards, 11th in the AFC, on a team that spent the season juggling quarterbacks... Watson averaged 19.2 yards per catch. Only Miami's Mark Duper had a higher average among AFC players with 25 receptions or more... His gangly body makes his speed deceptive. Defensive backs usually don't figure him out until he's behind them... Signed as a free agent in 1979 after graduating from Temple... Born May 28, 1957, in Baltimore... Led the AFC in reception yardage in 1981 with 1,244 yards. He also led the NFL that year with 13 TDs.

RULON JONES 26 6-6 260   Defensive End

Didn't rule like Rulon had hoped last season... He had just four sacks and may find his starting job in jeopardy if he can't find his way to the quarterback more frequently... Two years ago he was looked upon as the next great Bronco pass-rusher in the mold of Lyle Alzado, but has had only seven sacks the past two years. Denver can't wait much longer for the fire to return in Jones' eye... Still, he had 20 sacks in his first two seasons and a return to that form could transform Denver defense into a major force... Born March 25, 1958, in Salt Lake City... Missed just one game in four years at Utah State.

DENNIS SMITH 25 6-3 200   Strong Safety

Right man for the right position . . . Strong enough to handle any tight end even though he often gives away 30 pounds and is fast enough to run with the quickest of them . . . Began his pro career as a cornerback because of the presence of perennial All-Pro Bill Thompson. But an aging Thompson could not hold Smith off after his 1981 rookie year . . . Smith intercepted four passes in 1983 . . . Born Feb. 3, 1959, in Santa Monica, Cal. . . . Denver made Smith its first pick in 1981 after he had finished a career at USC which took him to two Rose Bowls and the Bluebonnet Bowl. Only bowl left is the Super Bowl . . . He was a 7-foot high-jumper in college.

STEVE FOLEY 30 6-2 190   Free Safety

Comeback Kid . . . Foley shattered his right forearm in a goal-line collision with San Diego's Wes Chandler in the 1982 season-opener and he never came back. So it was questionable how well he might play last season. Well, his five interceptions were second on the team and he didn't miss a game . . . Foley led Denver in interceptions for four years and is third in career interceptions with 33 . . . Twice has been forced to change positions and once changed leagues . . . He was a quarterback at Tulane who didn't have the arm for the NFL. So he signed with Jacksonville of the World Football League and he was switched to defense . . . Was orginally a cornerback before Denver converted him . . . Born Nov. 11, 1953 in New Orleans.

SAMMY WINDER 25 5-11 203   Running Back

A blue-collar running back . . . Winder has no great individual talent, but he is tenacious and powerful and that combination made him the 12th-leading rusher in the AFC with 757 yards . . . Gained his yards the hard way, averaging less than four yards per carry . . . Did have one 52-yard burst, but mostly he piles up yardage by piling into piles . . . Born July 15, 1959, in Madison, Miss. . . . Career rushing leader while at Southern Mississippi . . . Has given Denver sizeable payoff on its fifth-pick of 1982.

TOM JACKSON 33 5-11 220   Outside Linebacker

He's still Action Jackson, although he's not in the middle of as much of it as he once was . . . Loves to talk, both to his opponents and anyone else who will listen . . . Now that Randy Gradishar is retired, Jackson is the spiritual leader of Denver's defense and his penchant for the big play should serve him well there . . . As the years have passed, however, his legs aren't what they used to be. Still, he led the club with 5½ sacks . . . Born April 4, 1951, in Cleveland . . . He once ran 4.5 40s . . . Teams still don't look forward to trying to get around his end . . . He was Missouri Valley Player of the Year while at Louisville.

STAN BLINKA 6-2 230 27   Outside Linebacker

If he hits you, he makes you Blinka . . . His game has always been stepping up to stop the run, which he'll get the chance to do for the Broncos this season . . . But he has large shoes to fill . . . Denver acquired him to replace seven-time All-Pro Randy Gradishar . . . That is a tall order, expecially when you realize Blinka's next trip to the Pro Bowl will be his first . . . Born April 29, 1957, in Columbus, Ohio . . . He was a standup, 205-pound defensive end at Sam Houston State College before they converted him to linebacker . . . He lost his starting job in New York and then became a victim of this past offseason's shakeup in the Jets' hangar.

COACH DAN REEVES: He may have seen his team turn the

corner last year, making the playoffs for the first time in his three-year tenure . . . Reeves now appears to have some things in place. Broncos got a taste of playoff life and believe John Elway will be the next great NFL quarterback . . . Reeves thinks he's in a similar position to the one Chuck Noll was in during his early years in Pittsburgh. Noll had to wait for Terry Bradshaw to mature. Now Reeves is waiting for Elway . . . Reeves is 21-20 since leaving the Dallas Cowboys in 1981, when he became the youngest head coach in the NFL at 37 . . . Brought Tom Landry's multiple offense with him from Dallas, but he had problems force-feeding it to a rookie like Elway . . . Born Jan. 19, 1944, in Americus, Ga. . . . Dallas signed him as a free agent out of South Carolina and converted him from a college quarterback to an NFL running back . . . He became the fifth most productive back in Dallas history by the time he retired in 1972 . . . Had been a player-coach for three years and then a Dallas assistant in '72 and after a one-year retirement he came back to the Cowboys until '79 . . . Was Landry's offensive coordinator in 1977 and '78.

BIGGEST PLAY

Long-time defensive coordinator Joe Collier could still conjure up the feeling.

"It was a play so symbolic of the many mini-miracles we had that year that as Tom was running, we felt we were watching something bigger than all of us," Collier would recall seven years later.

The Denver Broncos and Baltimore Colts were tied with the best record in the AFC, 9-1, and were locking horns on Nov. 27, 1977, with much to settle.

Just 7:40 was left to play and the Broncos were clinging to a one-point lead, 14-13. But Bert Jones had the Colts kicking. They had moved to the Denver 29 when, on third-and-seven, Jones went once too often to his favorite receiver.

Don McCauley would catch 11 passes for 112 yards, but this most important pass would never reach him.

As Jones spiraled the ball into the flat, linebacker Tom Jackson, who had read the play perfectly, came up in full stride, stepped in front of McCauley and intercepted the pass. For 73 yards he ran untouched, scoring the touchdown that broke the game open.

The way things turned out, the Broncos, unbeatable at home all year, finished with the best record in the AFC by that one-game margin and thus kept the home-field advantage right up to the Super Bowl.

INDIVIDUAL BRONCO RECORDS

Rushing

Most Yards Game:	183	Otis Armstrong, vs Houston, 1974
Season:	1,407	Otis Armstrong, 1974
Career:	6,323	Floyd Little, 1967-75

Passing

Most TD Passes Game:	5	Frank Tripucka, vs Buffalo, 1962
Season:	24	Frank Tripucka, 1960
Career:	74	Craig Morton, 1977-82

Receiving

Most TD Passes Game:	3	Lionel Taylor, vs Buffalo, 1960
	3	Bob Scarpitto, vs Buffalo, 1966
	3	Haven Moses, vs Houston, 1973
	3	Steve Watson, vs Baltimore, 1981
Season:	13	Steve Watson, 1981
Career:	44	Lionel Taylor, 1960-66
	44	Haven Moses, 1972-81

Scoring

Most Points Game:	21	Gene Mingo, vs Los Angeles, 1960
Season:	137	Gene Mingo, 1962
Career:	736	Jim Turner, 1971-79
Most TDs Game:	3	Lionel Taylor, vs Buffalo, 1960
	3	Don Stone, vs San Diego, 1962
	3	Bob Scarpitto, vs Buffalo, 1966
	3	Floyd Little, vs Minnesota, 1972
	3	Floyd Little, vs Cincinnati, 1973
	3	Haven Moses, vs Houston, 1973
	3	Otis Armstrong, vs Houston, 1974
	3	Jon Keyworth, vs Kansas City, 1974
	3	Steve Watson, vs Baltimore, 1981
Season:	13	Floyd Little, 1972
	13	Floyd Little, 1973
	13	Steve Watson, 1981
Career:	54	Floyd Little, 1967-75

HOUSTON OILERS

TEAM DIRECTORY: Pres./Owner: K.S. (Bud) Adams Jr.; Exec. VP/GM: Ladd Herzeg; VP/Player Personnel: Mike Holovak; Dir. Adm.: Rick Nichols; Dir. Media Rel.: Bob Hyde: Head Coach: Hugh Campbell. Home field: Astrodome (50,452). Colors: Scarlet, Columbia blue and white.

SCOUTING REPORT

OFFENSE: Earl Campbell isn't all they have going for them these days. There is a Moon over Houston now and his name is Warren and he's a winner.

"I've personally been able to become a winner in other situations so why should I stop now?" Moon says. "I think the Oilers are much better than people give them credit for."

Since no one gives the 2-14 Oilers credit for anything, Moon is probably right. And with him at quarterback he's also right about the Oilers being better.

Moon left Canada for one of the richest contracts in history, but he brings more than a bulging money belt. The only quarterback in history to pass for 5,000 yards, Moon did it twice for the Edmonton Eskimos and it's no coincidence he did it for new Oiler coach Hugh Campbell.

At 6-3, 210, Moon has size, running ability and a big-league arm. He'll have no trouble getting the ball to wide receiver Tim Smith, who has the speed to go deep and the hands to catch 83 passes. To complement Smith there are Butch Johnson, who came from Dallas in the Mike Renfro deal, and Herkie Walls.

Moon should help open the inside for Campbell, who doesn't need much of an opening to produce big yardage. Before last season began there were whispers that Earl was washed up. But after rushing for 1,301 yards and 12 TDs, the whispers stopped and the applause started. He'll keep them clapping now that he says he's happy again.

The line is young and has four potential stars—No. 2 overall draft pick Dan Steinkuhler, Mike Munchak, Bruce Matthews and Harvey Salem. They join David Carter and veteran Doug France to form a phalanx of blockers.

DEFENSE: The Oilers were fourth against the pass, but that's because every team in the league ran over them. They allowed an average of 174.2 yards a game rushing, which is enough real estate to build a condo development on.

Obviously that has to stop and so do opposing runners. But one wonders how they'll do it.

The line features more unknown faces than a spies' convention. Bob Hamm, Brian Sochia and Jesse Baker are the starters, with only Baker secure. The return of Ken Kennard and Mike Stensrud might help, but Stensrud was beaten out by Sochia a year ago.

Unless the line does more than expected, the linebackers will have to stop most everything again. Gregg Bingham and Robert Abraham may be up to the job, but Avon Riley and Robert Brazile are not. Brazile is running out of gas after seven Pro Bowl seasons.

The secondary could be a bright spot with the return of Mike

Earl Campbell, inspired by Warren Moon, should be even better.

OILERS VETERAN ROSTER

HEAD COACH—Hugh Campbell. Assistant Coaches—Bill Allerheiligen, O. Kay Dalton, John Devlin, Gene Gaines, Jerry Glanville, Kenny Houston, Bruce Lemmerman, Bob Padilla, Al Roberts, Bill Walsh.

No.	Name	Pos.	Ht.	Wt.	NFL Exp.	College
56	Abraham, Robert	LB	6-1	215	3	North Carolina State
87	Arnold, Walt	TE	6-3	234	5	New Mexico
80	Bailey, Harold	WR	6-2	196	3	Oklahoma State
75	Baker, Jesse	DE	6-5	272	6	Jacksonville State
54	Bingham, Gregg	LB	6-1	225	12	Purdue
25	Bostic, Keith	S	6-1	212	2	Michigan
52	Brazile, Robert	LB	6-4	237	10	Jackson State
24	Brown, Steve	CB-KR	5-11	188	2	Oregon
81	Bryant, Steve	WR	6-2	191	3	Purdue
34	Campbell, Earl	RB	5-11	238	7	Texas
58	#Carter, David	C	6-2	260	8	Western Kentucky
40	Craft, Donald	RB	6-0	205	3	Louisville
88	Dressel, Chris	TE	6-4	231	2	Stanford
35	Edwards, Stan	RB	6-0	210	3	Michigan
78	Foster, Jerome	DE	6-2	258	2	Ohio State
77	France, Doug	T	6-5	266	9	Ohio State
90	Hamm, Bob	DE	6-4	248	2	Nevada-Reno
36	Hartwig, Carter	S	6-0	207	6	Southern California
21	Hatchett, Derrick	CB	5-11	184	5	Texas
23	Hill, Greg	CB	6-1	189	2	Oklahoma State
84	#Holston, Mike	WR	6-3	188	4	Morgan State
66	Howell, Pat	G	6-6	260	6	Southern California
50	Hunt, Daryl	LB	6-3	235	6	Oklahoma
6	James, John	P	6-3	196	13	Florida
86	Johnson, Butch	WR	6-1	187	9	Cal-Riverside
57	Joiner, Tim	LB	6-4	224	2	Louisiana State
22	Kay, Bill	CB	6-1	190	4	Purdue
4	Kempf, Florian	K	5-9	170	3	Pennsylvania
71	Kennard, Ken	DE	6-2	255	8	Angelo State
10	Luck, Oliver	QB	6-2	193	3	West Virginia
74	Matthews, Bruce	G-T	6-4	269	2	Southern California
89	McCloskey, Mike	TE	6-5	240	2	Penn State
26	Meadows, Darryl	S	6-1	199	2	Toledo
1	*Moon, Warren	QB	6-3	210	1	Washington
30	Moriarty, Larry	RB	6-1	228	2	Notre Dame
63	Munchak, Mike	G	6-3	275	3	Penn State
12	Ransom, Brian	QB	6-2	205	2	Tennessee State
37	Reinfeldt, Mike	S	6-2	192	9	Wisconsin-Milwaukee
53	Riley, Avon	LB	6-3	225	4	UCLA
85	Roaches, Carl	KR-WR	5-8	170	5	Texas A&M
73	Salem, Harvey	T	6-6	264	2	California
62	#Schuhmacher, John	G	6-3	267	4	Southern California
83	Smith, Tim	WR	6-2	203	5	Nebraska
72	Sochia, Brian	MG	6-3	250	2	Northwest Oklahoma
67	Stensrud, Mike	MG	6-5	285	6	Iowa State
68	#Studdard, Les	C	6-4	260	3	Texas
76	#Towns, Morris	T	6-4	263	8	Missouri
1	Thompson, Ted	LB	6-1	219	10	Southern Methodist
20	Tullis, Willie	CB	6-0	193	4	Troy State
86	Walls, Herkie	WR	5-8	154	2	Texas
79	Whitley, Wilson	MG	6-3	265	7	Houston
33	Wilson, J. C.	CB-S	6-0	184	7	Pittsburgh

#Unsigned at press time
*Played in CFL

TOP FIVE DRAFT CHOICES

Rd.	Name	Sel. No.	Pos.	Ht.	Wt.	College
1	Steinkuhler, Dean	2	T	6-3	270	Nebraska
2	Smith, Doug	29	DE	6-6	270	Auburn
2	Eason, Bo	54	DB	6-2	203	Cal-Davis
3	Meads, Johnny	58	LB	6-2	220	Nicholls State
4	Studaway, Mark	85	DE	6-3	237	Tennessee

Reinfeldt at free safety after recovering from a broken ankle. Two interesting battles shape up at strong safety (between Keith Bostic and former starter Carter Hartwig, who moved to free safety) and left corner (between Steve Brown and Derrick Hatchett). The only sure thing is right corner Willie Tullis.

KICKING GAME: Florian Kempf only missed three kicks all year and is now the most accurate kicker in the game. Punter John James should be named Jesse for the way he's robbing the Oilers. They need help here.

THE ROOKIES: The Oilers had the second pick in the draft and used it to shore up their last open offensive line spot for the next decade when they signed Nebraska's Steinkuhler. After that the needs were defensive and they took Auburn tackle Doug Smith and Cal-Davis safety Bo Eason. Scouts say Eason's ready to become a starter.

OUTLOOK: "I've seen the films and see signs the Oilers have turned the corner," Hugh Campbell says. In the past, there has always been a Mack truck around that corner but now there is the brightness of a new Moon so they should be better. When you only win twice, what else can you expect?

OILER PROFILES

WARREN MOON 27 6-3 210   **Quarterback**

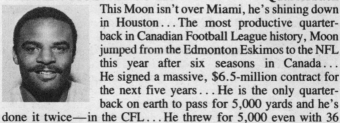

This Moon isn't over Miami, he's shining down in Houston ... The most productive quarterback in Canadian Football League history, Moon jumped from the Edmonton Eskimos to the NFL this year after six seasons in Canada ... He signed a massive, $6.5-million contract for the next five years ... He is the only quarterback on earth to pass for 5,000 yards and he's done it twice—in the CFL ... He threw for 5,000 even with 36 TDs in 1982 and followed last season with 5,648 yards, 32 TDs ... His team won the Grey Cup each of his first five seasons in Edmonton ... A rollout quarterback at U. of Washington who opted for the CFL rather than play a backup's role in the NFL ... Born Nov. 18, 1956, in Los Angeles.

EARL CAMPBELL 29 5-11 238   Running Back

He's the Earl of Football once again . . . Answered those critics who said his body was giving out by rushing for 1,301 yards (just 98 below his career average) on 322 carries. That left him second in the AFC in rushing . . . He has now rushed for over 1,000 yards five times in six years . . . His 1,934 yards in 1981 is the second-highest total in history . . . Houston shopped him around in the offseason, but the asking price was equal to the national budget of most Central American countries. No takers . . . No one is happier about that than new coach Hugh Campbell . . . He won the 1977 Heisman Trophy while at Texas . . . Born March 29, 1955, in Tyler, Tex.

OLIVER LUCK 24 6-2 193   Quarterback

Apparently, he has none. Luck that is . . . After serving a year on injured-reserve list and then backing up Archie Manning for half of last season, Luck was given a break. Manning was traded and Luck stepped ahead of Gifford Nielsen as the starter . . . But now the Oilers have gone for the Moon . . . No denying that Luck played solidly for a poor, poor team, however. He completed 57.1 percent of his passes for 1,375 yards . . . Born April 5, 1960, in Cleveland . . . He was the most prolific passer in West Virginia history until Jeff Hostetler came along . . . Brilliant student, but not just of football . . . Received a B in freshman calculus at West Virginia, which was the only blemish on an otherwise perfect academic record.

MIKE MUNCHAK 24 6-3 275   Guard

His reputation as s destroyer of defenders is beginning to grow as fast as he did . . . Didn't miss a start and some would argue he didn't miss a block, either . . . Found the perfect way to get out of spring mini-camp last year. He got married . . . Munchak anchors a young and improving offensive line that may soon rival any in the NFL despite the club's many other problems . . . Missed well over half of his rookie year because of the strike and an injury in the first game after contract problems were settled . . . In a minor surprise, Houston made him the first lineman taken in 1982, drafting him ahead of Penn State teammate Sean Farrell . . . Born March 5, 1960, in Scranton, Pa.

TIM SMITH 27 6-2 203   Wide Receiver

Who is this guy and where does he think he's going?... Usually, he was going into open territory last season... Smith emerged from the shadows of the unknown by catching 81 passes for 1,176 yards and six touchdowns... This topped his three-year career totals by 79 catches and six touchdowns... On Sept. 25 he caught 11 passes (over five times his career total) against Buffalo... Born March 20, 1957, in Tucson, Ariz.... Led the Big Eight in receptions with 31 in his senior year at Nebraska... His early pro career suffered from his having played college ball in a conference that believes you don't win if you don't run and run and run.

FLORIAN KEMPF 28 5-9 170   Kicker

It may sound like it, but he doesn't work for Lawrence Welk... Extremely accurate inside the 40. In fact, he's as accurate as you can get. He's never missed a kick of less than 40 yards in two years with the Oilers... Kempf was 17-of-20 last season... He never played college football, opting for an All-Ivy career in soccer at Penn... He then played three seasons in the North American Soccer League with the Philadelphia Fury. But when they left for Montreal, Kempf left the game for football... Born May 25, 1956, in Philadelphia... He knows how tenuous his job is. He failed in tryouts with the Eagles, Colts and Patriots and still works in the University of Pennsylvania's admission office in the offseason.

BRUCE MATTHEWS 23 6-4 269   Offensive Tackle

His presence made Earl Campbell smile... He took one game to get the hang of pounding on NFL defenders. After sitting on the bench opening day, the former USC All-American started the final 15 games and his powerful run-blocking proved his value... He still needs work on pass protection, but the Oilers believe he one day will become as dominating as Cincinnati's Anthony Munoz... Born Aug. 8, 1961, in Arcadia, Cal.... Pro football is in his genes. His dad, Clay Sr., played for the San Francisco 49ers and his brother, Clay Jr., was a USC All-American before becoming a starting linebacker with the Cleveland Browns.

KEITH BOSTIC 23 6-1 212   Strong Safety

He has a love affair with contact . . . Despite not starting until the fifth game of the season, Bostic finished third on the Oilers with 91 tackles and third in sacks with three as a crazed blitzer . . . He was a second-round draft choice a year ago after finishing an All-Big-10 career at Michigan . . . He is, however, aggressive to a fault, something the Oilers are trying to correct . . . Born Jan. 17, 1961, in Ann Arbor, Mich. . . . He continued to play on special teams last year even after becoming a starter . . . Bostic was the ninth defensive back and 42nd player overall taken in 1982.

ROBERT BRAZILE 31 6-4 237   Outside Linebacker

Time finally took its toll last season on one of the game's great linebackers. For the first time in eight years Brazile was not a Pro Bowl selection . . . He still can run and still can hit, but that speed is starting to fade . . . Still, he made 90 tackles and continued to make the big plays that kept him an All-Pro even when the Oilers kept hitting dry wells each NFL season . . . Last year Brazile caused three fumbles, recovered three and had two sacks . . . Born Feb. 7, 1953, in Mobile, Ala. . . . He was the top linebacker in college football in 1974, his final year at Jackson State.

ROBERT ABRAHAM 24 6-1 215   Inside Linebacker

They call him Abe, but he's no Lincoln. He didn't set anyone free in his first season as a starter . . . Abraham made 83 solo tackles and had his head in on a total of 117 hits . . . According to the Oilers' conditioning tests, Abraham is the best athlete on the team . . . He won a trip to Tahiti and Bora Bora for himself and his wife by registering the top score in a conditioning test at mini-camp that included a 33-inch vertical leap, a standing broad jump of 10 feet, and 42 dips . . . Beat out Daryl Hunt last season only a year after Hunt led the club in tackles . . . Born July 13, 1960, in Myrtle Beach, S.C. . . . Led North Carolina State in tackles his junior and senior years before the Oilers tapped him.

COACH HUGH CAMPBELL: This man's a mover and Oiler fans are hopeful he's also a shaker...In the past three years, Campbell has coached in the Canadian League, the USFL and now the NFL...He should feel at home, however, now that Houston has signed quarterback Warren Moon. Moon was Campbell's quarterback for five CFL champion seasons in Edmonton...In six years in the CFL, Campbell was 81-22-5, a winning percentage of .773...More important, his playoff record was 11-1, with five Grey Cup championships...If he does for the 1984 Oilers in his first season as their coach what he did for the Eskimos in his last year there, all will be well. He took an Edmonton team that was in last place at midseason and ran off 11 wins and a Grey Cup title...He moved to the Los Angeles Express last season and was not as successful. His team finished 8-10, his first losing team since his Whitworth College squad went 4-5 in 1973...He was one of the finest wide receivers in Washington State history, catching 176 passes for 2,452 yards between 1960-62. He was an All-American and then went to the Saskatchewan Rough Riders in 1963 where he was dubbed "Gluey Hughie" for catching a six-year total of 321 passes...Later was head coach at Whitworth College before taking over at Edmonton...Born May 21, 1941, in San Jose, Cal.

BIGGEST PLAY

They had won the first one, but it is through defending titles that real champions are crowned.

And the defense of the first AFL championship was not going well for the Houston Oilers on Dec. 24, 1961. The sunshine was bright at Balboa Stadium as the Oilers fought desperately to hold off the San Diego Chargers, the same team they had defeated, 24-16, a year earlier in the league's first title game, but San Diego was rolling as the clock ticked down.

Houston led, 10-3, but San Diego quarterback Jack Kemp had the Chargers on the Oiler 37, thanks to a pass interference call. Now the clock was running again and Kemp was dropping back to throw. He looked right, left and then right again.

Finally he felt he had them fooled so he fired. But Houston safety Julian Spence was not fooled. As Kemp watched in shoc'

Spence leaped up and cut the ball off in mid-spiral before it could reach Don Norton's hands.

The game was over. The championship had been preserved.

"A lot of teams win it once, but there is a lot more satisfaction in defending a championship," Oiler owner Bud Adams says 25 years later. "It was the biggest play in our history. I know that."

INDIVIDUAL OILER RECORDS

Rushing

Most Yards Game:	216	Billy Cannon, vs New York, 1961
Season:	1,934	Earl Campbell, 1980
Career:	8,296	Earl Campbell, 1978-83

Passing

Most TD Passes Game:	7	George Blanda, vs New York, 1961
Season:	36	George Blanda, 1961
Career:	165	George Blanda, 1960-66

Receiving

Most TD Passes Game:	3	Bill Groman, vs New York, 1960
	3	Bill Groman, vs New York, 1961
	3	Billy Cannon, vs New York, 1961
	3	Charlie Hennigan, vs San Diego, 1961
	3	Charlie Hennigan, vs Buffalo, 1963
	3	Charles Frazier, vs Denver, 1966 (twice)
	3	Dave Casper, vs Pittsburgh, 1981
Season:	17	Bill Groman, 1961
Career:	51	Charlie Hennigan, 1960-66

Scoring

Most Points Game:	30	Billy Cannon, vs New York, 1961
Season:	115	George Blanda, 1960
Career:	596	George Blanda, 1960-66
Most TDs Game:	5	Billy Cannon, vs New York, 1961
Season:	19	Earl Campbell, 1979
Career:	69	Earl Campbell, 1978-83

INDIANAPOLIS COLTS

TEAM DIRECTORY: Pres./Tres.: Robert Irsay; VP: Harriet Irsay; VP/Gen. Counsel: Michael Chernoff; Dir. Player Personnel: Jack Bushofsky; Dir. Pro Personnel: Bob Terpening; Dir. Pub. Rel.: Walt Gutowski; Head Coach: Frank Kush. Home field: Hoosier Dome (61,000). Colors: Royal blue and white.

SCOUTING REPORT

OFFENSE: The most offensive thing the Colts have done in years was to slink out of Baltimore at midnight last winter and move to Indianapolis' new domed stadium. Still, things are on the upswing under Frank Kush despite that retreat.

Curtis Dickey will rush to the acclaim of Indianapolis fans.

Baltimore improved its record form 0-8-1 to 7-9, the biggest jump in the NFL, with just 14 holdovers left from the team Kush inherited in '81. One reason for that improvement is the building of a line and running game where once none existed.

The Colts finished second in the NFL in rushing with Curtis Dickey's 1,122 yards leading the way. Dickey and Randy McMillan (802 yards) give the Colts as powerful an inside-outside running game as there is in the league, and their running lanes should grow even wider as Chris Hinton, Ray Donaldson and the rest of a young line mature.

But Kush has yet to solve one passing problem that seems unlikely to pass soon—his lack of a quarterback. Mike Pagel is a courageous and competitive fellow, but he's no NFL passer. The Colts, once rulers of the airways with Johnny Unitas, finished last in the league in passing. That may result in the emergence of local hero Mark Herrmann as the new starter. It can't hurt.

DEFENSE: The numbers didn't reflect the growing strength of this group, but the won-lost record did. The Colts allowed nearly 30 fewer yards rushing per game and began to break open games with a defense that causes turnovers with constant pressure.

The line is young and energetic. Nose tackle Leo Wisniewski is strong and getting stronger, defensive end Donnell Thompson appears to be coming into his own, and beware of young Steve Parker, a pass-rusher out of Northwestern who may be something special.

Linebackers are where it's at in Indianapolis with rookie Vernon Maxwell having become an instant "impact" player last year. Blitzing from outside linebacker, he finished with 11 sacks, 17 quarterback pressures and six forced fumbles. He is a force and a game-breaker with the potential to become the AFC's Lawrence Taylor. Now if Kush can light a fire under Johnie Cooks, the Colts will be awesome with reliable Barry Krauss and Greg Bracelin holding down the other spots.

The secondary is nothing special but safety Nesby Glasgow can play.

KICKING GAME: Perhaps the best total game in the NFL with unknown Raul Allegre converting everything he kicked (he was 30-for-35, including 14 of 17 between 40 and 55 yards) and punter Rohn Stark leading the NFL with a 45.3-yard average. You can't ask for more than that.

THE ROOKIES: Kush went for additional defensive help and got it with Vanderbilt defensive back Leonard Coleman and

COLTS VETERAN ROSTER

HEAD COACH—Frank Kush. Assistant Coaches—Zeke Bratkowski, George Catavolos, Gunther Cunningham, Hal Hunter, Richard Mann, Roger Theder, Rick Venturi, Mike Westhoff.

No.	Name	Pos.	Ht.	Wt.	NFL Exp.	College
74	Abramowitz, Sid	T	6-6	279	2	Tulsa
2	Allegre, Raul	K	5-9	165	2	Texas
26	Anderson, Kim	CB	5-11	185	5	Arizona State
30	Anderson, Larry	S	6-1	192	7	Louisiana Tech
72	Baldischwiler, Karl	T	6-5	265	7	Oklahoma
97	Ballard, Quinton	NT	6-3	276	3	Elon
81	Beach, Pat	TE	6-4	240	3	Washington State
90	Bell, Mark E.	DE	6-5	235	5	Colorado State
85	Bouza, Matt	WR	6-3	211	3	California
52	Bracelin, Greg	LB	6-2	215	5	California
45	Burroughs, Jim	CB	6-1	198	5	Michigan State
80	Butler, Raymond	WR	6-3	197	5	Southern California
98	Cooks, Johnie	LB	6-4	234	5	Mississippi State
33	Dickey, Curtis	RB	6-1	214	5	Texas A&M
53	Donaldson Ray	C	6-3	269	5	Georgia
50	Feasel, Grant	C	6-8	278	2	Abilene Christian
25	Glasgow, Nesby	S	5-10	184	6	Washington
69	Griffin, Wade	T	6-5	231	6	Mississippi
88	Henry, Bernard	WR	6-1	180	3	Arizona State
9	Herrmann, Mark	QB	6-4	190	4	Purdue
75	Hinton, Chris	T	6-4	280	2	Northwestern
51	Jones, Ricky	LB	6-2	222	8	Tuskegee
29	#Kafentzis, Mark	S	5-10	185	3	Hawaii
55	Krauss, Barry	LB	6-3	247	6	Alabama
56	Maxwell, Vernon	LB	6-2	219	2	Arizona State
32	McMillan, Randy	RB	6-1	222	4	Pittsburgh
76	Mills, Jim	T	6-9	271	2	Hawaii
23	Moore, Alvin	RB	5-11	190	2	Arizona State
84	Oatis, Victor	WR	6-0	179	2	N.W. Louisiana
49	Odom, Clifton	LB	6-2	233	4	Texas-Arlington
60	Padjen, Gary	LB	6-2	241	3	Arizona State
18	Pagel, Mike	QB	6-2	201	3	Arizona State
78	Parker, Steve	DE	6-4	235	2	Eastern Illinois
20	Porter, Ricky	RB	5-11	195	2	Slippery Rock
87	Porter, Tracy	WR	6-2	195	4	Louisiana State
21	Randle, Tate	CB	6-0	198	3	Texas Tech
8	Reed, Mark	QB	6-3	203	3	Moorehead (Minn.)
83	Sherwin, Tim	TE	6-6	245	4	Boston College
79	Sinnott, John	T	6-4	275	3	Brown
54	#Shiver, Sanders	LB	6-2	236	9	Carson-Newman
86	Smith, Phil	WR	6-3	188	2	San Diego State
3	Stark, Rohn	P	6-3	199	3	Florida State
12	Taylor, Jim Bob	QB	6-2	200	2	Georgia Tech
89	Thompson, Aundra	WR	6-0	186	8	East Texas State
99	Thompson, Donnell	DE	6-4	263	4	North Carolina
64	Utt, Ben	T	6-5	267	3	Georgia Tech
71	Waechter, Henry	DE	6-6	260	3	Nebraska
44	Williams, Kendall	CB	5-9	190	2	Arizona State
39	Williams, Newton	RB	5-10	204	3	Arizona State
69	Wisniewski, Leo	NT	6-1	264	3	Penn State
73	Wright, Steve	G-T	6-6	250	4	Northern Iowa
49	Young, Dave	TE	6-5	240	3	Purdue

#Unsigned at press time

TOP FIVE DRAFT CHOICES

Rd.	Name	Sel. No.	Pos.	Ht.	Wt.	College
1	Coleman, Leonard	8	DB	6-2	208	Vanderbilt
1	Solt, Ron	19	G	6-3	265	Maryland
2	Winter, Blaise	35	DT	6-3	260	Syracuse
3	Scott, Chris	66	DT	6-4	245	Purdue
4	Curry, Craig	93	DB	6-0	187	Texas

defensive tackles Blaise Winter of Syracuse and Chris Scott of Purdue. Maryland guard Ron Solt is "solidly built and tough," according to scouts. Maybe tough enough to earn a starting job.

OUTLOOK: They're on their way back. Kush has this team believing in itself and it has others believing in it. Depth is still a problem so injuries could retard the progress, but if the Colts stay healthy, their defense will make them a spoiler.

COLT PROFILES

CHRIS HINTON 23 6-4 280   Offensive Tackle

His place in NFL history is secure regardless of what he does with the rest of his career... "Thanks to John Elway I'll be a trivia question for ever," Hinton says... He came to the Colts in the trade that sent Elway to the Denver Broncos after Elway refused to play in Baltimore... Thus Hinton will always be the lineman whose asking price was a quarterback who was the first player taken in an NFL draft... Baltimore got the last laugh. Elway spent much of the year on the bench in confusion while Hinton blocked his way to the Pro Bowl... A powerhouse, Hinton held up the left side of the offense... Fourth player drafted in 1983... Weighed 218 when he entered Northwestern. Four years later he had gained 60 pounds and become an All-American... Born July 31, 1961, in Chicago.

ROHN STARK 25 6-3 199   Punter

He kicks 'em high and deep... So deep he led the NFL with an average boot of 45.3 yards... A year earlier, as a rookie, he finished second with 44.4 average, so he's no flash in the foot... Hang time on his punts is 5.1 seconds, which means you don't run many of them back too far too often... Seven of his kicks went over 60 yards... Has never had a punt blocked... Was the highest-drafted punter since Russell Erxleben went No. 1 in 1979... He is right-handed but left-footed... Born May 4, 1959, in Minneapolis... Coached high jumpers at Florida State, where he was an All-American in both football and track.

CURTIS DICKEY 27 6-1 214   **Running Back**

Fourth time was the charm . . . It finally all came together for him last season after three years of being hit more often than Tex Cobb . . . Dickey rushed for 1,122 yards, his first 1,000-yard season, as the young Colts' line finally gave him something other than headaches . . . Showed what his 4.26 speed over 40 yards can do if given room to run . . . Also caught 26 passes for 483 yards, an 18.6-yard average . . . Born Nov. 27, 1956, in Madisonville, Tex. . . . All-time leading ground-gainer at Texas A&M, where he ran for 3,703 yards . . . His speed and power are what made him a top pick in 1980 . . . He was talked out of jumping to the USFL by Frank Kush and team owner Robert Irsay's checkbook.

VERNON MAXWELL 22 6-2 219   **Outside Linebacker**

A very nasty fellow . . . Led team in sacks with 11 . . . He's a big-play guy who caused six fumbles, including one in overtime against New England that was returned for the winning TD . . . Had 17 quarterback pressures, which was second on the club . . . Figured in 92 tackles, including 68 solo shots, also a team best . . . Another Arizona State product . . . Was the first player drafted on the second round in '82 . . . Explosive tackler who is often just too strong for blocking backs to handle on the blitz . . . Born Oct. 25, 1961, in Birmingham, Ala. . . . Occasionally his undisciplined style got him in trouble, but more often it put his opponents there.

RAY DONALDSON 26 6-3 269   **Center**

One of the best centers in the NFL, but he's playing an anonymous position on an anonymous team, which doesn't make for much recognition . . . Also has the misfortune of playing in a conference—the AFC East—with four of the best centers in the game . . . Arrived from the University of Georgia in 1980 as one of only two black centers in the league. The other is Miami's Dwight Stephenson . . . He's started three of his four years as a pro . . . Nimble of foot and mind . . . Until Chris Hinton arrived, Donaldson was the only lineman in Baltimore who shouldn't have been arrested for impersonating a blocker . . . Born May 18, 1958, in Rome, Ga. . . . Is only beginning to earn what he deserves, but recognition will be on the way as the team improves.

MIKE PAGEL 23 6-2 201 Quarterback

Appears to be in for a fight this summer . . . His statistics fell off markedly from a year ago despite Colts' improvement . . . Some felt team prospered despite its quarterback . . . Threw for just 2,353 yards and had 17 passes intercepted against 12 TDs thrown . . . Such ratios usually produce unemployment checks, not Super Bowl checks . . . Lost starting job to Mark Herrmann for a short time and with the move to Indianapolis, Herrmann will be the hometown hero . . . Pagel completed less than 50 percent of his throws and Kush didn't like it . . . Born Sept. 13, 1960, in Douglass, Ariz. . . . Was taken on the fourth round out of Arizona State, a surprise move after Colts drafted Ohio State's All-American quarterback Art Schlichter first. But Pagel beat him out in their rookie year. The question now is can he hold on?

JOHNIE COOKS 25 6-4 234 Inside Linebacker

He was in the doghouse more times than Snoopy last year . . . Does he still have the fires burning inside after a two-year battle with coach Frank Kush over where he should play—and how? . . . He showed what he does best when he scooped up Tony Collins' fumble in overtime and sprinted for a 52-yard TD to beat the Patriots on Opening Day last year . . . Clearly a game-breaker, he has exceptional size, speed, agility and hostility . . . But Johnie, don't be so hostile toward your coach . . . Made 67 tackles while being benched twice and shifted from the outside to the inside . . . Born Nov. 23, 1958, in Leland, Miss. . . . An All-American at Mississippi State . . . Cooks prefers playing inside over outside linebacker. Kush likes his speed outside. Therein lies the problem. If they solve it, the Colts have a star. If they don't, the Colts have trouble.

DONNELL THOMPSON 25 6-4 263 Defensive End

Continuing to mature into a steady and dangerous pass-rusher . . . Career started slower than dripping water and people were beginning to wonder if he'd ever live up to his billing. But last year Thompson had four sacks and 15 quarterback pressures so it seems he's just a step away from greatness . . . If he can start on the road to the quarterback a bit sooner, he'll become a legend in a hurry... No. 1 draft choice four years ago from North Carolina... Born Oct. 27, 1958, in Lumberton, N.C.... Has started all but one of the game's he's played in.

LEO WISNIEWSKI 24 6-1 264   Nose Tackle

A nose tackle with a nose for the ball... Usually the nose man merely tries to hold his ground, take up space and survive an onslaught of blockers, but Wisniewski finished second on the Colts with 95 tackles and led the club with 18 quarterback pressures, unheard-of numbers from his position... He was the Pennsylvania state high-school heavyweight wrestling champion, which was good preparation for his present line of work... Born Nov. 6, 1959, in Hancock, Mich.... Co-captain of the 1981 Penn State team... May be on his way to becoming the best lineman on a fast-improving unit.

RAUL ALLEGRE 25 5-9 165   Kicker

Raul All-Leg-re... He made 30 of 35 field goals, including 14 of 17 from 40 yards or longer and four of five from beyond 50... Scored 112 points, more than double the next Colt... He made his first nine kicks, including four from 45 yards or more... Had four against Denver (the only miss was a 64-yarder) and five against the Eagles... Started kicking at University of Montana after moving from native Mexico, to Shelton, Wash. ... Transferred to Texas to study civil engineering after two years. He made the Longhorn team as a walk-on... Acquired before the season began in a trade with Dallas. The rest is history... Born June 15, 1959, in Torreon, Mexico.

COACH FRANK KUSH: You'll never mistake him for Mr. Nice

Guy... If you look up the word tough in the dictionary, Frank Kush's picture is next to it... Is rapidly turning the Colts into a contender by weeding out anyone he feels hasn't given 100 percent on every down... Latest victim was cornerback Derrick Hatchett, a former No. 1 draft choice... After an 0-8-1 season in his first year in Baltimore two seasons ago the

Colts were a surprising 7-9 last year. That record might have been even better but they faded at the end, losing five of their last six games after injuries began to take their toll on a young team without depth... "My coaching philosophy is, a disciplined approach which emphasizes conditioning and the fundamentals of the game, in addition to mental preparation," Kush says. "But above all else, everyone must be motivated toward the same objective —success."... He found his motivation in the coal fields around Windber, Pa., where he was born on Jan. 20, 1929, as one of 15 children... Kush was an All-American defensive guard at Michigan State at 175 pounds... Had a 175-54-1 record in 22 years as the head coach at Arizona State before being forced out after one of his players accused him of hitting him on the sidelines. Kush was acquitted, but left Arizona for the Hamiliton Tiger Cats of the CFL, where his team was 11-4-1.

BIGGEST PLAY

The breath was coming hard and heavy for Alan Ameche as he bent over in the Baltimore Colts' huddle and listened to quarterback John Unitas call his number.

It had turned cold and dark on Dec. 28, 1958, at Yankee Stadium. The shadows had grown long, for the hour was late and the NFL championship game was into overtime for the first time in history. The score was 17-17.

Now the Colts had driven 79 yards in 12 plays and the ball sat serenely on the Giants' one-yard line. A Steve Myrha field goal seemed a certainty, but Baltimore chose to go for a sudden-death victory by putting the ball into the massive hands of Alan Ameche, thereby risking a fumble and eternal damnation in Baltimore.

But Ameche wasn't thinking about fumbles. He had gained just 30 yards at that moment, but this last three feet of Yankee Stadium real estate, if covered, would turn this day around.

He took the handoff and headed to his right, his shoulders low and his head bowed. As he hit the line a huge hole suddenly opened and he drove forward, falling into the end zone before Jimmy Patton could stop him. Colts 23, Giants 17.

The Colts were the champions of the world and the game still called "the greatest one ever played" was over.

INDIVIDUAL COLT RECORDS

Rushing

Most Yards Game:	198	Norm Bulaich, vs N.Y. Jets, 1971
Season:	1,200	Lydell Mitchell, 1976
Career:	5,487	Lydell Mitchell, 1972-77

Passing

Most TD Passes Game:	5	Gary Cuozzo, vs Minnesota, 1965
Season:	32	John Unitas, 1959
Career:	287	John Unitas, 1956-72

Receiving

Most TD Passes Game:	3	Jim Mutscheller, vs Green Bay, 1957
	3	Raymond Berry, vs Dallas, 1960
	3	Raymond Berry, vs Green Bay, 1960
	3	Jimmy Orr, vs Washington, 1962
	3	Jimmy Orr, vs Los Angeles, 1964
	3	Roger Carr, vs Cincinnati, 1976
Season:	14	Raymond Berry, 1959
Career:	68	Raymond Berry, 1955-67

Scoring

Most Points Game:	24	Lenny Moore, vs Chicago, 1958
	24	Lenny Moore, vs Los Angeles, 1960
	24	Lenny Moore, vs Minnesota, 1961
	24	Lydell Mitchell, vs Buffalo, 1975
Season:	120	Lenny Moore, 1964
Career:	678	Lenny Moore, 1956-67
Most TDs Game:	4	Lenny Moore, vs Chicago, 1958
	4	Lenny Moore, vs Los Angeles, 1960
	4	Lenny Moore, vs Minnesota, 1961
	4	Lydell Mitchell, vs Buffalo, 1975
Season:	20	Lenny Moore, 1964
Career:	113	Lenny Moore, 1956-67

KANSAS CITY CHIEFS

TEAM DIRECTORY: Owner: Lamar Hunt; Pres.: Jack Steadman; VP/GM: Jim Schaaf; Dir. Administration: Don Steadman; Dir. Player Personnel: Les Miller; Dir. Pub. Rel.: Bob Sprenger; Head Coach: John Mackovic. Home field: Arrowhead Stadium (78,094). Colors: Red and gold.

SCOUTING REPORT

OFFENSE: They kept the ball in the air more than most volleyball teams and nothing has changed except, believe it or not, perhaps the quarterback.

Bill Kenney is coming off a season in which he passed for 4,348 yards but the word is coach John Mackovic believes Todd Blackledge has a better arm and a better chance of putting the Chiefs in the end zone. This situation bears watching because Kenney can throw it long, short and in between. If Blackledge is better, it's bombs away.

With all that airing out of the football, it's no surprise a new star was born in receiver Carlos Carson. Carson was second in the NFL with 1,351 yards on 80 receptions. He is a legitimate threat to give defensive backs acid indigestion. So, too, is veteran Henry Marshall, who caught 50 passes and finally got the chance to exhibit his skills after too many years as a decoy.

Despite their passing success, however, Mackovic knows he cannot continue to throw 85 percent of the time and win. Then again, he also knows he has no running game. The Chiefs proved that by finishing last in the NFL. Theotis Brown is no breakaway threat and Billy Jackson (499 yards) is giving all he's got. Kansas City thought it had solved the problem by signing Ken Lacy, the No. 3 rusher in the USFL in its first season when he ran for 1,180 yards, but his contract won't expire until Nov. 30. That sums up the Chiefs' running success.

The line is young and sound and could produce rushing yardage as well as protect the quarterback if Mackovic could find a runner to put behind them who didn't stay there.

DEFENSE: If they can ever get defensive ends Art Still and Mike Bell together somewhere besides the trainer's room, this could be a formidable defense.

Bell finally survived a full year and led the club in sacks, but Still had a series of nagging injuries, lost too much weight and ran into constant double-teaming. The result was a noticeable slip in his performance. Look out if they ever come together, though.

Carlos Carson was second in NFL in pass-receiving yardage.

The linebackers are all mobile and some are even hostile. Jerry Blanton is fast emerging as someone to reckon with. Gary Spani and Thomas Howard are capable and young Calvin Daniels may step ahead of Charles Jackson at outside linebacker.

The secondary lost an All-Pro safety in Gary Barbaro but added one when his replacement, Deron Cherry, intercepted seven passes and belted anyone who moved. Cherry joined perennial All-Pro cornerback Gary Green (now gone to L.A. Rams) in the Pro Bowl.

KICKING GAME: Nick Lowery (24 for 30) is one of the most consistent kickers in the game. Jim Arnold's net 32.6 yards per punt, however, makes him suspect. J.T. Smith and Anthony Hancock handle the returns, which is better than not handling them.

CHIEFS VETERAN ROSTER

HEAD COACH—John Mackovic. Assistant Coaches—Bud Carson, Walt Corey, Dan Daniel, Doug Graber, J. D. Helm, C. T. Hewgley, Rod Humenuik, Pete McCulley, Willie Peete, Jim Vechiarella, Richard Williamson.

No.	Name	Pos.	Ht.	Wt.	NFL Exp.	College
6	Arnold, Jim	P	6-2	212	2	Vanderbilt
77	Baldinger, Rich	T	6-4	280	2	Wake Forest
85	Beckman, Ed	TE	6-4	239	8	Florida State
99	Bell, Mike	DE	6-4	260	5	Colorado State
14	Blackledge, Todd	QB	6-3	225	2	Penn State
57	Blanton, Jerry	LB	6-1	236	6	Kentucky
27	Brown, Theotis	RB	6-3	225	6	UCLA
66	Budde, Brad	G	6-4	260	5	Southern California
34	Burruss, Lloyd	S	6-0	202	4	Maryland
88	Carson, Carlos	WR	5-11	174	5	Louisiana State
20	Cherry, Deron	S	5-11	190	4	Rutgers
65	Condon, Tom	G	6-3	275	11	Boston College
50	Daniels, Calvin	LB	6-3	236	3	North Carolina
75	Gardner, Ellis	T-G	6-4	263	2	Georgia Tech
82	Hancock, Anthony	WR-KR	6-0	187	3	Tennessee
56	Haynes, Louis	LB	6-0	227	3	North Texas State
60	Herkenhoff, Matt	T	6-4	272	9	Minnesota
52	#Howard, Thomas	LB	6-2	215	8	Texas Tech
43	Jackson, Billy	RB	5-10	215	4	Alabama
51	Jackson, Charles	LB	6-3	222	7	Washington
22	Jakes, Van	CB	5-11	185	2	Kent State
9	Kenney, Bill	QB	6-4	211	6	Northern Colorado
64	Kirchner, Mark	T-G	6-3	261	2	Baylor
55	Klug, Dave	LB	6-4	230	3	Concordia (Minn.)
91	Kremer, Ken	NT	6-4	252	6	Ball State
29	Lewis, Albert	CB	6-2	190	2	Grambling
71	Lindstrom, Dave	DE	6-6	255	7	Boston University
62	Lingner, Adam	C-G	6-4	240	2	Illinois
8	Lowery, Nick	K	6-4	189	5	Dartmouth
72	Lutz, Dave	T	6-5	280	2	Georgia Tech
74	Mangiero, Dino	NT	6-2	264	5	Rutgers
89	Marshall, Henry	WR	6-2	220	9	Missouri
48	McAlister, Ken	LB	6-5	220	3	San Francisco
83	Paige, Stephone	WR	6-1	180	2	Fresno State
58	Potter, Steve	LB	6-3	235	4	Virginia
79	Prater, Dean	DE	6-5	245	2	Oklahoma State
42	Ricks, Lawrence	RB	5-9	194	2	Michigan
38	Roquemore, Durwood	S	6-1	180	3	Texas A&I
70	Rourke, Jim	T-G	6-5	263	5	Boston College
53	Rush, Bob	C	6-5	264	7	Memphis State
81	Scott, Willie	TE	6-4	245	4	South Carolina
86	Smith, J. T.	WR-KR	6-2	185	7	North Texas State
23	Smith, Lucious	CB	5-10	190	5	Cal State-Fullerton
59	Spani, Gary	LB	6-2	228	7	Kansas State
67	Still, Art	DE	6-7	252	7	Kentucky
31	Thomas, Jewerl	RB	5-10	228	5	San Jose State
35	Thomas, Ken	RB	5-9	211	2	San Jose State
54	Walker, James	LB	6-1	250	2	Kansas State
87	Wetzel, Ron	TE	6-5	242	2	Arizona State
92	Yakavonis, Ray	NT	6-5	250	4	East Stroudsburg State
61	#Zamberlin, John	LB	6-2	226	6	Pacific Lutheran

#Unsigned at press time

TOP FIVE DRAFT CHOICES

Rd.	Name	Sel. No.	Pos.	Ht.	Wt.	College
1	Maas, Bill	5	DT	6-2	265	Pittsburgh
1	Alt, John	21	T	6-7	275	Iowa
2	Radecic, Scott	34	LB	6-3	237	Penn State
3	Heard, Herman	61	RB	6-0	184	Southern Colorado
4	Robinson, Mark	90	DB	5-11	206	Penn State

OUTLOOK: They are in the toughest division in football and they're still trying to survive with only half a gun. You can't pass to victory if you can't run to the line of scrimmage and the Chiefs run only for their life. The defense will keep them in most games and the pass offense will win some. But until they can run the ball, they won't be much better than 8-8.

THE ROOKIES: Chiefs have been looking for a nose guard and top choice Bill Maas of Pittsburgh should be it. Tough and strong, he has a good inside pass rush and was seldom handled one on one. Iowa tackle Jon Alt is a great athlete (a tight end until his junior year) who can already pass-block, a must in this offense.

CHIEF PROFILES

BILL KENNEY 29 6-4 211   Quarterback

It's safe to say Kenney took to new coach John Mackovic's passing fancies...Kenney took it to 4,348 yards passing, in fact, best in the AFC...Only two players—Dan Fouts (three times) and Lynn Dickey—ever passed for more yardage in a single season...Despite attempting more passes (603) than anyone but Fouts (who threw 609 in 1981) Kenney completed 57.4 percent of his throws...Kenney is a pure passer who is as mobile as the Rockies...Born Jan. 20, 1955, in San Francisco...Only his second season as a starter after backing up Steve Fuller for most of his first two years...He didn't become a full-time quarterback until his senior year at Colorado...He was a two-time loser, having been cut by both Miami and Washington before the Chiefs gave him a home.

CARLOS CARSON 25 5-11 174   Wide Receiver

It took an injury to get him in the lineup and he's been making people hurt ever since...Carson replaced J.T. Smith with six games to play in 1982 and he never looked back...If he had last season (looked back, that is) all he would have seen was some defender hopelessly chasing him...Carson finished fifth in the NFL with 80 receptions and led the AFC with 1,351 yards gained, an average of just under 17 yards per catch...Born Dec. 28, 1958, in Lake Worth, Fla....First got his reputation as a deep threat while at LSU, where he once caught six straight touchdown passes.

GARY SPANI 28 6-2 228   Inside Linebacker

He's like sonar. Once he zeros in, he always gets his man...Spani was involved in 90 tackles last season, dropping to fourth on the team. That was his lowest finish ever, but some of that came from opposing teams deciding to test teammate Jerry Blanton...Spani has averaged nearly 10 tackles per game throughout his six-year pro career...After becoming the only consensus All-American ever to play at Kansas State, Spani stepped into the Chiefs' lineup in 1978 as a rookie starter and has remained unmovable...Born Jan. 9, 1956, in Satanta, Kan.

DERON CHERRY 25 5-11 190   Free Safety

Chiefs originally signed Cherry as a punter in 1981. So much for scouting...Cherry stepped in and replaced All-Pro Gary Barbaro last season after Barbaro jumped to the USFL. Barbaro was soon forgotten after Cherry intercepted seven passes and made his own trip to the Pro Bowl...His is a rags-to-riches story. Released in 1981 after failing as a punter, Cherry was re-signed after injuries depleted Kansas City's defense. A year later he was the Chiefs' nickel back and now he's worth a million...Born Sept. 12, 1959, in Palmyra, N.J....Majored in biology at Rutgers and now hopes to become a dentist...Punishing tackler.

ART STILL 28 6-7 252   Defensive End

He seldom is—still, that is...Double- and triple-teamed more often than Dr. J but he still manages to find his way to the ball...Sack production, however, was down. He had just three last season and he must do more if the Chiefs are ever to be a winner...Missed the Pro Bowl for the first time in four years, which the Chiefs are hoping will shake him up...If it does, he'll be shaking up some quarterbacks...Born Dec. 5, 1955, in Camden, N.J....The Chiefs built their defense around

KANSAS CITY CHIEFS   223

him after drafting him first in 1978 after he finished an All-America senior season at Kentucky.

MIKE BELL 27 6-4 260   Defensive End

For once he didn't get his bell rung all season, which has the Chiefs breathing easier... Bell spent part of three of his first four seasons in the NFL on the injured-reserve list, but he came through the past two seasons with a clean bill of health... His fitness showed in his stats. He had 10 sacks, more than double anyone else on the team... Bell and Art Still had played to-gether in just 30 of their first 57 games as teammates before last season because of Bell's frequent trips to the hospital... Born Aug. 30, 1957, in Wichita, Kan.... Twin brother Mark was a defensive end with Seattle.

JERRY BLANTON 27 6-1 236   Inside Linebacker

He makes running backs blanch... Another free agent who made good... Blanton came to Kan-sas City in 1979 after failing a tryout with Buf-falo... He played briefly for Hamilton in the CFL before the Chiefs gave him a chance ... Blanton backed up Whitney Paul as an out-side linebacker before switching inside in 1980 and earning a starting job near the end of that season... Led Chiefs with 136 tackles last season... Born Dec. 20, 1956, in Toledo, Ohio... Blanton was a teammate of Art Still at Kentucky.

NICK LOWERY 28 6-4 189   Kicker

He may not have the reputation, but he's been the most productive kicker in the NFL since 1980... Converted 80 percent of his kicks last year (24 of 30) for 116 points. That left him second in AFC scoring to Pittsburgh's Gary Anderson... He has kicked 89 field goals over the past four years with a success ratio of 76 percent... His 58-yard boot against Washing-ton broke his old club record... For some reason he has not been to the Pro Bowl in three years, which is just about the time he started kicking like a Pro Bowler... Born May 27, 1956, in Mu-nich, Germany, where his father was in the Foreign Ser-vice... Dartmouth grad... He didn't miss a kick last year under 42 yards.

HENRY MARSHALL 30 6-2 220   Wide Receiver

He's the Marshall that counts in Kansas City these days... Marshall flourished under the Chiefs' new wide-open passing game, catching a career-high 50 passes for 788 yards... That was good enough to rank him in the AFC's top 20 receivers for the first time... Has been a starter since his rookie season nine years ago, but has played most of his career on a team that believed a pass was something you made at a waitress... Born Aug. 9, 1954, in Broxton, Ga.... The fact that he ranks fourth all-time among Chief receivers gives you an idea of what he's had to face before coach John Mackovic arrived. And the story was the same at Missouri, where he played on a wishbone team... The way Marshall figures it, he has a lot of catching and catching up to do.

COACH JOHN MACKOVIC: Figures they wouldn't put air in the ball if it wasn't meant to be thrown... Mackovic took a moribund Chiefs' offense and turned it into an aerial circus in his first season as head coach... His first team nearly doubled Kansas City's all-time passing record of 2,929 yards by throwing for 4,684... When he took the job a year ago he said, "Success is a journey, not a destination." Apparently he's

flying on this trip... Mackovic was the Dallas Cowboys' quarterback coach in 1981-82 before personally taking Bill Kenney under his wing last season. He then took Kenney's wing and showed him how to use it to pass for 4,348 of those yards... Yet even with all that yardage, the new Chiefs were only 6-10, which means Mac needs to come up with a new gimmick if he wants to hold his job... Born Oct. 1, 1943, in Barberton, Ohio... Got his first taste of passing as a quarterback at Wake Forest in 1962-64. Fourteen years later he returned to his alma mater and revived a dead football program... The Demon Deacons were in need of an exorcist after winning just 13 games the previous six years. Mackovic was it, going from 1-10 to 8-3 with a Tangerine Bowl in two years. That was Wake Forest's first bowl appearance since 1949.

BIGGEST PLAY

At last it was a game.

The heavily favored Minnesota Vikings had just scored their first touchdown of Super Bowl IV with 4:32 to play in the third quarter to cut the Kansas City Chiefs' lead to 16-7 and at last it seemed the long dormant Vikings were ready to explode in New Orleans.

It was Jan. 11, 1970, the final day of the American Football League's existence. The AFL had won its battle, forcing the NFL

Nick Lowery's 58-yarder against Redskins set a club mark.

to merge the following season. But even after the peace treaty was signed the rivalry lived on.

Thus the final game between the best teams in those leagues was for far more than a championship. It was for pride and the Chiefs' Otis Taylor knew all about pride.

More important, he also knew the Vikings' confidence was growing as the Chiefs regained possession. He wanted that stopped. So with a shake of his hips he stopped it.

There was 1:22 left in the quarter when Taylor ran a short hitch pattern and quarterback Len Dawson hit him with a perfect throw. As Taylor caught it, Viking defender Earsell Mackbee slammed into him. But the ever-elusive Taylor had braced himself and as Mackbee hit him, Taylor rolled those hips and was gone.

Forty-six yards later Taylor was in the end zone alone and the Chiefs were on their way to a 23-7 victory and a spot alone atop the world of professional football.

INDIVIDUAL CHIEF RECORDS

Rushing

Most Yards Game:	193	Joe Delaney, vs Houston, 1981
Season:	1,121	Joe Delaney, 1981
Career:	4,451	Ed Podolak, 1969-77

Passing

Most TD Passes Game:	6	Len Dawson, vs Denver, 1964
Season:	30	Len Dawson, 1964
Career:	237	Len Dawson, 1962-75

Receiving

Most TD Passes Game:	4	Frank Jackson, vs San Diego, 1964
Season:	12	Chris Burford, 1962
Career:	57	Otis Taylor, 1965-75

Scoring

Most Points Game:	30	Abner Haynes, vs Oakland, 1961
Season:	129	Jan Stenerud, 1968
Career:	1,231	Jan Stenerud, 1967-79
Most TDs Game:	5	Abner Haynes, vs Oakland, 1961
Season:	19	Abner Haynes, 1962
Career:	60	Otis Taylor, 1965-75

LOS ANGELES RAIDERS

TEAM DIRECTORY: Managing Gen. Partner: Al Davis; Exec. Asst.: Al LoCasale; Senior Administrators: Irv Kaze and Tom Grimes; Bus. Mgr.: Ken LaRue; Dir. Marketing/Promotions: Mike Ornstein; Head Coach: Tom Flores. Home field: Los Angeles Memorial Coliseum (92,600). Colors: Silver and black.

SCOUTING REPORT

OFFENSE: The Raiders have always believed in attacking their opponents and they have more weapons at their disposal than the Russian Army. Quarterback Jim Plunkett may be 37 but as he

QB Jim Plunkett helped make it happen in the Super Bowl.

showed in the playoffs, he can still throw when his bones don't ache. If they do, Marc Wilson is ready as he proved when he unseated Plunkett at midseason until he separated his shoulder.

The passing game will again try to stretch defenses to the breaking point with the long ball, but that does not mean they haven't made their concessions to time and change. That change began when Plunkett returned to the lineup. Turnovers from constant gambling on the deep pass had led him to the bench. Shorter, softer throws led him to the Super Bowl. You guess which he'll choose this year.

Of course, Cliff Branch, Malcolm Barnwell and Dokie Williams all can take it deep and will get the chance, but when the heat is on, Plunkett will look for tight end Todd Christensen. If you look closely you'll see their wide receivers tighter in the slots and running short motion more often, too.

Los Angeles also has made great use of the pass-catching of running back Marcus Allen (68 receptions). Once the Raiders only threw deep, which required their line to hold its blocks for inordinate periods of time. But Plunkett began dumping the ball more to Allen to avoid sacks and turnovers and had success with it.

Perhaps the most unbelievable thing about this offense is that its line may be better this year. Shelby Jordan, a marvelous passblocker, and young Don Mosebar are both ready to step in and start, which would put Charley Hannah, Bruce Davis and/or Mickey Marvin on the bench. All would start for most teams and Allen would happily run wild behind any of them.

DEFENSE: Attack. Attack. Attack.

That is the Raider way and it made them the fourth-best statistical defense in the game last year. They crush the run at the line of scrimmage and then smother the pass with a rush that produced 57 sacks and suffocating man-to-man coverage.

Defensive end Howie Long became an All-Pro in his third year and will stay there for some time. He combines speed, power and an attitude problem that is a problem for blockers. Rushmate Lyle Alzado decided not to retire and is tough as a cactus and nose tackle Reggie Kinlaw may be the most underrated lineman in the game. Add to this threesome young pass-rushers Bill Pickel and Greg Townsend and you have collisions waiting for a place to happen.

Linebacking is a strong point. Matt Millen and Bob Nelson jam the middle and no one runs around Rod Martin's end. The one weak spot may be where Ted Hendricks has long stood. Injuries and age (36) are taking a toll. But Jack Squirek (Joe Theismann still remembers him) may step in here.

RAIDERS VETERAN ROSTER

HEAD COACH—Tom Flores. Assistant Coaches—Sam Boghosian, Willie Brown, Chet Franklin, Larry Kennan, Earl Leggett, Bob Mischak, Steve Ortmayer, Art Shell, Charlie Sumner, Tom Walsh, Ray Willsey.

No.	Name	Pos.	Ht.	Wt.	NFL Exp.	College
32	Allen, Marcus	RB	6-2	210	3	Southern California
77	Alzado, Lyle	DE	6-3	260	14	Yankton
10	Bahr, Chris	K	5-10	175	9	Penn State
56	Barnes, Jeff	LB	6-2	230	8	California
80	Barnwell, Malcolm	WR	5-11	185	4	Virginia Union
40	#Berns, Rick	RB	6-2	215	5	Nebraska
21	Branch, Cliff	WR	5-11	170	13	Colorado
54	Byrd, Darryl	LB	6-1	220	2	Illinois
57	Caldwell, Tony	LB	6-1	225	2	Washington
46	Christensen, Todd	TE	6-3	230	6	Brigham Young
50	Dalby, Dave	C	6-3	250	13	UCLA
79	Davis, Bruce	T	6-6	280	6	UCLA
45	Davis, James	CB	6-0	195	3	Southern University
36	Davis, Mike	S	6-3	205	7	Colorado
8	Guy, Ray	P	6-3	190	12	Southern Mississippi
73	Hannah, Charley	G	6-5	260	8	Alabama
87	Hasselbeck, Don	TE	6-7	245	8	Colorado
37	Hawkins, Frank	RB	5-9	200	4	Nevada-Reno
37	Hayes, Lester	CB	6-0	200	8	Texas A&M
22	Haynes, Mike	CB	6-2	202	9	Arizona State
83	Hendricks, Ted	LB	6-7	240	16	Miami
48	Hill, Kenny	S	6-0	195	4	Yale
11	#Humm, David	QB	6-2	190	10	Nebraska
31	Jensen, Derrick	TE-RB	6-1	220	6	Texas-Arlington
64	Jordan, Shelby	T	6-7	285	9	Washington (Mo.)
33	King, Kenny	RB	5-11	205	6	Oklahoma
62	Kinlaw, Reggie	DT	6-2	245	5	Oklahoma
70	Lawrence, Henry	T	6-4	270	11	Florida A&M
75	Long, Howie	DE	6-5	270	4	Villanova
60	Marsh, Curt	G	6-5	270	3	Washington
53	Martin, Rod	LB	6-2	220	8	Southern California
63	Marvin, Mickey	G	6-4	265	8	Tennessee
26	McElroy, Vann	S	6-2	190	3	Baylor
23	McKinney, Odis	S	6-2	190	7	Colorado
55	Millen, Matt	LB	6-2	255	4	Penn State
28	Montgomery, Cleotha	WR	5-8	180	4	Abilene Christian
72	Mosebar, Don	T	6-6	270	2	Southern California
82	Muhammad, Calvin	WR	5-11	190	3	Texas Southern
76	Muransky, Ed	T	6-7	275	3	Michigan
51	Nelson, Bob	LB	6-4	235	8	Nebraska
25	Phillips, Irvin	CB	6-1	190	3	Arkansas Tech
71	Pickel, Bill	DE	6-5	260	2	Rutgers
16	Plunkett, Jim	QB	6-2	215	14	Stanford
34	Pruitt, Greg	RB	5-10	190	12	Oklahoma
68	Robinson, Johnny	DT-DE	6-2	255	4	Louisiana Tech
52	Romano, Jim	C	6-3	255	3	Penn State
58	Squirek, Jack	LB	6-4	225	3	Illinois
66	Sylvester, Steve	C-G	6-4	260	10	Notre Dame
93	Townsend, Greg	DE	6-3	240	2	Texas Christian
20	Watts, Ted	CB	6-0	195	4	Texas Tech
85	Williams, Dokie	WR	5-11	180	2	UCLA
38	Willis, Chester	RB	5-11	195	4	Auburn
6	Wilson, Marc	QB	6-6	205	5	Brigham Young

#Unsigned at press time

TOP FIVE DRAFT CHOICES

Rd.	Name	Sel. No.	Pos.	Ht.	Wt.	College
2	Jones, Sean	51	DE	6-7	270	Northeastern
3	McCall, Joe	84	RB	6-1	190	Pittsburgh
5	Parker, Andy	127	TE	6-5	226	Utah
6	Toran, Stacey	168	DB	6-3	206	Notre Dame
7	Willis, Mitch	183	DE	6-8	280	Southern Methodist

The secondary is simply the best in the game. Mike Haynes and Lester Hayes are masters of disaster at the corners, free safety Vann McElroy was an All-Pro in his second year and Mike Davis is steady at strong safety.

KICKING GAME: Ray Guy recovered from a sore knee so well that he averaged 42.8 yards a punt and kicker Chris Bahr was Mr Consistent. Returner Greg Pruitt made the Pro Bowl for the first time in six years so there's no problem here, either.

THE ROOKIES: As usual, the Raiders had no first-round choice but they still got a steal on the second round in Northeastern's 6-7 pass-rusher Sean Jones. He could become the next Howie Long. After that, it's tough to project many of their picks making this championship team.

OUTLOOK: Who is going to beat these guys without the use of nuclear weapons? The only question is how did they lose four games a year ago? They're the best team in football, plain and simple.

RAIDER PROFILES

JIM PLUNKETT 36 6-2 215   Quarterback

He has been resurrected more times than Lazarus . . . For the second time in four years Plunkett lost his job early in the year only to come back later and lead the Raiders to a Super Bowl win . . . Benched late in the season's seventh game in favor of Marc Wilson, Plunkett sat for three weeks until Wilson dislocated his shoulder. Plunkett went the next 3½ games without an interception and Los Angeles won nine of its last 10, including Super Bowl XVIII, with Jim at the controls . . . Born Dec. 5, 1947 in San Francisco . . . Switched from defensive end to quarterback as a freshman at Stanford and four years later owned the Heisman Trophy . . . Last season he threw for 2,935 yards and 20 touchdowns while completing 60.7 percent of his throws . . . High point personally was his 99-yard touchdown pass to Cliff Branch in a 37-35 loss to Washington.

MARC WILSON 27 6-6 205   Quarterback

Still in the wings, but he has proven his wing is ready to take flight... The problem is Jim Plunkett remains ahead of him... Wilson replaced Plunkett with 4:32 to play in last season's seventh game with the Raiders trailing, 38-22. Wilson closed the gap to 38-36 before time ran out... He remained the starter for the first time since 1981 for the next three games, but a dislocated shoulder put him out for the year... Finished 67 for 117 for 864 yards and eight TDs... His biggest day came in a 40-38 win over Dallas in which he passed for 318 yards and three touchdowns... Born Feb. 15, 1957, in Bremerton, Wash.... Majored in economics at Brigham Young and he can use what he learned now that he's signed a new contract that will bring him $1 million a year.

TODD CHRISTENSEN 28 6-3 230   Tight End

Finally got his chance to shine and he blinded defenders with his brilliance... Caught a record 92 passes for 1,247 yards and 12 touchdowns... His reception total led the NFL and broke Kellen Winslow's mark for a tight end... He is only the fifth Raider in their history to gain over 1000 yards receiving... Born Aug. 3, 1956, in Bellefont, Wash.... Keeps busy in dull moments by long-snapping for punts... Played with Marc Wilson at BYU before being drafted by Dallas in 1978... Washed out with the Cowboys and the New York Giants, both of whom saw him as a running back as well as a tight end. Dallas coach Tom Landry is still checking his computer for blown circuits for missing out on Christensen.

MARCUS ALLEN 24 6-2 210   Running Back

Told the Raiders he wanted the ball more late in the season and then he showed them why... Allen rushed for 121 yards against Pittsburgh, 154 against Seattle and 191 against Washington in the Super Bowl for a three-game playoff total of 466 yards rushing... Averaged 9.5 yards per carry in the Super Bowl and cruised to a 74-yard touchdown run in which he ran left, reversed his field and threaded his way through the entire Redskin defense... So why not give him the ball? The Raiders thought they did. He gained 1,014 yards rushing on 266 carrie and added 68 receptions (best among AFC running backs) fo another 500 yards... He has now won the Heisman Trophy, Rooki of the Year and Super Bowl MVP over the past three sea sons... Born March 26, 1960, in San Diego... Set NCAA recor at USC by rushing for 2,342 yards in 1981.

HOWIE LONG 24 6-5 270   Defensive En

So good his school retired football when h left... At least that's what he'd like you t believe was the reason Villanova dropped foot ball when he graduated... In just three year as a pro, Long has become what St. Louis Car dinal coach Jim Hanifan calls "the best pas rusher in the league."... His 13 sacks wer fifth best in the AFC and good enough to mak him All-Pro for the first time. It won't be the last... Althoug his strength is already legendary, it is his agility and speed tha sets him apart from most linemen... Born Jan. 6, 1960, in So merville, Mass.... Had five sacks in regular-season game agains Washington.

LESTER HAYES 29 6-0 200   Cornerbac

The Molester now has a chance to strik again... Ever since he intercepted 13 passes i 1980, Hayes has seen less combat than a pol itician's son. But with Mike Haynes now o the other corner, teams will be forced to loo his way at least occasionally... That shoul keep the four-time Pro Bowl starter happy. I also should let him pile up more than the tw interceptions he made a year ago... Born Jan. 22, 1955, in Hous ton... Played both linebacker and strong safety at Texas A&M before the Raiders converted him to cornerback.

ROD MARTIN 30 6-2 220   Outside Linebacke

Shaking his hand is like wrestling with a vis grip... It was the strength of those hands tha first got him drafted on the 12th round as a 200 pound linebacker out of USC... He was cut b the Raiders that season and also was picked u and released by the 49ers. But late in that 197 season the Raiders re-signed him... A year late Martin was starting and has been ever sinc

... Somehow remained almost unrecognized even after setting a Super Bowl record with three interceptions against the Eagles in 1980 ... But last year the world finally decided he could play. Martin was named Defensive Player of the Year and All-Pro for the first time ... Born April 7, 1954 in Welch, W.Va. ... He's missed just one game in the past seven years.

MIKE HAYNES 31 6-2 202   Cornerback

Held out and came out the big winner ... After sitting out seven weeks in a contract dispute with New England, Haynes finally was traded to the Raiders for two No. 1 draft picks. The Patriots got the choices, but Haynes got a choice world championship ring ... Played in five games, starting the last three, plus all three playoff victories ... Although he missed a trip to the Pro Bowl for only the second time in eight years, Haynes remains the game's finest cornerback ... He showed that early in Super Bowl XVIII when Joe Theismann threw three straight passes at Haynes and saw all three batted down ... Born July 1, 1953, in Denison, Tex. ... Two-time All-American at Arizona State.

VANN McELROY 24 6-2 190   Free Safety

This Preacher's son believes in punishment, at least when opposing receivers commit the sin of running through his territory ... Plays like Evel Knievel drove—in search of a pileup ... Took over as a starter at Jack Tatum's old position last year and played well enough to end up in Tatum's old position on the Pro Bowl team ... Led the AFC with eight interceptions, a position he should be used to after leading the nation in that category in 1980 as a junior at Baylor ... Born Jan. 13, 1960, in Birmingham, Ala. ... Second on the team in tackles, which is unusual for a defensive back, even one who plays like a linebacker.

MATT MILLEN 26 6-2 255   Inside Linebacker

Doesn't like contact. He favors collisions ... A powerful tackler who controls the middle of the Raider defense by holding his ground ... Showed what he does best in AFC championship game against Seattle when he repeatedly stepped into the holes designed for former Penn State teammate Curt Warner, the AFC's leading rusher ... Finished the day with six tackles, a closer relationship with Warner and a ticket to the Super Bowl ...Born March 12, 1958, in Hokendauqua, Pa....Believes in home remedies. Once had a calcium deposit that was keeping his arm bent at a 90-degree angle. He tried to straighten his arm in a vise. It must have worked.

COACH TOM FLORES: Seems to have the hang of this coaching thing...Has won two Super Bowls in five years as the Raiders' coach and his team is now 8-1 in playoff competition...He was Coach of the Year in 1982 when his team was 8-1 in the strike-shortened season...Called the "Ice Man" as a player because he seldom showed emotion. Now he's the "Ice Coach"...Rumor is he will smile if Raiders win another Super Bowl ...Flores has a 47-26 record, a .644 winning percentage, since taking over for John Madden in 1979...Born March 21, 1937, in Fresno, Cal....The son of Mexican farm workers, Flores was in the fields each summer until his play on other fields won him a scholarship to the College of the Pacific...Played one year in Canada and then in the AFL and NFL (after the merger)...Owns four Super Bowl rings, one as a backup quarterback with Kansas City in 1970, one as a Raider assistant in 1977 and the last two for his wins in 1981 and 1984.

BIGGEST PLAY

There were hands everywhere, but neither Ken Stabler nor Clarence Davis noticed them. Neither could afford that luxury.

It was fourth down on the Miami Dolphin eight with but 24 seconds left to play on the afternoon of Dec. 21, 1974. The then Oakland Raiders had one play left to overcome a 26-21 Dolphin lead or they would be knocked out of the AFC playoffs. The next play was obvious.

Stabler dropped back to pass and quickly felt pressure from Miami defensive end Vern Den Herder. He began to scramble while at the same time keeping his eyes riveted downfield.

Just as he was running out of time, Stabler spotted Davis drifting inside the end zone with an army of Dolphin defenders closing in on him.

Stabler cocked his arm to throw and was slammed from behind by Den Herder, but somehow he got the ball away.

The only problem was there was a defender falling into Davis from the front and another grabbing at him from behind. Davis saw none of this. He saw nothing but a football getting bigger and bigger as it somehow floated untouched through that sea of hands and dropped softly into his arms for an eight-yard touchdown and a 28-26 victory that would keep the Dolphins out of the Super Bowl for the first time in four years.

INDIVIDUAL RAIDER RECORDS

Rushing

Most Yards Game:	200	Clem Daniels, vs N.Y. Jets, 1963
Season:	1,273	Mark van Eeghen, 1977
Career:	5,907	Mark van Eeghen, 1974-81

Passing

Most TD Passes Game:	6	Tom Flores, vs Houston, 1963
	6	Daryle Lamonica, vs Buffalo, 1969
Season:	34	Daryle Lamonica, 1969
Career:	150	Ken Stabler, 1970-79

Receiving

Most TD Passes Game:	4	Art Powell, vs Houston, 1963
Season:	16	Art Powell, 1963
Career:	76	Fred Biletnikoff, 1965-78

Scoring

Most Points Game:	24	Art Powell, vs Houston, 1963
Season:	117	George Blanda, 1968
Career:	863	George Blanda, 1967-75
Most TDs Game:	4	Art Powell, vs Houston, 1963
Season:	16	Art Powell, 1975
	16	Pete Banaszak, 1975
Career:	77	Fred Biletnikoff, 1965-78

MIAMI DOLPHINS

TEAM DIRECTORY: Pres.: Joseph Robbie; Head Coach: Don Shula; Dir. Pro Scouting: Charley Winner; Dir. Player Personnel: Chuck Connor; Dir. Publicity: Chip Namias. Home field: Orange Bowl (75,206). Colors: Aqua and orange.

SCOUTING REPORT

OFFENSE: Only Don Shula could take a rookie quarterback and turn him into the AFC's leading passer. Dan Marino never spent a down wearing the confused look John Elway became known for and Shula is the reason why. Marino did the simple things well enough to pass for 2,210 yards and 20 TDs after taking over in the sixth game. With a gun for an arm, if his future were any brighter he'd be blinding.

The emergence of fleet wide receiver Mark Duper coincided

Joe Marino showed up everybody who passed him in the draft.

with Marino's rise. No accident there. The deep pass is back in Miami. Duper averaged 19.7 yards per catch and gained 1,003 yards on 51 receptions. If Jimmy Cefalo can come back from knee surgery, Miami's passing game will be as hot as its summer weather.

There is no Larry Csonka in the backfield, but Andra Franklin runs low, hard and often. Tony Nathan supplies outside speed and Shula is hopeful the David Overstreet he lured from Canada will eventually be the one who starred at Oklahoma and not the one who sleepwalked around Miami last year.

As always, the line is sound and smart. One change may emerge here, however. Third-year pro Roy Foster will be given every opportunity to beat out aging Pro Bowler Bob Kuechenberg at guard. Otherwise, Ed Newman, Dwight Stephenson, Eric Laakso and Jon Geisler remain unmoved and unmoveable.

DEFENSE: There is a new defensive coordinator but nothing much will change. The Killer Bees sting you when it counts. Even though they gave up too much yardage on the ground, they led the NFL in fewest points allowed.

Defensive end Doug Betters set the NFL on its ear with 16 sacks and took some of the heat off All-Pro nose tackle Bob Baumhower. Rumor has it Kim Bokamper may be hard-pressed to hold up the other end against the assault of young Mike 9006les because Shula believes Charles is stronger against the run and thus of more use to a defense whose only weakness was exposed in the playoffs by Seattle running back Curt Warner.

The linebacking could use a little shoring up with A.J. Duhe coming off both knee and shoulder surgery, but Charles Bowser now has a year under his belt as Larry Gordon's replacement, which should help group production. And Miami's top draftee, Jackie Shipp, is an important addition.

The secondary should benefit from the return of cornerback Don McNeal, who missed all of '83 with a ruptured Achilles. Otherwise, the Blackwoods—Glenn and Lyle—are safe at the safeties and Gerald Small is anything but on the other corner.

KICKING GAME: Reggie Roby's punts have to be retrieved by the space shuttle. Uwe von Schamann does what he can, which is seldom a miss inside 40 yards. Tom Vigorito's return from injuries will add spark to the return team and Fulton Walker is already a four-alarm fire under a kickoff. He averaged 26.7 yards a return last year.

THE ROOKIES: Miami went for need by drafting linebackers Shipp of Oklahoma and Jay Brophy of Miami on the first two

DOLPHINS VETERAN ROSTER

HEAD COACH—Don Shula. Assistant Coaches—Tom Keane, Bob Matheson, John Sandusky, Mike Scarry, David Shula, Chuck Studley, Carl Taseff, Junior Wade.

No.	Name	Pos.	Ht.	Wt.	NFL Exp.	College
70	Barnett, Bill	DE	6-4	250	5	Nebraska
73	Baumhower, Bob	DT	6-5	265	8	Alabama
34	#Bennett, Woody	RB	6-2	222	7	Miami
78	Benson, Charles	DE	6-3	267	2	Baylor
75	Betters, Doug	DE	6-7	260	7	Nevada-Reno
47	Blackwood, Glenn	S	6-0	188	6	Texas
42	Blackwood, Lyle	S	6-1	195	12	Texas Christian
58	Bokamper, Kim	DE	6-6	250	8	San Jose State
56	Bowser, Charles	LB	6-3	232	3	Duke
51	Brown, Mark	LB	6-2	218	2	Purdue
59	Brudzinski, Bob	LB	6-4	229	8	Ohio State
81	Cefalo, Jimmy	WR	5-11	188	6	Penn State
71	Charles, Mike	DT	6-4	283	2	Syracuse
76	#Clark, Steve	DT	6-4	255	3	Utah
83	Clayton, Mark	WR	5-9	172	2	Louisville
77	Duhe, A. J.	LB	6-4	240	8	Louisiana State
85	Duper, Mark	WR	5-9	193	3	N.W. State (Louisiana)
61	Foster, Roy	G-T	6-4	272	3	Southern California
37	Franklin, Andra	RB	5-10	228	4	Nebraska
79	#Giesler, Jon	T	6-5	260	6	Michigan
74	Green, Cleveland	T	6-3	262	6	Southern
84	Hardy, Bruce	TE	6-4	232	7	Arizona
88	Heflin, Vince	WR	6-2	185	3	Central State (Ohio)
53	Hester, Ron	LB	6-1	226	2	Florida State
31	Hill, Eddie	RB	6-2	206	6	Memphis State
11	Jensen, Jim	WR	6-4	215	4	Boston University
87	Johnson, Dan	TE	6-3	240	3	Iowa State
49	Judson, William	CB	6-1	187	3	South Carolina State
40	Kozlowski, Mike	S	6-0	198	5	Colorado
67	Kuechenberg, Bob	G	6-2	255	15	Notre Dame
68	#Laakso, Eric	T	6-4	265	7	Tulane
44	Lankford, Paul	CB	6-1	182	3	Penn State
13	Marino, Dan	QB	6-3	214	2	Pittsburgh
28	McNeal, Don	CB	5-11	192	4	Alabama
89	Moore, Nat	WR	5-9	188	11	Florida
22	Nathan, Tony	RB	6-0	206	6	Alabama
64	Newman, Ed	G	6-2	255	12	Duke
20	Overstreet, David	RB	5-11	208	2	Oklahoma
55	Rhone, Earnest	LB	6-2	224	9	Henderson State
4	Roby, Reggie	P	6-2	243	2	Iowa
80	Rose, Joe	TE	6-3	230	5	California
—	#Shull, Steve	LB	6-1	224	4	William & Mary
48	Small, Gerald	CB	5-11	192	7	San Jose State
45	Sowell, Robert	CB-S	5-11	175	2	Howard
57	Stephenson, Dwight	C	6-2	255	5	Alabama
10	Strock, Don	QB	6-5	220	11	Virginia Tech
52	Tautolo, Terry	LB	6-2	227	8	UCLA
54	Thomas, Rodell	LB	6-1	225	2	Alabama State
52	Tilley, Emmett	LB	5-11	240	2	Duke
60	Toews, Jeff	G	6-3	255	6	Washington
32	Vigorito, Tom	RB	5-10	190	3	Virginia
5	Von Schamann, Uwe	K	6-0	188	6	Oklahoma
41	Walker, Fulton	CB	5-10	196	4	West Virginia

#Unsigned at press time

TOP FIVE DRAFT CHOICES

Rd.	Name	Sel. No.	Pos.	Ht.	Wt.	College
1	Shipp, Jackie	14	LB	6-3	235	Oklahoma
2	Brophy, Jay	53	LB	6-3	227	Miami
4	Carter, Joe	109	RB	5-11	195	Alabama
5	May, Dean	138	QB	6-5	220	Louisville
6	Tatum, Rowland	165	LB	6-1	226	Ohio State

rounds. The Dolphins swapped picks with Buffalo on the first round to move up high enough to get Shipp, an undisciplined player who has trouble in pass coverage. But his forte is stopping the run, something Miami seldom did a year ago.

OUTLOOK: There are challengers, as always, in the AFC East but who's really going to beat the Dolphins? Dan Marino gives them the kind of passing that keeps every game within reach and the defense doesn't let anyone score enough to pull away. Look for a repeat here and maybe a Super Bowl visitor.

DOLPHIN PROFILES

DAN MARINO 22 6-3 214   Quarterback

The Arm Nobody Wanted, until now ... Marino's stock fell faster than Chrysler's did when he suffered through a disappointing senior season at Pitt ... A Heisman candidate before the 1982 campaign, he ended up being the sixth quarterback taken when Miami made him the 27th player drafted last year ... For six weeks he sat behind David Woodley as the Dolphins struggled. Finally he was given a chance and he responded by becoming the first rookie to lead the AFC in passing since the AFL-NFL merger ... Born Sept. 15, 1961, in Pittsburgh ... Someone in his hometown had an eye for an arm. Marino became a quarterback in the fourth grade ... Pitt retired his jersey. NFL defenses wish he'd stayed with his shirt.

DOUG BETTERS 28 6-7 260   Defensive End

Deadliest of the Killer Bees ... Betters finished second in the AFC and third in the NFL with 16 sacks, trailing only Mark Gastineau (19) and Fred Dean (17½) ... This was the first season he remained fully healthy since becoming a starter. That proved unhealthy for NFL quarterbacks ... Holds club record of forcing fumbles with 14 ... Born June 11, 1956, in Lincoln, Neb. ... Played three years as a defensive tackle at Montana before moving to Nevada-Reno with his coach, John Smith ... Although he grew up in the streets of Chicago, the mountains of Montana stayed with him. He sports the beard of a mountain man and spends the offseason in Pembroke Pines, Mont. ... He'll do anything to save a dollar. He once lived in his '65 van rather than rent an apartment . . . Stands seven feet tall in his spikes and helmet.

BOB BAUMHOWER 29 6-5 265   Defensive Tackle

Bobby, can you spare a dime? . . . Baumhower has plenty of them now. He is one of the highest-paid linemen in NFL history after signing a multi-million dollar contract before last season began . . . He now earns $360,000 in base pay alone in a job that used to leave a man unknown and underpaid . . . He led all Dolphin defensive linemen in tackles with 97 and had eight sacks . . . All-Pro once again so his money belt didn't get in his way . . . Born Aug. 4, 1955, in Portsmouth, Va. . . . Only Dolphin defensive tackle ever named All-Pro, he's begun to make it a habit. It's happened four times since he was drafted out of the University of Alabama . . . Owns a bilingual pet, an Amazon parrot named Ralph who speaks English and Spanish.

A.J. DUHE 28 6-4 240   Inside Linebacker

Decided he'd rather switch than fight two years ago when coach Don Shula suggested he move from defensive end to linebacker . . . He has since become a star of some magnitude . . . Combines great speed with quickness that allows him to roam from sideline to sideline and also cover any back in the league one-on-one in passing situations . . . Very, very active . . . Duhe loves to blitz and succeeded at it 5½ times last season . . . Born Nov. 27, 1955, in New Orleans . . . Averaged 72 tackles per year while at LSU . . . His wife, Frances, was the 1980 Orange Bowl queen . . . He is still remembered best for his three interceptions against the New York Jets in the 1982 AFC title game.

MARK DUPER 25 5-9 193   Wide Receiver

Super Duper sprinter with hands that match his speed . . . They haven't forgotten Paul Warfield in Miami, but Duper is making his image fade . . . Caught 51 passes last season for 1,033 yards, an average of 19.7 yards per catch . . . He and quarterback Dan Marino could be an item in the NFL for the next decade . . . Made his first Pro Bowl appearance in only his second season after spending 1982 making cameo appearances in Dolphin games . . . Born Jan. 25, 1959, in Pineville, La. . . . Runs the 40 in 4.37 seconds . . . Moreauville High School didn't have a football team so Duper hadn't tried the game until his junior year at Northwestern State College in Natchitoches, La.

DWIGHT STEPHENSON 26 6-2 255　　　　　Center

He was third center drafted in 1980 after Jim Ritcher (Buffalo) and Ray Donaldson (Baltimore) went before him. He's the pick of the litter now, though . . . Stephenson was a Pro Bowl starter and the AFC Offensive Lineman of the Year last season . . . Gets into his blocks quickly and has the agility and power to drive people back off the ball . . . Television commentator John Brodie first made Stephenson famous when he replayed a block on San Diego linebacker Cliff Thrift in which Stephenson drove Thrift straight back for eight yards . . . Born Nov. 20, 1957, in Murfreesboro, N.C. . . . Played so well for Bear Bryant at Alabama that Bryant called him "the best center I've ever coached."

REGGIE ROBY 23 6-2 243　　　　　Punter

His punts look like the launching of the space shuttle . . . A gaint among punters, Roby's kicks don't have hang time, they have orbit time . . . Averaged 43.1 yards per kick with 27 of his 74 punts landing inside the 20 . . . That was good enough to land him on the All-Rookie team . . . His longest punt traveled 64 yards . . . Roby twice led the nation in punting while at Iowa . . . Averaged 49.8 yards per kick in 1982 as a senior . . . Foot didn't seem too tired last year, but it should have been. He punted for 4½ miles of yardage while in college . . . Born July 30, 1961, in Waterloo, Iowa . . . Has a unique form of concentration. He picks a person out in the end-zone stands and tries to reach him with his kicks.

ANDRA FRANKLIN 25 5-10 228　　　　　Running Back

Delivers more headaches than a jackhammer . . . Inside power running is his game . . . Led the Dolphins with 746 yards rushing, but got them the hard way. He averaged only 3.3 yards per carry . . . His longest run of the season was only 18 yards, but he scored eight touchdowns, so you know how he got them . . . Spent his college days at Nebraska blocking for everyone else and the story seemed the same at Miami until he was pressed into service in 1981 when Woody Bennett was injured. Franklin responded by setting a Dolphin rookie record with 711 yards rushing... Born Aug. 22, 1959, in Anniston, Ala.... "He runs so close to the ground he's like a tank and when he turns those shoulders upfield no one is going to tackle him from an angle," says Dolphin tackle Eric Laakso.

ED NEWMAN 33 6-2 255   Guard

Buried treasure... Rode the bench for five years behind Larry Little before his chance came. Once he got it, though, he wasn't buried any longer. He's been an All-Pro three times... Can stop anyone's charge with his brute strength. He's the strongest Dolphin on record, having bench-pressed 510 pounds... He also once did ten repetitions with 400 pounds, which is ten more than most of us could do... Born June 4, 1951, in Woodbury, N.Y.... Named his cat "Monte Clark" after the Detroit Lions' coach who was his first pro line coach... Has a B.S. in psychology from Duke, although he uses his head in less intellectual ways during the season... Needed two throat operations in 1975 to remove a malignant tumor.

BOB KUECHENBERG 36 6-2 255   Guard

Mr. Lonely... Kuechenberg is the last active Dolphin to have played on all four of Miami's Super Bowl teams and in all 19 Miami playoff games... The amazing thing is that he's still going strong... Kuechenberg was a Pro Bowl reserve for the second straight year in 1983 after missing out the previous four years... He has played in 209 Dolphin games at center, guard and tackle... Born Oct. 14, 1947, in Gary, Ind.... One of nine children of a rodeo clown, he spent his youth riding in a gunnysack on his father's back... Years later, Notre Dame's fortunes were riding on Kuechenberg's back when, in 1968, he was voted the team's outstanding defensive lineman while he was also playing offensive tackle.

COACH DON SHULA: New Jersey Generals' owner Donald Trump offered Shula everything but Manhattan Island to jump to the USFL and coach his Generals, but Shula broke off negotiations once he decided it had turned into a media circus... Has had consistently more success with consistently less talent than any winning coach in the game... In his 20 years as a pro head coach he's won 213 games, making him the first coach to win over 200 games in the NFL in less than 20 years... Born Jan. 4, 1930, in Painesville, Ohio... At 54, Shula has no football worlds left to conquer, but he seems content to keep conquering the one he already rules... Since he arrived in Miami in 1970, Shula's teams are 142-57-2, including the only unbeaten, untied season (17-0) in NFL history, back-to-back Super Bowl champions (1972-73) and four Super Bowl appearances... Maybe Trump should have offered him Manhattan.

BIGGEST PLAY

It had dragged on long into the night of Dec. 25, 1971, and Garo Yepremian knew the time had arrived to end the struggle. It had to be stopped, this AFC playoff game, and it had to be done now or it would surely all slip away.

The Miami Dolphins had come back to tie the Kansas City Chiefs, 24-24, with 96 seconds left on a five-yard scoring pass from Bob Griese to Marv Fleming. After Chiefs' kicker Jan Stenerud missed a 32-yard field goal as time was running out, the second overtime game in playoff history had begun.

But now the game had passed from one sudden-death overtime into a second and both teams were at the point of exhaustion. There was nothing left for the Dolphins to give and Yepremian realized it.

Larry Csonka had just carried a load of Chiefs on a 29-yard run to the Kansas City 36 and all the world knew that was Miami's last gasp. Three plays netted just six yards and on came the tiny Cypriot soccer kicker who had already missed one chance when his 45-yard kick in overtime was short.

The world knew this, but Yepremian thought only of the spot 37 yards from the goal posts where Griese would place the ball.

Griese handled it smoothly and Yepremian sent the ball spiraling. The moment his foot struck leather he knew the longest game in NFL history—83 minutes and 40 seconds—was over, 27-24.

INDIVIDUAL DOLPHIN RECORDS

Rushing

Most Yards Game:	197	Mercury Morris, vs New England, 1973
Season:	1,258	Delvin Williams, 1978
Career:	6,737	Larry Csonka, 1968-74, 1979

Passing

Most TD Passes Game:	6	Bob Griese, vs St. Louis, 1977
Season:	22	Bob Griese, 1977
Career:	192	Bob Griese, 1967-80

Receiving

Most TD Passes Game:	4	Paul Warfield, vs Detroit, 1973
Season:	12	Nat Moore, 1977
Career:	54	Nat Moore, 1974-83

Scoring

Most Points Game:	24	Paul Warfield, vs Detroit, 1973
Season:	117	Garo Yepremian, 1971
Career:	830	Garo Yepremian, 1970-78
Most TDs Game:	4	Paul Warfield, vs Detroit, 1973
Season:	13	Nat Moore, 1977
	13	Larry Csonka, 1979
Career:	57	Larry Csonka, 1968-74, 1979

NEW ENGLAND PATRIOTS

TEAM DIRECTORY: Pres.: William Sullivan Jr.; VP: Bucko Kilroy; GM: Patrick J. Sullivan; Dir. Pub. Rel./Sales: Tom Hoffman; Dir. Publications: Dave Wintergrass; Head Coach: Ron Meyer. Home field: Sullivan Stadium (61,297). Colors: Red, white and blue.

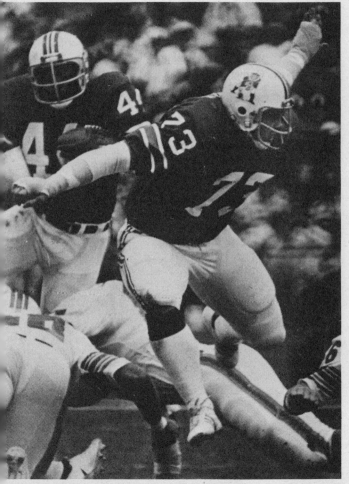

Unretired John Hannah made it to his seventh Pro Bowl.

SCOUTING REPORT

OFFENSE: Their ranking did not reflect it, but the Patriots seemed on their way to a major improvement in the passing game until quarterback Steve Grogan broke his leg in the 12th game. At the time, New England was averaging 21.5 points per game and had begun to convince teams they would do something other than run when they didn't have to punt.

Grogan will be back, but either the draft's No. 1 pick—Irving Fryar—or one of three second-year receivers—Stephen Starring, Darryal Wilson or Clarence Weathers—must join Stanley Morgan in the end zone as well as in the huddle. Tight end Derrick Ramsey led the club with six TDs so he already knows the way.

All this doesn't mean coach Ron Meyer has abandoned his love affair with the run. New England finished fifth in the NFL and Tony Collins became only the third back in Patriot history to rush for 1,000 yards, gaining 1,049. Meyer is now talking about going to a single-back offense with Collins carrying the load with Craig James, the ex-SMU star who did his best running when he left the USFL's Washington Federals to join the Patriots.

Fullback Mosi Tatupu rushed for 578 yards and topped the NFL with 5.5 yards-per-carry, making him an able replacement for the retired Mark van Eeghen.

The line, which averages 6-4½ and 280 pounds, is the biggest in football and with Pro Bowlers John Hannah and Brian Holloway anchoring a group that includes Pete Brock, Ron Wooten and Bob Cryder, it is one of the best.

DEFENSE: Despite having his front seven decimated by injuries, coordinator Rod Rust built a unit that finished third in the NFL in points allowed, which is the only statistic that matters.

Defensive end Ken Sims, who appeared in the best shape of his career in preseason, was lost for 10 weeks with a fractured fibula, and nose tackle Lester Williams started only one game because of injuries and a weight problem that has been solved. New England is counting heavily on both to restore a semblance of a pass rush, which is all that kept this defense from greatness.

Linebacking remains the strong point with Andre Tippett on the verge of stardom and second-year man Johnny Rembert ready to challenge veteran Steve Nelson for a starting inside job beside Clayton Weishuhn.

As always, the secondary remains strong. The trade of All-Pro cornerback Mike Haynes for what eventually turned out to be the No. 1 pick in this year's draft was barely noticed because of the play of eighth-round pick Ronnie Lippett. Ray Clayborn was a

PATRIOTS VETERAN ROSTER

HEAD COACH—Ron Meyer. Assistant Coaches—Tommy Brasher, Cleve Bryant, LeBaron Caruthers, Steve Endicott, Lew Erber, Bill Muir, Rod Rust, Dante Scarnecchia, Steve Sidwell, Steve Walters.

No.	Name	Pos.	Ht.	Wt.	NFL Exp.	College
85	#Adams, Julius	DE	6-3	270	13	Texas Southern
55	Blackmon, Don	LB	6-3	235	4	Tulsa
58	Brock, Pete	C	6-5	270	9	Colorado
3	Camarillo, Rich	P	5-11	191	4	Washington
26	Clayborn, Ray	CB	6-0	186	8	Texas
33	Collins, Anthony	RB	5-11	203	4	East Carolina
91	Crump, George	DE	6-4	260	2	East Carolina
75	Cryder, Bob	T	6-4	282	7	Alabama
87	Dawson, Lin	TE	6-3	240	4	North Carolina State
47	Dombroski, Paul	CB-S	6-0	185	5	Linfield
11	Eason, Tony	QB	6-4	212	2	Illinois
1	Franklin, Tony	K	5-8	182	6	Texas A&M
59	Golden, Tim	LB	6-1	220	3	Florida
14	Grogan, Steve	QB	6-4	210	10	Kansas State
68	Haley, Darryl	T	6-4	265	3	Utah
73	Hannah, John	G	6-3	282	12	Alabama
70	Henson, Luther	NT	6-0	275	3	Ohio State
76	Holloway, Brian	T	6-7	288	4	Stanford
51	Ingram, Brian	LB	6-4	235	3	Tennessee
32	*James, Craig	RB	6-0	215	1	Southern Methodist
38	James, Roland	S	6-2	191	5	Tennessee
83	Jones, Cedric	WR	5-11	184	3	Duke
19	Kerrigan, Mike	QB	6-3	205	2	Northwestern
22	Lee, Keith	CB-S	5-11	193	4	Colorado State
42	Lippett, Ronnie	CB	5-11	180	2	Miami
31	Marion, Fred	S	6-2	191	3	Miami
50	McGrew, Larry	LB	6-5	233	4	Southern California
67	Moore, Steve	T	6-4	285	2	Tennessee State
86	Morgan, Stanley	WR	5-11	181	8	Tennessee
57	Nelson, Steve	LB	6-2	230	11	North Dakota State
98	Owens, Dennis	NT	6-1	258	3	North Carolina State
35	Peoples, George	RB	6-0	215	3	Auburn
88	Ramsey, Derrick	TE	6-5	235	7	Kentucky
52	Rembert, Johnny	LB	6-3	234	2	Clemson
95	Reynolds, Ed	LB	6-5	230	2	Virginia
65	Rogers, Doug	DE	6-5	260	3	Stanford
25	Sanford, Rick	S	6-1	192	6	South Carolina
77	Sims, Ken	DE	6-5	271	3	Texas
27	Smith, Ricky	CB-S-KR	6-0	182	3	Alabama State
81	Starring, Stephen	WR	5-10	172	2	McNeese State
30	Tatupu, Mosi	RB	6-0	227	7	Southern California
56	Tippett, Andre	LB	6-3	241	3	Iowa
82	Weathers, Clarence	WR	5-9	170	2	Delaware State
24	Weathers, Robert	RB	6-2	222	3	Arizona State
53	Weishuhn, Clayton	LB	6-2	221	3	Angelo State
62	Wheeler, Dwight	C	6-3	274	6	Tennessee State
80	#Williams, Brooks	TE	6-4	226	7	North Carolina
72	Williams, Lester	NT	6-3	272	3	Miami
90	Williams, Toby	DE	6-3	254	2	Nebraska
88	Wilson, Darryal	WR	6-0	182	2	Tennessee
61	Wooten, Ron	G	6-4	273	3	North Carolina

#Unsigned at press time
*Played in USFL

TOP FIVE DRAFT CHOICES

Rd.	Name	Sel. No.	Pos.	Ht.	Wt.	College
1	Fryar, Irving	1	WR	6-0	200	Nebraska
2	Williams, Ed	43	LB	6-4	238	Texas
3	Williams, Jon	70	RB	5-10	195	Penn State
5	Fairchild, Paul	124	G	6-3	255	Kansas
6	Gibson, Ernest	151	DB	5-10	176	Furman

Pro Bowl alternate and Rick Sanford had seven interceptions and appears to have a home at free safety.

KICKING GAME: This was the team's weakness. The Pats went through three kickers before settling on unknown Joaquin Zendejas at season's end. Then they made a trade for Tony Franklin. You get the picture.

Punting, however, is the opposite story. Rich Camarillo is one of the league's best. He led the NFL with a net average of 37.1 yards and was second in gross average at 44.6

Ricky Smith made every return an adventure, but he broke some, averaging 21.8 yards per kickoff and 10.5 per punt.

THE ROOKIES: New England went for broke. Several weeks before the draft it traded two first-round picks to Cincinnati for the No. 1 choice and then spent $2.65 million to sign Fryar, Nebraska's game-breaking receiver. His 4.3 speed should help loosen the double coverage on Morgan. Texas pass-rusher Ed Williams could help and Kansas kicker Bruce Kallmeyer could beat out veteran Tony Franklin.

OUTLOOK: Bright. New England finished second in the AFC East last season with the second youngest team in football. If Grogan returns to form and Fryar has hands to go with his speed, Morgan will be aided and the Patriots will improve on their 8-8 record.

PATRIOT PROFILES

STEVE GROGAN 31 6-4 210   Quarterback

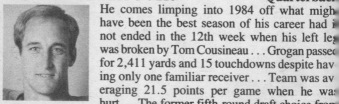

He comes limping into 1984 off what might have been the best season of his career had it not ended in the 12th week when his left leg was broken by Tom Cousineau . . . Grogan passed for 2,411 yards and 15 touchdowns despite having only one familiar receiver . . . Team was averaging 21.5 points per game when he was hurt . . . The former fifth-round draft choice from Kansas reestablished himself as the starting quarterback after a two-year battle with Matt Cavanaugh . . . Still, some critics now are hollering for young Tony Eason . . . Born July 24, 1953, in San Antonio . . . Still returns to Ottawa, Kan., with his family to drive a combine for his father-in-law during the June harvest.

BRIAN HOLLOWAY 25 6-7 288   Offensive Tackle

One of the largest members of the NFL's largest line, a group that averages 6-4½, 280...A No. 1 draft choice from Stanford three years ago, Holloway finally came into his own last season as a Pro Bowl selection for the first time...It was a year of firsts for Holloway. His wife, Bette, had their first child during the season...Born July 25, 1959, in Omaha, Neb....He is the son of a retired Air Force pilot who works in Washington as a lobbyist for Ford Motor Co....Enjoys carpentry and has rebuilt farm houses in upstate New York, where he and his wife opened a health club...Was an outstanding shot-putter at Stanford.

TONY COLLINS 25 5-11 203   Running Back

When he was drafted on the second round in 1981, everyone said "Tony who?" He showed them last season by becoming only the third back in Patriot history to run for 1,000 yards when he gained 1,049...Finished sixth in the AFC and set a club record with 212 yards against the New York Jets on Sept. 18...Despite appearing normal-sized, his legs aren't. He squats 609 pounds...Born May 27, 1959, in Sanford, Fla....Patriots' leading rusher all three years in NFL...Second-youngest child in a family of 16 that included nine boys and seven girls...Size of family may account for his speed, which was needed to get to dinner first.

RAYMOND CLAYBORN 29 6-0 186   Cornerback

The bridesmaid finally got to the altar...After two years as first alternate to the Pro Bowl, Clayborn got to the game last year when an injury sidelined Louis Wright...He did it the hard way, though, making the team without an interception..."If I could catch, I'd have had five or six," he says. "Of course, if I could catch, I'd be a receiver."...May have hands of stone but he can use them. He deflected 22 passes while facing the best receiver each week...Born Jan. 2, 1955, in Fort Worth, Tex....Once roomed with Earl Campbell and Alfred Jenkins at Texas...His 10-year-old punt-return record in the SWC was broken last fall, but by then even Clayborn had forgotten going 95 yards against Boston College in 1974.

JOHN HANNAH 33 6-3 282   Offensive Guard

They call him "Hawg," but they smile when they do . . . Set a club record by being named to the Pro Bowl for the seventh time . . . Played the final weeks with a torn rotator cuff in his left shoulder and never said a word . . . Actually, he didn't say much all year after coming out of retirement in August. With less than a week of practice he played a full half in his first game . . . Born April 4, 1951, in Canton, Ohio . . . Owns and operates a huge chicken farm in the same Alabama town where his father's farm machinery business is based . . . The $500,000 he makes this season should keep the chickens in feed . . . Was an All-American at Alabama . . . Father, Herb, played for the New York Giants.

RONNIE LIPPETT 23 5-11 180   Cornerback

Small investment, big dividend . . . Lippett, an eighth-round draft choice last season from Miami, was supposed to be too small. But when Mike Haynes refused to report, Lippett stepped in and led the team with 26 pass deflections . . . Broke his hand on a Saturday against Notre Dame his senior year, was operated on Monday, missed a week of practice and returned the next Saturday . . . Joined former teammates Lester Williams and Fred Marion in New England . . . Born Dec. 10, 1960, in Melbourne, Fla. . . . Seldom speaks unless spoken to and never discusses an opposing receiver.

RICH CAMARILLO 24 5-11 191   Punter

Superfoot . . . Camarillo doesn't punt footballs, he launches them . . . Led NFL in net average at 37.1 yards per kick and was second to Baltimore's Rohn Stark in gross average at 44.6 yards . . . Had four punts over 60 yards, including a 70-yarder in the snow against New Orleans, longest in the NFL in '83 . . . "He is the best punter in the NFL," coach Ron Meyer insists . . . The Patriots weren't saying that in 1981 when he was released after three preseason games. He re-signed eight weeks later . . . Born Nov. 29, 1959, in Whittier, Cal. . . . His hobbies make sense but not to his bosses. He enjoys cliff-diving and hot-air ballooning . . . Played his college ball at Washington.

MOSI TATUPU 29 6-0 227   **Running Back**

The Snowin' Samoan . . . Had the first 100-yard game of his six-year career on Dec. 4 when he ran through a blizzard against New Orleans for 128 yards . . . Finished second on the club with 578 yards rushing and led the NFL with a 5.5 yards-per-carry average . . . Also tied the club record with three rushing TDs against the Los Angeles Rams . . . Won five game balls last year for his special teams play . . . Born April 26, 1955, in Pago Pago, American Samoa . . . Son of a former Samoan boxing champion . . . Mosi doesn't fight, but his pets do. He raises Pit Bull terriers.

PETE BROCK 30 6-5 270   **Center**

Proved to be a Brock of granite . . . Headed toward All-Pro when he tore knee cartilage on the opening play of New England's 17-6 win over Miami Nov. 13. Despite the pain he silently played the entire game—70 more plays—before being operated on two days later . . . Missed two weeks before returning to play against his brother Stan and the Saints as promised . . . One of three Brock brothers to play in the NFL. Will played with Detroit and Kansas City before knee injuries laid him low . . . Born July 14, 1954, in Portland, Ore. . . . Once shared the center position with Bill Lenkaitis in unique fashion—Brock played the second and fourth quarters, "Link" the first and third.

ANDRE TIPPETT 24 6-3 241   **Outside Linebacker**

What he showed last season is just the Tip of this iceberg . . . The Silent Sentry led New England with 8½ sacks as its designated passrusher . . . The hope is that his speed and strength will make him an AFC version of Fred Dean . . . Plays left end in the four-man front and outside LB in the 3-4 . . . Should know how to use his hands. He holds a second-degree black belt and placed third and fourth in open tournaments in Massachusetts during the offseason . . . Also was a *Karate Illustrated* coverboy . . . Former All-American at Iowa who had 35 sacks in three seasons . . . Born Dec. 27, 1959, in Birmingham, Ala. . . . As a senior, he led Iowa to its first Rose Bowl since 1959.

COACH RON MEYER: No longer seen as Capt. Bligh... After  a stormy first season in which many Patriot veterans rebelled at his obsession with discipline, Meyer loosened the reins last year and his team responded by finishing second in the AFC East... Remained in the playoff picture until season's final weekend despite losing his starting quarterback and nearly all of his front seven on defense to injuries at one time or another... Since taking over a 2-14 team, Meyer's record is 13-12 with one playoff appearance and a second missed on the season's last day... New broom sweeps clean. He has brought in 27 new faces in two years and now has the second-youngest team in the NFL with 23 first- or second-year players last season... Born Feb. 17, 1941, in Westerville, Ohio... A walk-on at Purdue, Meyer won a scholarship as defensive back and led the team in minutes played as a junior and senior... Began coaching at Purdue after graduation, where he spent six years as an assistant... A legend as a college recruiter. He built a 12-1 team at Nevada-Las Vegas two years after the team was 1-10. Then turned SMU from a 3-8 train wreck into a national power in six years by recruiting the likes of Eric Dickerson and Craig James.

BIGGEST PLAY

It is still the moment they remember in New England, even though it was a tragic one. In fact, seven years later the man who insisted all along he'd been framed could not forget it on the day he retired.

The Patriots had finished the 1976 season 11-3 and were playing the Oakland Raiders in the AFC playoffs on Dec. 18, 1976. Everyone felt the winner would ultimately represent the AFC in the Super Bowl and all afternoon it seemed clear that winner would be New England.

Time was finally running out on the Raiders late in the fourth quarter with the Patriots ahead, 21-17. New England needed only to stop Oakland on one more play and its long quest for a playoff victory would be over.

On third-and-18 from the Patriot 27, Raider quarterback Ken Stabler tried to pass to Calvin Garrett, a former Patriot, but the ball was seemingly tipped by defensive end Ray Hamilton as Stabler and Hamilton fell in a heap.

The pass fell incomplete and Hamilton smiled at the thought of just one more play to stop, a play everyone knew would have to be another pass attempt.

But right at that moment he heard a whistle and saw the flag.

"My only regret in football is that I made a great play and I'm remembered for costing us the playoffs," Hamilton says now.

The rest is history. In a controversial call, Hamilton was flagged for roughing the passer: the ball was moved to the New England 13 and five plays later, with time all but out, Stabler rolled to his left and dove in for the score and a 24-21 victory. Football in New England never quite recovered.

INDIVIDUAL PATRIOT RECORDS

Rushing

Most Yards Game:	212	Tony Collins, N.Y. Jets 1983
Season:	1,458	Jim Nance, 1966
Career:	5,453	Sam Cunningham, 1973-79, 1981-82

Passing

Most TD Passes Game:	5	Babe Parilli, vs Buffalo, 1964
	5	Babe Parilli, vs Miami, 1967
	5	Steve Grogan, vs N.Y. Jets, 1979
Season:	31	Babe Parilli, 1964
Career:	136	Steve Grogan, 1975-83

Receiving

Most TD Passes Game:	3	Billy Lott, vs Buffalo, 1961
	3	Gino Cappelletti, vs Buffalo, 1964
	3	Jim Whalen, vs Miami, 1967
	3	Harold Jackson, vs N.Y. Jets, 1979
Season:	12	Stanley Morgan, 1979
Career:	42	Gino Cappelletti, 1960-70

Scoring

Most Points Game:	28	Gino Cappelletti, vs Houston, 1965
Season:	155	Gino Cappelletti, 1964
Career:	1,130	Gino Cappelletti, 1960-70
Most TDs Game:	3	Billy Lott, vs Buffalo, 1961
	3	Billy Lott, vs Oakland, 1961
	3	Larry Garron, vs Oakland, 1964
	3	Gino Cappelletti, vs Buffalo, 1964
	3	Larry Garron, vs San Diego, 1966
	3	Jim Whalen, vs Miami, 1967
	3	Sam Cunningham, vs Buffalo, 1974
	3	Mack Herron, vs Buffalo, 1974
	3	Sam Cunningham, vs Buffalo, 1975
	3	Harold Jackson, vs N.Y. Jets, 1979
	3	Tony Collins, vs N.Y. Jets, 1983
	3	Mosi Tatupu, vs L.A. Rams, 1983
Season:	13	Steve Grogan, 1976
	13	Stanley Morgan, 1979
Career:	49	Sam Cunningham, 1973-79, 1981-82

NEW YORK JETS

TEAM DIRECTORY: Chairman: Leon Hess; Pres.: Jim Kensil; Dir. Player Personnel: Mike Hickey; Dir. Pro Personnel: Jim Royer; Dir. Pub. Rel.: Frank Ramos; Head Coach: Joe Walton. Home field: Giants Stadium (76,891). Colors: Kelly green and white.

SCOUTING REPORT

OFFENSE: When Joe Walton took over as head coach last season it seemed the offense was set. A year earlier, under his direction, it finished fourth in the NFL and now he was the head coach so things could only get better.

This year they still can because they got nothing but worse in 1983. New York went from one step from the Super Bowl to one step from oblivion with a 7-9 record. Much of the reason for that was an offense that tumbled to 11th in the NFL and was outscored, 72-28, in the first quarter, the worst margin in the league. Not surprisingly, changes have been made.

The first to go was quarterback Richard Todd, who was traded to New Orleans, a decision that means Walton will live or die with untested Ken O'Brien.

"We committed ourselves to Ken O'Brien in the future and this will speed up his process," Walton says.

It certainly will since he didn't throw a pass as a rookie last year after being a surprise first-round pick out of the University of California-Davis. He is big, raw-boned and possesses a rifle arm. But so did Todd and what good did it do him?

In fairness to Walton, he was forced to play for seven weeks without 1982 AFC rushing leader Freeman McNeil (separated shoulder) and eight weeks without third-down specialist Bruce Harper. The two were only available together for one quarter all year. But McNeil (654 yards) announced his comeback with a 100-yard game so all seems well again.

Wide receiver Wesley Walker had the most catches of his career (61) and could be greatly aided if Johnny (Lam) Jones continues to play as he did the second half of last season when he caught 31 passes for 502 yards. That is the kind of explosion this offense needs to take off once again. If it does not, however, the explosion will be in Walton's office.

DEFENSE: Mark Gastineau led the NFL with 19 sacks and Joe Klecko adjusted so well to his move from end to tackle that all should have been fine here.

When it came to pass defense, it was fine, finishing seventh

Starting QB Ken O'Brien will throw his first pass as a pro.

in the NFL. But with Jerry Holmes, its best cornerback, having jumped to the USFL, and Darrol Ray unhappy, they had to do something. So they made saftey/cornerback Russell Carter their top draft pick. New York was 23rd in the league against the rush, which explains why defensive lineman Ron Faurot was No. 2 pick.

Walton was so disappointed in the overall production that he traded linemen Kenny Neil and Abdul Salaam to San Diego for a second-round pick, thus breaking up what many felt was the

JETS VETERAN ROSTER

HEAD COACH—Joe Walton. Assistant Coaches—Bill Baird, Ralph Baker, Ray Callahan, Mike Faulkner, Joe Gardi, Bobby Hammond, Rich Kotite, Larry Pasquale, Jim Ringo.

No.	Name	Pos.	Ht.	Wt.	NFL Exp.	College
60	Alexander, Dan	G	6-4	260	8	Louisiana State
35	Augustyniak, Mike	RB	5-11	226	4	Purdue
31	Barber, Marion	RB	6-3	224	3	Minnesota
78	Bennett, Barry	DT-DE	6-4	257	7	Concordia
64	Bingham, Guy	C-G-T	6-3	255	5	Montana
89	Brown, Preston	WR-KR	5-11	187	4	Vanderbilt
86	Bruckner, Nick	WR	5-11	185	2	Syracuse
51	Buttle, Greg	LB	6-3	232	9	Penn State
88	Coombs, Tom	TE	6-3	227	3	Idaho
50	Crable, Bob	LB	6-3	232	3	Notre Dame
52	Eliopulos, Jim	LB	6-2	229	2	Wyoming
65	Fields, Joe	C	6-2	253	10	Widener
38	Floyd, George	S-CB	5-11	190	2	Eastern Kentucky
81	Gaffney, Derrick	WR	6-1	182	7	Florida
99	Gastineau, Mark	DE	6-5	265	6	East Central Oklahoma
94	Guilbeau, Rusty	DE	6-4	260	3	McNeese State
42	Harper, Bruce	RB-KR	5-8	177	8	Kutztown
34	Hector, Johnny	RB	5-11	197	2	Texas A&M
40	Jackson, Bobby	CB	5-10	180	7	Florida State
80	Jones, Johnny (Lam)	WR	5-11	180	5	Texas
73	Klecko, Joe	DT-DE	6-3	263	8	Temple
30	Klever, Rocky	RB	6-3	225	2	Montana
5	Leahy, Pat	K	6-0	189	11	St. Louis University
22	Lewis, Kenny	RB	6-0	196	4	Virginia Tech
59	Lilja, George	C	6-4	250	3	Michigan
71	Luscinski, Jim	T-G	6-5	275	2	Norwich
29	Lynn, Johnny	CB-S	6-0	198	5	UCLA
93	Lyons, Marty	DT	6-5	265	6	Alabama
68	McElroy, Reggie	T	6-6	270	2	West Texas State
24	McNeil, Freeman	RB	5-11	218	4	UCLA
56	Mehl, Lance	LB	6-3	233	5	Penn State
20	Mullen, Davlin	CB-KR	6-1	177	2	Western Kentucky
7	O'Brien, Ken	QB	6-4	210	2	Cal-Davis
62	Pellegrini, Joe	C-G	6-4	252	3	Harvard
79	Powell, Marvin	T	6-5	260	8	Southern California
15	Ramsey, Chuck	P	6-2	189	8	Wake Forest
28	Ray, Darrol	S	6-1	198	5	Oklahoma
76	Rudolph, Ben	DT-DE	6-5	266	4	Long Beach State
10	Ryan, Pat	QB	6-3	210	7	Tennessee
48	Schroy, Ken	S	6-2	198	8	Maryland
82	Shuler, Mickey	TE	6-3	231	7	Penn State
87	Sohn, Kurt	WR-KR	5-11	180	3	Fordham
21	Springs, Kirk	S-CB	6-0	192	4	Miami (Ohio)
70	Waldemore, Stan	G-T	6-4	269	7	Nebraska
85	Walker, Wesley	WR	6-0	179	8	California
72	Ward, Chris	T	6-3	269	7	Ohio State
57	Woodring, John	LB	6-2	232	4	Brown

TOP FIVE DRAFT CHOICES

Rd.	Name	Sel. No.	Pos.	Ht.	Wt.	College
1	Carter, Russell	10	DB	6-3	193	Southern Methodist
1	Faurot, Ron	15	DE	6-8	255	Arkansas
2	Sweeney, Jim	37	C	6-3	250	Pittsburgh
2	Dennison, Glenn	39	TE	6-3	225	Miami
3	Clifton, Kyle	64	LB	6-3	215	Texas Christian

best pass rush in the league two years ago. So now what? Ben Rudolph moves into Neil's old spot or Klecko moves over to allow Barry Bennett in at tackle. Either way, there are questions.

Lance Mehl is becoming one of the game's most solid linebackers and Bob Crable gives the Jets muscle in the middle so this group remains a strong point even in a time of change.

KICKING GAME: Pat Leahy came on strong for the second straight year, making his last seven kicks and nine of his last 13. Meanwhile, punter Chuck Ramsey was true to form, averaging 39.7 yards a kick. If Bruce Harper returns, so will exciting returns.

THE ROOKIES: Four of their first six picks were defenders, so that should tell you Walton's concerns. SMU's Carter is counted on to step in and start and Arkansas' Faurot should fill one of the holes in the decimated line. Keep an eye on fourth-round linebacker Bobby Bell, whose dad, Bobby Sr., was one of the NFL's best.

OUTLOOK: The Jets expected to reach the Super Bowl last year and forgot you have to earn it. That's a lesson learned, but what can you expect from a team with a quarterback who has never played and a defense that has been overhauled? Improvement.

There is too much talent here to finish 7-9 again. But there may not be enough to reach the playoffs.

JET PROFILES

KEN O'BRIEN 23 6-4 210   Quarterback

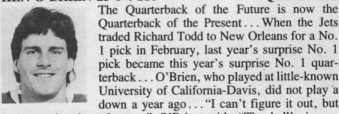

The Quarterback of the Future is now the Quarterback of the Present . . . When the Jets traded Richard Todd to New Orleans for a No. 1 pick in February, last year's surprise No. 1 pick became this year's surprise No. 1 quarterback . . . O'Brien, who played at little-known University of California-Davis, did not play a down a year ago . . . "I can't figure it out, but it opens the door for me," O'Brien said. "The ball's in my court." . . . If he keeps it out of defender's hands, the job will be, too . . . Born Nov. 27, 1960, in Brooklyn, N.Y., but he grew up in Sacramento, Cal. . . . He was the fifth quarterback taken in the 1983 draft, meaning he was selected before eventual AFC Rookie of the Year Dan Marino.

MARK GASTINEAU 27 6-5 265   Defensive End

The John Travolta of the NFL has had his Sack Dance outlawed... Loved to dance over fallen quarterbacks, but such outbursts have now been banned by a vote of NFL owners and coaches... Did it 19 times last year without knowing he'd be legislated into becoming a wallflower... But he says he'll dance on. "Let them try to call a penalty with 60,000 screaming New York fans watching," Gastineau growls... Named All-Pro for third straight season... Fastest pass-rushing feet in the AFC. And he's got size, too... Born Nov. 20, 1956, in Ardmore, Okla.... First (and only) player out of East Central Oklahoma State drafted into the NFL when he was taken on the second round in 1979... In quiet moments he competes in rodeos.

JOE KLECKO 30 6-3 263   Defensive Tackle

Bionic Man... Returned from major knee surgery that nearly finished his career in 1982 and made smooth transition from end to tackle. So smooth, in fact, he was selected to the Pro Bowl for the second time... Second on Jets in sacks with six, well below his team record 20½ set in 1981... Comeback came as no surprise to those who know him. "I'm never going to get complacent," Klecko says. "Too many people forget the hard times. Not me. That would be stupid."... Born Oct. 15, 1953, in Chester, Pa.... Once played sandlot football under assumed name of Jim Jones... Was discovered driving a truck by Temple equipment man Joe DiGregorio, who convinced coach Wayne Hardin to offer him a scholarship... Once sparred with Joe Frazier.

JOE FIELDS 30 6-2 253   Center

Fast becoming one of the AFC's best, but how did it happen?... Given little chance to make the '75 Jets after being drafted on the 14th round out of Widener College... Unimpressive in rookie camp, where it was felt he was slowed by baby fat. He hit the weights and worked snapping the ball to his wife and made the team... Remains a dedicated weightlifter... Born Nov. 14, 1953, in Woodbury, N.J.... Two-time All-Pro who might have made it again had his team not fallen apart... Known as "The General" because when he speaks, people respond.

LANCE MEHL 26 6-3 233   Outside Linebacker

Quiet but deadly... "He's kind of a cruiser," says Jets' linebacker coach Ralph Baker. "He cruises in, makes the tackle and cruises to the huddle. There's no fanfare about it."... Someone noticed, though. He was chosen the Jets' MVP, first time a defensive player was chosen since 1971... Led Jets in tackles for third straight year with 121... Added 84 assists... Born Feb. 14, 1958, in Belleaire, Ohio... His seven interceptions were the best by an LB in NFL... Wasn't drafted until the third round despite Penn State coach Joe Paterno saying Mehl may have been the best inside linebacker he ever coached.

BOB CRABLE 24 6-3 232   Middle Linebacker

Found a home in the middle of the Jets' defense... New York's top pick in 1981 and took over as a starter in the seventh game of his rookie year. He led team in tackles in seven of the remaining 10 games... Second in tackles last year with 179... Has a nose for the ball and uses it. He caused four fumbles last year ... Former Notre Dame All-American who is the Fighting Irish's all-time leading tackler... Born Sept. 22, 1959, in Cincinnati... Is the first LB ever taken on the first round by the Jets... They like his style. So would a kamikaze pilot.

FREEMAN McNEIL 25 5-11 218   Running Back

Maybe the strike-shortened 1982 season seemed like a good idea to McNeil... For the second year he played in just nine games, although last season there was no choice... Separated his shoulder and missed seven games. Thus, after leading the NFL in rushing in 1982 with 786 yards, he fell to 15th in the AFC with 654... That doesn't mean he's lost anything but a little shoulder bone... Announced he was back with a 102-yard performance against the Colts... Born April 22, 1959, in Jackson, Miss.... Runs low, hard and with acceleration, although avoiding people is not his specialty... Averaged 4.1 yards per carry... According to teammate Scott Dierking, "He runs like he's being chased by killer bees."

BRUCE HARPER 29 5-8 177   Running Back

Although never a starter, his absence made the Jets grow fonder... Missed the first three games with a knee injury and the final four with cracked ribs. The Jets lost four of those games... But in the nine he did play in, Harper produced as consistently as always... He gained 354 yards rushing and caught 48 passes (his specialty) for 413 more... Has gained over 2,000 combined yards twice, one of only five players to do so... Born June 20, 1955, in Englewood, N.J.... First back in history at Kutztown State College to rush for 1,000 yards... Had led AFC four times in combined yardage (rushing, receiving and returns).

MARVIN POWELL 29 6-5 260   Offensive Tackle

Despite a down season, he was named to the Pro Bowl for the fifth straight time... Blocks out everything in sight, especially Democrats. He campaigned for the Reagan-Bush team four years ago... In six NFL seasons he has earned more honors than any Jet lineman... Looks like a reaper (a grim one) when he turns the corner on a sweep... Born Aug. 30, 1955, in Fort Bragg, N.C.... Calls himself a "Churchillian conservative" after his idol, Winston Churchill... Was All-Everything at USC... Studies in the offseason at New York Law School.

WESLEY WALKER 29 6-0 179   Wide Receiver

He doesn't walk, he runs... He also still can fly after seven years of terrorizing NFL secondaries... Despite Jets' woes, he had most catches of his career with 61 for 868 yards and seven TDs... That was most receptions by a Jet receiver since George Sauer hauled in 66 in 1968... Only one Jet receiver has more career receiving yardage than Walker's 5,112. That's Don Maynard, the NFL record-holder... Born May 26, 1955, in San Bernadino, Cal.... Legally blind in one eye, but you'd never know it. "It's not so bad," Walker says. "If I close my good eye, I can still get around the house. I just can't read my eye chart."... Dad is a Vietnam vet... Was a high-school sprint champion in California and set all sorts of records catching passes from Vince Ferragamo, Steve Bartkowski and the late Joe Roth at the University of California at Berkeley.

COACH JOE WALTON: Why me?...That should have been  Walton's question all season...Took over a finalist in AFC championship game of 1982 and then saw team collapse because of injury and increased hat sizes..."In 1982 we were one step away," Walton says. "In 1983 we might have been 300 steps away."...His team lost five games by seven points or less, two of which went down the tubes in the final 30 seconds...Also faced incredible injury situation. He had Freeman McNeil, his best rusher, and Bruce Harper, his third-down specialist, together for only one quarter all season...Spent 14 years as an NFL assistant before getting his chance...Second-best player ever to come out of Beaver Falls, Pa., birthplace of Joe Namath...Although only 5-10, 185, he played tight end and linebacker at the University of Pittsburgh...Was a second-round Washington draft choice and played there for four years before being traded to the Giants. Was a tight end for them for three straight seasons in which they reached the championship game ...This quiet man got loud when his Jets went into a tailspin. But nothing helped.

BIGGEST PLAY

Ralph Baker couldn't believe his eyes. He stared at the ball as it lay quietly on the turf of Shea Stadium on this brisk, windy afternoon—Dec. 29, 1968—and then he stared up into the eyes of Oakland Raider running back Charlie Smith, who appeared utterly without interest in the football.

Baker began to move forward as Smith turned and walked away.

It was the fading minutes of the 1968 AFL championship game and the Raiders were trailing, 27-23, but were driving under the leadership of quarterback Daryle Lamonica. Lamonica had just turned and thrown a lateral pass in the direction of Smith, but the ball had come up short, hitting the ground in front of Smith and rolling free.

It was, Smith thought, just another incomplete pass.

But Ralph Baker knew better.

As Smith turned curiously to watch, Baker roared upfield and dove on the ball, which was awarded to the Jets because an incomplete lateral pass is nothing more than a fumble. As Baker dove on the ball, the Jets were headed for a date with destiny and the Baltimore Colts in Super Bowl III and they had Ralph Baker's quick feet and quicker mind to thank for it.

INDIVIDUAL JET RECORDS

Rushing

Most Yards Game:	180	Matt Snell, vs Houston, 1964
Season:	1,005	John Riggins, 1975
Career:	5,135	Emerson Boozer, 1966-75

Passing

Most TD Passes Game:	6	Joe Namath, vs Baltimore, 1972
Season:	26	Al Dorow, 1960
	26	Joe Namath, 1967
Career:	170	Joe Namath, 1965-76

Receiving

Most TD Passes Game:	3	Art Powell, vs Denver, 1960
	3	Don Maynard, vs Denver, 1963
	3	Don Maynard, vs San Diego, 1967
	3	Don Maynard, vs Miami, 1968
	3	Rich Caster, vs Baltimore, 1972
	3	Wesley Walker, vs Detroit, 1982
Season:	14	Art Powell, 1960
	14	Don Maynard, 1965
Career:	88	Don Maynard, 1960-72

Scoring

Most Points Game:	19	Jim Turner, vs Buffalo, 1968
Season:	145	Jim Turner, 1968
Career:	697	Jim Turner, 1964-70
Most TDs Game:	3	Art Powell, vs Denver, 1960
	3	Don Maynard, vs Denver, 1963
	3	Emerson Boozer, vs Denver, 1967
	3	Emerson Boozer, vs Miami, 1967
	3	Don Maynard, vs San Diego, 1967
	3	Billy Joe, vs Boston, 1968
	3	Don Maynard, vs Miami, 1968
	3	Emerson Boozer, vs Buffalo, 1972
	3	Rich Caster, vs Baltimore, 1972
	3	Emerson Boozer, vs New England, 1972 (twice)
	3	John Riggins, vs San Diego, 1974
	3	Kevin Long, vs Buffalo, 1978
	3	Kevin Long, vs Detroit, 1979
	3	Wesley Walker, vs Detroit, 1982
Season:	14	Art Powell, 1960
	14	Don Maynard, 1965
	14	Emerson Boozer, 1972
Career:	88	Don Maynard, 1960-72

PITTSBURGH STEELERS

TEAM DIRECTORY: Chairman: Art Rooney; Pres.: Daniel Rooney; VP: John McGinley; VP: Art Rooney Jr.; Dir. Player Personnel: Dick Haley; Dir. Publicity: Joe Gordon; Head Coach: Chuck Noll. Home field: Three Rivers Stadium (59,000). Colors: Black and gold.

SCOUTING REPORT

OFFENSE: For the first time in 10 years the Steeler quarterback job doesn't belong to Terry Bradshaw. Of course, it doesn't yet belong to anyone else, either.

Franco Harris needs 363 yards to snap Jim Brown's mark.

Bradshaw is struggling to recover from an elbow injury that kept him out of all but one quarter last season. It has been over a year since his operation and he still cannot throw deep or hard without pain.

Mindful of that, Chuck Noll traded for Miami's David Woodley. Woodley lost his job to Dan Marino but is a proven winner if his supporting cast is strong. Unfortunately, his arm is not and his presence could force Pittsburgh to greatly alter its attack. Something, however, has to be done to improve the passing game. In seven of their 10 wins the Steelers rushed for more yards than they passed, which happens about as often as the federal government balances the budget.

Pittsburgh ranked fourth in the NFL in rushing yardage and averaged 4.3 yards a shot, but those figures are misleading. If you deduct the production of departed quarterback Cliff Stoudt and the other non-running backs, the average dips below four yards a carry, which is unacceptable.

Franco Harris gained 1,000 yards again but probably for the last time. He ran for just 397 in the final eight games and his average per carry slipped to 3.6 yards. He's run his race. Frank Pollard, who gained 608 yards, may be asked to shoulder the load. He's not Harris and neither is Walter Abercrombie.

The long pass was almost non-existent last year. John Stallworth played in just four games and never two in succession. He must come back. All that is behind him are Calvin Sweeney, Greg Hawthorne and Wayne Capers. Plus rookie Louis Lipps.

The line, too, is not what it was. Tackle Larry Brown has gone from All-Pro to always fragile. Ted Petersen, Tunch Ilkin, Steve Courson, Craig Wolfley and Mike Webster start, but guards Emil Boures and Rick Donnalley may earn jobs.

DEFENSE: The Steel Curtain has come down, but Pittsburgh still was third in the NFL with an almost completely new cast of Steel.

Six linemen perform regularly, depending on the situation. Gary Dunn plays the nose or a tackle spot. Keith Willis and Keith Gary handle the pass rush from their DE positions and will challenge Tom Beasley and John Goodman for spots in the 3-4 as well.

Linebacker remains the strength of the Steelers. Jack Lambert may be missing some teeth but his talent remains intact. Robin Cole could move inside to compete with Loren Toews. If he does, Mike Merriweather and Bryan Hinkle will hold down the outside.

The secondary must replace retired Mel Blount, probably with 5-9 Harvey Clayton, who can run. Dwayne Woodruff is a fixture

STEELERS VETERAN ROSTER

HEAD COACH—Chuck Noll. Assistant Coaches—Ron Blackledge, Tony Dungy, Dennis Fitzgerald, Dick Hoak, Jed Hughes, Jon Kolb, Bill Meyers, Tom Moore.

No.	Name	Pos.	Ht.	Wt.	NFL Exp.	College
34	Abercrombie, Walter	RB	5-11	210	3	Baylor
1	Anderson, Gary	K	5-11	156	3	Syracuse
65	Beasley, Tom	DE-NT	6-5	248	7	Virginia Tech
25	Best, Greg	S	5-10	185	2	Kansas State
54	Bingham, Craig	LB	6-2	211	3	Syracuse
71	Boures, Emil	G-C	6-1	261	3	Pittsburgh
12	Bradshaw, Terry	QB	6-3	210	14	Louisiana Tech
79	Brown, Larry	T	6-4	270	14	Kansas
80	Capers, Wayne	WR	6-2	193	2	Kansas
33	Clayton, Harvey	CB	5-9	170	2	Florida State
56	Cole, Robin	LB	6-2	220	8	New Mexico
5	Colquitt, Craig	P	6-1	182	6	Tennessee
77	Courson, Steve	G	6-1	270	7	South Carolina
89	Cunningham, Bennie	TE	6-5	260	9	Clemson
45	Davis, Russell	RB	6-1	224	5	Michigan
55	Donnalley, Rick	C-G	6-2	255	3	North Carolina
88	Dunaway, Craig	TE	6-2	233	2	Michigan
67	Dunn, Gary	NT	6-3	260	8	Miami
20	#French, Ernest	S	5-11	195	2	Alabama A&M
86	Garrity, Gregg	WR	5-10	171	2	Penn State
92	Gary, Keith	DE	6-3	255	2	Oklahoma
95	Goodman, John	DE	6-6	250	4	Oklahoma
32	Harris, Franco	RB	6-2	225	13	Penn State
43	Harris, Tim	RB	5-9	206	2	Washington State
27	Hawthorne, Greg	WR-RB	6-2	225	6	Baylor
53	Hinkle, Bryan	LB	6-1	220	3	Oregon
62	Ilkin, Tunch	T	6-3	255	5	Indiana State
29	Johnson, Ron	S	5-10	200	7	Eastern Michigan
90	Kohrs, Bob	LB	6-3	235	4	Arizona State
58	Lambert, Jack	LB	6-4	220	11	Kent State
50	Little, David	LB	6-1	220	4	Florida
16	Malone, Mark	QB	6-4	223	5	Arizona State
57	Merriweather, Mike	LB	6-2	215	3	Pacific
64	Nelson, Edmund	NT-DE	6-3	270	3	Auburn
44	Odom, Henry	RB-KR	5-10	200	2	South Carolina State
66	Petersen, Ted	T	6-5	245	7	Eastern Illinois
30	Pollard, Frank	RB	5-10	218	5	Baylor
87	Rodgers, John	TE	6-2	220	3	Louisiana Tech
31	Shell, Donnie	S	5-11	190	11	South Carolina State
81	Skansi, Paul	WR-KR	5-11	190	2	Washington
82	Stallworth, John	WR	6-2	191	11	Alabama A&M
85	Sweeney, Calvin	WR	6-2	190	5	Southern California
51	Toews, Loren	LB	6-3	222	12	California
41	Washington, Sam	CB	5-8	180	3	Mississippi Valley State
52	Webster, Mike	C	6-1	255	11	Wisconsin
93	Willis, Keith	DE	6-1	251	3	Northeastern
61	Wingle, Blake	G	6-2	267	2	UCLA
73	Wolfley, Craig	G	6-1	265	5	Syracuse
16	Woodley, David	QB	6-2	204	5	Louisiana State
49	Woodruff, Dwayne	CB	5-11	198	6	Louisville
22	Woods, Rick	S	6-0	196	3	Boise State

#Unsigned at press time

TOP FIVE DRAFT CHOICES

Rd.	Name	Sel. No.	Pos.	Ht.	Wt.	College
1	Lipps, Louis	23	WR	5-11	188	Southern Mississippi
2	Kolodziejski, Chris	52	TE	6-3	230	Wyoming
4	Thompson, Weegie	108	WR	6-6	220	Florida State
4	Long, Terry	111	G	6-0	280	East Carolina
5	Hughes, Van	135	DT	6-3	270	S.W. Texas State

at left corner and safeties Donnie Shell, Rick Woods and Ron Johnson will split time with Shell slowly being phased out.

KICKING GAME: Perhaps the strong point of the team. Gary Anderson led the AFC in scoring, made 87 percent of his kicks and can hit from 60 yards. Punter Craig Colquitt recovered from an Achilles tendon injury and averaged 41.9 yards a punt. Exactly 25 percent of his kicks landed inside the 20.

THE ROOKIES: Receiving was a problem and the Steelers tried to solve it with Southern Mississippi's Lipps, a first-rounder who runs the 40 in 4.5 and catches the ball in a crowd. Sleeper could be tight end Chris Kolodziejski, a raw prospect who showed flashes of brilliance as a senior at Wyoming.

OUTLOOK: There are more holes to fill than any time since the first playoff team in 1972. How well Noll plugs them will decide if the glory is over for the Steelers. He is one of the game's great coaches. This year he'll have to be.

STEELER PROFILES

DAVID WOODLEY 25 6-2 204   Quarterback

Out of the frying pan and into the fire . . . Traded by Miami over the winter after Dan Marino made his presence unnecessary, Woodley now finds himself fighting the legend of Terry Bradshaw . . . Despite losing his job at Miami midway through last season, Woodley could point to winning years—the Dolphins were 22-13 in games he started over four seasons . . . Born Oct. 25, 1958, in Shreveport, La. . . . He scored more touchdowns running than passing while at LSU, which explains why he was only the 214th player drafted in 1980 . . . He is intelligent and a leader, but his arm does not allow him to throw deep or to the sidelines effectively . . . Defenses appeared to finally figure that out last year and thus massed to stop his short passing game . . . Even if he has problems, he won't be happy riding the bench after being the youngest quarterback ever to start in a Super Bowl.

TERRY BRADSHAW 35 6-3 210   Quarterback

His hair is gone and maybe so has his arm, but his heart is intact... After missing the first 14 games because of elbow problems, Bradshaw started a key game against the New York Jets and delivered two first-half touchdown passes before his arm went numb again... That effort pushed Pittsburgh into the playoffs, but it also may have pushed Bradshaw one step closer to retirement... "We're not sure about Terry," coach Chuck Noll said last winter. "He hasn't shown any improvement."... That comment caused Bradshaw to explode. "He should keep his mouth shut. As far as I'm concerned I'm going to play."... Born Sept. 2, 1948, in Shreveport, La.... All-American at Louisiana Tech... The Steelers still believe in him, but this time it may not be enough.

FRANCO HARRIS 34 6-2 225   Running Back

He has Jim Brown talking to himself (and everyone else) about a comeback... That's because Harris is now within 462 yards of Brown's all-time rushing record of 12,412 yards... Last year was Harris' eighth 1,000-yard season, his first in four years... Brown and Harris' other critics say he heads for the sidelines too often, but he's gained 11,950 yards so he must have gone upfield some time... Born March 7, 1950, at Fort Dix, N.J.... Difficult as it is to believe, Harris spent most of his time at Penn State blocking... He holds or shares 29 NFL records, including 25 in postseason play... With six more touchdowns, Harris will move into third place in that category on the all-time list... The way he's going, Harris might pass Brown even if Brown does come back.

KEITH WILLIS 25 6-1 251   Defensive End

Who was that guy?... That was the question NFL quarterbacks were asking last season after the unknown Willis set a Steeler record with 14 sacks... He was one of 15 first-year players to make the Steelers in 1982 after coming out of Northeastern... That's right, Northeastern... "When I got their scholarship offer, I thought I was going to Northwestern," Willis says... Either way, he's a Steeler of the future now... Born

July 29, 1959, in Newark, N.J.... Molded in the image of Fred Dean because of his superior speed for a big man... Plans to turn an experimental degree program in therapeutic recreation into a career working with the handicapped, juvenile delinquents and geriatric patients.

JACK LAMBERT 32 6-4 220   Inside Linebacker

Still has gaps in his teeth and fills the gaps in the Steeler defense... Led team in tackles for 10th consecutive year with 159, 66 more than any other Steeler... He is the only linebacker in history to be selected to the Pro Bowl nine times... He has yet to show any signs of slowing down... Born July 8, 1952, in Mantua, Ohio... High-school stadium where he was a quarterback renamed in his honor... A No. 2 draft choice in 1974 out of Kent State, Lambert became Rookie of the Year and the only rookie to start on the Steel Curtain defense... The steel in that curtain has now been replaced, but the man in the middle of it goes on.

MIKE WEBSTER 32 6-1 255   Center

His biceps have biceps... Muscle is his game and he plays it to perfection... He is believed to be the strongest player in the game... He won that title once in an NFL power-lifting competition, then chose never to defend the title... Has been All-AFC for the past six years... Started every game at center since 1977... When his pro career began in 1973, he was a 225-pound rookie from Wisconsin. Things certainly have changed... Born March 18, 1952, in Tomahawk, Wisc.... Cools his heels in the offseason ice-fishing if the ice is strong enough to hold him.

GARY ANDERSON 25 5-11 156   Placekicker

As accurate as William Tell and just as lethal... In just his second year as a pro, Anderson led the AFC in kick-scoring with 119 points while setting a Steeler record for field goal accuracy (87.1 percent)... That broke his own mark of 83.3 percent set the previous year... Not bad for a guy who never saw a game until his family moved from South Africa to Pennsylvania when he was a teenager... Born July 16, 1959, in Parys, Orange Free State, South Africa... Father was a pro soccer player in England before becoming a Baptist minister... He missed just four field goals last year, but that's nothing. He's missed just two extra points in his life.

CALVIN SWEENEY 29 6-2 190   Wide Receiver

Trying to break out of the shadows, but they are long ones... Led Steelers last year with 39 receptions, but that isn't enough to make them forget Lynn Swann, John Stallworth or even Jim Smith... Erasing some of those memories is his goal, but he must improve the preciseness of his patterns if he's ever going to come close to that goal... Two-time MVP on USC track team as a hurdler and 440 man... Born Jan. 12, 1955, in Riverside, Cal.... He doubled the number of catches he made in his entire career last season.

MIKE MERRIWEATHER 23 6-2 215 Outside Linebacker

The Great Ham is gone, but this guy can bring home the bacon... Merriweather replaced the legendary Jack Ham last season and finished second on the team with 93 tackles... He ranges from sideline to sideline using his speed to best advantage... Saw more playing time as a rookie in 1982 than any Steeler rookie linebacker since Jack Lambert arrived a decade earlier... Merriweather was listed as the starter from the opening day of training camp and his play made Chuck Noll look like Jeane Dixon... Born Nov. 26, 1960, in St. Albans, N.Y.... Four-year starter at University of Pacific.

JOHN STALLWORTH 32 6-2 191   Wide Receiver

When he went down, so did the Steeler passing game and he was down most of the year... Caught only eight passes for an even 100 yards and played in just four games... Never played in successive games because of chronic hamstring problems and a bad ankle... He averaged over six TDs a season for the past six years before being shut out last year... With the retirement of Lynn Swann, Stallworth had gone into 1983 hoping it would be his season of glory. Better luck this year . . . He needs just 30 catches and 59 yards to pass Swann as the all-time leading Steeler receiver . . . Born Aug. 26, 1952, in Tuscaloosa, Ala. . . . Alabama A&M retired his uniform after he graduated in 1974 . . . He'd like to give the Steelers a reason to do the same.

COACH CHUCK NOLL: The Mirror Man . . . Took Steelers into the playoffs each of the past two years with teams that didn't belong there . . . Not even the loss of Terry Bradshaw, Lynn Swann, John Stallworth, Jim Smith and diminished performance from tackle Larry Brown could keep him from going 10-6 and reaching the first round of postseason play . . . Noll is the only coach to go four-for-four in Super Bowl competition . . . He has a 133-81-1 record in 15 years with the Steelers . . . Pulled off key offseason trade with Miami for quarterback David Woodley after Cliff Stoudt jumped to the USFL and Terry Bradshaw's elbow continued to prevent him from throwing . . . Is rebuilding the Steelers' defense by switching from the 4-3 to the 3-4 and replacing the old hands with some new faces . . . They say he coaches more than many head coaches but with this crew he has to . . . Born Jan. 5, 1932, in Cleveland, Ohio . . . Played seven years with the Browns after graduating from Dayton.

BIGGEST PLAY

There was only one chance left and Terry Bradshaw was desperate.

Only 22 seconds remained in the Dec. 23, 1972, playoff game with the Oakland Raiders and Bradshaw was facing a fourth-and-10 situation at his own 40 with his team trailing, 7-6. Obviously, he had to pass, but no one was open.

Bradshaw began to scramble, searching downfield for someone, anyone, to throw to. Finally he spotted Frenchy Fuqua and he fired in his direction.

The ball and Raider safety Jack Tatum intersected with Fuqua at the same moment on the Raider 35 and the pass ricocheted off someone and back upfield.

As it did, Franco Harris, who originally was blocking for Bradshaw, sprinted upfield alone in the hope Bradshaw might see him. Bradshaw had not, but as the ball spun wildly back toward the Steelers, Harris increased his speed, caught it in full stride just six inches off the ground at Oakland's 42 and sprinted up the sideline with nothing in sight but the goal line.

At the 15, Raider defensive back Jimmy Warren, who had sprinted from across the field, closed in but Harris saw him and slammed a stiff arm into his helmet that dropped Warren in his tracks.

Five strides later Harris was in the end zone and the Steelers had their first playoff win, 13-6, thanks to the "Immaculate Reception."

INDIVIDUAL STEELER RECORDS

Rushing

Most Yards Game:	218	John Fuqua, vs Philadelphia, 1970
Season:	1,246	Franco Harris, 1975
Career:	11,950	Franco Harris, 1972-83

Passing

Most TD Passes Game:	5	Terry Bradshaw, vs Atlanta, 1981
Season:	28	Terry Bradshaw, 1978
Career:	210	Terry Bradshaw, 1970-82

Receiving

Most TD Passes Game:	4	Roy Jefferson, vs Atlanta, 1968
Season:	12	Buddy Dial, 1961
Career:	51	Lynn Swann, 1974-82

Scoring

Most Points Game:	24	Ray Mathews, vs Cleveland, 1954
	24	Roy Jefferson, vs Atlanta, 1968
Season:	123	Roy Gerela, 1973
Career:	770	Roy Gerela, 1971-78
Most TDs Game:	4	Ray Mathews, vs Cleveland, 1954
	4	Roy Jefferson, vs Atlanta, 1968
Season:	14	Franco Harris, 1976
Career:	93	Franco Harris, 1972-82

SAN DIEGO CHARGERS

TEAM DIRECTORY: Pres.: Eugene Klein; GM: John Sanders; Asst. to Pres.: Jack Teele; Asst. GM: Tank Younger; Dir. Pub. Rel.: Rick Smith; Head Coach: Don Coryell. Home field: San Diego Jack Murphy Stadium (60,100). Colors: Blue, gold and white.

SCOUTING REPORT

OFFENSE: Air Coryell was the offense that bent defenses but never broke them. San Diego tumbled from preseason Super Bowl contender to a 7-9 finish primarily because its offense produced yards (387.4 per game) but not points. The Chargers scored 17 or less six times last season. In the previous three years that had happened only seven times in 47 games, including playoffs.

The points should return, however, if quarterback Dan Fouts stays sound and Pete Johnson rushes as he did at Cincinnati. Fouts was injured for several weeks and sore for several months but still threw for 2,975 yards.

Everything here starts and ends with Fouts and his receivers. Fouts is the NFL's most productive quarterback and, you can argue, its best. His corps of tight end Kellen Winslow and Eric Sievers and wide receivers Charlie Joiner and Wes Chandler is one of the best. And if the 36-year-old Joiner begins to show his age, Bobby Duckworth (21.1 yards per catch, 5 TDs) is ready.

The running game was inadequate despite a sound veteran line and a superb horse in Chuck Muncie. Muncie gained just 886 yards, but he scored 13 TDs and simply cannot be tackled when he chooses not to be.

Johnson, the Bengals' leading rusher for seven seasons, scored 14 touchdowns in a 12-game season (out four games on suspension) and came in the trade for tiny James Brooks and should make up in sheer power what Brooks was with his speed. But don't expect coach Don Coryell to abandon his passing game. He will have Fouts throwing until his arm or opposing defenses give out.

DEFENSE: In San Diego they think defense is something they put around "d'yard." Even after a complete retooling of the unit with five rookies and a switch to the 3-4, the Chargers couldn't stop anyone. They finished 26th in total defense, which wouldn't be bad except they also gave up 104 more points than their offense scored.

This area should improve, however, because youth is on its

His receivers—and Charger fans—hope for a healthy Dan Fouts.

side. Billy Ray Smith, last year's top draft pick, has to have figured out by now how to play linebacker after a year spent tackling air. He got no help from the rookie next to him, Mike Green. Both will be stronger and smarter this time around.

The return of cornerback Gill Byrd, another No. 1 choice a year ago, from a mysterious head injury will solidify a pass defense that received an unexpected boost from rookie Danny Walters' seven interceptions. That gives San Diego the best set of corners it's ever had. One problem, however, is that no pass rush has been

CHARGERS VETERAN ROSTER

HEAD COACH—Don Coryell. Assistant Coaches—Tom Bass, Marv Braden, Earnel Durden, Dave Levy, Al Saunders, Doug Shively, Jim Wagstaff, Chuck Weber, Ernie Zampese.

No.	Name	Pos.	Ht.	Wt.	NFL Exp.	College
91	Ackerman, Rick	NT	6-4	254	3	Memphis State
6	Benirschke, Rolf	K	6-1	179	8	Cal-Davis
50	Bradley, Carlos	LB	6-0	226	4	Wake Forest
61	#Brown, Don	T	6-6	262	2	Santa Clara
7	Buford, Maury	P	6-0	185	3	Texas Tech
22	Byrd, Gill	CB	5-11	191	2	San Jose State
89	Chandler, Wes	WR	6-0	183	7	Florida
77	Claphan, Sam	T	6-6	267	4	Oklahoma
82	Duckworth, Bobby	WR	6-3	197	3	Arkansas
78	Ehin, Chuck	DE	6-4	254	2	Brigham Young
72	Elko, Bill	G	6-5	277	2	Louisiana State
56	Evans, Larry	LB	6-2	220	9	Mississippi College
76	Ferguson, Keith	DE	6-5	241	4	Ohio State
84	Fortune, Hosea	WR	6-0	175	2	Rice
14	Fouts, Dan	QB	6-3	205	12	Oregon
48	Fox, Tim	S	5-11	186	9	Ohio State
75	Gissinger, Andy	T	6-5	277	3	Syracuse
69	Gofourth, Derrel	G-C	6-3	260	8	Oklahoma State
58	Green, Mike	LB	6-0	226	2	Oklahoma State
28	Greene, Ken	S	6-3	203	7	Washington State
43	Gregor, Bob	S	6-2	190	4	Washington State
20	Henderson, Reuben	CB	6-1	188	4	San Diego State
88	Holohan, Pete	TE	6-4	240	4	Notre Dame
41	Jackson, Earnest	RB	5-10	208	2	Texas A&M
40	Jodat, Jim	RB	5-11	213	8	Carthage
79	Johnson, Gary	DE	6-2	255	10	Grambling
—	Johnson, Pete	RB	6-0	249	8	Ohio State
18	#Joiner, Charlie	WR	5-11	180	16	Grambling
—	Kelly, Brian	LB	6-3	222	12	California Lutheran
18	King, Linden	LB	6-5	245	7	Colorado State
64	#Loewen, Chuck	G-T	6-4	264	4	South Dakota State
51	Lowe, Woodrow	LB	6-0	226	9	Alabama
11	Luther, Ed	QB	6-3	210	5	San Jose State
62	Macek, Don	C	6-2	260	9	Boston College
12	Mathison, Bruce	QB	6-3	210	2	Nebraska
60	McKnight, Dennis	C-G	6-3	260	3	Drake
24	McPherson, Miles	CB	6-0	183	3	New Haven
46	Muncie, Chuck	RB	6-3	228	10	California
—	Neil, Kenny	DE-DT	6-4	255	4	Iowa State
55	#Nelson, Derrie	LB	6-1	234	2	Nebraska
—	Salaam, Abdul	DT	6-3	269	9	Kent State
66	Shields, Billy	T	6-8	284	10	Georgia Tech
85	Sievers, Eric	TE	6-3	233	4	Maryland
54	Smith, Billy Ray	LB	6-3	239	2	Arkansas
47	Smith, Sherman	RB	6-4	225	9	Miami (Ohio)
59	Thrift, Clifford	LB	6-1	230	6	E. Central Oklahoma
23	Walters, Danny	CB	6-1	187	2	Arkansas
67	White, Ed	G	6-2	279	16	California
63	Wilkerson, Doug	G	6-3	258	15	North Carolina Central
45	Williams, Henry	CB	6-0	180	3	San Diego State
80	Winslow, Kellen	TE	6-6	251	6	Missouri
49	#Young, Andre	S	6-0	203	3	Louisiana Tech

#Unsigned at press time

TOP FIVE DRAFT CHOICES

Rd.	Name	Sel. No.	Pos.	Ht.	Wt.	College
1	Cade, Mossy	6	DB	6-0	189	Texas
2	Guendling, Mike	33	LB	6-3	242	Northwestern
5	James, Lionel	118	KR	5-7	166	Auburn
6	Guthrie, Keith	144	DT	6-3	269	Texas A&M
7	Bendross, Jesse	174	WR	6-1	185	Alabama

seen in these parts since Fred Dean rushed off to San Francisco three years ago. Dean is not back, but second-year nose tackle Bill Elko and veteran defensive end Gary Johnson are and they must do something to improve this area or those young corners will all feel like Byrd did a year ago.

KICKING GAME: Rolf Benirschke was not as accurate as he has been in the past and accuracy is what he's selling because he lacks leg strength, as his 3-of-10 beyond 40 yards showed. Punter Maury Buford gets distance (43.9-yard average) but they don't always hang like they should. Brooks' returns are worth the price of a ticket.

THE ROOKIES: Don Coryell appears to have finally decided he needs more than points to win in the NFL. For the second year he loaded up on defenders, taking Texas corner Mossy Cade first and Northwestern linebacker Mike Guendling second. But the talent pool was so slim that Guendling may be a gamble because his 4.8 speed is not suited for his position—outside linebacker.

OUTLOOK: If San Diego doesn't score, it doesn't win even if its defense is improved. And if San Diego is to score, it's up to Fouts to make it happen. If he does, the Chargers are in the hunt. But if recent history on defense is repeated, San Diego will bag itself before the hunt is over.

CHARGER PROFILES

DAN FOUTS 33 6-3 205   Quarterback

Proved once again that he's not exactly the *Venus de Milo*. This guy has an arm...He is probably the only quarterback in the game who could miss six games and still throw for 2,975 yards. That's two good seasons for some quarterbacks...Fouts holds the NFL mark for passing yards in a season with 4,802 and he has thrown for 4,000 yards three times. Only three other quarterbacks in history have ever done it once...Shoulder injury knocked him out for six weeks, but he still finished third in the AFC with a 63.2 percent completion average...Born June 10, 1951, in San Francisco, where his dad was once the play-by-play announcer for the 49ers while Dan was their ballboy.

CHUCK MUNCIE 31 6-3 228   Running Back

You try and tackle him . . . He's removed more fillings than a short-order dentist with his bruising running style and marvelously muscled body . . . Tacklers say he's a wrecking ball . . . His 13 touchdowns ranked him sixth in the NFL in scoring among non-kickers . . . Rushed for 886 yards in 235 carries, but people were disappointed. He has so much ability they were even disappointed when he rushed for 1,144 yards two years ago . . . Born March 17, 1953, in Uniontown, Pa. . . . He was the runnerup to Archie Griffin in the 1975 Heisman Trophy vote after a brilliant career at California.

WES CHANDLER 28 6-0 183   Wide Receiver

The fly boy of Air Coryell . . . After spending frustrating years in New Orleans, Chandler came to the right place when he was traded to the Chargers in 1981 . . . He was so happy that he became the only NFL receiver to gain over 1,000 yards in strike-shortened 1982 . . . Injuries slowed him to 58 catches and 845 yards last year, but he still ran through the middle of a defense better than any receiver in the game . . . He is fearless . . . Born Aug. 22, 1956, in New Smyrna Beach, Fla. . . . He was a No. 1 draft pick in 1978 after being named Florida Amateur Athlete of the Year for his footwork at the University of Florida.

KELLEN WINSLOW 26 6-6 251   Tight End

Superman would seem to fit. In fact, it's Don Shula's description of him. "When you think about Winslow, you think about Superman," Shula says. "He does it all, climbs the highest buildings." . . . Winslow has the size to knock over those buildings and the speed to avoid them before they hit the ground . . . He has revolutionized his position because of his speed-power combination . . . Made his fourth consecutive trip to the Pro Bowl after catching 88 passes for 1,172 yards . . . Born Nov. 5, 1957 in East St. Louis, Mo. . . . For some reason he didn't play football until his senior year in high school, but seemed to get the hang of this game while at Missouri.

CHARLIE JOINER 36 5-11 180   Wide Receiver

Old Man River, he just keeps rolling . . . Last season, at 35, Joiner rolled to 65 receptions and 960 yards . . . He no longer has all the speed he once did, but he remains what 49er coach Bill Walsh calls "the most intelligent and perceptive receiver the game has ever seen." . . . His greatest skill is the machine-like precision of his routes . . . He will tie Jackie Smith for most seasons by an NFL receiver this year, 16 . . . He has survived while still running dangerous, middle-distance pass routes . . . Born Oct. 14, 1947, in Many, La. . . . That was a fitting place to start because he's made many catches since he left there for Grambling.

PETE JOHNSON 30 6-0 249   Fullback

This load of granite wanted out of Cincinnati and they obliged by trading him for Jim Brooks . . . After sitting out the first four games because of an NFL suspension for drug use, Johnson rolled over tacklers, rushing 210 times for 763 yards in 12 games . . . Scored 14 touchdowns, one below his career high . . . He led the Bengals in rushing for seven years . . . Born March 2, 1954, in Peach County, Ga. . . . Johnson holds every Big Ten scoring record, including 58 career touchdowns during his time as an Ohio State All-American.

GILL BYRD 23 5-11 191   Cornerback

Mysterious head and neck injuries put him out of commission and threatened his career in his rookie season . . . But now he reportedly is fully healed and ready to prove the Chargers did not waste one of their three No. 1 picks a year ago . . . Byrd did manage one interception before his problems laid him low . . . He was a walk-on as a freshman at San Jose State. He played so well the coaches decided to redshirt him. He started his next four years . . . Sadly, injuries have been as close to him as his shoulder pads the past three years. He tore up a knee as a junior and then had to play six games his senior year with a cast on a broken right hand. . . . Born Feb. 20, 1961, in San Francisco . . . Works as a financial analyst for an aerospace firm when he's not selling real estate . . . Or playing football.

DANNY WALTERS 23 6-1 187   Cornerback

The afterthought who made everyone think . . . Walters was drafted on the fourth round well behind No. 1 pick Gill Byrd last year. But by season's end Walters led the Chargers with seven interceptions, more than three times that of his closest teammate . . . He is still learning his position, which he has played for only three years . . . Walters was originally a running back and then a wide receiver at Arkansas, where he once backed up San Diego teammate Bobby Duckworth . . . Born Nov. 4, 1960, in Prescott, Ark. . . . His 4.4 speed allowed him to outrun many of his rookie mistakes, so just wait until he knows what he's doing.

BILLY RAY SMITH 23 6-3 239   Inside Linebacker

Went over like the Hindenburg last year, but all hope is not yet lost . . . Simply did not react well to position switch from standup defensive end at Arkansas to professional inside linebacker . . . The Chargers counted heavily on Smith, making him their No. 1 pick . . . He was the fifth player drafted overall and the first defender . . . San Diego coaches still believe he will be the next Randy Gradishar because he has speed, size and agility above the norm . . . Born Aug. 10, 1961, in Fayetteville, Ark. . . . His father, Billy Ray Sr., played 14 years in the NFL as an All-Pro defensive lineman with the Baltimore Colts.

ROLF BENIRSCHKE 29 6-1 179   Kicker

Did not have a great year, but still became the NFL's all-time leading kicker with his first two kicks . . . Entered 1983 season with a .737 conversion percentage, far ahead of Toni Fritsch and Efren Herrera . . . Finished 15-of-24 and scored 88 points . . . Remains one of sport's most inspirational stories . . . He was at death's door four years ago but came back from severe intestinal disorder that dropped 50 pounds off his already thin body... Has suffered through four operations and never complained... His father, Kurt, is internationally-known pathologist and conservationist who is director of research at the San Diego Zoo... Born Feb. 7, 1955, in Boston... He donates $50 to the zoo for every field goal he makes.

COACH DON CORYELL: Air Coryell is still in business, but its leader may not be if the Chargers repeat last season's disappointing 6-10 showing... Coryell changed the game in the 1970s with his all-out passing philosophy... He had some big successes, including twice reaching the AFC championship game, but his teams have never made it to the Super Bowl and many are beginning to wonder if you can pass your way to all-out NFL success... He is no Ice Man on the sidelines. He rants, he raves, he runs up and down. When his afternoon is done he often looks worse off than his players... Last season was his only losing year in 26 of coaching, so look for the Chargers to charge back into the AFC West race... Born Oct. 17, 1924, in Seattle... You'd think he'd go easy on the passing. After all he once was a defensive back at Washington... Since coming to San Diego his record is 53-32... During World War II Coryell joined the Army as a private in the ski troops after high school. Three-and-a-half years later he was discharged as a first lieutenant and a paratrooper... His first coaching job may have been his easiest—he was an assistant at Punahou Academy in Honolulu.

BIGGEST PLAY

His body ached and his mind was numb, but somehow Charlie Joiner knew he had to leave the locker room again.

The final Monday night game of the season, on Dec. 17, 1979, was tied, 7-7, with 2:58 to play in the third quarter and the San Diego Chargers were a team in need.

Five years earlier they were at rock-bottom, scandal-ridden, perennial losers. But now they stood 12-3, within one victory of

an AFC West title and their first playoff appearance since 1965
But on this night nothing was going right and the game was in
danger of slipping away. At that point, quarterback Dan Fouts
made a decision. He would call on a battered Charlie Joiner.

Joiner had already been knocked out twice by the Denver Broncos. Twice he had been taken to the locker room and twice he
had returned. Now he was groggy and aching. But he was also
willing.

With the ball on the Denver 32, Joiner began churning out his
pass route. Suddenly he shook his shoulders to the post and cor
nerback Steve Foley went with them as Joiner broke to the flag
For an instant, Foley was frozen.

By the time he melted free, Charlie Joiner was gone, hauling
in a scoring pass in the corner of the end zone that sent San Diego
on its way to a 17-7 win and a trip to the playoffs.

INDIVIDUAL CHARGER RECORDS
Rushing

Most Yards Game:	206	Keith Lincoln, vs Boston, 1964
Season:	1,162	Don Woods, 1974
Career:	4,963	Paul Lowe, 1960-67

Passing

Most TD Passes Game:	6	Dan Fouts, vs Oakland, 1981
Season:	33	Dan Fouts, 1981
Career:	201	John Hadl, 1962-72

Receiving

Most TD Passes Game:	5	Kellen Winslow, vs Oakland, 1981
Season:	14	Lance Alworth, 1965
Career:	81	Lance Alworth, 1962-70

Scoring

Most Points Game:	30	Kellen Winslow, vs Oakland, 1981
Season:	118	Rolf Benirschke, 1980
Career:	585	Rolf Benirschke, 1977-83
Most TDs Game:	5	Kellen Winslow, vs Oakland, 1981
Season:	19	Chuck Muncie, 1981
Career:	83	Lance Alworth, 1962-70

SEATTLE SEAHAWKS

TEAM DIRECTORY: Pres./GM: Mike McCormack; Asst. GM: Chuck Allen; Dir. Player Personnel: Dick Mansperger; Dir. Pub. Rel.: Gary Wright; Dir. Publicity: Dave Neubert; Head Coach: Chuck Knox. Home field: Kingdome (64,757). Colors: Blue, green and silver.

SCOUTING REPORT

OFFENSE: Chuck Knox came to Seattle saying he needed a running back. Curt Warner came to Seattle saying he needed the football. After their arrival last fall, opposing teams came to Seattle saying they needed some Alka Seltzer. The Seahawks had turned into one tough bird.

Knox built a ball-control offense with Warner, who became

What a year it was for rookie Curt Warner, AFC's top rusher.

the first rookie to lead the AFC in rushing since 1978. He also was the single reason why Seattle increased its rushing average 32 yards per game. Warner produced over 1,000 yards more than any of his teammates (1,449) and is not likely to slip. He has size, speed and an uncanny ability to use his blockers.

At last there are some. Knox traded for Reggie McKenzie and Blair Bush and they joined Robert Pratt, Ron Essink and Steve August to build a surprisingly smooth-operating line.

As big a move as the acquisition of Warner was the emergence of quarterback Dave Krieg. When the season opened he was so unknown the CIA could have used his name as a password. But after unseating Jim Zorn, Krieg's dropback style and strong arm made it clear he will do the passing here for quite some time.

Steve Largent remains the key receiver, although Warner coming out of the backfield is equally dangerous and tight end Charle Young still has some life in him.

DEFENSE: They weren't supposed to stop anyone and often they didn't, ranking next-to-last in team defense. But the Seahawks play a swarming, gambling style that counterbalances its weaknesses by creating havoc.

They ranked second in football in turnover differential and proved they could rush the passer out of Knox's 3-4. Seattle got 24 sacks out of defensive ends Jacob Green (16) and Jeff Bryant, second-best sack pair in the NFL. And nose tackle Joe Nash holds his own in the middle.

Linebackers Michael Jackson and Keith Butler thrived in the 3-4, a defense that capitalized on their skills. Shelton Robinson played like a backup who has to become a starter inside this year. If he is, Joe Norman is out. Bruce Scholtz quietly led them all in tackles.

The secondary is anchored by the Hit Man—Kenny Easley. Easley switched positions with John Harris, moving from free safety to strong, and both prospered. The corners, however, could be a problem. Rookie Terry Taylor might help solve it.

KICKING GAME: Norm Johnson missed three of seven kicks between 30-40 yards but was 8-for-10 beyond 40. You figure that out. Punter Jeff West averaged just 39.5 yards, but somehow he holds his job. As units, they can cover and return kicks, leading the league in both categories. Zach Dixon topped the NFL in kick returns and had the two longest runbacks in Seattle history.

THE ROOKIES: Biggest need was an offensive tackle, but none suited Knox, so he tried to bolster his defense with Southern

SEAHAWKS VETERAN ROSTER

HEAD COACH—Chuck Knox. Assistant Coaches—Tom Catlin, George Dyer, Chick Harris, Ralph Hawkins, Ken Meyer, Steve Moore, Ray Prochaska, Rusty Tillman, Joe Vitt.

No.	Name	Pos.	Ht.	Wt.	NFL Exp.	College
76	#August, Steve	T	6-5	258	8	Tulsa
65	Bailey, Edwin	G	6-5	265	4	South Carolina State
22	Brown, Dave	CB	6-2	190	10	Michigan
32	#Bryant, Cullen	FB	6-1	236	12	Colorado
77	Bryant, Jeff	DE	6-5	260	3	Clemson
59	Bush, Blair	C	6-3	252	7	Washington
53	Butler, Keith	LB	6-4	225	7	Memphis State
83	Castor, Chris	WR	6-0	170	2	Duke
31	Dixon, Zachary	RB	6-1	204	6	Temple
33	Doornink, Dan	RB	6-3	210	7	Washington State
35	Dufek, Don	S	6-0	195	8	Michigan
66	Dugan, Bill	G	6-3	271	4	Penn State
45	Easley, Ken	S	6-3	206	4	UCLA
64	Essink, Ron	T	6-6	260	5	Grand Valley State
50	Flones, Brian	LB	6-1	228	3	Washington State
56	Gaines, Greg	LB	6-3	220	3	Tennessee
79	Green, Jacob	DE	6-3	247	5	Texas A&M
75	#Hardy, Robert	NT	6-2	250	5	Jackson State
44	Harris, John	S	6-2	200	7	Arizona State
69	Hernandez, Matt	T	6-6	260	2	Purdue
63	Hicks, Mark	LB	6-2	225	2	Arizona State
46	Hughes, David	RB	6-0	220	4	Boise State
70	Irvin, Darrell	DE	6-4	255	5	Oklahoma
29	#Jackson, Harold	WR	5-10	175	17	Jackson State
55	Jackson, Michael	LB	6-1	220	6	Washington
—	Jackson, Terry	CB	5-11	197	7	San Diego State
85	Johns, Paul	WR	5-11	170	4	Tulsa
9	#Johnson, Norm	K	6-2	193	3	UCLA
62	Kauahi, Kani	C	6-2	260	3	Hawaii
17	Krieg, Dave	QB	6-1	185	5	Milton
37	#Lane, Eric	RB	6-0	195	4	Brigham Young
80	Largent, Steve	WR	5-11	184	9	Tulsa
67	McKenzie, Reggie	G	6-5	255	13	Michigan
51	Merriman, Sam	LB	6-3	225	2	Idaho
88	#Metzelaars, Pete	TE	6-7	240	3	Wabash
21	Moyer, Paul	S	6-1	201	2	Arizona State
72	Nash, Joe	NT	6-3	250	3	Boston College
52	#Norman, Joe	LB	6-1	220	5	Indiana
61	Pratt, Bob	G	6-4	250	11	North Carolina
57	Robinson, Shelton	LB	6-2	233	3	North Carolina
58	Scholtz, Bruce	LB	6-6	240	3	Texas
42	Simpson, Keith	CB	6-1	195	7	Memphis State
86	Tice, Mike	TE	6-7	250	4	Maryland
89	Walker, Byron	WR	6-4	190	3	Citadel
28	Warner, Curt	RB	5-11	205	2	Penn State
8	#West, Jeff	P	6-2	2-5	9	Cincinnati
54	Williams, Eugene	LB	6-1	220	3	Tulsa
87	#Young, Charle	TE	6-4	234	12	Southern California
10	Zorn, Jim	QB	6-2	200	9	Cal Poly-Pomona

#Unsigned at press time

TOP FIVE DRAFT CHOICES

Rd.	Name	Sel. No.	Pos.	Ht.	Wt.	College
1	Taylor, Terry	22	DB	5-10	175	Southern Illinois
2	Turner, Daryl	49	WR	6-3	198	Michigan State
3	Young, Fred	76	LB	6-1	220	New Mexico State
4	Hagood, Rickey	86	DT	6-3	285	South Carolina
6	Kaiser, John	162	LB	6-3	218	Arizona

Illinois corner Terry Taylor, the fastest of the top-rated DBs at 4.45; New Mexico LB Fred Young and South Carolina tackle Rickey Hagood. Michigan State receiver Daryl Turner was drafted second because Steve Largent is talking retirement and Turner is talking speed.

OUTLOOK: Their bubble may burst this year. Warner will run, Krieg will throw and Largent will catch, but Knox did it with mirrors last year. Seattle snuck into the AFC championship game but won't slip unnoticed by anyone this year. There is still no depth, especially at running back, and the defense can't expect to save itself again by falling on fumbles. A repeat trip to the playoffs from this division will be difficult.

SEAHAWK PROFILES

DAVE KRIEG 25 6-1 185   **Quarterback**

His college coach got him to Seattle and now Krieg got the Seahawks into the AFC championship game in his first year as a starter ...There was little interest in his credentials after his college career was over at Milton College in 1980. But his coach knew someone in Seahawk's front office and he convinced them to give Krieg a chance. The rest is history ...Krieg moved ahead of Jim Zorn for good last season, starting 11 games and leading the Seahawks to a 7-4 record and two playoff wins...Born Oct. 20, 1958, in Iola, Wisc....Finished second in the AFC in passing, completing 60.5 percent of his throws for 2,139 yards and 18 touchdowns, which doubled his career totals...Possesses an extremely strong arm.

JIM ZORN 31 6-2 200   **Quarterback**

Lost his job but none of his popularity in Seattle...Until last year he was really the only quarterback the Seahawks had ever known. But his scrambling style didn't fit into new coach Chuck Knox's more conservative philosophy ...Zorn quietly rode the bench, completing just 103 of 205 passes for 1,166 yards, his lowest totals in seven years...Born May 10, 1953 in Whittier, Cal....Played at Cal Poly Pomona before signing with the Dallas Cowboys as a free agent...Dallas cut him and the

Seahawks brought him to Seattle in their first season the following year . . . Many expect he could be traded before the season begins, but if he isn't, it will give Seattle an All-Free-Agent quarterbacking duo.

CURT WARNER 23 5-11 205   Running Back

There was nothing curt about most of his runs. They were lengthy rambles . . . Warner burst upon the NFL scene as a rookie last season, leading the AFC in rushing with 1,449 yards and 14 touchdowns. He also caught 42 passes . . . Warner was the first rookie to lead the AFC in rushing since Earl Campbell . . . He is the most danger- ous runner in Seattle since Hugh McElhenney was running for the University of Washington three decades ago . . . Born March 18, 1961, in Pineville, W.Va. . . . Twice gained 1,000 yards while at Penn State . . . He broke Seattle's season- rushing record by 644 yards, so what does he do for an encore?

KEN EASLEY 25 6-3 206   Safety

He's the "AM-PM Man." When he hits a re- ceiver it's morning, but by the time that guy wakes up it's nightfall . . . He is the only Sea- hawk defender ever named to the Pro Bowl, which he made for the second straight time last year . . . A rare three-time All-American at UCLA, Easley was the fourth player drafted in 1981 and immediately made an impression on the NFL by being named Rookie Defensive Player of the Year . . . Born Jan. 15, 1959, in Chesapeake, Va. . . . He led the Seahawks with seven interceptions, tying him for second place in the AFC . . . Intimidation remains his style, but he has the speed to cover anyone.

ZACK DIXON 28 6-1 204   Kick Returner

Zack was on track once he arrived in Seat- tle . . . After opening the season with the Colts, Dixon was released and landed on his feet with the Seahawks . . . From that point on his feet were flying . . . He led the NFL with 1,171 yards on 51 kick returns, 49 made for Seattle . . . His 94-yard kickoff return for a touchdown against St. Louis was the first kick returned for a score in Seattle history . . . Born March 5, 1956, in Dorchester, Mass. . . . He was a junior college All-American running back before transferring to Temple, where he averaged nearly five yards per carry... In one season he had the two longest kick returns in Seahawk history—the 94 and a 59-yarder.

STEVE LARGENT 29 5-11 184   Wide Receiver

Bum Phillips still says he is the one that got away... When both were in Houston in 1976 Phillips traded Largent to Seattle for an eighth-round draft choice. Bum thought Largent had eighth-round speed... Phillips was right. Largent can't run. But football is not a track meet and eight years later no one has slowed down Largent yet... No one in the game runs better patterns... He caught 72 passes last season for 1,074 yards, marking the fifth time in the past six years he's gone over 1,000 yards... Born Sept. 28, 1954, in Tulsa, Okla.... He played his college ball in his hometown, where he led the nation in touchdown receptions in 1974 and '75 with 14 each year for Tulsa.

JACOB GREEN 27 6-3 247   Defensive End

Hit his stride, and a load of quarterbacks, last season... Green set club records with 16 sacks... Believe it or not, he also produced the longest interception return in the NFL in 1983 with a 73-yard run for a touchdown against the Cleveland Browns... He and teammate Jeff Bryant were the second-best sack pair in the AFC... Green now has 37 sacks in 55 games... He relies on speed and nimble feet to shake free of blockers... Born Jan. 21, 1957, in Pasadena, Tex.... He was a college roommate of Colts' running back Curtis Dickey at Texas A&M, where both were All-Americans.

JEFF BRYANT 24 6-5 260   Defensive End

They call him "Boogey," perhaps because of the way he dances on quarterbacks... Bryant is the other half of Seattle's Sack Pack, having joined Jacob Green to produce a tandem total of 24 sacks... Had eight sacks in his second pro season to rank behind Green... They perform their specialties far differently. Where Green's thing is speed, Bryant lives with power. Bryant bench-presses 425 pounds, squats 600 and dead-lifts 680... Born May 22, 1960, in Atlanta... Bryant was an undefeated high-school wrestler, which doesn't hurt you when you spend your afternoons wrestling with blockers ... Bryant was a surprise first-round pick in 1982 after getting little recognition on Clemson's 12-0 1981 national champions.

DAVE BROWN 31 6-2 190   Cornerback

One of the originals ... Brown came to Seattle in the allocation draft in 1976 that helped stock the then-expansion Seahawks ... Along with Steve Largent, he is the only original Seahawk still in the starting lineup nine years later ... Brown's six interceptions showed he can still cover even as the years pass ... He has started every Seattle game for which he was physically able ... Originally a No. 1 draft choice of the Pittsburgh Steelers in 1975 and played on their Super Bowl X champions ... Born Jan. 16, 1953, in Akron, Ohio ... Unanimous All-American in 1974 while at Michigan.

BLAIR BUSH 27 6-3 252   Center

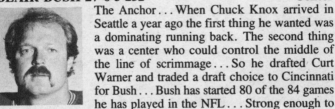

The Anchor ... When Chuck Knox arrived in Seattle a year ago the first thing he wanted was a dominating running back. The second thing was a center who could control the middle of the line of scrimmage ... So he drafted Curt Warner and traded a draft choice to Cincinnati for Bush ... Bush has started 80 of the 84 games he has played in the NFL ... Strong enough to handle nose men and quick enough to get out after inside linebackers ... Born Nov. 25, 1956, in Fort Hood, Tex. ... He co-captained his team at Washington before becoming Cincinnati's No. 1 pick in 1978 ... Once had 21 pins in 26 wrestling matches as a high-school senior.

COACH CHUCK KNOX: He did it again ... In his first season

in Seattle, Knox took a loser and made it a winner just as he had with the Buffalo Bills and Los Angeles Rams ... Seahawks were 4-5 in 1982 and had never made a playoff appearance in their seven-year history. But after Knox replaced interim coach Mike McCormack for the 1983 season, Seattle finished 9-7 despite the toughest schedule in the NFL and ended up in the AFC title game . . . Knox did the same thing in 1973 when he took a 6-7-1 Ram team and converted it into a 12-2 division winner . . . He arrived in Buffalo in 1978 facing a worse situation. The Bills were 3-11 the previous season, but one year with Chuck and they were 11-5 and the AFC East title-holder . . . He is the first coach in NFL history to take three different teams into the playoffs . . . Born April 27, 1932, in Sewickley, Pa. . . . He was a tiny tackle at tiny Juniata College, where he later began his coaching career . . . Once a conservative, ball-control advocate, Knox now lets his quarterbacks throw on some down other than third. But he's still a believer in defense and a dominating running back first . . . Has a 100-58-1 record for the eighth-best winning percentage in NFL history. In those 11 years as a head coach his teams have won six division titles and eight of his teams have reached the playoffs.

BIGGEST PLAY

Dave Krieg had never been in this situation, but then neither had anyone else he was looking at.

The Seattle Seahawks were in unfamiliar yet familiar territory. They were trailing the Miami Dolphins, 20-17, last Dec. 31. Nothing strange there. But they were doing so in the AFC playoffs, a place Seattle had never been.

But with exactly 2:00 left it seemed Cinderella had finally lost her slipper. The Dolphins had just scored after Gerald Small intercepted Krieg's pass intended for Steve Largent and the longshot Seahawks seemed doomed.

But Krieg had the innocence of youth on his side. And more important, he also had the cagy Largent. With the ball sitting at the Miami 42 on first-and-10, Krieg figured there was no need to waste any of the two minutes he had left.

Taking the snap, he dropped back to pass as Largent worked through the Dolphin zone defense, first eluding Small and then safety Glenn Blackwood as he broke to the post and then back deep to the corner. As he made his final out, Largent shot past Blackwood and took Krieg's pass over his shoulder for a 40-yard gain as Blackwood dragged him down at the two.

One play later, Curt Warner scored and the Seahawks owned a stunning 24-20 win and a ticket to the AFC championship game.

INDIVIDUAL SEAHAWK RECORDS

Rushing

Most Yards Game:	207	Curt Warner, vs Kansas City, 1983
Season:	1,449	Curt Warner, 1983
Career:	3,429	Sherman Smith, 1976-82

Passing

Most TD Passes Game:	4	Steve Myer, vs Tampa Bay, 1977
	4	Jim Zorn, vs Buffalo, 1977
	4	Jim Zorn, vs San Diego, 1977
	4	Jim Zorn, vs New Orleans, 1979
	4	Jim Zorn, vs New England, 1980
Career:	107	Jim Zorn, 1976-83

Receiving

Most TD Passes Game:	3	Steve Largent, vs St. Louis, 1983
Season:	11	Steve Largent, 1983
Career:	60	Steve Largent, 1976-83

Scoring

Most Points Game:	18	David Sims, vs New York Jets, 1978
	18	David Sims, vs Cleveland, 1978
	18	Sherman Smith, vs Cleveland, 1979
	18	Steve Largent, vs St. Louis, 1983
	18	Curt Warner, vs Kansas City, 1983
Season:	103	Norm Johnson, 1983
Career:	366	Steve Largent, 1976-83
Most TDs Game:	3	David Sims, vs New York Jets, 1978
	3	David Sims, vs Cleveland, 1978
	3	Sherman Smith, vs Cleveland, 1979
	3	Steve Largent, vs St. Louis, 1983
	3	Curt Warner, vs Kansas City, 1983
Season:	15	David Sims, 1978
Career:	60	Steve Largent, 1976-83

OFFICIAL 1983 NFL STATISTICS

(Compiled by Elias Sports Bureau)

RUSHING

TOP TEN RUSHERS

	Att	Yards	Avg	Long	TD
Dickerson, Eric, Rams	390	1808	4.6	t85	18
Andrews, William, Atl.	331	1567	4.7	27	7
Warner, Curt, Sea.	335	1449	4.3	60	13
Payton, Walter, Chi.	314	1421	4.5	t49	6
Riggins, John, Wash.	375	1347	3.6	44	24
Dorsett, Tony, Dall.	289	1321	4.6	77	8
Campbell, Earl, Hou.	322	1301	4.0	42	12
Anderson, Ottis, St.L.	296	1270	4.3	43	5
Pruitt, Mike, Clev.	293	1184	4.0	27	10
Rogers, George, N.O.	256	1144	4.5	t76	5

NFC – INDIVIDUAL RUSHERS

	Att	Yards	Avg	Long	TD
Dickerson, Eric, Rams	390	1808	4.6	t85	18
Andrews, William, Atl.	331	1567	4.7	27	7
Payton, Walter, Chi.	314	1421	4.5	t49	6
Riggins, John, Wash.	375	1347	3.6	44	24
Dorsett, Tony, Dall.	289	1321	4.6	77	8
Anderson, Ottis, St.L.	296	1270	4.3	43	5
Rogers, George, N.O.	256	1144	4.5	t76	5
Sims, Billy, Det.	220	1040	4.7	41	7

t = Touchdown
Leader based on most yards gained

For average per carry, Falcon William Andrews was tops—4.7.

	Att	Yards	Avg	Long	TD
Woolfolk, Butch, Giants	246	857	3.5	22	4
Tyler, Wendell, S.F.	176	856	4.9	39	4
Wilson, Wayne, N.O.	199	787	4.0	29	9
Washington, Joe, Wash.	145	772	5.3	41	0
Craig, Roger, S.F.	176	725	4.1	71	8
Ellis, Gerry, G.B.	141	696	4.9	71	4
Suhey, Matt, Chi.	149	681	4.6	39	4
Nelson, Darrin, Minn.	154	642	4.2	t56	1
Wilder, James, T.B.	161	640	4.0	t75	4
Carpenter, Rob, Giants	170	624	3.7	37	4
Springs, Ron, Dall.	149	541	3.6	t19	7
Brown, Ted, Minn.	120	476	4.0	43	10
Jones, James, Det.	135	475	3.5	18	6
Galbreath, Tony, Minn.	113	474	4.2	t52	4
Riggs, Gerald, Atl.	100	437	4.4	t40	8
Oliver, Hubert, Phil.	121	434	3.6	24	1
Gajan, Hokie, N.O.	81	415	5.1	58	4
Williams, Mike, Phil.	103	385	3.7	32	0
Mitchell, Stump, St.L.	68	373	5.5	46	3
Redden, Barry, Rams	75	372	5.0	t40	2
Carver, Mel, T.B.	114	348	3.1	16	0
Ivery, Eddie Lee, G.B.	86	340	4.0	21	2
Clark, Jessie, G.B.	71	328	4.6	42	0

	Att	Yards	Avg	Long	TD
McMahon, Jim, Chi.	55	307	5.6	32	2
Montana, Joe, S.F.	61	284	4.7	18	2
Owens, James, T.B.	96	266	2.8	15	5
Morris, Wayne, St.L.	75	257	3.4	17	2
Ring, Bill, S.F.	64	254	4.0	25	2
Bussey, Dexter, Det.	57	249	4.4	26	0
Theismann, Joe, Wash.	37	234	6.3	22	1
Haddix, Michael, Phil.	91	220	2.4	11	2
Meade, Mike, G.B.	55	201	3.7	15	1
Newsome, Tim, Dall.	44	185	4.2	20	2
Huckleby, Harlan, GB.	50	182	3.6	20	4
Hipple, Eric, Det.	41	171	4.2	27	3
Morris, Joe, Giants	35	145	4.1	16	0
Evans, Vince, Chi.	22	142	6.5	27	1
Montgomery, Wilbert, Phil. .	29	139	4.8	32	0
Thompson, Vince, Det.	40	138	3.5	10	1
Jaworski, Ron, Phil.	25	129	5.2	29	1
Lomax, Neil, St.L.	27	127	4.7	35	2
Love, Randy, St.L.	35	103	2.9	16	2
Harrington, Perry, Phil. ...	23	98	4.3	35	1
Young, Rickey, Minn.	39	90	2.3	9	2
Wonsley, Otis, Wash.	25	88	3.5	9	0
Johnson, Billy, Atl.	15	83	5.5	36	0
Rogers, Jimmy, N.O.	26	80	3.1	13	0
Thompson, Leonard, Det.	4	72	18.0	t40	1
Gentry, Dennis, Chi.	16	65	4.1	17	0
Brunner, Scott, Giants	26	64	2.5	12	0
Cain, Lynn, Atl.	19	63	3.3	10	1
Hayes, Jeff, Wash.	2	63	31.5	48	0
Brown, Charlie, Wash.	4	53	13.3	17	0
Ferrell, Earl, St.L.	7	53	7.6	21	1
Giaquinto, Nick, Wash.	14	53	3.8	11	0
Green, Roy, St.L.	4	49	12.3	25	0
Tuggle, John, Giants	17	49	2.9	t7	1
Redwine, Jarvis, Minn.	10	48	4.8	21	0
Moore, Jeff, S.F.	15	43	2.9	14	1
Guman, Mike, Rams	7	42	6.0	11	0
LeCount, Terry, Minn.	2	42	21.0	40	0
Orosz, Tom, S.F.	2	39	19.5	23	0
Bartkowski, Steve, Atl.	16	38	2.4	10	1
Lofton, James, G.B.	9	36	4.0	13	0
Newhouse, Robert, Dall.	9	34	3.8	8	0
Gault, Willie, Chi.	4	31	7.8	22	0
White, Danny, Dall.	18	31	1.7	22	4
Armstrong, Adger, T.B.	7	30	4.3	7	0
Alexander, Robert, Rams	7	28	4.0	15	0
Dils, Steve, Minn.	16	28	1.8	8	0

Rob Carpenter was second in Giant rushing to Butch Woolfolk.

	Att	Yards	Avg	Long	TD
Morton, Michael, T.B.	13	28	2.2	5	0
Parsons, Bob, Chi.	1	27	27.0	27	0
Rutledge, Jeff, Giants	7	27	3.9	14	0
Thompson, Jack, T.B.	26	27	1.0	10	0
Thomas, Calvin, Chi.	8	25	3.1	9	0
Monroe, Carl, S.F.	10	23	2.3	5	0
Campfield, Billy, Giants ...	2	21	10.5	13	0
Wilson, Tim, N.O.	8	21	2.6	7	0
Kane, Rick, Det.	4	19	4.8	9	0
Clark, Dwight, S.F.	3	18	6.0	9	0
Ferragamo, Vince, Rams	22	17	0.8	8	0
Austin, Cliff, N.O.	4	16	4.0	5	0
Lewis, Gary, G.B.	4	16	4.0	11	1
Merkens, Guido, N.O.	1	16	16.0	16	0
Groth, Jeff, N.O.	1	15	15.0	15	0
Giacomarro, Ralph, Atl.	2	13	6.5	13	0
Harrell, Willard, St.L.	4	13	3.3	8	0
Holly, Bob, Wash.	4	13	3.3	13	0
Hutchison, Anthony, Chi. ...	6	13	2.2	5	1
Nichols, Mark, Det.	1	13	13.0	13	0
Pearson, Drew, Dall.	2	13	6.5	10	0
Dickey, Lynn, G.B.	21	12	0.6	4	3
Hart, Jim, St.L.	5	12	2.4	13	0
Manning, Archie, Hou.-Minn.	3	12	4.0	11	0
Moroski, Mike, Atl.	2	12	6.0	7	0
Evans Reggie, Wash.	16	11	0.7	5	4
Komlo, Jeff, T.B.	2	11	5.5	11	0
Sharpe, Luis, St.L.	1	11	11.0	11	0
Walker, Rick, Wash.	2	10	5.0	11	0
Jones, Mike, Minn.	1	9	9.0	9	0
Lisch, Rusty, St.L.	2	9	4.5	5	0
Robinson, Bo, Atl.	3	9	3.0	7	0
Cavanaugh, Matt, S.F.	1	8	8.0	8	0
Danielson, Gary, Det.	6	8	1.3	8	0
Ellard, Henry, Rams	3	7	2.3	12	0
Everett, Major, Phil.	5	7	1.4	7	0
Margerum, Ken, Chi.	1	7	7.0	7	0
White, Sammy, Minn.	1	7	7.0	7	0
King, Horace, Det.	3	6	2.0	4	0
Moorehead, Emery, Chi.	5	6	1.2	5	0
Runager, Max, Phil.	1	6	6.0	6	0
Williams, Richard, Atl.	1	5	5.0	5	0
Middleton, Terdell, T.B. ...	2	4	2.0	2	0
Eddings, Floyd, Giants	1	3	3.0	3	0
Golsteyn, Jerry, T.B.	5	3	0.6	2	0
Goodlow, Eugene, N.O.	1	3	3.0	3	0
Kramer, Tommy, Minn.	8	3	0.4	8	0

	Att	Yards	Avg	Long	TD
Ramson, Eason, S.F.	1	3	3.0	3	0
Solomon, Freddie, S.F.	1	3	3.0	3	0
Wilson, Dave, N.O.	5	3	0.6	5	1
Baschnagel, Brian, Chi.	2	2	1.0	2	0
Bright, Leon, Giants	1	2	2.0	2	0
Hill, Tony, Dall.	1	2	2.0	2	0
Lewis, Leo, Minn.	1	2	2.0	2	0
Miller, Junior, Atl.	1	2	2.0	2	0
Miller, Mike, Giants	1	2	2.0	2	0
Benjamin, Guy, S.F.	1	1	1.0	1	0
Carter, Gerald, T.B.	1	0	0.0	0	0
Cromwell, Nolan, Rams	1	0	0.0	0	0
Garrett, Alvin, Wash.	2	0	0.0	4	0
Johnson, Butch, Dall.	1	0	0.0	0	0
Pastorini, Dan, Phil.	1	0	0.0	0	0
Perrin, Benny, St.L.	1	0	0.0	0	0
Pisarcik, Joe, Phil.	3	-1	-0.3	0	0
Kemp, Jeff, Rams	3	-2	-0.7	0	0
Wilson, Wade, Minn.	3	-3	-1.0	2	0
House, Kevin, T.B.	1	-4	-4.0	-4	0
Whitehurst, David, G.B.	2	-4	-2.0	0	0
Bailey, Stacey, Atl.	2	-5	-2.5	0	0
Coleman, Greg, Minn.	1	-9	-9.0	-9	0
Erxleben, Russell, N.O.	2	-9	-4.5	1	0
Farmer, George, Rams	1	-9	-9.0	-9	0
Black, Mike, Det.	2	-10	-5.0	0	0
Grant, Otis, Rams	2	-10	-5.0	1	0
Hogeboom, Gary, Dall.	6	-10	-1.7	-1	0
Stabler, Ken, N.O.	9	-14	-1.6	0	0
Duckett, Kenny, N.O.	2	-16	-8.0	2	0
Monk, Art, Wash.	3	-19	-6.3	2	0

AFC — INDIVIDUAL RUSHERS

	Att	Yards	Avg	Long	TD
Warner, Curt, Sea.	335	1449	4.3	60	13
Campbell, Earl, Hou.	322	1301	4.0	42	12
Pruitt, Mike, Clev.	293	1184	4.0	27	10
Cribbs, Joe, Buff.	263	1131	4.3	45	3
Dickey, Curtis, Balt.	254	1122	4.4	56	4
Collins, Anthony, N.E.	219	1049	4.8	t50	10
Allen, Marcus, Raiders	266	1014	3.8	19	9
Harris, Franco, Pitt.	279	1007	3.6	19	5
Muncie, Chuck, S.D.	235	886	3.8	t34	12
McMillan, Randy, Balt.	198	802	4.1	t39	5

James Wilder led the Buccaneers in rushing yardage.

	Att	Yards	Avg	Long	TD
Johnson, Pete, Cin.	210	763	3.6	t16	14
Winder, Sammy, Den.	196	757	3.9	52	3
Franklin, Andra, Mia.	224	746	3.3	18	8
Nathan, Tony, Mia.	151	685	4.5	40	3
McNeil, Freeman, Jets	160	654	4.1	19	1
Pollard, Frank, Pitt.	135	608	4.5	32	4
Crutchfield, Dwayne,Jets-Hou	140	578	4.1	17	3
Tatupu, Mosi, N.E.	106	578	5.5	55	4
Hawkins, Frank, Raiders	110	526	4.8	32	6
Alexander, Charles, Cin. ...	153	523	3.4	12	3
Brooks, James, S.D.	127	516	4.1	61	3
Jackson, Billy, K.C.	152	499	3.3	19	2
Green, Boyce, Clev.	104	497	4.8	29	3
Brown, Theotis, Sea.-K.C. ..	130	481	3.7	t49	8
Stoudt, Cliff, Pitt.	77	479	6.2	23	4
Abercrombie, Walter, Pitt. .	112	446	4.0	t50	4
Pagel, Mike, Balt.	54	441	8.2	33	0
Weathers, Robert, N.E.	73	418	5.7	77	1
Overstreet, David, Mia.	85	392	4.6	44	1
van Eeghen, Mark, N.E.	95	358	3.8	11	2
Harper, Bruce, Jets	51	354	6.9	t78	1
Moriarty, Larry, Hou.	65	321	4.9	80	3
Hughes, David, Sea.	83	313	3.8	26	1
King, Kenny, Raiders	82	294	3.6	16	1
Moore, Booker, Buff.	60	275	4.6	21	0
Wilson, Stanley, Cin.	56	267	4.8	18	1
Poole, Nathan, Den.	81	246	3.0	19	4
Preston, Dave, Den.	57	222	3.9	28	1
Moore, Alvin, Balt.	57	205	3.6	13	1
Bennett, Woody, Mia.	49	197	4.0	25	2
Willhite, Gerald, Den.	43	188	4.4	t24	3
Leaks, Roosevelt, Buff.	58	157	2.7	12	1
Kinnebrew, Larry, Cin.	39	156	4.0	17	3
Pruitt, Greg, Raiders	26	154	5.9	18	2
Anderson, Ken, Cin.	22	147	6.7	29	1
Craft, Donald, Hou.	55	147	2.7	8	0
Elway, John, Den.	28	146	5.2	23	1
Wilson, Marc, Raiders	13	122	9.4	23	0
Schonert, Turk, Cin.	29	117	4.0	15	2
Thomas, Jewerl, K.C.	44	115	2.6	11	0
Dierking, Scott, Jets	28	113	4.0	31	3
Grogan, Steve, N.E.	23	108	4.7	17	2
Todd, Richard, Jets	35	101	2.9	17	0
Walker, Dwight, Clev.	19	100	5.3	15	0
Doornink, Dan, Sea.	40	99	2.5	9	2
Parros, Rick, Den.	30	96	3.2	13	1
Smith, Sherman, S.D.	24	91	3.8	20	0

	Att	Yards	Avg	Long	TD
Ferguson, Joe, Buff.	20	88	4.4	19	0
Bryant, Cullen, Sea.	27	87	3.2	9	0
Hector, Johnny, Jets	16	85	5.3	42	0
Plunkett, Jim, Raiders	26	78	3.0	20	0
Woodley, David, Mia.	19	78	4.1	15	0
Barber, Marion, Jets	15	77	5.1	13	1
Tate, Rodney, Cin.	25	77	3.1	13	0
Williams, Newton, Balt.	28	77	2.8	13	0
Zorn, Jim, Sea.	30	71	2.4	t18	1
Kenney, Bill, K.C.	23	59	2.6	11	3
Sipe, Brian, Clev.	26	56	2.2	9	0
Krieg, Dave, Sea.	16	55	3.4	t10	2
Luck, Oliver, Hou.	17	55	3.2	17	0
Thomas, Ken, K.C.	15	55	3.7	28	0
Myles, Jesse, Den.	8	52	6.5	16	0
Augustyniak, Mike, Jets	18	50	2.8	6	2
Hawthorne, Greg, Pitt.	5	47	9.4	20	0
Marino, Dan, Mia.	28	45	1.6	15	2
Walls, Herkie, Hou.	5	44	8.8	14	0
Nielsen, Gifford, Hou.	8	43	5.4	20	0
Davis, Johnny, Clev.	13	42	3.2	16	0
Edwards, Stan, Hou.	16	40	2.5	9	0
Eason, Tony, N.E.	19	39	2.1	12	0
Jackson, Ernest, S.D.	11	39	3.5	6	0
Dixon, Zachary, Balt.-Sea. .	9	32	3.6	7	0
Verser, David, Cin.	2	31	15.5	29	0
DeBerg, Steve, Den.	13	28	2.2	11	1
Hunter, Tony, Buff.	2	28	14.0	24	0
Ricks, Lawrence, K.C.	21	28	1.3	10	0
Weathers, Clarence, N.E. ...	1	28	28.0	28	0
Reed, Mark, Balt.	2	27	13.5	18	0
Chandler, Wes, S.D.	2	25	12.5	23	0
Kofler, Matt, Buff.	4	25	6.3	11	0
Lewis, Kenny, Jets	5	25	5.0	7	0
Ryan, Pat, Jets	4	23	5.8	25	0
Berns, Rick, Raiders	6	22	3.7	13	0
Martin, Mike, Cin.	2	21	10.5	15	0
Branch, Cliff, Raiders	1	20	20.0	20	0
Carson, Carlos, K.C.	2	20	10.0	18	0
Jones, Bobby, Clev.	1	19	19.0	19	0
Upchurch, Rick, Den.	6	19	3.2	9	0
Riddick, Robb, Buff.	4	18	4.5	12	0
Kubiak, Gary, Den.	4	17	4.3	8	1
McDonald, Paul, Clev.	3	17	5.7	10	0
Watson, Steve, Den.	3	17	5.7	10	0
Smith, Tim, Hou.	2	16	8.0	9	0
Harris, Tim, Pitt.	2	15	7.5	10	0

	Att	Yards	Avg	Long	TD
Kerrigan, Mike, N.E.	1	14	14.0	14	0
Morgan, Stanley, N.E.	1	13	13.0	13	0
Barnwell, Malcolm, Raiders .	1	12	12.0	12	0
Hill, Eddie, Mia.	2	12	6.0	10	0
Johns, Paul, Sea.	2	12	6.0	26	0
Williams, Van, Buff.	3	11	3.7	5	0
Hadnot, James, K.C.	4	10	2.5	7	0
Jones, Lam, Jets	4	10	2.5	9	0
Clayton, Mark, Mia.	2	9	4.5	9	0
Holt, Harry, Clev.	3	8	2.7	4	0
Stark, Rohn, Balt.	1	8	8.0	8	0
Montgomery, Cleotha, Raiders	2	7	3.5	5	0
Odom, Henry, Pitt.	2	7	3.5	4	0
Prestridge, Luke, Den.	1	7	7.0	7	0
Allen, Gary, Hou.	1	5	5.0	5	0
Cappelletti, John, S.D.	1	5	5.0	5	0
Crosby, Ron, Jets	1	5	5.0	5	0
Jensen, Derrick, Raiders ...	1	5	5.0	5	0
Bradshaw, Terry, Pitt.	1	3	3.0	3	0
Dressel, Chris, Hou.	1	3	3.0	3	0
Franklin, Byron, Buff.	1	3	3.0	3	0
Renfro, Mike, Hou.	1	3	3.0	3	0
Adams, Willis, Clev.	1	2	2.0	2	0
Collinswoth, Cris, Cin.	2	2	1.0	8	0
Hall, Dino, Clev.	1	2	2.0	2	0
Hardy, Bruce, Mia.	1	2	2.0	2	0
Kreider, Steve, Cin.	1	2	2.0	2	0
Lane, Eric, Sea.	3	1	0.3	7	0
Scott, Willie, K.C.	1	1	1.0	1	0
Blackledge, Todd, K.C.	1	0	0.0	0	0
Brown, Curtis, Hou.	3	0	0.0	t1	1
Harris, Duriel, Mia.	1	0	0.0	0	0
Herrmann, Mark, Balt.	1	0	0.0	0	0
James, John, Hou.	1	0	0.0	0	0
Mathison, Bruce, S.D.	1	0	0.0	0	0
Willis, Chester, Raiders ...	5	0	0.0	4	0
Humm, David, Raiders	1	-1	-1.0	-1	0
Krauss, Barry, Balt.	1	-1	-1.0	-1	0
Christensen, Jeff, Cin.	1	-2	-2.0	-2	0
Sweeney, Calvin, Pitt.	1	-2	-2.0	-2	0
Belk, Rocky, Clev.	1	-5	-5.0	-5	0
Fouts, Dan, S.D.	12	-5	-0.4	3	1
Sievers, Eric, S.D.	1	-7	-7.0	-7	0
Wright, James, Den.	1	-11	-11.0	-11	0
Guy, Ray, Raiders	2	-13	-6.5	-3	0
Luther, Ed, S.D.	9	-14	-1.6	8	0
Strock, Don, Mia.	6	-16	-2.7	0	0

TOP TEN SCORERS – KICKERS

	XP	XPA	FG	FGA	PTS
Moseley, Mark, Wash.	62	63	33	47	161
Haji-Sheikh, Ali, Giants	22	23	35	42	127
Wersching, Ray, S.F.	51	51	25	30	126
Septien, Rafael, Dall.	57	59	22	27	123
Anderson, Gary, Pitt.	38	39	27	31	119
Lowery, Nick, K.C.	44	45	24	30	116
Stenerud, Jan, G.B.	52	52	21	26	115
Bahr, Chris, Raiders	51	53	21	27	114
Murray, Ed, Det.	38	38	25	32	113
Allegre, Raul, Balt.	22	24	30	35	112

TOP TEN SCORERS – NON-KICKERS

	TD	TDR	TDP	TDM	PTS
Riggins, John, Wash.	24	24	0	0	144
Dickerson, Eric, Rams	20	18	2	0	120
Green, Roy, St.L.	14	0	14	0	84
Johnson, Pete, Cin.	14	14	0	0	84
Warner, Curt, Sea.	14	13	1	0	84
Muncie, Chuck, S.D.	13	12	1	0	78
Quick, Mike, Phil.	13	0	13	0	78
Allen, Marcus, Raiders	12	9	2	1	72
Campbell, Earl, Hou.	12	12	0	0	72
Christensen, Todd, Raiders	12	0	12	0	72
Craig, Roger, S.F.	12	8	4	0	72
Pruitt, Mike, Clev.	12	10	2	0	72

TOP TEN PASS RECEIVERS BY YARDS

	Yards	No	Avg	Long	TD
Quick, Mike, Phil.	1409	69	20.4	t83	13
Carson, Carlos, K.C.	1351	80	16.9	t50	7
Lofton, James, G.B.	1300	58	22.4	t74	8
Christensen, Todd, Raiders	1247	92	13.6	45	12
Green, Roy, St.L.	1227	78	15.7	t71	14
Brown, Charlie, Wash.	1225	78	15.7	t75	8
Smith, Tim, Hou.	1176	83	14.2	t47	6
Winslow, Kellen, S.D.	1172	88	13.3	46	8
Gray, Earnest, Giants	1139	78	14.6	62	5
Watson, Steve, Den.	1133	59	19.2	t78	5

San Diego's Kellen Winslow had 14 receptions in one game.

PASSING

NFC INDIVIDUAL QUALIFIERS

	Att	Comp	Pct Comp	Yards
Bartkowski, Steve, Atl.	432	274	63.4	3167
Theismann, Joe, Wash.	459	276	60.1	3714
Montana, Joe, S.F.	515	332	64.5	3910
Lomax, Neil, St.L.	354	209	59.0	2636
Dickey, Lynn, G.B.	484	289	59.7	4458
White, Danny, Dall.	533	334	62.7	3980
McMahon, Jim, Chi.	295	175	59.3	2184
Ferragamo, Vince, Rams	464	274	59.1	3276
Jaworski, Ron, Phil.	446	235	52.7	3315
Thompson, Jack, T.B.	423	249	58.9	2906
Dils, Steve, Minn.	444	239	53.8	2840
Hipple, Eric, Det.	387	204	52.7	2577
Stabler, Ken, N.O.	311	176	56.6	1988
Brunner, Scott, Giants	386	190	49.2	2516

AFC INDIVIDUAL QUALIFIERS

	Att	Comp	Pct Comp	Yards
Marino, Dan, Mia.	296	173	58.4	2210
Krieg, Dave, Sea.	243	147	60.5	2139
Fouts, Dan, S.D.	340	215	63.2	2975
Anderson, Ken, Cin.	297	198	66.7	2333
Plunkett, Jim, Raiders	379	230	60.7	2935
Grogan, Steve, N.E.	303	168	55.4	2411
Kenney, Bill, K.C.	603	346	57.4	4348
DeBerg, Steve, Den.	215	119	55.3	1617
Sipe, Brian, Clev.	496	291	58.7	3566
Todd, Richard, Jets	518	308	59.5	3478
Ferguson, Joe, Buff.	508	281	55.3	2995
Zorn, Jim, Sea.	205	103	50.2	1166
Pagel, Mike, Balt.	328	163	49.7	2353
Luck, Oliver, Hou.	217	124	57.1	1375
Stoudt, Cliff, Pitt.	381	197	51.7	2553
Luther, Ed, S.D.	287	151	52.6	1875
Elway, John, Den.	259	123	47.5	1663

PUNTING

TOP TEN PUNTERS

	No	Yards	Long	Avg
Stark, Rohn, Balt.	91	4124	68	45.3
Camarillo, Rich, N.E.	81	3615	70	44.6
Buford, Maury, S.D.	63	2763	60	43.9
Roby, Reggie, Mia.	74	3189	64	43.1
Guy, Ray, Raiders	78	3336	67	42.8
Garcia, Frank, T.B.	95	4008	64	42.2
Colquitt, Craig, Pitt.	80	3352	58	41.9
McInally, Pat, Cin.	67	2804	60	41.9
Runager, Max, Phil.	59	2459	55	41.7
Prestridge, Luke, Den.	87	3620	60	41.6
Scribner, Bucky, G.B.	69	2869	70	41.6

Avg Gain	TD	Pct TD	Long	Int	Pct Int	Rating Points
7.33	22	5.1	t76	5	1.2	97.6
8.09	29	6.3	84	11	2.4	97.0
7.59	26	5.0	t77	12	2.3	94.6
7.45	24	6.8	t71	11	3.1	92.0
9.21	32	6.6	t75	29	6.0	87.3
7.47	29	5.4	t80	23	4.3	85.6
7.40	12	4.1	t87	13	4.4	77.6
7.06	22	4.7	t61	23	5.0	75.9
7.43	20	4.5	t83	18	4.0	75.1
6.87	18	4.3	80	21	5.0	73.3
6.40	11	2.5	68	16	3.6	66.8
6.66	12	3.1	t80	18	4.7	64.7
6.39	9	2.9	48	18	5.8	61.4
6.52	9	2.3	62	22	5.7	54.3

Avg Gain	TD	Pct TD	Long	Int	Pct Int	Rating Points
7.47	20	6.8	t85	6	2.0	96.0
8.80	18	7.4	t50	11	4.5	95.0
8.75	20	5.9	t59	15	4.4	92.5
7.86	12	4.0	t80	13	4.4	85.6
7.74	20	5.3	t99	18	4.7	82.7
7.96	15	5.0	t76	12	4.0	81.4
7.21	24	4.0	53	18	3.0	80.8
7.52	9	4.2	54	7	3.3	79.9
7.19	26	5.2	t66	23	4.6	79.1
6.71	18	3.5	t64	26	5.0	70.3
5.90	26	5.1	t43	25	4.9	69.3
5.69	7	3.4	43	7	3.4	64.8
7.17	12	3.7	t72	17	5.2	64.0
6.34	8	3.7	66	13	6.0	63.4
6.70	12	3.1	52	21	5.5	60.6
6.53	7	2.4	46	17	5.9	56.6
6.42	7	2.7	t49	14	5.4	54.9

Total Punts	TB	Blk	Opp Ret	Ret Yds	In 20	Net Avg
91	9	0	55	642	20	36.3
81	11	0	48	392	25	37.1
63	8	0	35	299	13	36.6
75	11	1	32	229	26	36.5
78	10	0	35	334	17	35.9
96	12	1	59	603	16	33.0
80	7	0	44	418	20	34.9
69	9	2	41	310	13	33.5
59	5	0	37	339	12	34.2
87	7	0	55	524	19	34.0
70	7	1	43	384	11	33.5

Packer James Lofton's longest of eight TDs was a 74-yarder.

Bronco Steve Watson had 78-yard TD among 59 catches.

Tim Smith, Oilers' No. 1 receiver, welcomes Warren Moon.

TOP TEN INTERCEPTORS

	No	Yards	Avg	Long	TD
Murphy, Mark, Wash.	9	127	14.1	48	0
Reece, Beasley, Giants-T.B.	8	103	12.9	29	0
Washington, Lionel, St.L. ..	8	92	11.5	26	0
Riley, Ken, Cin.	8	89	11.1	t42	2
McElroy, Vann, Raiders	8	68	8.5	28	0
Wright, Eric, S.F.	7	164	23.4	t60	2
Poe, Johnnie, N.O.	7	146	20.9	t31	1
Frazier, Leslie, Chi.	7	135	19.3	58	1
Easley, Ken, Sea.	7	106	15.1	48	0
Cherry, Deron, K.C.	7	100	14.3	41	0
Mehl, Lance, Jets	7	57	8.1	t34	1
Walters, Danny, S.D.	7	55	7.9	33	0
McNorton, Bruce, Det.	7	30	4.3	15	0
Sanford, Rick, N.E.	7	24	3.4	16	0

TOP TEN KICKOFF RETURNERS

	No	Yards	Avg	Long	TD
Walker, Fulton, Mia.	36	962	26.7	78	0
Brown, Steve, Hou.	31	795	25.6	t93	1
Nelson, Darrin, Minn.	18	445	24.7	50	0
Williams, Kendall, Balt.	20	490	24.5	90	0
Morton, Michael, T.B.	30	689	23.0	50	0
Dixon, Zachary, Balt.-Sea. ..	51	1171	23.0	t94	1
Nelms, Mike, Wash.	35	802	22.9	41	0
Springs, Kirk, Jets	16	364	22.8	64	0
Bright, Leon, Giants	21	475	22.6	36	0
Williams, Van, Buff.	22	494	22.5	60	0

TOP TEN PUNT RETURNERS

	No	FC	Yards	Avg	Long	TD
Ellard, Henry, Rams	16	4	217	13.6	t72	1
Springs, Kirk, Jets	23	4	287	12.5	t76	1
Pruitt, Greg, Raiders	58	18	666	11.5	t97	1
Johns, Paul, Sea.	28	5	316	11.3	t75	1
Thomas, Zack, Den.	33	9	368	11.2	t70	1
McLemore, Dana, S.F.	31	6	331	10.7	t56	1
Johnson, Billy, Atl.	46	4	489	10.6	t71	1
Smith, Ricky, N.E.	38	12	398	10.5	55	0
Jenkins, Ken, Det.	23	1	230	10.0	43	0
Martin, Mike, Cin.	23	3	227	9.9	19	0

NFL STANDINGS
1921–1983

1921

	W	L	T	Pct.
Chicago Staleys	10	1	1	.909
Buffalo All-Americans	9	1	2	.900
Akron, Ohio, Pros	7	2	1	.778
Green Bay Packers	6	2	2	.750
Canton, Ohio, Bulldogs	4	3	3	.571
Dayton Triangles	4	3	1	.571
Rock Island Independents	5	4	1	.556
Chicago Cardinals	2	3	2	.400
Cleveland Indians	2	6	0	.250
Rochester Jeffersons	2	6	0	.250
Detroit Heralds	1	7	1	.125
Columbus Panhandles	0	6	0	.000
Cincinnati Celts	0	8	0	.000

1922

	W	L	T	Pct.
Canton, Ohio, Bulldogs	10	0	2	1.000
Chicago Bears	9	3	0	.750
Chicago Cardinals	8	3	0	.727
Toledo Maroons	5	2	2	.714
Rock Island Independents	4	2	1	.667
Dayton Triangles	4	3	1	.571
Green Bay Packers	4	3	3	.571
Racine, Wis., Legion	5	4	1	.556
Akron, Ohio, Pros	3	4	2	.429
Buffalo All-Americans	3	4	1	.429
Milwaukee Badgers	2	4	3	.333
Marion, O., Oorang Indians	2	6	0	.250
Minneapolis Marines	1	3	0	.250
Evansville Crimson Giants	0	2	0	.000
Louisville Brecks	0	3	0	.000
Rochester Jeffersons	0	3	1	.000
Hammond, Ind., Pros	0	4	1	.000
Columbus Panhandles	0	7	0	.000

1923

	W	L	T	Pct.
Canton, Ohio, Bulldogs	11	0	1	1.000
Chicago Bears	9	2	1	.818
Green Bay Packers	7	2	1	.778
Milwaukee Badgers	7	2	3	.778
Cleveland Indians	3	1	3	.750
Chicago Cardinals	8	4	0	.667
Duluth Kelleys	4	3	0	.571
Buffalo All-Americans	5	4	3	.556
Columbus Tigers	5	4	1	.556
Racine, Wis., Legion	4	4	2	.500
Toledo Maroons	2	3	2	.400
Rock Island Independents	2	3	3	.400

Minneapolis Marines	2	5	2	.286
St. Louis All-Stars	1	4	2	.200
Hammond, Ind., Pros	1	5	1	.167
Dayton Triangles	1	6	1	.143
Akron, Ohio, Indians	1	6	0	.143
Marion, O., Oorang Indians	1	10	0	.091
Rochester Jeffersons	0	2	0	.000
Louisville Brecks	0	3	0	.000

1924

	W	L	T	Pct.
Cleveland Bulldogs	7	1	1	.875
Chicago Bears	6	1	4	.857
Frankford Yellowjackets	11	2	1	.846
Duluth Kelleys	5	1	0	.833
Rock Island Independents	6	2	2	.750
Green Bay Packers	8	4	0	.667
Buffalo Bisons	6	4	0	.600
Racine, Wis., Legion	4	3	3	.571
Chicago Cardinals	5	4	1	.556
Columbus Tigers	4	4	0	.500
Hammond, Ind., Pros	2	2	1	.500
Milwaukee Badgers	5	8	0	.385
Dayton Triangles	2	7	0	.222
Kansas City Cowboys	2	7	0	.222
Akron, Ohio, Indians	1	6	0	.143
Kenosha, Wis., Maroons	0	5	1	.000
Minneapolis Marines	0	6	0	.000
Rochester Jeffersons	0	7	0	.000

1925

	W	L	T	Pct.
Chicago Cardinals	11	2	1	.846
Pottsville, Pa., Maroons	10	2	0	.833
Detroit Panthers	8	2	2	.800
New York Giants	8	4	0	.667
Akron, Ohio, Indians	4	2	2	.667
Frankford Yellowjackets	13	7	0	.650
Chicago Bears	9	5	3	.643
Rock Island Independents	5	3	3	.625
Green Bay Packers	8	5	0	.615
Providence Steamroller	6	5	1	.545
Canton, Ohio, Bulldogs	4	4	0	.500
Cleveland Bulldogs	5	8	1	.385
Kansas City Cowboys	2	5	1	.286
Hammond, Ind., Pros	1	3	0	.250
Buffalo Bisons	1	6	2	.143
Duluth Kelleys	0	3	0	.000
Rochester Jeffersons	0	6	1	.000
Milwaukee Badgers	0	6	0	.000
Dayton Triangles	0	7	1	.000
Columbus Tigers	0	9	0	.000

1926

	W	L	T	Pct.
Frankford Yellowjackets	14	1	1	.933
Chicago Bears	12	1	3	.923
Pottsville, Pa., Maroons	10	2	1	.833
Kansas City Cowboys	8	3	1	.727
Green Bay Packers	7	3	3	.700
Los Angeles Buccaneers	6	3	1	.667
New York Giants	8	4	1	.667
Duluth Eskimos	6	5	2	.545
Buffalo Rangers	4	4	2	.500
Chicago Cardinals	5	6	1	.455
Providence Steamroller	5	7	0	.417
Detroit Panthers	4	6	2	.400
Hartford Blues	3	7	0	.300
Brooklyn Lions	3	8	0	.273
Milwaukee Badgers	2	7	0	.222
Akron, Ohio, Indians	1	4	3	.200
Dayton Triangles	1	4	1	.200
Racine, Wis., Legion	1	4	0	.200
Columbus Tigers	1	6	0	.143
Canton, Ohio, Bulldogs	1	9	3	.100
Hammond, Ind., Pros	0	4	0	.000
Louisville Colonels	0	4	0	.000

1927

	W	L	T	Pct.
New York Giants	11	1	1	.917
Green Bay Packers	7	2	1	.778
Chicago Bears	9	3	2	.750
Cleveland Bulldogs	8	4	1	.667
Providence Steamroller	8	5	1	.615
New York Yankees	7	8	1	.467
Frankford Yellowjackets	6	9	3	.400
Pottsville, Pa., Maroons	5	8	0	.385
Chicago Cardinals	3	7	1	.300
Dayton Triangles	1	6	1	.143
Duluth Eskimos	1	8	0	.111
Buffalo Bisons	0	5	0	.000

1928

	W	L	T	Pct.
Providence Steamroller	8	1	2	.889
Frankford Yellowjackets	11	3	2	.786
Detroit Wolverines	7	2	1	.778
Green Bay Packers	6	4	3	.600
Chicago Bears	7	5	1	.583
New York Giants	4	7	2	.364
New York Yankees	4	8	1	.333
Pottsville, Pa., Maroons	2	8	0	.200
Chicago Cardinals	1	5	0	.167
Dayton Triangles	0	7	0	.000

1929

	W	L	T	Pct.
Green Bay Packers	12	0	1	1.000
New York Giants	13	1	1	.929
Frankford Yellowjackets	9	4	5	.692
Chicago Cardinals	6	6	1	.500
Boston Bulldogs	4	4	0	.500
Orange, N.J., Tornadoes	3	4	4	.429
Stapleton Stapes	3	4	3	.429
Providence Steamroller	4	6	2	.400
Chicago Bears	4	9	2	.308
Buffalo Bisons	1	7	1	.125
Minneapolis Red Jackets	1	9	0	.100
Dayton Triangles	0	6	0	.000

1930

	W	L	T	Pct.
Green Bay Packers	10	3	1	.769
New York Giants	13	4	0	.765
Chicago Bears	9	4	1	.692
Brooklyn Dodgers	7	4	1	.636
Providence Steamroller	6	4	1	.600
Stapleton Stapes	5	5	2	.500
Chicago Cardinals	5	6	2	.455
Portsmouth, O., Spartans	5	6	3	.455
Frankford Yellowjackets	4	14	1	.222
Minneapolis Red Jackets	1	7	1	.125
Newark Tornadoes	1	10	1	.091

1931

	W	L	T	Pct.
Green Bay Packers	12	2	0	.857
Portsmouth, O., Spartans	11	3	0	.786
Chicago Bears	8	5	0	.615
Chicago Cardinals	5	4	0	.556
New York Giants	7	6	1	.538
Providence Steamroller	4	4	3	.500
Stapleton Stapes	4	6	1	.400
Cleveland Indians	2	8	0	.200
Brooklyn Dodgers	2	12	0	.143
Frankford Yellowjackets	1	6	1	.143

1932

	W	L	T	Pct.
Chicago Bears	7	1	6	.875
Green Bay Packers	10	3	1	.769
Portsmouth, O., Spartans	6	2	4	.750
Boston Braves	4	4	2	.500
New York Giants	4	6	2	.400
Brooklyn Dodgers	3	9	0	.250
Chicago Cardinals	2	6	2	.250
Stapleton Stapes	2	7	3	.222

1933

EASTERN DIVISION

	W	L	T	Pct.	Pts.	OP
N.Y. Giants	11	3	0	.786	244	101
Brooklyn	5	4	1	.556	93	54
Boston	5	5	2	.500	103	97
Philadelphia	3	5	1	.375	77	158
Pittsburgh	3	6	2	.333	67	208

WESTERN DIVISION

	W	L	T	Pct.	Pts.	OP
Chi. Bears	10	2	1	.833	133	82
Portsmouth	6	5	0	.545	128	87
Green Bay	5	7	1	.417	170	107
Cincinnati	3	6	1	.333	38	110
Chi. Cardinals	1	9	1	.100	52	101

NFL Championship: Chicago Bears 23, N.Y. Giants 21

1934

EASTERN DIVISION	W	L	T	Pct.	Pts.	OP
N.Y. Giants	8	5	0	.615	147	107
Boston	6	6	0	.500	107	94
Brooklyn	4	7	0	.364	61	153
Philadelphia	4	7	0	.364	127	85
Pittsburgh	2	10	0	.167	51	206

WESTERN DIVISION	W	L	T	Pct.	Pts.	OP
Chi. Bears	13	0	0	1.000	286	86
Detroit	10	3	0	.769	238	59
Green Bay	7	6	0	.538	156	112
Chi. Cardinals	5	6	0	.455	80	84
St. Louis	1	2	0	.333	27	61
Cincinnati	0	8	0	.000	10	243

NFL Championship: N.Y. Giants 30, Chicago Bears 13

1935

EASTERN DIVISION	W	L	T	Pct.	Pts.	OP
N.Y. Giants	9	3	0	.750	180	96
Brooklyn	5	6	1	.455	90	141
Pittsburgh	4	8	0	.333	100	209
Boston	2	8	1	.200	65	123
Philadelphia	2	9	0	.182	60	179

WESTERN DIVISION	W	L	T	Pct.	Pts.	OP
Detroit	7	3	2	.700	191	111
Green Bay	8	4	0	.667	181	96
Chi. Bears	6	4	2	.600	192	106
Chi. Cardinals	6	4	2	.600	99	97

NFL Championship: Detroit 26, N.Y. Giants 7
One game between Boston and Philadelphia was canceled.

1936

EASTERN DIVISION	W	L	T	Pct.	Pts.	OP
Boston	7	5	0	.583	149	110
Pittsburgh	6	6	0	.500	98	187
N.Y. Giants	5	6	1	.455	115	163
Brooklyn	3	8	1	.273	92	161
Philadelphia	1	11	0	.083	51	206

WESTERN DIVISION	W	L	T	Pct.	Pts.	OP
Green Bay	10	1	1	.909	248	118
Chi. Bears	9	3	0	.750	222	94
Detroit	8	4	0	.667	235	102
Chi. Cardinals	3	8	1	.273	74	143

NFL Championship: Green Bay 21, Boston 6

1937

EASTERN DIVISION	W	L	T	Pct.	Pts.	OP
Washington	8	3	0	.727	195	120
N.Y. Giants	6	3	2	.667	128	109
Pittsburgh	4	7	0	.364	122	145
Brooklyn	3	7	1	.300	82	174
Philadelphia	2	8	1	.200	86	177

WESTERN DIVISION	W	L	T	Pct.	Pts.	OP
Chi. Bears	9	1	1	.900	201	100
Green Bay	7	4	0	.636	220	122
Detroit	7	4	0	.636	180	105
Chi. Cardinals	5	5	1	.500	135	165
Cleveland	1	10	0	.091	75	207

NFL Championship: Washington 28, Chicago Bears 21

1938

EASTERN DIVISION	W	L	T	Pct.	Pts.	OP
N.Y Giants	8	2	1	.800	194	79
Washington	6	3	2	.667	148	154
Brooklyn	4	4	3	.500	131	161
Philadelphia	5	6	0	.455	154	164
Pittsburgh	2	9	0	.182	79	169

WESTERN DIVISION	W	L	T	Pct.	Pts.	OP
Green Bay	8	3	0	.727	223	118
Detroit	7	4	0	.636	119	108
Chi. Bears	6	5	0	.545	194	148
Cleveland	4	7	0	.364	131	215
Chi. Cardinals	2	9	0	.182	111	168

NFL Championship: N.Y. Giants 23, Green Bay 17

1939

EASTERN DIVISION	W	L	T	Pct.	Pts.	OP
N.Y. Giants	9	1	1	.900	168	85
Washington	8	2	1	.800	242	94
Brooklyn	4	6	1	.400	108	219
Philadelphia	1	9	1	.100	105	200
Pittsburgh	1	9	1	.100	114	216

WESTERN DIVISION	W	L	T	Pct.	Pts.	OP
Green Bay	9	2	0	.818	233	153
Chi. Bears	8	3	0	.727	298	157
Detroit	6	5	0	.545	145	150
Cleveland	5	5	1	.500	195	164
Chi. Cardinals	1	10	0	.091	84	254

NFL Championship: Green Bay 27, N.Y. Giants 0

1940

EASTERN DIVISION	W	L	T	Pct.	Pts.	OP
Washington	9	2	0	.818	245	142
Brooklyn	8	3	0	.727	186	120
N.Y. Giants	6	4	1	.600	131	133
Pittsburgh	2	7	2	.222	60	178
Philadelphia	1	10	0	.091	111	211

WESTERN DIVISION	W	L	T	Pct.	Pts.	OP
Chi. Bears	8	3	0	.727	238	152
Green Bay	6	4	1	.600	238	155
Detroit	5	5	1	.500	138	153
Cleveland	4	6	1	.400	171	191
Chi. Cardinals	2	7	2	.222	139	222

NFL Championship: Chicago Bears 73, Washington 0

1941

EASTERN DIVISION	W	L	T	Pct.	Pts.	OP
N.Y. Giants	8	3	0	.727	238	114
Brooklyn	7	4	0	.636	158	127
Washington	6	5	0	.545	176	174
Philadelphia	2	8	1	.200	119	218
Pittsburgh	1	9	1	.100	103	276

WESTERN DIVISION	W	L	T	Pct.	Pts.	OP
Chi. Bears	10	1	0	.909	396	147
Green Bay	10	1	0	.909	258	120
Detroit	4	6	1	.400	121	195
Chi. Cardinals	3	7	1	.300	127	197
Cleveland	2	9	0	.182	116	244

Western Division playoff: Chicago Bears 33, Green Bay 14
NFL Championship: Chicago Bears 37, N.Y. Giants 9

1942

EASTERN DIVISION	W	L	T	Pct.	Pts.	OP
Washington	10	1	0	.909	227	102
Pittsburgh	7	4	0	.636	167	119
N.Y. Giants	5	5	1	.500	155	139
Brooklyn	3	8	0	.273	100	168
Philadelphia	2	9	0	.182	134	239

WESTERN DIVISION	W	L	T	Pct.	Pts.	OP
Chi. Bears	11	0	0	1.000	376	84
Green Bay	8	2	1	.800	300	215
Cleveland	5	6	0	.455	150	207
Chi. Cardinals	3	8	0	.273	98	209
Detroit	0	11	0	.000	38	263

NFL Championship: Washington 14, Chicago Bears 6

1943

EASTERN DIVISION	W	L	T	Pct.	Pts.	OP
Washington	6	3	1	.667	229	137
N.Y. Giants	6	3	1	.667	197	170
Phil-Pitt	5	4	1	.556	225	230
Brooklyn	2	8	0	.200	65	234

WESTERN DIVISION	W	L	T	Pct.	Pts.	OP
Chi. Bears	8	1	1	.889	303	157
Green Bay	7	2	1	.778	264	172
Detroit	3	6	1	.333	178	218
Chi. Cardinals	0	10	0	.000	95	238

Eastern Division playoff: Washington 28, N.Y. Giants 0
NFL Championship: Chicago Bears 41, Washington 21

1944

EASTERN DIVISION	W	L	T	Pct.	Pts.	OP
N.Y. Giants	8	1	1	.889	206	75
Philadelphia	7	1	2	.875	267	131
Washington	6	3	1	.667	169	180
Boston	2	8	0	.200	82	233
Brooklyn	0	10	0	.000	69	166

WESTERN DIVISION	W	L	T	Pct.	Pts.	OP
Green Bay	8	2	0	.800	238	141
Chi. Bears	6	3	1	.667	258	172
Detroit	6	3	1	.667	216	151
Cleveland	4	6	0	.400	188	224
Card-Pitt	0	10	0	.000	108	328

NFL Championship: Green Bay 14, N.Y. Giants 7

1945

EASTERN DIVISION	W	L	T	Pct.	Pts.	OP
Washington	8	2	0	.800	209	121
Philadelphia	7	3	0	.700	272	133
N.Y. Giants	3	6	1	.333	179	198
Boston	3	6	1	.333	123	211
Pittsburgh	2	8	0	.200	79	220

WESTERN DIVISION	W	L	T	Pct.	Pts.	OP
Cleveland	9	1	0	.900	244	136
Detroit	7	3	0	.700	195	194
Green Bay	6	4	0	.600	258	173
Chi. Bears	3	7	0	.300	192	235
Chi. Cardinals	1	9	0	.100	98	228

NFL Championship: Cleveland 15, Washington 14

1946

EASTERN DIVISION	W	L	T	Pct.	Pts.	OP
N.Y. Giants	7	3	1	.700	236	162
Philadelphia	6	5	0	.545	231	220
Washington	5	5	1	.500	171	191
Pittsburgh	5	5	1	.500	136	117
Boston	2	8	1	.200	189	273

WESTERN DIVISION	W	L	T	Pct.	Pts.	OP
Chi. Bears	8	2	1	.800	289	193
Los Angeles	6	4	1	.600	277	257
Green Bay	6	5	0	.545	148	158
Chi. Cardinals	6	5	0	.545	260	198
Detroit	1	10	0	.091	142	310

NFL Championship: Chicago Bears 24, N.Y. Giants 14

1947

EASTERN DIVISION	W	L	T	Pct.	Pts.	OP
Philadelphia	8	4	0	.667	308	242
Pittsburgh	8	4	0	.667	240	259
Boston	4	7	1	.364	168	256
Washington	4	8	0	.333	295	367
N.Y. Giants	2	8	2	.200	190	309

WESTERN DIVISION	W	L	T	Pct.	Pts.	OP
Chi. Cardinals	9	3	0	.750	306	231
Chi. Bears	8	4	0	.667	363	241
Green Bay	6	5	1	.545	274	210
Los Angeles	6	6	0	.500	259	214
Detroit	3	9	0	.250	231	305

Eastern Division playoff: Philadelphia 21, Pittsburgh 0
NFL Championship: Chicago Cardinals 28, Philadelphia 21

1948

EASTERN DIVISION	W	L	T	Pct.	Pts.	OP
Philadelphia	9	2	1	.818	376	156
Washington	7	5	0	.583	291	287
N.Y. Giants	4	8	0	.333	297	388
Pittsburgh	4	8	0	.333	200	243
Boston	3	9	0	.250	174	372

WESTERN DIVISION	W	L	T	Pct.	Pts.	OP
Chi. Cardinals	11	1	0	.917	395	226
Chi. Bears	10	2	0	.833	375	151
Los Angeles	6	5	1	.545	327	269
Green Bay	3	9	0	.250	154	290
Detroit	2	10	0	.167	200	407

NFL Championship: Philadelphia 7, Chicago Cardinals 0

1949

EASTERN DIVISION	W	L	T	Pct.	Pts.	OP
Philadelphia	11	1	0	.917	364	134
Pittsburgh	6	5	1	.545	224	214
N.Y. Giants	6	6	0	.500	287	298
Washington	4	7	1	.364	268	339
N.Y. Bulldogs	1	10	1	.091	153	368

WESTERN DIVISION	W	L	T	Pct.	Pts.	OP
Los Angeles	8	2	2	.800	360	239
Chi. Bears	9	3	0	.750	332	218
Chi. Cardinals	6	5	1	.545	360	301
Detroit	4	8	0	.333	237	259
Green Bay	2	10	0	.167	114	329

NFL Championship: Philadelphia 14, Los Angeles 0

1950

AMERICAN CONFERENCE	W	L	T	Pct.	Pts.	OP
Cleveland	10	2	0	.833	310	144
N.Y. Giants	10	2	0	.833	268	150
Philadelphia	6	6	0	.500	254	141
Pittsburgh	6	6	0	.500	180	195
Chi. Cardinals	5	7	0	.417	233	287
Washington	3	9	0	.250	232	326

NATIONAL CONFERENCE	W	L	T	Pct.	Pts.	OP
Los Angeles	9	3	0	.750	466	309
Chi. Bears	9	3	0	.750	279	207
N.Y. Yanks	7	5	0	.583	366	367
Detroit	6	6	0	.500	321	285
Green Bay	3	9	0	.250	244	406
San Francisco	3	9	0	.250	213	300
Baltimore	1	11	0	.083	213	462

American Conference playoff: Cleveland 8, N.Y. Giants 3
National Conference playoff: Los Angeles 24, Chicago Bears 14
NFL Championship: Cleveland 30, Los Angeles 28

1951

AMERICAN CONFERENCE	W	L	T	Pct.	Pts.	OP
Cleveland	11	1	0	.917	331	152
N.Y. Giants	9	2	1	.818	254	161
Washington	5	7	0	.417	183	296
Pittsburgh	4	7	1	.364	183	235
Philadelphia	4	8	0	.333	234	264
Chi. Cardinals	3	9	0	.250	210	287

NATIONAL CONFERENCE	W	L	T	Pct.	Pts.	OP
Los Angeles	8	4	0	.667	392	261
Detroit	7	4	1	.636	336	259
San Francisco	7	4	1	.636	255	205
Chi. Bears	7	5	0	.583	286	282
Green Bay	3	9	0	.250	254	375
N.Y. Yanks	1	9	2	.100	241	382

NFL Championship: Los Angeles 24, Cleveland 17

1952

AMERICAN CONFERENCE

	W	L	T	Pct.	Pts.	OP
Cleveland	8	4	0	.667	310	213
N.Y. Giants	7	5	0	.583	234	231
Philadelphia	7	5	0	.583	252	271
Pittsburgh	5	7	0	.417	300	273
Chi. Cardinals	4	8	0	.333	172	221
Washington	4	8	0	.333	240	287

NATIONAL CONFERENCE

	W	L	T	Pct.	Pts.	OP
Detroit	9	3	0	.750	344	192
Los Angeles	9	3	0	.750	349	234
San Francisco	7	5	0	.583	285	221
Green Bay	6	6	0	.500	295	312
Chi. Bears	5	7	0	.417	245	326
Dallas	1	11	0	.083	182	427

National Conference playoff: Detroit 31, Los Angeles 21
NFL Championship: Detroit 17, Cleveland 7

1953

EASTERN CONFERENCE

	W	L	T	Pct.	Pts.	OP
Cleveland	11	1	0	.917	348	162
Philadelphia	7	4	1	.636	352	215
Washington	6	5	1	.545	208	215
Pittsburgh	6	6	0	.500	211	263
N.Y. Giants	3	9	0	.250	179	277
Chi. Cardinals	1	10	1	.091	190	337

WESTERN CONFERENCE

	W	L	T	Pct.	Pts.	OP
Detroit	10	2	0	.833	271	205
San Francisco	9	3	0	.750	372	237
Los Angeles	8	3	1	.727	366	236
Chi. Bears	3	8	1	.273	218	262
Baltimore	3	9	0	.250	182	350
Green Bay	2	9	1	.182	200	338

NFL Championship: Detroit 17, Cleveland 16

1954

EASTERN CONFERENCE

	W	L	T	Pct.	Pts.	OP
Cleveland	9	3	0	.750	336	162
Philadelphia	7	4	1	.636	284	230
N.Y. Giants	7	5	0	.583	293	184
Pittsburgh	5	7	0	.417	219	263
Washington	3	9	0	.250	207	432
Chi. Cardinals	2	10	0	.167	183	347

WESTERN CONFERENCE

	W	L	T	Pct.	Pts.	OP
Detroit	9	2	1	.818	337	189
Chi. Bears	8	4	0	.667	301	279
San Francisco	7	4	1	.636	313	251
Los Angeles	6	5	1	.545	314	285
Green Bay	4	8	0	.333	234	251
Baltimore	3	9	0	.250	131	279

NFL Championship: Cleveland 56, Detroit 10

1955

EASTERN CONFERENCE

	W	L	T	Pct.	Pts.	OP
Cleveland	9	2	1	.818	349	218
Washington	8	4	0	.667	246	222
N.Y. Giants	6	5	1	.545	267	223
Chi. Cardinals	4	7	1	.364	224	252
Philadelphia	4	7	1	.364	248	231
Pittsburgh	4	8	0	.333	195	285

WESTERN CONFERENCE

	W	L	T	Pct.	Pts.	OP
Los Angeles	8	3	1	.727	260	231
Chi. Bears	8	4	0	.667	294	251
Green Bay	6	6	0	.500	258	276
Baltimore	5	6	1	.455	214	239
San Francisco	4	8	0	.333	216	298
Detroit	3	9	0	.250	230	275

NFL Championship: Cleveland 38, Los Angeles 14

1956

EASTERN CONFERENCE

	W	L	T	Pct.	Pts.	OP
N.Y. Giants	8	3	1	.727	264	197
Chi. Cardinals	7	5	0	.583	240	182
Washington	6	6	0	.500	183	225
Cleveland	5	7	0	.417	167	177
Pittsburgh	5	7	0	.417	217	250
Philadelphia	3	8	1	.273	143	215

WESTERN CONFERENCE

	W	L	T	Pct.	Pts.	OP
Chi. Bears	9	2	1	.818	363	246
Detroit	9	3	0	.750	300	188
San Francisco	5	6	1	.455	233	284
Baltimore	5	7	0	.417	270	322
Green Bay	4	8	0	.333	264	342
Los Angeles	4	8	0	.333	291	307

NFL Championship: N.Y. Giants 47, Chicago Bears 7

1957

EASTERN CONFERENCE	W	L	T	Pct.	Pts.	OP
Cleveland	9	2	1	.818	269	172
N.Y. Giants	7	5	0	.583	254	211
Pittsburgh	6	6	0	.500	161	178
Washington	5	6	1	.455	251	230
Philadelphia	4	8	0	.333	173	230
Chi. Cardinals	3	9	0	.250	200	299

WESTERN CONFERENCE	W	L	T	Pct.	Pts.	OP
Detroit	8	4	0	.667	251	231
San Francisco	8	4	0	.667	260	264
Baltimore	7	5	0	.583	303	235
Los Angeles	6	6	0	.500	307	278
Chi. Bears	5	7	0	.417	203	211
Green Bay	3	9	0	.250	218	311

Western Conference playoff: Detroit 31, San Francisco 27
NFL Championship: Detroit 59, Cleveland 14

1958

EASTERN CONFERENCE	W	L	T	Pct.	Pts.	OP
N.Y. Giants	9	3	0	.750	246	183
Cleveland	9	3	0	.750	302	217
Pittsburgh	7	4	1	.636	261	230
Washington	4	7	1	.364	214	268
Chi. Cardinals	2	9	1	.182	261	356
Philadelphia	2	9	1	.182	235	306

WESTERN CONFERENCE	W	L	T	Pct.	Pts.	OP
Baltimore	9	3	0	.750	381	203
Chi. Bears	8	4	0	.667	298	230
Los Angeles	8	4	0	.667	344	278
San Francisco	6	6	0	.500	257	324
Detroit	4	7	1	.364	261	276
Green Bay	1	10	1	.091	193	382

Eastern Conference playoff: N.Y. Giants 10, Cleveland 0
NFL Championship: Baltimore 23, N.Y. Giants 17, sudden-death overtime

1959

EASTERN CONFERENCE	W	L	T	Pct.	Pts.	OP
N.Y. Giants	10	2	0	.833	284	170
Cleveland	7	5	0	.583	270	214
Philadelphia	7	5	0	.583	268	278
Pittsburgh	6	5	1	.545	257	216
Washington	3	9	0	.250	185	350
Chi. Cardinals	2	10	0	.167	234	324

WESTERN CONFERENCE	W	L	T	Pct.	Pts.	OP
Baltimore	9	3	0	.750	374	251
Chi. Bears	8	4	0	.667	252	196
Green Bay	7	5	0	.583	248	246
San Francisco	7	5	0	.583	255	237
Detroit	3	8	1	.273	203	275
Los Angeles	2	10	0	.167	242	315

NFL Championship: Baltimore 31, N.Y. Giants 16

1960 AFL

EASTERN DIVISION	W	L	T	Pct.	Pts.	OP
Houston	10	4	0	.714	379	285
N.Y. Titans	7	7	0	.500	382	399
Buffalo	5	8	1	.385	296	303
Boston	5	9	0	.357	286	349

WESTERN DIVISION	W	L	T	Pct.	Pts.	OP
L.A. Chargers	10	4	0	.714	373	336
Dall. Texans	8	6	0	.571	362	253
Oakland	6	8	0	.429	319	388
Denver	4	9	1	.308	309	393

AFL Championship: Houston 24, L.A. Chargers 16

1960 NFL

EASTERN CONFERENCE	W	L	T	Pct.	Pts.	OP
Philadelphia	10	2	0	.833	321	246
Cleveland	8	3	1	.727	362	217
N.Y. Giants	6	4	2	.600	271	261
St. Louis	6	5	1	.545	288	230
Pittsburgh	5	6	1	.455	240	275
Washington	1	9	2	.100	178	309

WESTERN CONFERENCE	W	L	T	Pct.	Pts.	OP
Green Bay	8	4	0	.667	332	209
Detroit	7	5	0	.583	239	212
San Francisco	7	5	0	.583	208	205
Baltimore	6	6	0	.500	288	234
Chicago	5	6	1	.455	194	299
L.A. Rams	4	7	1	.364	265	297
Dall. Cowboys	0	11	1	.000	177	369

NFL Championship: Philadelphia 17, Green Bay 13

1961 AFL

EASTERN DIVISION	W	L	T	Pct.	Pts.	OP	WESTERN DIVISION	W	L	T	Pct.	Pts.	OP
Houston	10	3	1	.769	513	242	San Diego	12	2	0	.857	396	219
Boston	9	4	1	.692	413	313	Dall. Texans	6	8	0	.429	334	343
N.Y. Titans	7	7	0	.500	301	390	Denver	3	11	0	.214	251	432
Buffalo	6	8	0	.429	294	342	Oakland	2	12	0	.143	237	458

AFL Championship: Houston 10, San Diego 3

1961 NFL

EASTERN CONFERENCE	W	L	T	Pct.	Pts.	OP	WESTERN CONFERENCE	W	L	T	Pct.	Pts.	OP
N.Y. Giants	10	3	1	.769	368	220	Green Bay	11	3	0	.786	391	223
Philadelphia	10	4	0	.714	361	297	Detroit	8	5	1	.615	270	258
Cleveland	8	5	1	.615	319	270	Baltimore	8	6	0	.571	302	307
St. Louis	7	7	0	.500	279	267	Chicago	8	6	0	.571	326	302
Pittsburgh	6	8	0	.429	295	287	San Francisco	7	6	1	.538	346	272
Dall. Cowboys	4	9	1	.308	236	380	Los Angeles	4	10	0	.286	263	333
Washington	1	12	1	.077	174	392	Minnesota	3	11	0	.214	285	407

NFL Championship: Green Bay 37, N.Y. Giants 0

1962 AFL

EASTERN DIVISION	W	L	T	Pct.	Pts.	OP	WESTERN DIVISION	W	L	T	Pct.	Pts.	OP
Houston	11	3	0	.786	387	270	Dall. Texans	11	3	0	.786	389	233
Boston	9	4	1	.692	346	295	Denver	7	7	0	.500	353	334
Buffalo	7	6	1	.538	309	272	San Diego	4	10	0	.286	314	392
N.Y. Titans	5	9	0	.357	278	423	Oakland	1	13	0	.071	213	370

AFL Championship: Dallas Texans 20, Houston 17, sudden-death overtime

1962 NFL

EASTERN CONFERENCE	W	L	T	Pct.	Pts.	OP	WESTERN CONFERENCE	W	L	T	Pct.	Pts.	OP
N.Y. Giants	12	2	0	.857	398	283	Green Bay	13	1	0	.929	415	148
Pittsburgh	9	5	0	.643	312	363	Detroit	11	3	0	.786	315	177
Cleveland	7	6	1	.538	291	257	Chicago	9	5	0	.643	321	287
Washington	5	7	2	.417	305	376	Baltimore	7	7	0	.500	293	288
Dall. Cowboys	5	8	1	.385	398	402	San Francisco	6	8	0	.429	282	331
St. Louis	4	9	1	.308	287	361	Minnesota	2	11	1	.154	254	410
Philadelphia	3	10	1	.231	282	356	Los Angeles	1	12	1	.077	220	334

NFL Championship: Green Bay 16, N.Y. Giants 7

1963 AFL

EASTERN DIVISION	W	L	T	Pct.	Pts.	OP	WESTERN DIVISION	W	L	T	Pct.	Pts.	OP
Boston	7	6	1	.538	317	257	San Diego	11	3	0	.786	399	255
Buffalo	7	6	1	.538	304	291	Oakland	10	4	0	.714	363	282
Houston	6	8	0	.429	302	372	Kansas City	5	7	2	.417	347	263
N.Y. Jets	5	8	1	.385	249	399	Denver	2	11	1	.154	301	473

Eastern Division playoff: Boston 26, Buffalo 8
AFL Championship: San Diego 51, Boston 10

1963 NFL

EASTERN CONFERENCE	W	L	T	Pct.	Pts.	OP	WESTERN CONFERENCE	W	L	T	Pct.	Pts.	OP
N.Y. Giants	11	3	0	.786	448	280	Chicago	11	1	2	.917	301	144
Cleveland	10	4	0	.714	343	262	Green Bay	11	2	1	.846	369	206
St. Louis	9	5	0	.643	341	283	Baltimore	8	6	0	.571	316	285
Pittsburgh	7	4	3	.636	321	295	Detroit	5	8	1	.385	326	265
Dallas	4	10	0	.286	305	378	Minnesota	5	8	1	.385	309	390
Washington	3	11	0	.214	279	398	Los Angeles	5	9	0	.357	210	350
Philadelphia	2	10	2	.167	242	381	San Francisco	2	12	0	.143	198	391

NFL Championship: Chicago 14, N.Y. Giants 10

1964 AFL

EASTERN DIVISION	W	L	T	Pct.	Pts.	OP	WESTERN DIVISION	W	L	T	Pct.	Pts.	OP
Buffalo	12	2	0	.857	400	242	San Diego	8	5	1	.615	341	300
Boston	10	3	1	.769	365	297	Kansas City	7	7	0	.500	366	306
N.Y. Jets	5	8	1	.385	278	315	Oakland	5	7	2	.417	303	350
Houston	4	10	0	.286	310	355	Denver	2	11	1	.154	240	438

AFL Championship: Buffalo 20, San Diego 7

1964 NFL

EASTERN CONFERENCE	W	L	T	Pct.	Pts.	OP	WESTERN CONFERENCE	W	L	T	Pct.	Pts.	OP
Cleveland	10	3	1	.769	415	293	Baltimore	12	2	0	.857	428	225
St. Louis	9	3	2	.750	357	331	Green Bay	8	5	1	.615	342	245
Philadelphia	6	8	0	.429	312	313	Minnesota	8	5	1	.615	355	296
Washington	6	8	0	.429	307	305	Detroit	7	5	2	.583	280	260
Dallas	5	8	1	.385	250	289	Los Angeles	5	7	2	.417	283	339
Pittsburgh	5	9	0	.357	253	315	Chicago	5	9	0	.357	260	379
N.Y. Giants	2	10	2	.167	241	399	San Francisco	4	10	0	.286	236	330

NFL Championship: Cleveland 27, Baltimore 0

1965 AFL

EASTERN DIVISION	W	L	T	Pct.	Pts.	OP	WESTERN DIVISION	W	L	T	Pct.	Pts.	OP
Buffalo	10	3	1	.769	313	226	San Diego	9	2	3	.818	340	227
N.Y. Jets	5	8	1	.385	285	303	Oakland	8	5	1	.615	298	239
Boston	4	8	2	.333	244	302	Kansas City	7	5	2	.583	322	285
Houston	4	10	0	.286	298	429	Denver	4	10	0	.286	303	392

AFL Championship: Buffalo 23, San Diego 0

1965 NFL

EASTERN CONFERENCE	W	L	T	Pct.	Pts.	OP	WESTERN CONFERENCE	W	L	T	Pct.	Pts.	OP
Cleveland	11	3	0	.786	363	325	Green Bay	10	3	1	.769	316	224
Dallas	7	7	0	.500	325	280	Baltimore	10	3	1	.769	389	284
N.Y. Giants	7	7	0	.500	270	338	Chicago	9	5	0	.643	409	275
Washington	6	8	0	.429	257	301	San Francisco	7	6	1	.538	421	402
Philadelphia	5	9	0	.357	363	359	Minnesota	7	7	0	.500	383	403
St. Louis	5	9	0	.357	296	309	Detroit	6	7	1	.462	257	295
Pittsburgh	2	12	0	.143	202	397	Los Angeles	4	10	0	.286	269	328

Western Conference playoff: Green Bay 13, Baltimore 10, sudden-death overtime

NFL Championship: Green Bay 23, Cleveland 12

1966 AFL

EASTERN DIVISION	W	L	T	Pct.	Pts.	OP	WESTERN DIVISION	W	L	T	Pct.	Pts.	OP
Buffalo	9	4	1	.692	358	255	Kansas City	11	2	1	.846	448	276
Boston	8	4	2	.667	315	283	Oakland	8	5	1	.615	315	288
N.Y. Jets	6	6	2	.500	322	312	San Diego	7	6	1	.538	335	284
Houston	3	11	0	.214	335	396	Denver	4	10	0	.286	196	381
Miami	3	11	0	.214	213	362							

AFL Championship: Kansas City 31, Buffalo 7

1966 NFL

EASTERN CONFERENCE	W	L	T	Pct.	Pts.	OP	WESTERN CONFERENCE	W	L	T	Pct.	Pts.	OP
Dallas	10	3	1	.769	445	239	Green Bay	12	2	0	.857	335	163
Cleveland	9	5	0	.643	403	259	Baltimore	9	5	0	.643	314	226
Philadelphia	9	5	0	.643	326	340	Los Angeles	8	6	0	.571	289	212
St. Louis	8	5	1	.615	264	265	San Francisco	6	6	2	.500	320	325
Washington	7	7	0	.500	351	355	Chicago	5	7	2	.417	234	272
Pittsburgh	5	8	1	.385	316	347	Detroit	4	9	1	.308	206	317
Atlanta	3	11	0	.214	204	437	Minnesota	4	9	1	.308	292	304
N.Y. Giants	1	12	1	.077	263	501							

NFL Championship: Green Bay 34, Dallas 27

Super Bowl I: Green Bay (NFL) 35, Kansas City (AFL) 10

1967 AFL

EASTERN DIVISION

	W	L	T	Pct.	Pts.	OP
Houston	9	4	1	.692	258	199
N.Y. Jets	8	5	1	.615	371	329
Buffalo	4	10	0	.286	237	285
Miami	4	10	0	.286	219	407
Boston	3	10	1	.231	280	389

WESTERN DIVISION

	W	L	T	Pct.	Pts.	OP
Oakland	13	1	0	.929	468	238
Kansas City	9	5	0	.643	408	254
San Diego	8	5	1	.615	360	352
Denver	3	11	0	.214	256	409

AFL Championship: Oakland 40, Houston 7

1967 NFL

EASTERN CONFERENCE

Capitol Division

	W	L	T	Pct.	Pts.	OP
Dallas	9	5	0	.643	342	268
Philadelphia	6	7	1	.462	351	409
Washington	5	6	3	.455	347	353
New Orleans	3	11	0	.214	233	379

Century Division

	W	L	T	Pct.	Pts.	OP
Cleveland	9	5	0	.643	334	297
N.Y. Giants	7	7	0	.500	369	379
St. Louis	6	7	1	.462	333	356
Pittsburgh	4	9	1	.308	281	320

WESTERN CONFERENCE

Coastal Division

	W	L	T	Pct.	Pts.	OP
Los Angeles	11	1	2	.917	398	196
Baltimore	11	1	2	.917	394	198
San Francisco	7	7	0	.500	273	337
Atlanta	1	12	1	.077	175	422

Central Division

	W	L	T	Pct.	Pts.	OP
Green Bay	9	4	1	.692	332	209
Chicago	7	6	1	.538	239	218
Detroit	5	7	2	.417	260	259
Minnesota	3	8	3	.273	233	294

Conference Championships: Dallas 52, Cleveland 14; Green Bay 28, Los Angeles 7
NFL Championship: Green Bay 21, Dallas 17
Super Bowl II: Green Bay (NFL) 33, Oakland (AFL) 14

1968 AFL

EASTERN DIVISION

	W	L	T	Pct.	Pts.	OP
N.Y. Jets	11	3	0	.786	419	280
Houston	7	7	0	.500	303	248
Miami	5	8	1	.385	276	355
Boston	4	10	0	.286	229	406
Buffalo	1	12	1	.077	199	367

WESTERN DIVISION

	W	L	T	Pct.	Pts.	OP
Oakland	12	2	0	.857	453	233
Kansas City	12	2	0	.857	371	170
San Diego	9	5	0	.643	382	310
Denver	5	9	0	.357	255	404
Cincinnati	3	11	0	.214	215	329

Western Division playoff: Oakland 41, Kansas City 6
AFL Championship: N.Y. Jets 27, Oakland 23

1968 NFL

EASTERN CONFERENCE

Capitol Division

	W	L	T	Pct.	Pts.	OP
Dallas	12	2	0	.857	431	186
N.Y. Giants	7	7	0	.500	294	325
Washington	5	9	0	.357	249	358
Philadelphia	2	12	0	.143	202	351

Century Division

	W	L	T	Pct.	Pts.	OP
Cleveland	10	4	0	.714	394	273
St. Louis	9	4	1	.692	325	289
New Orleans	4	9	1	.308	246	327
Pittsburgh	2	11	1	.154	244	397

WESTERN CONFERENCE

Coastal Division

	W	L	T	Pct.	Pts.	OP
Baltimore	13	1	0	.929	402	144
Los Angeles	10	3	1	.769	312	200
San Francisco	7	6	1	.538	303	310
Atlanta	2	12	0	.143	170	389

Central Division

	W	L	T	Pct.	Pts.	OP
Minnesota	8	6	0	.571	282	242
Chicago	7	7	0	.500	250	333
Green Bay	6	7	1	.462	281	227
Detroit	4	8	2	.333	207	241

Conference Championships: Cleveland 31, Dallas 20; Baltimore 24, Minnesota 14
NFL Championship: Baltimore 34, Cleveland 0
Super Bowl III: N.Y. Jets (AFL) 16, Baltimore (NFL) 7

1969 AFL

EASTERN DIVISION	W	L	T	Pct.	Pts.	OP
N.Y. Jets	10	4	0	.714	353	269
Houston	6	6	2	.500	278	279
Boston	4	10	0	.286	266	316
Buffalo	4	10	0	.286	230	359
Miami	3	10	1	.231	233	332

WESTERN DIVISION	W	L	T	Pct.	Pts.	OP
Oakland	12	1	1	.923	377	242
Kansas City	11	3	0	.786	359	177
San Diego	8	6	0	.571	288	276
Denver	5	8	1	.385	297	344
Cincinnati	4	9	1	.308	280	367

Divisional playoffs: Kansas City 13, N.Y. Jets 6; Oakland 56, Houston 7
AFL Championship: Kansas City 17, Oakland 7

1969 NFL

EASTERN CONFERENCE

Capitol Division	W	L	T	Pct.	Pts.	OP
Dallas	11	2	1	.846	369	223
Washington	7	5	2	.583	307	319
New Orleans	5	9	0	.357	311	393
Philadelphia	4	9	1	.308	279	377

Century Division	W	L	T	Pct.	Pts.	OP
Cleveland	10	3	1	.769	351	300
N.Y. Giants	6	8	0	.429	264	298
St. Louis	4	9	1	.308	314	389
Pittsburgh	1	13	0	.071	218	404

WESTERN CONFERENCE

Coastal Division	W	L	T	Pct.	Pts.	OP
Los Angeles	11	3	0	.786	320	243
Baltimore	8	5	1	.615	279	268
Atlanta	6	8	0	.429	276	268
San Francisco	4	8	2	.333	277	319

Central Division	W	L	T	Pct.	Pts.	OP
Minnesota	12	2	0	.857	379	133
Detroit	9	4	1	.692	259	188
Green Bay	8	6	0	.571	269	221
Chicago	1	13	0	.071	210	339

Conference Championships: Cleveland 38, Dallas 14; Minnesota 23, Los Angeles 20
NFL Championship: Minnesota 27, Cleveland 7
Super Bowl IV: Kansas City (AFL) 23, Minnesota (NFL) 7

1970

AMERICAN CONFERENCE

Eastern Division	W	L	T	Pct.	Pts.	OP
Baltimore	11	2	1	.846	321	234
Miami*	10	4	0	.714	297	228
N.Y. Jets	4	10	0	.286	255	286
Buffalo	3	10	1	.231	204	337
Boston	2	12	0	.143	149	361

Central Division	W	L	T	Pct.	Pts.	OP
Cincinnati	8	6	0	.571	312	255
Cleveland	7	7	0	.500	286	265
Pittsburgh	5	9	0	.357	210	272
Houston	3	10	1	.231	217	352

Western Division	W	L	T	Pct.	Pts.	OP
Oakland	8	4	2	.667	300	293
Kansas City	7	5	2	.583	272	244
San Diego	5	6	3	.455	282	278
Denver	5	8	1	.385	253	264

NATIONAL CONFERENCE

Eastern Division	W	L	T	Pct.	Pts.	OP
Dallas	10	4	0	.714	299	221
N.Y. Giants	9	5	0	.643	301	270
St. Louis	8	5	1	.615	325	228
Washington	6	8	0	.429	297	314
Philadelphia	3	10	1	.231	241	332

Central Division	W	L	T	Pct.	Pts.	OP
Minnesota	12	2	0	.857	335	143
Detroit*	10	4	0	.714	347	202
Chicago	6	8	0	.429	256	261
Green Bay	6	8	0	.429	196	293

Western Division	W	L	T	Pct.	Pts.	OP
San Francisco	10	3	1	.769	352	267
Los Angeles	9	4	1	.692	325	202
Atlanta	4	8	2	.333	206	261
New Orleans	2	11	1	.154	172	347

*Wild Card qualifier for playoffs
Divisional playoffs: Baltimore 17, Cincinnati 0; Oakland 21, Miami 14
AFC Championship: Baltimore 27, Oakland 17
Divisional playoffs: Dallas 5, Detroit 0; San Francisco 17, Minnesota 14
NFC Championship: Dallas 17, San Francisco 10
Super Bowl V: Baltimore (AFC) 16, Dallas (NFC) 13

1971

AMERICAN CONFERENCE						NATIONAL CONFERENCE					
Eastern Division						**Eastern Division**					
	W	L	T	Pct.	Pts.	OP		W	L	T	Pct.	Pts.	OP
Miami	10	3	1	.769	315	174	Dallas	11	3	0	.786	406	222
Baltimore*	10	4	0	.714	313	140	Washington*	9	4	1	.692	276	190
New England	6	8	0	.429	238	325	Philadelphia	6	7	1	.462	221	302
N.Y. Jets	6	8	0	.429	212	299	St. Louis	4	9	1	.308	231	279
Buffalo	1	13	0	.071	184	394	N.Y. Giants	4	10	0	.286	228	362

Central Division						**Central Division**					
	W	L	T	Pct.	Pts.	OP		W	L	T	Pct.	Pts.	OP
Cleveland	9	5	0	.643	285	273	Minnesota	11	3	0	.786	245	139
Pittsburgh	6	8	0	.429	246	292	Detroit	7	6	1	.538	341	286
Houston	4	9	1	.308	251	330	Chicago	6	8	0	.429	185	276
Cincinnati	4	10	0	.286	284	265	Green Bay	4	8	2	.333	274	298

Western Division						**Western Division**					
	W	L	T	Pct.	Pts.	OP		W	L	T	Pct.	Pts.	OP
Kansas City	10	3	1	.769	302	208	San Francisco	9	5	0	.643	300	216
Oakland	8	4	2	.667	344	278	Los Angeles	8	5	1	.615	313	260
San Diego	6	8	0	.429	311	341	Atlanta	7	6	1	.538	274	277
Denver	4	9	1	.308	203	275	New Orleans	4	8	2	.333	266	347

*Wild Card qualifier for playoffs
Divisional playoffs: Miami 27, Kansas City 24, sudden-death overtime; Baltimore 20, Cleveland 3
AFC Championship: Miami 21, Baltimore 0
Divisional playoffs: Dallas 20, Minnesota 12; San Francisco 24, Washington 20
NFC Championship: Dallas 14, San Francisco 3
Super Bowl VI: Dallas (NFC) 24, Miami (AFC) 3

1972

AMERICAN CONFERENCE						NATIONAL CONFERENCE					
Eastern Division						**Eastern Division**					
	W	L	T	Pct.	Pts.	OP		W	L	T	Pct.	Pts.	OP
Miami	14	0	0	1.000	385	171	Washington	11	3	0	.786	336	218
N.Y. Jets	7	7	0	.500	367	324	Dallas*	10	4	0	.714	319	240
Baltimore	5	9	0	.357	235	252	N.Y. Giants	8	6	0	.571	331	247
Buffalo	4	9	1	.321	257	377	St. Louis	4	9	1	.321	193	303
New England	3	11	0	.214	192	446	Philadelphia	2	11	1	.179	145	352

Central Division						**Central Division**					
	W	L	T	Pct.	Pts.	OP		W	L	T	Pct.	Pts.	OP
Pittsburgh	11	3	0	.786	343	175	Green Bay	10	4	0	.714	304	226
Cleveland*	10	4	0	.714	268	249	Detroit	8	5	1	.607	339	290
Cincinnati	8	6	0	.571	299	229	Minnesota	7	7	0	.500	301	252
Houston	1	13	0	.071	164	380	Chicago	4	9	1	.321	225	275

Western Division						**Western Division**					
	W	L	T	Pct.	Pts.	OP		W	L	T	Pct.	Pts.	OP
Oakland	10	3	1	.750	365	248	San Francisco	8	5	1	.607	353	249
Kansas City	8	6	0	.571	287	254	Atlanta	7	7	0	.500	269	274
Denver	5	9	0	.357	325	350	Los Angeles	6	7	1	.464	291	286
San Diego	4	9	1	.321	264	344	New Orleans	2	11	1	.179	215	361

*Wild Card qualifier for playoffs
Divisional playoffs: Pittsburgh 13, Oakland 7; Miami 20, Cleveland 14
AFC Championship: Miami 21, Pittsburgh 17
Divisional playoffs: Dallas 30, San Francisco 28; Washington 16, Green Bay 3
NFC Championship: Washington 26, Dallas 3
Super Bowl VII: Miami (AFC) 14, Washington (NFC) 7

1973

AMERICAN CONFERENCE						NATIONAL CONFERENCE					
Eastern Division						**Eastern Division**					
	W	L	T	Pct.	Pts.	OP					
	W	L	T	Pct.	Pts.	OP		W	L	T	Pct.	Pts.	OP

AMERICAN CONFERENCE							NATIONAL CONFERENCE						
Eastern Division							**Eastern Division**						
	W	L	T	Pct.	Pts.	OP		W	L	T	Pct.	Pts.	OP
Miami	12	2	0	.857	343	150	Dallas	10	4	0	.714	382	203
Buffalo	9	5	0	.643	259	230	Washington*	10	4	0	.714	325	198
New England	5	9	0	.357	258	300	Philadelphia	5	8	1	.393	310	393
Baltimore	4	10	0	.286	226	341	St. Louis	4	9	1	.321	286	365
N.Y. Jets	4	10	0	.286	240	306	N.Y. Giants	2	11	1	.179	226	362
Central Division							**Central Division**						
Cincinnati	10	4	0	.714	286	231	Minnesota	12	2	0	.857	296	168
Pittsburgh*	10	4	0	.714	347	210	Detroit	6	7	1	.464	271	247
Cleveland	7	5	2	.571	234	255	Green Bay	5	7	2	.429	202	259
Houston	1	13	0	.071	199	447	Chicago	3	11	0	.214	195	334
Western Division							**Western Division**						
Oakland	9	4	1	.679	292	175	Los Angeles	12	2	0	.857	388	178
Denver	7	5	2	.571	354	296	Atlanta	9	5	0	.643	318	224
Kansas City	7	5	2	.571	231	192	New Orleans	5	9	0	.357	163	312
San Diego	2	11	1	.179	188	386	San Francisco	5	9	0	.357	262	319

*Wild Card qualifier for playoffs
Divisional playoffs: Oakland 33, Pittsburgh 14; Miami 34, Cincinnati 16
AFC Championship: Miami 27, Oakland 10
Divisional playoffs: Minnesota 27, Washington 20; Dallas 27, Los Angeles 16
NFC Championship: Minnesota 27, Dallas 10
Super Bowl VIII: Miami (AFC) 24, Minnesota (NFC) 7

1974

AMERICAN CONFERENCE							NATIONAL CONFERENCE						
Eastern Division							**Eastern Division**						
	W	L	T	Pct.	Pts.	OP		W	L	T	Pct.	Pts.	OP
Miami	11	3	0	.786	327	216	St. Louis	10	4	0	.714	285	218
Buffalo*	9	5	0	.643	264	244	Washington*	10	4	0	.714	320	196
New England	7	7	0	.500	348	289	Dallas	8	6	0	.571	297	235
N.Y. Jets	7	7	0	.500	279	300	Philadelphia	7	7	0	.500	242	217
Baltimore	2	12	0	.143	190	329	N.Y. Giants	2	12	0	.143	195	299
Central Division							**Central Division**						
Pittsburgh	10	3	1	.750	305	189	Minnesota	10	4	0	.714	310	195
Cincinnati	7	7	0	.500	283	259	Detroit	7	7	0	.500	256	270
Houston	7	7	0	.500	236	282	Green Bay	6	8	0	.429	210	206
Cleveland	4	10	0	.286	251	344	Chicago	4	10	0	.286	152	279
Western Division							**Western Division**						
Oakland	12	2	0	.857	355	228	Los Angeles	10	4	0	.714	263	181
Denver	7	6	1	.536	302	294	San Francisco	6	8	0	.429	226	236
Kansas City	5	9	0	.357	233	293	New Orleans	5	9	0	.357	166	263
San Diego	5	9	0	.357	212	285	Atlanta	3	11	0	.214	111	271

*Wild Card qualifier for playoffs
Divisional playoffs: Oakland 28, Miami 26; Pittsburgh 32, Buffalo 14
AFC Championship: Pittsburgh 24, Oakland 13
Divisional playoffs: Minnesota 30, St. Louis 14; Los Angeles 19, Washington 10
NFC Championship: Minnesota 14, Los Angeles 10
Super Bowl IX: Pittsburgh (AFC) 16, Minnesota (NFC) 6

1975

AMERICAN CONFERENCE

Eastern Division

	W	L	T	Pct.	Pts.	OP
Baltimore	10	4	0	.714	395	269
Miami	10	4	0	.714	357	222
Buffalo	8	6	0	.571	420	355
New England	3	11	0	.214	258	358
N.Y. Jets	3	11	0	.214	258	433

Central Division

	W	L	T	Pct.	Pts.	OP
Pittsburgh	12	2	0	.857	373	162
Cincinnati*	11	3	0	.786	340	246
Houston	10	4	0	.714	293	226
Cleveland	3	11	0	.214	218	372

Western Division

	W	L	T	Pct.	Pts.	OP
Oakland	11	3	0	.786	375	255
Denver	6	8	0	.429	254	307
Kansas City	5	9	0	.357	282	341
San Diego	2	12	0	.143	189	345

NATIONAL CONFERENCE

Eastern Division

	W	L	T	Pct.	Pts.	OP
St. Louis	11	3	0	.786	356	276
Dallas*	10	4	0	.714	350	268
Washington	8	6	0	.571	325	276
N.Y. Giants	5	9	0	.357	216	306
Philadelphia	4	10	0	.286	225	302

Central Division

	W	L	T	Pct.	Pts.	OP
Minnesota	12	2	0	.857	377	180
Detroit	7	7	0	.500	245	262
Chicago	4	10	0	.286	191	379
Green Bay	4	10	0	.286	226	285

Western Division

	W	L	T	Pct.	Pts.	OP
Los Angeles	12	2	0	.857	312	135
San Francisco	5	9	0	.357	255	286
Atlanta	4	10	0	.286	240	289
New Orleans	2	12	0	.143	165	360

*Wild Card qualifier for playoffs
Divisional playoffs: Pittsburgh 28, Baltimore 10; Oakland 31, Cincinnati 28
AFC Championship: Pittsburgh 16, Oakland 10
Divisional playoffs: Los Angeles 35, St. Louis 23; Dallas 17, Minnesota 14
NFC Championship: Dallas 37, Los Angeles 7
Super Bowl X: Pittsburgh (AFC) 21, Dallas (NFC) 17

1976

AMERICAN CONFERENCE

Eastern Division

	W	L	T	Pct.	Pts.	OP
Baltimore	11	3	0	.786	417	246
New England*	11	3	0	.786	376	236
Miami	6	8	0	.429	263	264
N.Y. Jets	3	11	0	.214	169	383
Buffalo	2	12	0	.143	245	363

Central Division

	W	L	T	Pct.	Pts.	OP
Pittsburgh	10	4	0	.714	342	138
Cincinnati	10	4	0	.714	335	210
Cleveland	9	5	0	.643	267	287
Houston	5	9	0	.357	222	273

Western Division

	W	L	T	Pct.	Pts.	OP
Oakland	13	1	0	.929	350	237
Denver	9	5	0	.643	315	206
San Diego	6	8	0	.429	248	285
Kansas City	5	9	0	.357	290	376
Tampa Bay	0	14	0	.000	125	412

NATIONAL CONFERENCE

Eastern Division

	W	L	T	Pct.	Pts.	OP
Dallas	11	3	0	.786	296	194
Washington*	10	4	0	.714	291	217
St. Louis	10	4	0	.714	309	267
Philadelphia	4	10	0	.286	165	286
N.Y. Giants	3	11	0	.214	170	250

Central Division

	W	L	T	Pct.	Pts.	OP
Minnesota	11	2	1	.821	305	176
Chicago	7	7	0	.500	253	216
Detroit	6	8	0	.429	262	220
Green Bay	5	9	0	.357	218	299

Western Division

	W	L	T	Pct.	Pts.	OP
Los Angeles	10	3	1	.750	351	190
San Francisco	8	6	0	.571	270	190
Atlanta	4	10	0	.286	172	312
New Orleans	4	10	0	.286	253	346
Seattle	2	12	0	.143	229	429

*Wild Card qualifier for playoffs
Divisional playoffs: Oakland 24, New England 21; Pittsburgh 40, Baltimore 14
AFC Championship: Oakland 24, Pittsburgh 7
Divisional playoffs: Minnesota 35, Washington 20; Los Angeles 14, Dallas 12
NFC Championship: Minnesota 24, Los Angeles 13
Super Bowl XI: Oakland (AFC) 32, Minnesota (NFC) 14

1977

AMERICAN CONFERENCE

Eastern Division

	W	L	T	Pct.	Pts.	OP
Baltimore	10	4	0	.714	295	221
Miami	10	4	0	.714	313	197
New England	9	5	0	.643	278	217
N.Y. Jets	3	11	0	.214	191	300
Buffalo	3	11	0	.214	160	313

Central Division

	W	L	T	Pct.	Pts.	OP
Pittsburgh	9	5	0	.643	283	243
Houston	8	6	0	.571	299	230
Cincinnati	8	6	0	.571	238	235
Cleveland	6	8	0	.429	269	267

Western Division

	W	L	T	Pct.	Pts.	OP
Denver	12	2	0	.857	274	148
Oakland*	11	3	0	.786	351	230
San Diego	7	7	0	.500	222	205
Seattle	5	9	0	.357	282	373
Kansas City	2	12	0	.143	225	349

NATIONAL CONFERENCE

Eastern Division

	W	L	T	Pct.	Pts.	OP
Dallas	12	2	0	.857	345	212
Washington	9	5	0	.643	196	189
St. Louis	7	7	0	.500	272	287
Philadelphia	5	9	0	.357	220	207
N.Y. Giants	5	9	0	.357	181	265

Central Division

	W	L	T	Pct.	Pts.	OP
Minnesota	9	5	0	.643	231	227
Chicago*	9	5	0	.643	255	253
Detroit	6	8	0	.429	183	252
Green Bay	4	10	0	.286	134	219
Tampa Bay	2	12	0	.143	103	223

Western Division

	W	L	T	Pct.	Pts.	OP
Los Angeles	10	4	0	.714	302	146
Atlanta	7	7	0	.500	179	129
San Francisco	5	9	0	.357	220	260
New Orleans	3	11	0	.214	232	336

*Wild Card qualifier for playoffs
Divisional playoffs: Denver 34, Pittsburgh 21; Oakland 37, Baltimore 31, sudden-death overtime
AFC Championship: Denver 20, Oakland 17
Divisional playoffs: Dallas 37, Chicago 7; Minnesota 14, Los Angeles 7
NFC Championship: Dallas 23, Minnesota 6
Super Bowl XII: Dallas (NFC) 27, Denver (AFC) 10

1978

AMERICAN CONFERENCE

Eastern Division

	W	L	T	Pct.	Pts.	OP
New England	11	5	0	.688	358	286
Miami*	11	5	0	.688	372	254
N.Y. Jets	8	8	0	.500	359	364
Buffalo	5	11	0	.313	302	354
Baltimore	5	11	0	.313	239	421

Central Division

	W	L	T	Pct.	Pts.	OP
Pittsburgh	14	2	0	.875	356	195
Houston*	10	6	0	.625	283	298
Cleveland	8	8	0	.500	334	356
Cincinnati	4	12	0	.250	252	284

Western Division

	W	L	T	Pct.	Pts.	OP
Denver	10	6	0	.625	282	198
Oakland	9	7	0	.563	311	283
Seattle	9	7	0	.563	345	358
San Diego	9	7	0	.563	355	309
Kansas City	4	12	0	.250	243	327

NATIONAL CONFERENCE

Eastern Division

	W	L	T	Pct.	Pts.	OP
Dallas	12	4	0	.750	384	208
Philadelphia*	9	7	0	.563	270	250
Washington	8	8	0	.500	273	283
St. Louis	6	10	0	.375	248	296
N.Y. Giants	6	10	0	.375	264	298

Central Division

	W	L	T	Pct.	Pts.	OP
Minnesota	8	7	1	.531	294	306
Green Bay	8	7	1	.531	249	269
Detroit	7	9	0	.438	290	300
Chicago	7	9	0	.438	253	274
Tampa Bay	5	11	0	.313	241	259

Western Division

	W	L	T	Pct.	Pts.	OP
Los Angeles	12	4	0	.750	316	245
Atlanta*	9	7	0	.563	240	290
New Orleans	7	9	0	.438	281	298
San Francisco	2	14	0	.125	219	350

*Wild Card qualifier for playoffs
First-round playoff: Houston 17, Miami 9
Divisional playoffs: Houston 31, New England 14; Pittsburgh 33, Denver 10
AFC Championship: Pittsburgh 34, Houston 5
First-round playoff: Atlanta 14, Philadelphia 13
Divisional playoffs: Dallas 27, Atlanta 20; Los Angeles 34, Minnesota 10
NFC Championship: Dallas 28, Los Angeles 0
Super Bowl XIII: Pittsburgh (AFC) 35, Dallas (NFC) 31

1979

AMERICAN CONFERENCE

Eastern Division

	W	L	T	Pct.	Pts.	OP
Miami	10	6	0	.625	341	257
New England	9	7	0	.563	411	326
N.Y. Jets	8	8	0	.500	337	383
Buffalo	7	9	0	.438	268	279
Baltimore	5	11	0	.313	271	351

Central Division

	W	L	T	Pct.	Pts.	OP
Pittsburgh	12	4	0	.750	416	262
Houston*	11	5	0	.688	362	331
Cleveland	9	7	0	.563	359	352
Cincinnati	4	12	0	.250	337	421

Western Division

	W	L	T	Pct.	Pts.	OP
San Diego	12	4	0	.750	411	246
Denver*	10	6	0	.625	289	262
Seattle	9	7	0	.563	378	372
Oakland	9	7	0	.563	365	337
Kansas City	7	9	0	.438	238	262

NATIONAL CONFERENCE

Eastern Division

	W	L	T	Pct.	Pts.	OP
Dallas	11	5	0	.688	371	313
Philadelphia*	11	5	0	.688	339	282
Washington	10	6	0	.625	348	295
N.Y. Giants	6	10	0	.375	237	323
St. Louis	5	11	0	.313	307	358

Central Division

	W	L	T	Pct.	Pts.	OP
Tampa Bay	10	6	0	.625	273	237
Chicago*	10	6	0	.625	306	249
Minnesota	7	9	0	.438	259	337
Green Bay	5	11	0	.313	246	316
Detroit	2	14	0	.125	219	365

Western Division

	W	L	T	Pct.	Pts.	OP
Los Angeles	9	7	0	.563	323	309
New Orleans	8	8	0	.500	370	360
Atlanta	6	10	0	.375	300	388
San Francisco	2	14	0	.125	308	416

Wild Card qualifier for playoffs
First-round playoff: Houston 13, Denver 7
Divisional playoffs: Houston 17, San Diego 14; Pittsburgh 34, Miami 14
AFC Championship: Pittsburgh 27, Houston 13
First-round playoff: Philadelphia 27, Chicago 17
Divisional playoffs: Tampa Bay 24, Philadelphia 17; Los Angeles 21, Dallas 19
NFC Championship: Los Angeles 9, Tampa Bay 0
Super Bowl XIV: Pittsburgh (AFC) 31, Los Angeles (NFC) 19

1980

AMERICAN CONFERENCE

Eastern Division

	W	L	T	Pct.	Pts.	OP
Buffalo	11	5	0	.688	320	260
New England	10	6	0	.625	441	325
Miami	8	8	0	.500	266	305
Baltimore	7	9	0	.438	355	387
N.Y. Jets	4	12	0	.250	302	395

Central Division

	W	L	T	Pct.	Pts.	OP
Cleveland	11	5	0	.688	357	310
Houston*	11	5	0	.688	295	251
Pittsburgh	9	7	0	.563	352	313
Cincinnati	6	10	0	.375	244	312

Western Division

	W	L	T	Pct.	Pts.	OP
San Diego	11	5	0	.688	418	327
Oakland*	11	5	0	.688	364	306
Kansas City	8	8	0	.500	319	336
Denver	8	8	0	.500	310	323
Seattle	4	12	0	.250	291	408

NATIONAL CONFERENCE

Eastern Division

	W	L	T	Pct.	Pts.	OP
Philadelphia	12	4	0	.750	384	222
Dallas*	12	4	0	.750	454	311
Washington	6	10	0	.375	261	293
St. Louis	5	11	0	.313	299	350
N.Y. Giants	4	12	0	.250	249	425

Central Division

	W	L	T	Pct.	Pts.	OP
Minnesota	9	7	0	.563	317	308
Detroit	9	7	0	.563	334	272
Chicago	7	9	0	.437	304	264
Tampa Bay	5	10	1	.343	271	341
Green Bay	5	10	1	.343	231	371

Western Division

	W	L	T	Pct.	Pts.	OP
Atlanta	12	4	0	.750	405	272
Los Angeles*	11	5	0	.688	424	289
San Francisco	6	10	0	.375	320	415
New Orleans	1	15	0	.063	291	487

Wild Card qualifier for playoffs
First-round playoff: Oakland 27, Houston 7
Divisional playoffs: San Diego 20, Buffalo 14; Oakland 14, Cleveland 12
AFC Championship: Oakland 34, San Diego 27
First-round playoff: Dallas 34, Los Angeles 13
Divisional playoffs: Philadelphia 31, Minnesota 16; Dallas 30, Atlanta 27
NFC Championship: Philadelphia 20, Dallas 7
Super Bowl XV: Oakland (AFC) 27, Philadelphia (NFC) 10

1981

AMERICAN CONFERENCE

Eastern Division

	W	L	T	Pct.	Pts.	OP
Miami	11	4	1	.719	345	275
N.Y. Jets*	10	5	1	.656	355	287
Buffalo*	10	6	0	.625	311	276
Baltimore	2	14	0	.125	259	533
New England	2	14	0	.125	322	370

Central Division

	W	L	T	Pct.	Pts.	OP
Cincinnati	12	4	0	.750	421	304
Pittsburgh	8	8	0	.500	356	297
Houston	7	9	0	.438	281	355
Cleveland	5	11	0	.313	276	375

Western Division

	W	L	T	Pct.	Pts.	OP
San Diego	10	6	0	.625	478	390
Denver	10	6	0	.625	321	289
Kansas City	9	7	0	.563	343	290
Oakland	7	9	0	.438	273	343
Seattle	6	10	0	.375	322	388

NATIONAL CONFERENCE

Eastern Division

	W	L	T	Pct.	Pts.	OP
Dallas	12	4	0	.750	367	277
Philadelphia*	10	6	0	.625	368	221
N.Y. Giants*	9	7	0	.563	295	257
Washington	8	8	0	.500	347	349
St. Louis	7	9	0	.438	315	408

Central Division

	W	L	T	Pct.	Pts.	OP
Tampa Bay	9	7	0	.563	315	268
Detroit	8	8	0	.500	397	322
Green Bay	8	8	0	.500	324	361
Minnesota	7	9	0	.438	325	369
Chicago	6	10	0	.375	253	324

Western Division

	W	L	T	Pct.	Pts.	OP
San Francisco	13	3	0	.813	357	250
Atlanta	7	9	0	.438	426	355
Los Angeles	6	10	0	.375	303	351
New Orleans	4	12	0	.250	207	378

*Wild card qualifier for playoffs

First-round playoff: Buffalo 31, N.Y. Jets 27
Divisional playoffs: San Diego 41, Miami 38 (OT); Cincinnati 28, Buffalo 21
AFC Championship: Cincinnati 27, San Diego 7
First-round playoff: N.Y. Giants 27, Philadelphia 21
Divisional playoffs: Dallas 38, Tampa Bay 0; San Francisco 38, N.Y. Giants 24
NFC Championship: San Francisco 28, Dallas 27
Super Bowl XVI: San Francisco (NFC) 26, Cincinnati (AFC) 21

*1982

AMERICAN CONFERENCE

	W	L	T	Pct.	Pts.	OP
L.A. Raiders	8	1	0	.889	260	200
Miami	7	2	0	.778	198	131
Cincinnati	7	2	0	.778	232	177
Pittsburgh	6	3	0	.667	204	146
San Diego	6	3	0	.667	288	221
N.Y. Jets	6	3	0	.667	245	166
New England	5	4	0	.556	143	157
Cleveland	4	5	0	.444	140	182
Buffalo	4	5	0	.444	150	154
Seattle	4	5	0	.444	127	147
Kansas City	3	6	0	.333	176	184
Denver	2	7	0	.222	148	226
Houston	1	8	0	.111	136	245
Baltimore	0	8	1	.063	113	236

NATIONAL CONFERENCE

	W	L	T	Pct.	Pts.	OP
Washington	8	1	0	.889	190	128
Dallas	6	3	0	.667	226	145
Green Bay	5	3	1	.611	226	169
Minnesota	5	4	0	.556	187	198
Atlanta	5	4	0	.556	183	199
St. Louis	5	4	0	.556	135	170
Tampa Bay	5	4	0	.556	158	178
Detroit	4	5	0	.444	181	176
New Orleans	4	5	0	.444	129	160
N.Y. Giants	4	5	0	.444	164	160
San Francisco	3	6	0	.333	209	206
Chicago	3	6	0	.333	141	174
Philadelphia	3	6	0	.333	191	195
L.A. Rams	2	7	0	.222	200	250

*Top eight teams in each Conference qualified for playoffs under format necessitated by strike-shortened season

First-round playoffs: Miami 28, New England 13; L.A. Raiders 27, Cleveland 10; N.Y. Jets 44, Cincinnati 17; San Diego 31, Pittsburgh 28
Second-round playoffs: N.Y. Jets 17, L.A. Raiders 14; Miami 34, San Diego 13
AFC Championship: Miami 14, N.Y. Jets 0
First-round playoffs: Green Bay 41, St. Louis 16; Washington 31, Detroit 7; Minnesota 30, Atlanta 24; Dallas 30, Tampa Bay 17
Second-round playoffs: Washington 21, Minnesota 7; Dallas 37, Green Bay 26
NFC Championship: Washington 31, Dallas 17
Super Bowl XVII: Washington 27, Miami 17

1983

AMERICAN CONFERENCE

Eastern Division

	W	L	T	Pct.	Pts.	OP
Miami	12	4	0	.750	389	250
New England	8	8	0	.500	274	289
Buffalo	8	8	0	.500	283	351
Baltimore	7	9	0	.438	264	354
N.Y. Jets	7	9	0	.438	313	331

Central Division

	W	L	T	Pct.	Pts.	OP
Pittsburgh	10	6	0	.625	355	303
Cleveland	9	7	0	.562	356	342
Cincinnati	7	9	0	.438	346	302
Houston	2	14	0	.125	288	460

Western Division

	W	L	T	Pct.	Pts.	OP
L.A. Raiders	12	4	0	.750	442	338
Seattle*	9	7	0	.562	403	397
Denver*	9	7	0	.562	302	327
San Diego	6	10	0	.375	358	462
Kansas City	6	10	0	.375	386	367

NATIONAL CONFERENCE

Eastern Division

	W	L	T	Pct.	Pts.	OP
Washington	14	2	0	.875	541	332
Dallas*	12	4	0	.750	479	360
St. Louis	8	7	1	.531	374	428
Philadelphia	5	11	0	.313	233	322
N.Y. Giants	3	12	1	.219	267	347

Central Division

	W	L	T	Pct.	Pts.	OP
Detroit	9	7	0	.562	347	286
Green Bay	8	8	0	.500	429	439
Chicago	8	8	0	.500	311	301
Minnesota	8	8	0	.500	316	348
Tampa Bay	2	14	0	.125	241	380

Western Division

	W	L	T	Pct.	Pts.	OP
San Francisco	10	6	0	.625	432	293
L.A. Rams*	9	7	0	.562	361	344
New Orleans	8	8	0	.500	319	337
Atlanta	7	9	0	.438	370	389

*Wild card qualifier for playoffs

First-round playoff: Seattle 31, Denver 7
Divisional playoffs: Seattle 27, Miami 20; L.A. Raiders 38, Pittsburgh 10
AFC Championship: L.A. Raiders 30, Seattle 14
First-round playoff: L.A. Rams 24, Dallas 17
Divisional playoffs: San Francisco 24, Detroit 23; Washington 51, L.A. Rams 7
NFC Championship: Washington 24, San Francisco 21
Super Bowl XVIII: L.A. Raiders 38, Washington 9

1984 NFL DRAFT

Player	Order No.	Pos.	College	Club	Round
Acorn, Fred	57	DB	Texas	Tampa Bay	3
Allen, Patrick	100	DB	Utah State	Houston	4
Alt, John	21	T	Iowa	Kansas City	1
Anderson, Alfred	67	RB	Baylor	Minnesota	3
Anderson, Brad	212	WR	Arizona	Chicago	8
Anderson, Ernest	74	RB	Oklahoma State	Detroit	3
Andrews, Tom	98	G	Louisville	Chicago	4
Anthony, Tyrone	69	RB	North Carolina	New Orleans	3
Armstrong, Tron	122	WR	Eastern Kentucky	New York Jets	5
Atkins, Renwick	187	T	Kansas	Detroit	7
Auer, Scott	229	T	Michigan State	Kansas City	9
Aughtman, Dowe	304	DT	Auburn	Dallas	11
Azelby, Joe	263	LB	Harvard	Buffalo	10
Baack, Steve	75	DE	Oregon	Detroit	3
Baldwin, Tom	234	DT	Tulsa	New York Jets	9
Banks, Carl	3	LB	Michigan State	New York Giants	1
Barker, Leo	177	LB	New Mexico State	Cincinnati	7
Barnes, Zack	230	DT	Alabama State	San Diego	9
Baugh, Kevin	197	WR	Penn State	Houston	8
Bayless, Martin	101	DB	Bowling Green	St. Louis	4
Bell, Bobby	91	LB	Missouri	New York Jets	4
Bell, Greg	26	RB	Notre Dame	Buffalo	1
Bellinger, Rodney	77	DB	Miami	Buffalo	3
Bendross, Jesse	174	WR	Alabama	San Diego	7
Bennett, Ben	148	QB	Duke	Atlanta	6
Benson, Cliff	132	TE	Purdue	Atlanta	5
Benson, Thomas	36	LB	Oklahoma	Atlanta	2
Beverly, Dwight	147	RB	Illinois	Indianapolis	6
Bias, Moe	328	LB	Illinois	Los Angeles Rams	12
Blados, Brian	28	T	North Carolina	Cincinnati	1
Bolden, Rickey	96	TE	Southern Methodist	Cleveland	4
Bolzan, Scott	238	T	Northern Illinois	New England	9
Bourgeau, Michel	291	DE	Boise State	New Orleans	11
Boyle, Jim	250	T	Tulane	Miami	9
Brady, Ed	215	LB	Illinois	Los Angeles Rams	8
Brennan, Brian	104	WR	Boston College	Cleveland	4
Brewer, Chris	245	RB	Arizona	Denver	9
Brookins, Mitchell	95	WR	Illinois	Buffalo	4
Brophy, Jay	53	LB	Miami	Miami	2
Brown, Bud	305	DB	So. Mississippi	Miami	11
Brown, Chris	164	DB	Notre Dame	Pittsburgh	6
Browner, Keith	30	LB	Southern California	Tampa Bay	2
Bryan, Rick	9	DT	Oklahoma	Atlanta	1
Bussey, Barney	119	DB	South Carolina State	Cincinnati	5
Butkus, Mark	297	DT	Illinois	Chicago	11
Byner, Earnest	280	RB	East Carolina	Cleveland	10
Cade, Mossy	6	DB	Texas	San Diego	1
Call, Kevin	130	T	Colorado State	Indianapolis	5
Campbell, Scott	191	QB	Purdue	Pittsburgh	7
Cannon, Billy Jr.	25	LB	Texas A&M	Dallas	1
Cannon, Mark	294	C	Texas-Arlington	Green Bay	11
Carreker, Alphonso	12	DE	Florida State	Green Bay	1

WR Irving Fryar of Nebraska, No. 1 overall, is a Patriot.

OG Dean Steinkuhler of Nebraska, second pick, is an Oiler.

Player	Order No.	Pos.	College	Club	Round
Carroll, Jay	169	TE	Minnesota	Tampa Bay	7
Carter, Jimmie	178	LB	New Mexico	Detroit	7
Carter, Joe	109	RB	Alabama	Miami	4
Carter, Michael	121	DT	Southern Methodist	San Francisco	5
Carter, Russell	10	DB	Southern Methodist	New York Jets	1
Carvalho, Bernard	194	G	Hawaii	Miami	7
Casale, Mark	244	QB	Montclair State	Chicago	9
Case, Scott	32	DB	Oklahoma	Atlanta	2
Cephous, Frank	283	RB	UCLA	New York Giants	11
Chesley, John	277	TE	Oklahoma State	Miami	10
Clark, Randy	202	DB	Florida	Kansas City	8
Clark, Rod	157	LB	S.W. Texas State	St. Louis	6
Clifton, Kyle	64	LB	Texas Christian	New York Jets	3
Coleman, Leonard	8	DB	Vanderbilt	Indianapolis	1
Collins, Dwight	154	WR	Pittsburgh	Minnesota	6
Cone, Ronny	261	RB	Georgia Tech	New York Jets	10
Cooper, Evan	88	DB	Michigan	Philadelphia	4
Cornwell, Fred	81	TE	Southern California	Dallas	3
Craighead, Bob	219	RB	N.E. Louisiana	San Diego	8
Curry, Craig	93	DB	Texas	Indianapolis	4
D'Addio, Dave	106	RB	Maryland	Detroit	4
Daniel, Eugene	205	DB	Louisiana State	Indianapolis	8
David, Stan	182	DB	Texas Tech	Buffalo	7
Davis, Bruce	50	WR	Baylor	Cleveland	2
Davis, Russell	322	WR	Maryland	Buffalo	12
Dawson, Doug	45	G	Texas	St. Louis	2
De Ossie, Steve	110	LB	Boston College	Dallas	4
Dennison, Glenn	39	TE	Miami	New York Jets	2
Devane, William	320	DT	Clemson	Miami	12
Dodge, Kirk	175	LB	Nevada-Las Vegas	Atlanta	7
Donaldson, Jeff	226	DB	Colorado	Houston	9
Dooley, Joe	274	C	Ohio State	Los Angeles Rams	10
Dorsey, John	99	LB	Connecticut	Green Bay	4
Dumont, Jim	190	LB	Rutgers	Cleveland	7
Duncan, Clyde	17	WR	Tennessee	St. Louis	1
Eason, Bo	54	DB	Cal-Davis	Houston	2
Emans, Mark	323	LB	Bowling Green	Green Bay	12
Erenberg, Rich	247	RB	Colgate	Pittsburgh	9
Esiason, Boomer	38	QB	Maryland	Cincinnati	2
Essington, Randy	336	QB	Colorado	Los Angeles Raiders	12
Fairchild, Paul	124	G	Kansas	New England	5
Farley, John	92	RB	Cal State-Sacramento	Cincinnati	4
Faurot, Ron	15	DE	Arkansas	New York Jets	1
Fields, Jitter	123	DB	Texas	New Orleans	5
Fisher, Rod	309	DB	Oklahoma State	Los Angeles Rams	12
Flager, Charlie	292	G	Washington State	New England	11
Flynn, Tom	126	DB	Pittsburgh	Green Bay	5
Frank, John	56	TE	Ohio State	San Francisco	2
Franklin, Derrick	260	DB	Fresno State	Atlanta	10
Frizzell, William	259	DB	N. Carolina Central	Detroit	10
Fryar, Irving	1	WR	Nebraska	New England	1
Fuller, Jeff	139	LB	Texas A&M	San Francisco	5
Gallery, Jim	254	K	Minnesota	Tampa Bay	10
Garnett, Scott	218	DT	Washington	Denver	8
Gayle, Shaun	271	DB	Ohio State	Chicago	10
Geathers, James	42	DE	Wichita State	New Orleans	2
Gemza, Steve	302	T	UCLA	Seattle	11
Gibson, Ernest	151	DB	Furman	New England	6

Player	Order No.	Pos.	College	Club	Round
Gillespie, Fernandars	332	RB	William Jewell	Pittsburgh	12
Golden, Heyward	257	DB	South Carolina State	New York Giants	10
Goode, Conrad	87	T	Missouri	New York Giants	4
Goode, John	136	TE	Youngstown	St. Louis	5
Granger, Norm	137	RB	Iowa	Dallas	5
Gray, Paul	264	LB	Western Kentucky	New Orleans	10
Green, Lawrence	311	LB	Tenn.-Chattanooga	New York Giants	12
Griffin, Keith	279	RB	Miami	Washington	10
Griggs, Billy	203	TE	Virginia	New York Jets	8
Grimsley, John	141	LB	Kentucky	Houston	6
Guendling, Mike	33	LB	Northwestern	San Diego	2
Gunter, Michael	107	RB	Tulsa	Tampa Bay	4
Guthrie, Keith	144	DT	Texas A&M	San Diego	6
Hagood, Rickey	86	DT	South Carolina	Seattle	4
Haines, John	180	DT	Texas	Minnesota	7
Hamilton, Harry	176	DB	Penn State	New York Jets	7
Hamilton, Steve	55	DE	East Carolina	Washington	2
Hansen, Brian	237	P	Sioux Falls, S. D.	New Orleans	9
Hardy, Andre	116	RB	St. Mary's, Calif.	Philadelphia	5
Harmon, Derrick	248	RB	Cornell	San Francisco	9
Harper, Maurice	331	WR	La Verne	San Digeo	12
Harper, Michael	293	RB	Southern California	Los Angeles Rams	11
Harris, Clint	115	DB	East Carolina	New York Giants	5
Hathaway, Steve	317	LB	West Virginia	Indianapolis	12
Hayes, Joe	172	RB	Central State, Okla.	Philadelphia	7
Heard, Herman	61	RB	Southern Colorado	Kansas City	3
Heller, Ron	112	T	Penn State	Tampa Bay	4
Hestera, Dave	240	TE	Colorado	Kansas City	9
Hilgenberg, Joel	97	C	Iowa	New Orleans	4
Hoage, Terry	68	DB	Georgia	New Orleans	3
Hoffman, Gary	267	T	Santa Clara	Green Bay	10
Holle, Eric	117	DE	Texas	Kansas City	5
Hollins, Rich	246	WR	West Virginia	Detroit	9
Holmes, Don	318	WR	Mesa, Colo.	Atlanta	12
Hood, Winford	207	T	Georgia	Denver	8
Hostetler, Jeff	59	QB	West Virginia	New York Giants	3
Howe, Glen	233	T	So. Mississippi	Atlanta	9
Howell, Harper	319	TE	UCLA	New England	12
Howell, Leroy	236	DE	Appalachian State	Buffalo	9
Hughes, Van	135	DT	S.W. Texas State	Pittsburgh	5
Humphrey, Donnie	72	DT	Auburn	Green Bay	3
Humphries, Stefan	71	G	Michigan	Chicago	3
Hunley, Ricky	7	LB	Arizona	Cincinnati	1
Hunt, John	232	G	Florida	Dallas	9
Jackson, Aaron	262	LB	North Carolina	Cincinnati	10
Jackson, Jeff	206	LB	Auburn	Atlanta	8
Jackson, Kenny	4	WR	Penn State	Philadelphia	1
James, Lionel	118	KR	Auburn	San Diego	5
Jarmin, Murray	326	WR	Clemson	Denver	12
Jemison, Thad	310	WR	Ohio State	Tampa Bay	12
Jennings, Stanford	65	RB	Furman	Cincinnati	3
Johnson, Bobby	285	RB	San Jose State	Kansas City	11
Johnson, Mike	228	DE	Illinois	Houston	9
Jones, Anthony	306	TE	Wichita State	Washington	11
Jones, Daryll	181	DB	Georgia	Green Bay	7
Jones, David	214	C	Texas	Detroit	8
Jones, Don	227	WR	Texas A&M	Cleveland	9
Jones, Mike	321	RB	North Carolina A&T	Minnesota	12
Jones, Sean	51	DE	Northeastern	Los Angeles Raiders	2
Jordan, David	255	G	Auburn	New York Giants	10

The Giants made LB Carl Banks of Michigan State their No. 1.

Player	Order No.	Pos.	College	Club	Round
Jordan, Donald	330	RB	Houston	Chicago	12
Joyner, Willie	170	RB	Maryland	Houston	7
Kaiser, John	162	LB	Arizona	Seattle	6
Kallmeyer, Bruce	184	K	Kansas	New England	7
Kay, Clarence	186	TE	Georgia	Denver	7
Kern, Don	150	TE	Arizona State	Cincinnati	6
Keyton, James	211	T	Arizona State	New England	8
Kidd, John	128	P	Northwestern	Buffalo	5
Kidd, Keith	235	WR	Arkansas	Minnesota	9
Kiel, Blair	281	QB	Notre Dame	Tampa Bay	11
Koch, Pete	16	DE	Maryland	Cincinnati	1
Kolodziejski, Chris	52	TE	Wyoming	Pittsburgh	2
Kozerski, Bruce	231	C	Holy Cross	Cincinnati	9
Landry, Ronnie	221	RB	Mc Neese State	Miami	8
Lang, Gene	298	RB	Louisiana State	Denver	11
Lang, Mark	314	LB	Texas	Kansas City	12
Leiding, Jeff	129	LB	Texas	St. Louis	5
Levelis, Joe	166	G	Iowa	Dallas	6
Lewis, Carl	334	WR	Houston	Dallas	12
Lewis, David	20	TE	California	Detroit	1
Lewis, Loyd	196	G	Texas A&I	Minnesota	7
Lilly, Tony	78	DB	Florida	Denver	3
Lipps, Louis	23	WR	So. Mississippi	Pittsburgh	1
Lockhart, Eugene	152	LB	Houston	Dallas	6
Long, Terry	111	G	East Carolina	Pittsburgh	4
Love, Dwyane	301	RB	Houston	Los Angeles Rams	11
Lyles, Robert	114	LB	Texas Christian	Houston	5
Maas, Bill	5	DT	Pittsburgh	Kansas City	1
Mackey, Kyle	296	QB	East Texas State	St. Louis	11
Malancon, Rydell	94	LB	Louisiana State	Atlanta	4
Mallory, Rick	225	G	Washington	Tampa Bay	9
Mandley, Pete	47	WR	Northern Arizona	Detroit	2
Manuel, Lionel	171	WR	Pacific	New York Giants	7
Marshall, Wilber	11	LB	Florida	Chicago	1
Martin, Dan	288	T	Iowa State	New York Jets	11
Martin, Ed	193	LB	Indiana State	Dallas	7
Matsakis, Manny	200	K	Capital	Philadelphia	8
Maune, Neil	249	G	Notre Dame	Dallas	9
May, Dean	138	QB	Louisville	Miami	5
McCall, Joe	84	RB	Pittsburgh	Los Angeles Raiders	3
McFadden, Paul	312	K	Youngstown	Philadelphia	12
McGee, Buford	286	RB	Mississippi	San Diego	11
McIntyre, Guy	73	G	Georgia	San Francisco	3
McIvor, Rick	80	QB	Texas	St. Louis	3
McJunkin, Kirk	276	T	Texas	Pittsburgh	10
McKeaver, Steve	289	RB	Central State, Okla.	Cincinnati	11
McNanie, Sean	79	DE	San Diego State	Buffalo	3
McSwain, Rod	63	DB	Clemson	Atlanta	3
Meads, Johnny	58	LB	Nicholls State	Houston	3
Micho, Bobby	272	TE	Texas	Denver	10
Millard, Keith	13	DE	Washington State	Minnesota	1
Miller, Lee	239	DB	Cal State-Fullerton	San Francisco	9
Moritz, Dave	275	WR	Iowa	San Francisco	10
Morris, Randall	270	RB	Tennessee	Seattle	10
Mullins, Eric	161	WR	Stanford	Houston	6
Neal, Speedy	82	RB	Miami	Buffalo	3
Nelson, Byron	324	T	Arizona	New Orleans	12
Noga, Falaniko	201	LB	Hawaii	St. Louis	8

Rookie Bear, 11th pick, is DB Wilber Marshall of Florida.

Texas DB Mossy Cade was chosen 11th by San Diego.

Player	Order No.	Pos.	College	Club	Round
Norman, Tommy	287	WR	Jackson State	Atlanta	11
Nugent, Terry	158	QB	Colorado State	Cleveland	6
Paige, Tony	149	RB	Virginia Tech	New York Jets	6
Paine, Jeff	134	LB	Texas A&M	Kansas City	5
Parker, Andy	127	TE	Utah	Los Angeles Raiders	5
Parker, Paul	325	G	Oklahoma	St. Louis	12
Paulling, Bob	213	K	Clemson	St. Louis	8
Pegues, Jeff	125	LB	East Carolina	Washington	5
Pelluer, Steve	113	QB	Washington	Dallas	5
Pendleton, Kirk	307	WR	Brigham Young	San Francisco	11
Pickett, Edgar	295	LB	Clemson	Minnesota	11
Piepkorn, Dave	131	T	North Dakota State	Cleveland	5
Puzar, John	216	C	Cal State-Long Beach	Seattle	8
Radachowsky, George	188	DB	Boston College	Los Angeles Rams	7
Radecic, Scott	34	LB	Penn State	Kansas City	2
Ralph, Dan	163	DT	Oregon	Atlanta	6
Raquet, Steve	316	LB	Holy Cross	Cincinnati	12
Raridon, Scott	145	T	Nebraska	Philadelphia	6
Rasmussen, Randy	220	C	Minnesota	Pittsburgh	8
Rayfield, Stacy	209	DB	Texas-Arlington	Buffalo	8
Reasons, Gary	105	LB	N.W. Louisiana	New York Giants	4
Reimers, Bruce	204	T	Iowa State	Cincinnati	8
Revell, Mike	222	RB	Bethune-Cookman	Dallas	8
Reynolds, George	242	P	Penn State	Los Angeles Rams	9
Rice, Allen	140	RB	Baylor	Minnesota	5
Richardson, Eric	41	WR	San Jose State	Buffalo	2
Rivera, Ron	44	LB	California	Chicago	2
Robbins, Randy	89	DB	Arizona	Denver	4
Roberson, David	315	WR	Houston	New York Jets	12
Roberts, Bill	27	T	Ohio State	New York Giants	1
Robertson, John	284	T	East Carolina	Philadelphia	11
Robertson, Nakita	179	RB	Central Arkansas	Chicago	7
Robinson, Fred	198	DE	Miami	Tampa Bay	8
Robinson, Mark	90	DB	Penn State	Kansas City	4
Rockins, Chris	48	DB	Oklahoma State	Cleveland	2
Rogers, Don	18	DB	UCLA	Cleveland	1
Ross, Kevin	173	DB	Temple	Kansas City	7
Russell, Mike	252	LB	Toledo	Houston	9
Russell, Rusty	60	T	South Carolina	Philadelphia	3
Salonen, Brian	278	TE	Montana	Dallas	10
Saxon, Mike	300	P	San Diego State	Detroit	11
Schreiber, Adam	243	G	Texas	Seattle	9
Schroeder, Jay	83	QB	UCLA	Washington	3
Scott, Chris	66	DT	Purdue	Indianapolis	3
Scott, Jim	143	DE	Clemson	New York Giants	6
Scott, Victor	40	DB	Colorado	Dallas	2
Seale, Sam	224	WR	Western State, Colo.	Los Angeles Raiders	8
Shell, Todd	24	LB	Brigham Young	San Francisco	1
Shipp, Jackie	14	LB	Oklahoma	Miami	1
Singer, Curt	167	T	Tennessee	Washington	6
Slater, Bob	31	DT	Oklahoma	Washington	2
Slater, Sam	189	T	Weber State	Seattle	7
Slaton, Tony	155	C	Southern California	Buffalo	6
Smith, Aaron	159	LB	Utah State	Denver	6
Smith, Doug	29	DE	Auburn	Houston	2
Smith, Jeff	223	DB	Missouri	Washington	8
Smith, Jimmy	102	RB	Elon	Washington	4
Smith, Mark	195	WR	North Carolina	Washington	7
Smythe, Mark	269	DT	Indiana	St. Louis	10

The Jets went first for DB Russell Carter of SMU.

Player	Order No.	Pos.	College	Club	Round
Solt, Ron	19	G	Maryland	Indianapolis	1
Spencer, James	268	LB	Oklahoma State	Minnesota	10
Steinkuhler, Dean	2	T	Nebraska	Houston	1
Stephens, Hal	133	DE	East Carolina	Los Angeles Rams	5
Stevens, Rufus	146	WR	Grambling	Kansas City	6
Stowe, Bob	290	T	Illinois	Indianapolis	11
Streno, Glenn	327	C	Tennessee	Detroit	12
Studaway, Mark	85	DE	Tennessee	Houston	4
Sverchek, Paul	208	DT	Cal Poly-Obispo	Minnesota	8
Sweeney, Jim	37	C	Pittsburgh	New York Jets	2
Tate, Golden	120	WR	Tennessee State	Indianapolis	5
Tatum, Rowland	165	LB	Ohio State	Miami	6
Taylor, Lenny	313	WR	Tennessee	Green Bay	12
Taylor, Terry	22	DB	Southern Illinois	Seattle	1
Terrell, Clemon	210	RB	So. Mississippi	New Orleans	8
Thaxton, James	273	DB	Louisiana Tech	Detroit	10
Thomas, Curtland	335	WR	Missouri	Washington	12
Thomas, John	256	DB	Texas Christian	Philadelphia	10
Thompson, Lawrence	308	WR	Miami	Minnesota	11
Thompson, Weegie	108	WR	Florida State	Pittsburgh	4
Thorp, Don	156	DT	Illinois	New Orleans	6
Toran, Stacey	168	DB	Notre Dame	Los Angeles Raiders	6
Townsend, Andre	46	DE	Mississippi	Denver	2
Turner, Daryl	49	WR	Michigan State	Seattle	2
Vann, Norwood	253	TE	East Carolina	Los Angeles Rams	10
Veals, Elton	303	RB	Tulane	Pittsburgh	11
Vestman, Kurt	266	TE	Idaho	Chicago	10
Walker, John	241	RB	Texas	St. Louis	9
Walker, Quentin	185	RB	Virginia	St. Louis	7
Washington, Chris	142	LB	Iowa State	Tampa Bay	6
Weingrad, Mike	333	LB	Illinois	Miami	12
Wenglikowski, Al	258	LB	Pittsburgh	Kansas City	10
White, Craig	299	WR	Missouri	Buffalo	11
Williams, Derwin	192	WR	New Mexico	New England	7
Williams, Ed	43	LB	Texas	New England	2
Williams, Eric	62	DT	Washington State	Detroit	3
Williams, Gardner	282	DB	St. Mary's, Calif.	Los Angeles Raiders	11
Williams, Jon	70	RB	Penn State	New England	3
Willis, Mitch	183	DE	Southern Methodist	Los Angeles Raiders	7
Windham, David	251	LB	Jackson State	New England	9
Windham, Theodis	329	DB	Utah State	Seattle	12
Winter, Blaise	35	DT	Syracuse	Indianapolis	2
Witkowski, John	160	QB	Columbia	Detroit	6
Wonsley, George	103	RB	Mississippi State	Indianapolis	4
Woodard, Raymond	199	DT	Texas	San Diego	8
Wright, Brett	217	P	S.E. Louisiana	New York Jets	8
Wright, Randy	153	QB	Wisconsin	Green Bay	6
Young, Fred	76	LB	New Mexico State	Seattle	3
Ziegler, Brent	265	RB	Syracuse	Cincinnati	10

Nebraska's Mike Rozier, USFL's No. 1, is a Pittsburgh Mauler.

1984 USFL DRAFT

Player	Order No.	Pos.	College	Club	Round
Albritton, Vince	329	DB	Washington	Philadelphia	16
Allen, Brian	314	WR	Idaho	Oklahoma	15
Allen, Patrick	28	DB	Utah St.	Washington	2
Alt, John	47	T	Iowa	Oklahoma	3
Anderson, Cedric	285	WR	Ohio St.	Michigan	14
Andrews, Tom	124	T	Louisville	Memphis	6
Archer, David	172	QB	Iowa St.	Denver	9
Armstrong, Tron	49	WR	E. Kentucky	Chicago	3
Atkins, Rennie	118	G	Kansas	Birmingham	6
Baack, Steve	185	DE	Oregon	Philadelphia	9
Baird, Kerry	58	DB	Kentucky	Michigan	3
Batiste, Derrick	222	DB	McNeese St.	Oakland	11
Bates, Glenn	229	DB	Marshall	Pittsburgh	11
Battle, Ralph	340	DB	Jacksonville St.	Memphis	17
Bauer, Mark	397	T	Drake	Pittsburgh	19
Bayless, Martin	21	DB	Bowling Green	Memphis	1
Bell, Bobby	44	LB	Missouri	Chicago	3
Bell, Kerwin	221	RB	Kansas	Los Angeles	11
Bellinger, Rodney	41	DB	Miami (FL)	Houston	2
Bennett, Mitchell	261	WR	Lamar	New Jersey	13
Bennett, Roy	318	DB	Jackson St.	Jacksonville	15
Benson, Cliff	12	TE	Purdue	Oakland	1
Bentley, Albert	7	RB	Miami (FL)	Chicago	1
Bergmann, Paul	43	TE	UCLA	Jacksonville	3
Bertoldi, Tom	153	QB	No. Michigan	New Jersey	8
Biestek, Bob	165	RB	Boston College	Denver	8
Bolden, Rickey	73	TE	SMU	Oakland	4
Booze, William	326	WR	Cincinnati	Tampa Bay	16
Boren, Phillip	61	T	Arkansas	Birmingham	3
Bourgeau, Michel	220	DE	Boise St.	Chicago	11
Brennan, Brian	327	WR	Boston College	Denver	16
Bridges, Gary	129	DB	E. Illinois	Memphis	7
Brooks, Rod	325	DB	No. Alabama	Michigan	16
Brophy, Jay	74	LB	Miami (FL)	Tampa Bay	4
Broughton, Walter	36	RB	Jacksonville St.	Michigan	2
Brown, Don	365	LB	Defiance	Los Angeles	18
Brown, Emerson	308	RB	Cameron	New Orleans	15
Brown, Jim	349	TE	So. Mississippi	Birmingham	17
Brown, K.C.	217	G	Kansas	Los Angeles	11
Brown, Rodney	311	DB	C. Arkansas	Houston	15
Browne, Less	276	DB	Colorado St.	Pittsburgh	13
Browning, Dean	156	DT	Washington	Tampa Bay	8
Burningham, Rex	322	T	BYU	New Orleans	16
Bussey, Barney	4	DB	So. Carolina St.	Memphis	1
Buzzard, Danny	298	G	Texas Tech	San Antonio	15
Byrne, Jim	216	DT	Wisconsin-LaCrosse	Pittsburgh	11
Callahan, Mitch	90	DT	Arizona St.	Oakland	5
Campbell, Scott	77	QB	Purdue	Philadelphia	4
Cannon, Mark	63	C	Texas-Arlington	Tampa Bay	3
Carroll, Jay	192	TE	Minnesota	Pittsburgh	9

Player	Order No.	Pos.	College	Club	Round
Carswell, Ernie	167	DB	Alabama St.	Oklahoma	8
Carter, Joe	105	RB	Alabama	Memphis	5
Carter, Mike	197	DT	SMU	Los Angeles	10
Carter, Russell	10	DB	SMU	Denver	1
Carter, Steve	242	WR	Albany St.	Tampa Bay	12
Carter, Thomas	96	LB	San Diego St.	Oakland	5
Carvalho, Bernard	157	G	Hawaii	Oakland	8
Casale, Mark	195	QB	Montclair St.	New Jersey	10
Catano, Mark	247	T	Valdosta St.	Memphis	12
Caterbone, Mike	359	WR	Franklin & Marshall	Oklahoma	17
Cauthion, Keith	181	WR	Virginia Union	Birmingham	9
Cephous, Frank	46	RB	UCLA	San Antonio	3
Chaffin, Jeff	395	DE	UCLA	Philadelphia	19
Charphia, David	319	QB	Furman	Washington	16
Christie, Demosthenes	252	G	Morgan St.	Pittsburgh	12
Clark, Gary	6	WR	James Madison	Jacksonville	1
Clifton, Kyle	13	LB	TCU	Birmingham	1
Cole, Emmanuel	341	DT	Toledo	Houston	17
Cole, Terry	266	DE	Illinois	New Orleans	13
Collins, Clarence	55	WR	Illinois St.	New Jersey	3
Collins, Trent	401	DB	San Diego St.	Houston	19
Cooks, Rayford	317	DE	No. Texas St.	Houston	15
Corbin, Don	145	T	Kentucky	Pittsburgh	7
Corley, Anthony	144	RB	Nevada-Reno	Michigan	7
Cottingham, Reginald	339	DB	TCU	San Antonio	17
Courtney, Matt	79	DB	Idaho St.	Jacksonville	4
Craighead, Bobby	171	RB	N.E. Louisiana	San Antonio	9
Curtis, Larry	275	DB	Virginia Union	Birmingham	13
Cutts, Tim	237	P	Mississippi St.	New Jersey	12
Daly, John	292	WR	Dartmouth	Memphis	14
Daniel, Donnell	152	DB	So. Illinois	Chicago	8
Davis, Larry	313	RB	Luther	Pittsburgh	15
Davis, Ricky	291	DB	West Texas St.	San Antonio	14
Del Greco, Al	307	K	Auburn	Birmingham	15
Dennison, Glenn	65	TE	Miami (FL)	Houston	3
DeOssie, Steve	15	LB	Boston College	New Jersey	1
Dixon, Kevin	383	TE	So. Oregon	Oklahoma	19
Dodge, Kirk	113	LB	Nevada-Las Vegas	Los Angeles	6
Dodson, Lance	393	T	Washington	Los Angeles	19
Dorsey, John	143	LB	Connecticut	Philadelphia	7
Dorsey, Melvin	310	RB	W. Carolina	Memphis	15
Dukes, Richard	88	DB	W. Carolina	Memphis	5
Dumont, Jim	363	LB	Rutgers	New Jersey	18
Eason, Bo	19	DB	Cal-Davis	Oakland	1
Eddo, Mike	258	WR	BYU	Jacksonville	13
Edwards, Al Rickey	230	RB	Mississippi St.	Oklahoma	11
England, Jeff	335	G	So. Colorado	Oklahoma	16
Errico, Dan	345	DB	Rutgers	New Jersey	17
Etzel, Scott	177	C	No. Iowa	New Jersey	9
Fairchild, Paul	125	G	Kansas	Houston	6
Farley, John	140	RB	Sacramento St.	New Orleans	7
Faurot, Ron	2	DE	Arkansas	Oklahoma	1
Fernandes, Fred	236	WR	Utah St.	New Orleans	12
Fields, Milton	142	LB	Arkansas	Birmingham	7
Fitzpatrick, Tony	128	DT	Miami (FL)	Houston	7
Flager, Charlie	164	G	Washington St.	Arizona	8
Flint, Brandon	337	DT	BYU	Pittsburgh	17
Fowler, Todd	332	TE	Stephen F. Austin	Houston	16
Freeman, Reese	301	DT	No. Colorado	New Jersey	15

Player	Order No.	Pos.	College	Club	Round
Fryar, Irving	3	RB	Miami (FL)	Chicago	1
Futrell, Bobby	94	DB	Elizabeth City	Michigan	5
Galloway, Tim	212	DB	Holy Cross	Houston	11
Gardner, Mark	239	G	Hawaii	Los Angeles	12
Garcia, Jesse	250	K	N.E. Louisiana	San Antonio	12
Garnett, Scott	67	DT	Washington	Washington	4
Garron, Arnold	131	DB	New Hampshire	Denver	7
Gary, Paul	116	LB	W. Kentucky	Tampa Bay	6
Gayle, Shaun	288	DB	Ohio St.	Michigan	14
Gemza, Steve	256	T	UCLA	Memphis	13
Gibson, Ernest	45	DB	Furman	Memphis	3
Gill, Turner	104	QB	Nebraska	Houston	5
Goode, Conrad	23	T	Missouri	Oklahoma	1
Goode, John	86	TE	Youngstown St.	Oklahoma	5
Gordon, Scott	254	T	UCLA	Oklahoma	13
Granger, Norm	38	RB	Iowa	Oklahoma	2
Grant, Mike	362	LB	E. Carolina	Memphis	18
Gray, Mel	133	RB	Purdue	Chicago	7
Green, Bruce	347	LB	Texas Southern	Los Angeles	17
Green, George	259	DB	Western Carolina	Memphis	13
Green, Lawrence	136	LB	Tenn-Chattanooga	Washington	7
Green, Willie	186	DE	Mississippi Valley	Michigan	9
Grogan, Tom	287	QB	Iowa	Oakland	14
Griffin, Keith	215	RB	Miami (FL)	Oklahoma	11
Grimsley, John	60	LB	Kentucky	Denver	3
Guendling, Mike	269	LB	Northwestern	Philadelphia	13
Gunn, Carlton	159	DE	Carson-Newman	Memphis	8
Gunn, Duane	120	WR	Indiana	Washington	6
Gunter, Larry	278	DT	Lenoir-Rhyne	Memphis	14
Hagum, Dean	151	DT	Mesa College	Denver	8
Hamilton, Steve	80	DE	E. Carolina	Michigan	4
Hamilton, Waymon	199	RB	BYU	Washington	10
Hanks, Duan	286	WR	Stephen F. Austin	Philadelphia	14
Hardy, Andre	87	RB	St. Mary's	San Antonio	5
Harlien, Matt	375	T	Texas Tech	San Antonio	18
Harmon, Derrick	338	RB	Cornell	Oklahoma	17
Harper, Steve	331	TE	BYU	Jacksonville	16
Harris, Clint	110	DB	E. Carolina	Washington	6
Harris, R.L.	59	DB	Stephen F. Austin	Philadelphia	3
Harris, Willie	403	DB	No. Carolina	Philadelphia	19
Hart, Darrel	54	DB	Lane College	Oakland	3
Harter, Steve	316	T	Mt. Union	Memphis	15
Hauser, Pat	206	G	Cal St.-Northridge	Oklahoma	10
Hawkins, Reco	265	DB	Missouri	Birmingham	13
Hayes, Joe	277	RB	Central St. (OK)	Washington	14
Hedderly, Russ	243	LB	Kent St.	Michigan	12
Henderson, Willie	333	WR	Central St. (OK)	Memphis	16
Herrington, Mike	309	DE	Wisconsin	Tampa Bay	15
Herrmann, Doug	213	DT	Nebraska	Memphis	11
Hilgenberg, Joel	109	C	Iowa	Washington	6
Hill, Stewart	68	LB	Washington	Denver	4
Hines, Joe	400	DT	Penn St.	Denver	19
Hobert, Ken	42	QB	Idaho	Jacksonville	2
Hobbs, Curtis	163	WR	Nicholls St.	Jacksonville	8
Hoffman, Gary	190	T	Santa Clara	San Antonio	9
Holland, Brian	219	RB	Arizona	Denver	11
Hollie, Doug	30	DE	SMU	Pittsburgh	2
Holmes, Don	404	WR	Mesa College	Oakland	19
Hornback, Eddie	387	DE	Mississippi St.	New Jersey	19
Hornof, Tom	293	G	Missouri	Houston	14

Player	Order No.	Pos.	College	Club	Round
Howell, Harper	202	TE	UCLA	New Jersey	10
Howell, Leroy	134	DE	Appalachian St.	New Orleans	7
Hudson, Gordon	155	TE	BYU	Los Angeles	8
Hufford, Mike	283	T	Iowa	Tampa Bay	14
Ingram, Kevin	99	QB	E. Carolina	Tampa Bay	5
Jackson, Billy	173	LB	Mississippi St.	Houston	9
Jackson, Mark	334	DB	Abilene Christian	San Antonio	16
Jacobs, Jason	97	RB	Iowa St.	Michigan	5
Jackson, Chris	255	C	SMU	San Antonio	13
Jackson, Marvin	245	DB	Utah St.	Philadelphia	12
James, Daryl	290	RB	Yankton	Oklahoma	14
James, Keith	390	WR	No. Carolina A&T	Oakland	19
Jamison, George	35	LB	Cincinnati	Philadelphia	2
Jelesky, Tom	280	T	Purdue	Denver	14
Jenkins, Mark	271	G	Cincinnati	Michigan	13
Jenkins, Randy	141	QB	Kentucky	Tampa Bay	7
Jennings, Stanford	18	RB	Furman	Michigan	1
Jensen, Chris	226	WR	Lake Forest (IL)	Michigan	11
Johnson, Bobby	346	RB	Arkansas St.	Denver	17
Johnson, Bill	66	WR	Kansas	Philadelphia	3
Johnson, Hardis	150	WR	Florida St.	Jacksonville	7
Johnson, Tony	294	WR	Florida St.	Jacksonville	14
Jones, Mike	241	RB	No. Carolina A&T	Oakland	12
Johnson, Randy	184	RB	Texas-Arlington	Arizona	9
Jones, Sean	92	DE	Northeastern	Washington	5
Jordan, Eric	115	RB	Purdue	Oakland	6
Jordan, Buford	14	RB	McNeese St.	New Orleans	1
Kalafat, Jim	315	LB	Montana St.	San Antonio	15
Kallmeyer, Bruce	168	K	Kansas	Pittsburgh	8
Kapischke, Kurt	352	T	Augustana (IL)	Michigan	17
Kelley, Greg	360	LB	So. Mississippi	Pittsburgh	17
Kelly, Otto	161	RB	Nevada-Reno	Philadelphia	8
Kemp, Perry	211	WR	Cal St. (PA)	Jacksonville	11
Kennard, Derek	53	C	Nevada-Reno	Los Angeles	3
Kidd, Alvin	405	RB	Mississippi College	Washington	19
Kidd, Keith	32	WR	Arkansas	Washington	2
King, James	82	T	W. Kentucky	Chicago	4
Koontz, Henry	228	RB	Mississippi St.	New Jersey	11
Kozerski, Bruce	248	T	Holy Cross	Houston	12
Kragen, Greg	299	DT	Utah St.	Oklahoma	15
Landrum, Mike	198	TE	So. Mississippi	Birmingham	10
Landry, Ronnie	132	RB	McNeese St.	Pittsburgh	7
Lee, Lawrence	232	RB	Kentucky	Memphis	11
Lesnik, Ivan	323	DT	Arizona	Los Angeles	16
Levelis, Joe	62	T	Iowa	Oklahoma	3
Lipps, Louis	156	WR	So. Mississippi	Arizona	8
Long, Matt	240	C	San Diego St.	New Jersey	12
Long, Terry	76	G	E. Carolina	Washington	4
Louallen, Fletcher	282	DB	Livingston	Birmingham	14
Louthan, Marty	388	QB	Air Force	Denver	19
Lutu, Leroy	367	TE	Washington	Oakland	18
Lynch, Dan	342	G	Washington St.	Jacksonville	17
MacDonald, Mark	84	T	Boston College	Pittsburgh	4
Mack, Eric	394	TE	Kansas St.	Michigan	19
Mackey, Kyle	218	QB	E. Texas St.	Washington	11
Mackey, Willis Ray	370	RB	S.W. Texas	Denver	18
Madison, L.E.	223	LB	Kansas St.	Washington	11

Player	Order No.	Pos.	College	Club	Round
Madsen, Lynn	51	DT	Washington	New Jersey	3
Maggs, Don	29	T	Tulane	Pittsburgh	2
Mallory, Rick	224	G	Washington	Arizona	11
Marler, Chris	398	T	LA Tech	Philadelphia	19
Martin, Ed	121	LB	Indiana St.	Pittsburgh	6
Mason, Nate	377	QB	Nebraska	Houston	18
Massey, Dwayne	205	T	So. Mississippi	Pittsburgh	10
May, Dean	176	QB	Louisville	Chicago	9
McClelland, Kevin	225	LB	Kentucky	Tampa Bay	11
McCormick, Tom	267	C	Florida St.	Tampa Bay	13
McCurley, Chuck	126	TE	No. Alabama	Jacksonville	6
McDade, Clarence	191	LB	SMU	Oklahoma	9
McDowell, Felix	253	TE	E. Texas St.	Pittsburgh	13
McFadden, Paul	175	K	Youngstown St.	Chicago	9
McInnis, Mike	119	DE	Ark.-Pine Bluff	Philadelphia	6
McKeever, Vito	114	DB	Florida	Michigan	6
McLean, John	402	LB	Florida St.	Jacksonville	19
McNanie, Sean	31	DE	San Diego St.	Oakland	2
McQuaid, Dan	321	T	Nevada-Las Vegas	New Jersey	16
Meads, Johnny	56	LB	Nicholls St.	New Orleans	3
Millard, Keith	5	DE	Washington St.	Arizona	1
Monson, Dennis	263	DT	Nevada-Reno	Los Angeles	13
Moore, Tom	366	DB	Vanderbilt	Birmingham	18
Morgan, John	358	G	Texas-Arlington	San Antonio	17
Moritz, Dave	235	WR	Iowa	Washington	12
Morris, Raymond	166	LB	Texas-El Paso	San Antonio	8
Mosely, Andre	264	DB	No. Texas St.	Oakland	13
Motton, Ron	257	G	Nicholls St.	Houston	13
Myers, Milt	93	QB	Whitworth	Oklahoma	5
Naylor, Rick	246	LB	Notre Dame	Michigan	12
Neal, Alan	357	LB	So. Carolina St.	Memphis	17
Neal, Robert	78	RB	Miami (FL)	Tampa Bay	4
Nease, Mike	170	T	Tenn.-Chattanooga	Oklahoma	9
Nelson, Kevin	24	RB	UCLA	Los Angeles	1
Neuheisel, Rick	39	QB	UCLA	San Antonio	2
Newton, Mike	106	DB	Austin Peay	Tampa Bay	5
Nichols, Darryl	328	LB	Grambling	Arizona	16
Nicholson, Chris	376	DT	E. Illinois	Memphis	18
Noga, Falaniko	193	LB	Hawaii	Oakland	10
Norman, Tom	179	WR	Jackson St.	Los Angeles	9
O'Meara, Brian	147	T	SMU	San Antonio	7
O'Neal, Ken	160	TE	Idaho St.	Michigan	8
Page, Ken	227	DE	UCLA	Philadelphia	11
Parker, Andy	101	TE	Utah	Philadelphia	5
Patrick, Linnie	302	RB	Alabama	Michigan	15
Patterson, Elvis	210	DB	Kansas	Jacksonville	10
Paul, Gaylord	369	DB	S.W. Louisiana	New Orleans	18
Pelleur, Steve	111	QB	Washington	Oakland	6
Pendleton, Kirk	174	WR	BYU	Jacksonville	9
Pendergrass, Horace	361	DB	Elizabeth City	Washington	18
Pennison, Jay	270	C	Nicholls St.	Jacksonville	13
Peterson, Paul	386	QB	Idaho St.	Washington	19
Phillips, Eddie	207	RB	Iowa	San Antonio	10
Piepkorn, Dave	180	G	No. Dakota St.	Philadelphia	9
Pillman, Brian	204	LB	Miami (OH)	Denver	10
Pittman, Dwayne	83	RB	Arkansas St.	Oklahoma	4
Porter, Robert	306	DB	Holy Cross	Philadelphia	15
Powell, Alvin	122	G	Winston-Salem	Oklahoma	6
Preston, John	279	DB	Central St.	New Jersey	14

Player	Order No.	Pos.	College	Club	Round
Qualls, Carl	103	LB	Idaho St.	Jacksonville	5
Radachowsky, George	85	DB	Boston College	Philadelphia	5
Ralph, Dan	130	DT	Oregon	Arizona	7
Raquet, Steve	162	DE	Holy Cross	Oakland	8
Raridon, Scott	17	T	Nebraska	Philadelphia	1
Rasmussen, Randy	244	G	Minnesota	Chicago	12
Rayfield, Stacy	98	DB	Texas-Arlington	New Orleans	5
Reasons, Gary	27	LB	N.W. Louisiana	New Jersey	2
Reid, Alan	385	RB	Minnesota	Memphis	19
Reimers, Bruce	137	G	Iowa St.	Los Angeles	7
Retherford, Dave	378	WR	Purdue	Jacksonville	18
Reyes, Jeff	350	DE	Utah	New Orleans	17
Rhone, Ed	330	DE	Oregon	Oakland	16
Risher, Billy	381	WR	Furman	Memphis	19
Robertson, John	208	T	E. Carolina	Memphis	10
Robertson, Nakita	89	RB	Central Arkansas	Washington	5
Roberts, Frank	201	C	Tulane	New Orleans	10
Robinson, Fred	25	DE	Miami (FL)	Washington	2
Roche, Rich	355	LB	Syracuse	Jacksonville	17
Roe, Ken	379	LB	Florida St.	Jacksonville	18
Rogan, Dennis	233	RB	Weber St.	Houston	11
Rogers, Don	22	DB	UCLA	San Antonio	1
Rogers, Shawn	272	RB	Cal-Davis	Houston	13
Rose, Carlton	354	LB	Michigan	Michigan	17
Rosnagle, Ted	148	DB	Portland St.	Memphis	7
Rozier, Mike	1	RB	Nebraska	Pittsburgh	1
Russell, Mike	34	LB	Toledo	Chicago	2
Ryerson, Scott	351	K	Central Florida	Tampa Bay	17
Sales, Taft	48	LB	Missouri	Birmingham	3
Salonen, Brian	188	TE	Montana	Houston	9
Sanchez, Lupe	16	DB	UCLA	Arizona	1
Sandusky, Jim	75	WR	San Diego St.	Philadelphia	4
Saxon, Mike	268	P	San Diego St.	Arizona	13
Schellen, Mark	33	RB	Nebraska	New Orleans	2
Schofield, Gary	289	QB	Wake Forest	Pittsburgh	14
Scott, Chris	40	DT	Purdue	Memphis	2
Seale, Sam	312	WR	W. Colorado	Memphis	15
Seccareccia, Bob	380	T	Rhode Island	Houston	19
Seman, Steve	251	G	Idaho	Oklahoma	12
Seurer, Frank	95	QB	Kansas	Los Angeles	5
Shaw, Tony	234	DB	Nevada-Reno	Jacksonville	11
Shell, Todd	52	LB	BYU	Denver	3
Shipp, Greg	324	DB	So. Illinois	Birmingham	16
Shockley, Scott	200	T	Missouri	Tampa Bay	10
Simmons, Eddie	260	LB	Kansas	Memphis	13
Simmons, Ricky	70	WR	Nebraska	Washington	4
Singletary, Reggie	102	DT	Kansas St.	Michigan	5
Skudneski, Dave	384	DT	Ft. Lewis	Pittsburgh	19
Slater, Sam	108	T	Weber St.	Pittsburgh	5
Smith, Aaron	187	LB	Utah St.	Jacksonville	9
Smith, Allanda	8	DB	TCU	Washington	1
Smith, Jeff	57	DB	Missouri	Tampa Bay	3
Smith, Jimmy	100	RB	Elon	Arizona	5
Smith, Reggie	71	T	Kansas	Tampa Bay	4
Smith, Wayne	300	WR	Tulane	Pittsburgh	15
Smythe, Mark	178	DT	Indiana	New Orleans	9
Spek, Jeff	303	DE	San Diego St.	New Jersey	15
Spivak, Joe	391	G	Illinois St.	Birmingham	19
Stamps, Sylvester	373	RB	Jackson St.	Birmingham	18
Steinkuhler, Dean	117	G	Nebraska	Arizona	6

Player	Order No.	Pos.	College	Club	Round
Stephens, Hal	81	LB	E. Carolina	Memphis	4
Stevens, Rufus	107	WR	Grambling	Oklahoma	5
Stinnett, Ed	353	RB	BYU	Philadelphia	17
Sutton, Phil	146	DB	Minnesota	New Orleans	7
Swanke, Rob	169	DT	Boston College	Pittsburgh	9
Taliferro, Mike	72	DT	TCU	Denver	4
Taylor, Joe	284	DB	Washington St.	New Orleans	14
Taylor, Terry	26	DB	So. Illinois	Chicago	2
Thomas, Curtland	371	WR	Missouri	Philadelphia	18
Thomas, Donald Ray	295	DB	Tulane	Jacksonville	15
Thomas, John	138	DB	TCU	Oakland	7
Tillery, Glenn	368	WR	Duke	Tampa Bay	18
Tiumalu, Casey	281	RB	BYU	Los Angeles	14
Todd, Everette	231	DE	Rice	San Antonio	11
Tootle, Jeff	249	LB	Mesa College	Memphis	12
Towery, Rusty	127	QB	No. Alabama	Jacksonville	7
Townsend, Kent	274	DE	Baylor	San Antonio	13
Tucker, Mel	348	RB	Toledo	Oakland	17
Turner, Ricky	123	QB	Washington St.	San Antonio	6
Turner, Robert	297	DB	James Madison	Memphis	15
Verdin, Clarence	356	WR	S.W. Louisiana	Houston	17
Vestman, Kurt	336	TE	Idaho	Pittsburgh	16
Wade, Michael	396	WR	Iowa St.	Michigan	19
Walker, Del	374	RB	E. Stroudsburg St.	Oklahoma	18
Washington, Chris	50	LB	Iowa St.	Washington	3
Webster, Rodney	389	RB	Boise St.	Los Angeles	19
Weems, Orson	382	T	Arkansas	San Antonio	19
Weiler, Mark	343	LB	Indiana	Memphis	17
Wells, Mike	304	TE	San Diego St.	Denver	15
West, Doug	64	LB	UCLA	Memphis	3
White, Craig	214	DB	Minnesota	San Antonio	11
White, Craig	149	WR	Missouri	Houston	7
White, Eddie	320	TE	Arkansas	Memphis	16
Wilburn, Steve	154	DE	Illinois St.	Denver	8
Wilkening, Doug	273	RB	Nebraska	Memphis	13
Williams, Alphonso	364	WR	Nevada-Reno	Denver	18
Williams, Dennis	305	T	Tenn.-Chattanooga	Los Angeles	15
Williams, Eddie	209	DB	Miami (FL)	Arizona	10
Williams, Eric	20	DT	Washington St.	New Jersey	1
Williams, Gardner	372	DB	St. Mary's	Michigan	18
Williams, Leonard	182	RB	Western Carolina	Memphis	9
Williams, Robert	135	DB	E. Illinois	Birmingham	7
Willis, Mitch	69	DT	SMU	San Antonio	4
Wilson, Jay	344	LB	Missouri	Birmingham	17
Windham, David	262	LB	Jackson St.	Denver	13
Windham, Lamar	238	RB	Mississippi St.	Denver	12
Windham, Theodis	183	DB	Utah St.	Tampa Bay	0
Wise, Ben	203	LB	SMU	Houston	10
Witkowski, John	139	QB	Columbia	Philadelphia	7
Woodberry, Dennis	112	DB	So. Arkansas	Birmingham	6
Wright, Randy	189	QB	Wisconsin	Memphis	9
Young, Jon	392	DB	BYU	Philadelphia	19
Young, Steve	11	QB	BYU	Los Angeles	1
Zendejas, Tony	91	K	Nevada-Reno	Los Angeles	5
Zeno, Daric	296	WR	Central St. (OK)	Houston	15
Zimmerman, Gary	37	G	Oregon	Los Angeles	2
Zinamon, Bert	399	LB	Arkansas	San Antonio	19

Jerry Robinson: Eagles' most valuable defensive lineman.

1984
NFL SCHEDULE

*NIGHT GAME

SUNDAY, SEPT. 2
Atlanta at New Orleans
Cincinnati at Denver
Cleveland at Seattle
Kansas City at Pittsburgh
L.A. Raiders at Houston
Miami at Washington
New England at Buffalo
New York Jets at Indianapolis
Philadelphia at New York Giants
St. Louis at Green Bay
San Diego at Minnesota
San Francisco at Detroit
Tampa Bay at Chicago

MONDAY, SEPT. 3
*Dallas at L.A. Rams

THURSDAY, SEPT. 6
*Pittsburgh at New York Jets

SUNDAY, SEPT. 9
Buffalo at St. Louis
Cleveland at L.A. Rams
Indianapolis at Houston
Dallas at New York Giants
Denver at Chicago
Detroit at Atlanta
Green Bay at L.A. Raiders
Kansas City at Cincinnati
Minnesota at Philadelphia
New England at Miami
San Diego at Seattle
Tampa Bay at New Orleans

MONDAY, SEPT. 10
*Washington at San Francisco

SUNDAY, SEPT. 16
Atlanta at Minnesota
Chicago at Green Bay
Cincinnati at New York Jets
*Denver at Cleveland
Detroit at Tampa Bay
Houston at San Diego
L.A. Raiders at Kansas City
L.A. Rams at Pittsburgh
New Orleans at San Francisco

New York Giants at Washington
Philadelphia at Dallas
St. Louis at Indianapolis
Seattle at New England

MONDAY, SEPT. 17
*Miami at Buffalo

SUNDAY, SEPT. 23
Chicago at Seattle
Indianapolis at Miami
Green Bay at Dallas
Houston at Atlanta
Kansas City at Denver
L.A. Rams at Cincinnati
Minnesota at Detroit
New York Jets at Buffalo
Pittsburgh at Cleveland
St. Louis at New Orleans
San Francisco at Philadelphia
Tampa Bay at New York Giants
Washington at New England

MONDAY, SEPT. 24
*San Diego at L.A. Raiders

SUNDAY, SEPT. 30
Atlanta at San Francisco
Buffalo at Indianapolis
Cleveland at Kansas City
Dallas at Chicago
Detroit at San Diego
Green Bay at Tampa Bay
L.A. Raiders at Denver
Miami at St. Louis
New England at New York Jets
New Orleans at Houston
New York Giants at L.A. Rams
Philadelphia at Washington
Seattle at Minnesota

MONDAY, OCT. 1
*Cincinnati at Pittsburgh

SUNDAY, OCT. 7
Atlanta at L.A. Rams
Denver at Detroit
Houston at Cincinnati

Miami at Pittsburgh
Minnesota at Tampa Bay
New England at Cleveland
New Orleans at Chicago
New York Jets at Kansas City
Philadelphia at Buffalo
St. Louis at Dallas
San Diego at Green Bay
Seattle at L.A. Raiders
Washington at Indianapolis

MONDAY, OCT. 8
*San Francisco at N.Y. Giants

SUNDAY, OCT. 14
Buffalo at Seattle
Chicago at St. Louis
Cincinnati at New England
Indianapolis at Philadelphia
Dallas at Washington
Houston at Miami
L.A. Rams at New Orleans
Minnesota at L.A. Raiders
New York Giants at Atlanta
New York Jets at Cleveland
Pittsburgh at San Francisco
San Diego at Kansas City
Tampa Bay at Detroit

MONDAY, OCT. 15
*Green Bay at Denver

SUNDAY, OCT. 21
Chicago at Tampa Bay
Cleveland at Cincinnati
Denver at Buffalo
Detroit at Minnesota
Kansas City at New York Jets
L.A. Raiders at San Diego
Miami at New England
*New Orleans at Dallas
New York Giants at Philadelphia
Pittsburgh at Indianapolis
San Francisco at Houston
Seattle vs. Green Bay
    at Milwaukee
Washington at St. Louis

MONDAY, OCT. 22
L.A. Rams at Atlanta

SUNDAY, OCT. 28
Atlanta at Pittsburgh
Buffalo at Miami
Cincinnati at Houston
Indianapolis at Dallas
Denver at L.A. Raiders
Detroit at Green Bay
Minnesota at Chicago
New Orleans at Cleveland

New York Jets at New England
St. Louis at Philadelphia
San Francisco at L.A. Rams
Tampa Bay at Kansas City
Washington at New York Giants

MONDAY, OCT. 29
*Seattle at San Diego

SUNDAY, NOV. 4
Cincinnati at San Francisco
Cleveland at Buffalo
Green Bay at New Orleans
Houston at Pittsburgh
Kansas City at Seattle
L.A. Raiders at Chicago
L.A. Rams at St. Louis
Miami at New York Jets
New England at Denver
New York Giants at Dallas
Philadelphia at Detroit
San Diego at Indianapolis
Tampa Bay at Minnesota

MONDAY, NOV. 5
*Atlanta at Washington

SUNDAY, NOV. 11
Buffalo at New England
Chicago at L.A. Rams
Indianapolis at New York Jets
Dallas at St. Louis
Denver at San Diego
Detroit at Washington
Houston at Kansas City
Minnesota vs. Green Bay
    at Milwaukee
New Orleans at Atlanta
New York Giants at Tampa Bay
Philadelphia at Miami
Pittsburgh at Cincinnati
San Francisco at Cleveland

MONDAY, NOV. 12
*L.A. Raiders at Seattle

SUNDAY, NOV. 18
Cleveland at Atlanta
Dallas at Buffalo
Detroit at Chicago
Kansas City at L.A. Raiders
L.A. Rams vs. Green Bay
    at Milwaukee
Miami at San Diego
Minnesota at Denver
New England at Indianapolis
New York Jets at Houston
St. Louis at New York Giants
Seattle at Cincinnati
Tampa Bay at San Francisco
Washington at Philadelphia

MONDAY, NOV. 19
*Pittsburgh at New Orleans

THURSDAY, NOV. 22
Green Bay at Detroit
New England at Dallas

SUNDAY, NOV. 25
Atlanta at Cincinnati
Buffalo at Washington
Chicago at Minnesota
Indianapolis at L.A. Raiders
Houston at Cleveland
Kansas City at New York Giants
L.A. Rams at Tampa Bay
Philadelphia at St. Louis
San Diego at Pittsburgh
San Francisco at New Orleans
Seattle at Denver

MONDAY, NOV. 26
*New York Jets at Miami

THURSDAY, NOV. 29
*Washington at Minnesota

SUNDAY, DEC. 2
Cincinnati at Cleveland
Indianapolis at Buffalo
Dallas at Philadelphia
Denver at Kansas City
Detroit at Seattle
L.A. Raiders at Miami
New Orleans at L.A. Rams
N.Y. Giants at N.Y. Jets
Pittsburgh at Houston
St. Louis at New England
San Francisco at Atlanta
Tampa Bay at Green Bay

MONDAY, DEC. 3
*Chicago at San Diego

SATURDAY, DEC. 8
Buffalo at New York Jets
Minnesota at San Francisco

SUNDAY, DEC. 9
Atlanta at Tampa Bay
Cincinnati at New Orleans
Cleveland at Pittsburgh
Green Bay at Chicago
Houston at L.A. Rams
Miami at Indianapolis
New England at Philadelphia
New York Giants at St. Louis
San Diego at Denver

Seattle at Kansas City
Washington at Dallas

MONDAY, DEC. 10
*L.A. Raiders at Detroit

FRIDAY, DEC. 14
*L.A. Rams at San Francisco

SATURDAY, DEC. 15
Denver at Seattle
New Orleans at New York Giants

SUNDAY, DEC. 16
Buffalo at Cincinnati
Chicago at Detroit
Cleveland at Houston
Indianapolis at New England
Green Bay at Minnesota
Kansas City at San Diego
New York Jets at Tampa Bay
Philadelphia at Atlanta
Pittsburgh at L.A. Raiders
St. Louis at Washington

MONDAY, DEC. 17
*Dallas at Miami

Nationally Televised Games

(The CBS Radio Network will broadcast 37 games, including Monday night games and all postseason games, among others.)

REGULAR SEASON

Monday, Sept. 3—Dallas at Los Angeles Rams (night, ABC)
Thursday, Sept. 6—Pittsburgh at New York Jets (night, ABC)
Monday, Sept. 10—Washington at San Francisco (night, ABC)
Sunday, Sept. 16—Denver at Cleveland (night, ABC)
Monday, Sept. 17—Miami at Buffalo (night, ABC)
Monday, Sept. 24—San Diego at Los Angeles Raiders (night, ABC)
Monday, Oct. 1—Cincinnati at Pittsburgh (night, ABC)
Monday, Oct. 8—San Francisco at New York Giants (night, ABC)
Monday, Oct. 15—Green Bay at Denver (night, ABC)
Sunday, Oct. 21—New Orleans at Dallas (night, ABC)
Monday, Oct 22—Los Angeles Rams at Atlanta (night, ABC)
Monday, Oct. 29—Seattle at San Diego (night, ABC)
Monday, Nov. 5—Atlanta at Washington (night, ABC)
Monday, Nov. 12—Los Angeles Raiders at Seattle (night, ABC)
Monday, Nov. 19—Pittsburgh at New Orleans (night, ABC)
Thursday, Nov. 22—(Thanksgiving) Green Bay at Detroit (day, CBS)
⠀⠀⠀⠀⠀⠀⠀⠀⠀⠀⠀⠀⠀⠀⠀⠀⠀New England at Dallas (day, NBC)
Monday, Nov. 26—New York Jets at Miami (night, ABC)
Thursday, Nov. 29—Washington at Minnesota (night, ABC)
Monday, Dec. 3—Chicago at San Diego (night, ABC)
Saturday, Dec. 8—Buffalo at New York Jets (day, NBC)
⠀⠀⠀⠀⠀⠀⠀⠀⠀⠀⠀⠀⠀⠀Minnesota at San Francisco (day, CBS)
Monday, Dec. 10—Los Angeles Raiders at Detroit (night, ABC)
Friday, Dec. 14—Los Angeles Rams at San Francisco (night, ABC)
Saturday, Dec. 15—Denver at Seattle (day, NBC)
⠀⠀⠀⠀⠀⠀⠀⠀⠀⠀⠀⠀⠀⠀New Orleans at New York Giants (day, CBS)
Monday, Dec. 17—Dallas at Miami (night, ABC)

POSTSEASON

Sunday, Dec. 23—AFC and NFC First Round Playoffs (NBC and CBS)
Saturday, Dec. 29—AFC and NFC Divisional Playoffs (NBC and CBS)
Sunday, Dec. 30—AFC and NFC Divisional Playoffs (NBC and CBS)
Sunday, Jan. 6—AFC and NFC Championship Games (NBC and CBS)
Sunday, Jan. 20—Super Bowl XIX at Stanford Stadium, Palo Alto, Cal. (ABC)
Sunday, Jan. 27—AFC-NFC Pro Bowl, Honolulu, Hawaii (ABC)

MONDAY NIGHT GAMES (ABC)

Sept. 3—Dallas at L.A. Rams
Sept. 10—Washington at San Francisco
Sept. 17—Miami at Buffalo
Sept. 24—San Diego at L.A. Raiders
Oct. 1—Cincinnati at Pittsburgh
Oct. 8—San Francisco at N.Y. Giants
Oct. 15—Green Bay at Denver
Oct. 22—L.A. Rams at Atlanta

Oct. 29—Seattle at San Diego
Nov. 5—Atlanta at Washington
Nov. 12—L.A. Raiders at Seattle
Nov. 19—Pittsburgh at New Orleans
Nov. 26—N.Y. Jets at Miami
Dec. 3—Chicago at San Diego
Dec. 10—L.A. Raiders at Detroit
Dec. 17—Dallas at Miami

SUNDAY, THURSDAY, FRIDAY NIGHT GAMES (ABC)

Thursday, Sept. 6—Pittsburgh at N.Y. Jets
Sunday, Sept. 16—Denver at Cleveland
Sunday, Oct. 21—N.O. at Dallas

Thursday, Nov. 29—Wash. at Minn.
Friday, Dec. 14—L.A. Rams at S.F.

Seattle's Dave Krieg led AFC in passing yards per attempt.